T0230936

Morphological Aspects of Language Processing

Morphological Aspects of Language Processing

Edited by
Laurie Beth Feldman
The University at Albany, SUNY
Haskins Laboratories

 Psychology Press
Taylor & Francis Group

New York London

First Published by
Lawrence Erlbaum Associates, Inc., Publishers
365 Broadway
Hillsdale, New Jersey 07642

Transferred to Digital Printing 2009 by Psychology Press
270 Madison Ave, New York NY 10016
27 Church Road, Hove, East Sussex, BN3 2FA

Library of Congress Cataloging-in-Publication Data

Morphological aspects of language processing / edited by Laurie Beth
  Feldman.
        p. cm.
  Includes bibliographical references and indexes.
  ISBN 0-8058-1358-6
  1. Grammar, Comparative and general—Morphology—Psy-
chological aspects. 2. Psycholinguistics. I. Feldman, Laurie
Beth
P241.M598   1994
415—dc20   94-28968
                                                          CIP

Publisher's Note
The publisher has gone to great lengths to ensure the quality of this reprint
but points out that some imperfections in the original may be apparent.

To Misha, Ivan, and Petar

Contents

PART 2

Semantic Issues in Morphological Processing

PART 3

Phonological Issues in Morphological Processing

PART 4

Structural and Statistical Issues in Morphological Processing

Contributors

Harold Baayen, Interfaculty Research Unit for Language and Speech, Wundtlaan 1, 6525 XD Nijmegen, THE NETHERLANDS

Shlomo Bentin, Psychology Department, Hebrew University, 91905 Jerusalem, ISRAEL

Dianna Buijs, Department of SWI, Leiden University, Stationsplein 12, NL 2312-AK, Leiden, THE NETHERLANDS

Cristina Burani, Istituto di Psicologia del CNR, Viale Marx 15, I-00137 Roma, ITALY

Joan Bybee, Department of Linguistics, University of New Mexico, Albuquerque, New Mexico 87131 USA

Alfonso Caramazza, Cognitive Neuropsychology Laboratory, Dartmouth College, Hanover, New Hampshire 03755 USA

Joanne Carlisle, Learning Disabilities Center, 2299 Sheridan Road, Northwestern University, Evanston, Illinois 60208 USA

Dorianna Chialant, Cognitive Neuropsychology Laboratory, Dartmouth College, Hanover, New Hampshire 03755 USA

Bruce Derwing, Department of Linguistics, University of Alberta, Edmonton, CANADA T6G 2E7

Karen Emmorey, The Salk Institute for Biological Studies, 10010 N. Torrey Pines Road, La Jolla, California 92037 USA

Laurie Beth Feldman, Department of Psychology, SS112, The University at Albany, SUNY, Albany, New York 12222 USA

Anne Fowler, Haskins Laboratories, 270 Crown Street, New Haven, Connecticut 06511 USA

Carol A. Fowler, Haskins Laboratories, 270 Crown Street, New Haven, Connecticut 06511 USA

Ram Frost, Psychology Department, Hebrew University, 91905 Jerusalem, ISRAEL

Vicki Hanson, IBM Thomas Watson Research, P. O. Box 218, Yorktown Heights, New York 10598 USA

Patrick Hudson, Department of SWI, Leiden University, Stationsplein 12, NL 2312-AK, Leiden, THE NETHERLANDS

Leonard Katz, Department of Psychology, U20, University of Connecticut, Babbidge Road, Storrs, Connecticut 06269 USA

Aleksandar Kostić, Odeljenje za Psihologiju, Filozofski Fakultet, Cika Ljubina 18-20, 11000 Belgrade, YUGOSLAVIA

Alessandro Laudanna, Istituto di Psicologia del CNR, Viale Marx 15, I-00137 Roma, ITALY

Mira Peter, Department of Psychology, U20, University of Connecticut, Babbidge Road, Storrs, Connecticut 06269 USA

Karl Rexer, College of the Holy Cross, Department of Psychology, 1 College Street, Worcester, Massachusetts 01610 USA

Robert Schreuder, Interfaculty Research Unit for Language and Speech, Wundtlaan 1, 6525 XD Nijmegen, THE NETHERLANDS

Martha Smith, Department of Linguistics, University of Alberta, Edmonton, CANADA T6G 2E7

Philip T. Smith, Department of Psychology, University of Reading, Earley Gate, Whiteknights, Reading, RG6 2AL, UNITED KINGDOM

Joseph Stemberger, Department of Communication, University of Minnesota, Minneapolis, Minnesota 55455 USA

Jennifer Stolz, Department of Psychology, SS112, The University at Albany, SUNY, Albany, New York 12222 USA

Marcus Taft, School of Psychology, University of New South Wales, P. O. Box 1, Kensington NSW 2033, Sydney, AUSTRALIA

Grace Wiebe, Department of Linguistics, University of Alberta, Edmonton, CANADA T6G 2E7

Xiaoping Zhu, School of Psychology, University of New South Wales, P. O. Box 1, Kensington NSW 2033, Sydney, AUSTRALIA

Acknowledgment

The production of this volume was supported in part by a grant from the National Institute of Child Health and Human Development HD-01994 to Haskins Laboratories.

I wish to thank the following people for their contributions: Yvonne Manning-Jones was responsible for the design, layout, and production of all manuscripts and figures as well as for tranforming my image into a cover design. All of the chapters in the book were reviewed by other authors. In addition, Jacqueline Larabee provided editorial expertise. Finally, Carol Fowler provided a scholarly perspective on each chapter.

I could not have completed this project without their help.

—*Laurie Beth Feldman*

Introduction

Carol A. Fowler
Haskins Laboratories

Linguistic analysis of the lexical elements of a language reveals that many words have internal morphological structure. Word bases and affixes recur in different words, and, to a degree, bases may be associated with a common core of meaning; for their part, affixes may convey a meaning (e.g. *un-* in English) or may subserve a particular grammatical function. What does this have to do with the psychology of knowing a language?

It must have something to do with it, for language users use sublexical morphological elements of words productively. When we coin a new word (e.g., *videocassette recorder*), we may do so by putting existing morphemes into new combinations. Further, such new words, used in a sentence, acquire the appropriate inflections for their syntactic class and role in the sentence (*I have two videocassette recorders.*). Accordingly, there is not only a linguistics of morphology to be understood, there is a psychology as well. Following the lead of Senator Howard Baker, we should ask: What do language users know about morphology and when do we come to know it? More than that, we have to step back from the psychology of the individual to understand how language use fosters change in language forms. Why does the transparent *videocassette recorder* become the opaque *VCR*, and why do meanings of coined derived words drift? Why do *fantastic, terrific, awful,* and, more recently, *awesome* not retain the meanings of their original base forms *fantasy, terrify,* and *awe*, respectively?

To gain insight into possible answers to these questions and others, I urge researchers in the area of morphology to read every chapter in this volume, not just those closest to their own research interests. Having read the chapters before writing this Introduction, I recognize the unique and positive contribution that an edited volume of individually authored chapters can make. A single-authored book on morphology (e.g., the very fine *Morphology* [Amsterdam: John Benjamins, 1985] written by Joan Bybee, a contributor to this volume) can provide a focused, coherent outlook on its topic. An edited book cannot make that contribution, but it can make a contribution of a complementary sort. A multiple-authored book, with chapters that are written largely independently, provides a wonderfully honest picture of the diversity of theoretical questions addressed by researchers in the field and, provocatively, the diversity of answers offered to the same questions. This is where I expect researcher-readers to reap the most profit, because the diversity opens doors to future investigations.

Many chapters describe research of experimental psychologists interested in the representation of morphological knowledge in the mental lexicon. Other chapters describe research, largely of linguists, who remind us that, however language users represent morphologically complex words, the representations are subject to systematic, diachronic change of an understandable sort. Realistic models of the lexicon in adult, fluent users of the language, must reflect representations and organizations that not only could be learned by a child, but also are continually modified by language use.

The volume also includes the work of researchers concerned with the universality of representation of morphological structure. Is there only one way in which language users represent morphological structure in words, or is the way of representing structure affected by crosslinguistic variation in morphology? Is the lexicon of a speaker/reader of English different from that of a speaker/reader of the highly inflected Serbo-Croatian or Italian, the wholly uninflected Chinese, the nonconcatenative Hebrew, and the nonconcatenative and gestural American Sign Language? It is pleasing to see researchers worldwide taking advantage of the diversity of morphologies that languages of the world offer to bring this topic under scrutiny.

A question of increasing currency in this field as in others asks whether morphological structure is represented explicitly at all in a language user's mental lexicon. Not surprisingly, different answers are offered to this question by the authors of these chapters. In many accounts and models, morphological structure is explicit; further, some authors appear to show that experimental effects, ostensibly of morphological relatedness, cannot be explained instead as consequences of the orthographic, phonological, or semantic relatedness that morphologically related forms tend, confoundedly, to have. On the other side, however, one chapter offers simulations in which morphological structure is an "emergent" property of a network in which words can be similar or different in their spellings, pronunciations, and meanings. Perhaps compatibly, an author suggests caution in interpreting evidence of children's acquisition of morphological structure. Some omissions of morphemes may occur, for example, not because the form is a morpheme and because the child is learning morphemes as such, but because the morpheme's phonological implementation is currently difficult for the child to produce. Similar issues arise in research on the importance of morphological knowledge to the success with which children learn to read. If morphological awareness, comprehension, and production in the young beginning reader predict later reading success, are the measures of morphological knowledge mediated by phonological knowledge, or is morphology an independent knowledge source? Now that the question of explicitness has been raised, research tools have to be sharpened to address it. The book offers a look at a wide variety of tools currently in use.

A last issue, and another on which readers will find diversity of opinion, concerns the question of what lexicons really are. For some contributors to the volume, one lexicon is purely orthographic, and presumably an independent one represents the phonological forms of words. Because morphological structure is explicit in the orthographic lexicon, it must be redundantly explicit in the phonological one. Another view is that one lexicon, which begins life with phonological representations of words, acquires spellings of words when its owner learns to read. Could a challenge to the first view be a finding reported in this volume that, among profoundly deaf readers—whom one might least expect to access phonological information about words while reading—the difficulty of generating derived words from their base forms is affected not by orthographic differences between simple and complex forms but by conjoint orthographic and phonological differences? Let the reader decide.

I offer a brief look at the diversity of questions and answers to questions that the book offers. In doing so, I intentionally omit the names of authors whose research I mention so as not to direct attention to any particular chapter. I invite the reader to delve into them all.

PART 1

Visual and Orthographic Issues in Morphological Processing

On the Role of Spelling in Morpheme Recognition: Experimental Studies with Children and Adults*

1

Bruce L. Derwing, Martha L. Smith,† and Grace E. Wiebe
Department of Linguistics, University of Alberta

Two experiments were conducted to assess the effect of spelling knowledge on morpheme recognition (MR; i.e., skill in identifying the root morphemes of derived words). Both experiments involved a spelling test and an MR test. The expectation was that subjects who spelled the root portions of the derived words and the root words in the *same* way (S-spellers, e.g., <u>know</u>/<u>know</u>ledge or *<u>no</u>/*<u>no</u>ladge) would be more successful on the MR test than subjects who spelled the root portions *differently* (D-spellers, e.g., <u>know</u>/*<u>no</u>ladge). The first experiment was performed with children, so an MR test based on non-technical vocabulary had to be devised, and a six-question test battery was the result. Two of those questions (both versions of Derwing's, 1976, "Comes From" test, i.e., *"Does the [derived] word come from the [root] word?"*) served as the basis for the results reported here. The second experiment involved university students familiar with basic linguistic terminology. For these subjects the MR test consisted simply of asking them whether they thought the derived word contained the same root as the isolated word. While the results showed that S-spellers generally outperformed D-spellers on both MR tests, the

*The main findings of Smith's experiment were first presented at the 13th Annual Symposium of the Deseret Language and Linguistics Society at Brigham Young University, Provo, UT, and appeared in the proceedings as Smith and Derwing (1987). Permission from DLLS to reprint portions of that paper here is gratefully acknowledged. Thanks are also expressed to the students and staff of the Evansdale Elementary School in Edmonton and the Corinthia Park School in Leduc for their assistance with that study.

†Martha Smith is now a doctoral candidate at Harvard University.

3

results were reliable on less than half of the items, and only a few of these provided unambiguous evidence in favor of the proposed directionality of the effect. The conclusion was nonetheless supported that knowledge of spelling and other education-based factors can sometimes lead to large-scale individual differences in morpheme recognition, as in many other linguistic and metalinguistic skills, and some important implications of this result on standard theoretical and methodological practice in linguistics are discussed.

INTRODUCTION

Over the past half century or so, the field of linguistics in North America has largely been dominated by what Scinto (1986) terms the "phonocentric canon." The often unquestioned and unstated assumption of this canon is that "the voice is somehow primary and central to language and, by implication, other instantiations of language are only secondary reflections of the voice" (p. 2). Such a bias is clearly reflected in the Bloomfieldian dictum that "[W]riting is not language, but merely a way of recording language by means of visible marks" (Bloomfield, 1933, p. 21).

In other places, however, the central goal of linguistics has been characterized as that of establishing and codifying the "knowledge" that native speakers have of their language (Chomsky, 1965, and elsewhere). Clearly, not all linguistic knowledge derives from speech alone. In particular, since we live in a society where literacy is highly valued and widespread, the typical speaker can hardly avoid exposure to the written form of the language. Indeed, this experience with the written language can begin at a quite early age, as children often begin learning to read and write while they are still undergoing early linguistic and general cognitive development. Nor does one's knowledge of language cease to grow at any particular age, as even mature adults continue to make frequent discoveries about their language and its use. Moreover, since psycholinguistic research has largely utilized subjects who are literate or in the process of becoming literate, it is of some importance that workers in this field try to sort out intuitively acquired linguistic behavior from education-derived behavior (Jaeger, 1984).[1]

One place where there is prima facie evidence of interaction between knowledge derived from hearing/speaking the spoken language and seeing/writing the written one is in the area of morpheme recognition (MR; i.e., that particular aspect of general morphological knowledge that involves the identification of the minimal, meaningful components of morphologically complex words,

---

[1]It is also worthy of note that this is one of the difficulties of the one-step or "instantaneous" model of language acquisition (Chomsky & Halle, 1968) that takes in all of the data before proceeding with the analysis: universal, innate-driven sources of knowledge are inevitably confounded with individual, education-driven sources, thus overstating (perhaps grossly) and otherwise distorting the requirements of the supposed innate language faculty (cf. Derwing, 1990).

especially shared roots). Surprisingly little experimental research seems to have been carried out in this area, considering the central role that the morpheme notion has played in most linguistic theoretical accounts[2] and in psychological models of speech recognition and retrieval. Yet most of what is known or believed about morphemes is actually based more on what linguists have proposed or believed about language forms, rather than on any hard evidence related to the internalized knowledge of speakers. As noted in Derwing (1973), for example, linguists make frequent assumptions about the presumed synchronic morphological relatedness of forms—the assumed morphological connectedness of the words *fable* and *fabulous* (Chomsky & Halle, 1968, p. 196) provides a classical case in point—but until quite recently little empirical work has been done to substantiate such claims. (Note that it is not the indubitable historical or etymological relationship between these words that is in question here, but rather the synchronic claim that these words are morphologically related in the minds of contemporary speakers.) It is therefore important for the psychological veracity of such morphological models as proposed in both linguistics and psychology that we understand not only which morphemes are recognized by speakers, but also the bases upon which this recognition takes place.

BACKGROUND

Most prior work on the relationship between knowledge of spelling and morphological knowledge has taken the approach that it is the second that enhances the first, i.e., either that awareness of morphological relationship aids spelling (e.g., Carlisle, 1988; Fischer, Shankweiler, & Liberman, 1985) or that morphological awareness can be an important contributory factor in improving reading skill (e.g., Leong, 1989; and both the Carlisle and Fowler chapters in this volume). This paper takes a somewhat different tack and explores spelling as one factor (of several) that influences the identification of morphological relationships in the first place. While by no means challenging or denying the significance of the prior work, we wish to emphasize the fact that the relationship between spelling and morphological knowledge is undoubtedly reciprocal, and that spelling similarities can give rise to morphological insights perhaps at least as readily as morphological awareness can lead to improvements in the skills of writing and reading words in English (cf. Templeton & Scarborough-Franks, 1985, who also emphasize the important developmental

---

[2]It is, of course, possible, and perhaps even advisable, to view morphology as the study of rule-like relationships among words (Anderson, 1992), rather than in terms of the traditional structuralist notion of a concatenation of individual morphemic elements. Even in such a process framework, however, the identification of shared meaningful elements, especially roots, must presumably still provide speakers with their best clues as to which words are to be related to which other words, so even this theoretic framework ought to benefit considerably from a better understanding of how speakers do in fact identify these commonalities and the various factors that play a role in this activity.

role played by orthographic information in the accessing of some derivational morphological processes). We will give an informal report below on some of the early exploratory work in this area, which focuses largely on methodological issues, followed by the description of a new experimental study that attempts to approach the problem in a more systematic way.

FACTORS IN MORPHEME RECOGNITION

Since the (mental) lexicon is generally assumed to be the place where meaning and phonological form are psychologically linked, and since morphemes are taken to be the minimal or basic elements into which words can be meaningfully segmented, the two most likely factors to affect MR skill are those of phonetic (or phonological) and semantic (or meaning) similarity between the hypothetically related forms (Derwing, 1973, pp. 122-126). Consequently, these were the two factors that were first explored in Derwing (1976). A set of 50 potentially related word pairs that illustrated a small number of high frequency derivational relationships were selected to represent the full range of variation along the dimensions of phonetic and semantic similarity. In addition to the *fable/ fabulous* example already mentioned, this list included such word pairs as *teach/teacher, dirt/dirty, quiet/quietly, wonder/wonderful, number/numerous, awe/awful, hand/handle, moon/month, holy/holiday, hand/handkerchief, cup/ cupboard, lace/necklace,* and *puppy/dog,* as well as a few non-etymologically related pairs such as *ear/eerie* and *fry/Friday.*

Three different tests were devised in this investigation: one to measure perceived similarity in sound between words or parts of words (henceforth PS, for "phonetic similarity"), one to measure the perceived similarity in meaning between them (henceforth SS, for "semantic similarity"), and a third to measure the ability to identify any shared minimal, meaningful component parts (i.e., the MR skill itself). In Derwing's initial attempt, reasonably straightforward rating tasks were devised for the first two of these, but the third proved to be much more challenging.

To our knowledge, the first experimental attempt to tap the MR skill was done by Berko (1958). Though this classic paper is remembered and cited mainly for its so-called "wug test," i.e., the use of nonce-words (such as WUG) to assess the productive ability of speakers to deal with the English morphological inflections (such as plural, past, etc.), the paper also included a short section at the end that amounted to an MR test for root morphemes in a short list of English noun compounds (such as *Thanksgiving, blackboard,* and *football*). Specifically, what Berko did was to ask her subjects why such words were given the names they were. What she was looking for were examples of so-called "etymological responses," which would reveal an awareness of the morphological composition of these words. (Thus, as Berko notes, if a subject were to respond to the word *Thanksgiving* by saying something like, "Thanksgiving is called Thanksgiving because the pilgrims gave thanks," the last two words would betray an awareness that both *give* and *thank* were intrinsic parts of the larger word.) Derwing (1976) showed, however, that without further experimental controls, this test often gave counterintuitive results for such seemingly transparent cases as *dirty* and *quickly,* where only a small number of subjects (a mere 15% and 4%, respectively) made explicit mention of the root elements *dirt* and *quick.* (What subjects typically did instead was to provide paraphrases or other appropriate circumlocutions.) Though controls can readily be conceived that might have strengthened these results (e.g., by making it clear somehow in the instructions that etymological-like responses were the kind sought), Derwing took a different tack and introduced an entirely new task, called the "Comes From" (CF) test.

In the original version of the CF test, Derwing presented examples of potentially related word pairs (such as *teach/teacher, dirt/dirty, quiet/quietly,* etc.) to subjects and asked them whether or not they thought that the second word "came from" the first (in some vague and unspecified etymological sense). For example, "Do you think that the word *teacher* 'comes from' the word *teach?*" A five-point answer scale was used, where 4=No doubt about it, 3=Probably, 2=Can't decide, 1=Probably not and 0=No way.[3]

In sharp contrast with Berko's task, the CF test gave highly satisfactory results in two important respects, for a sample of 65 linguistically naive university undergraduate subjects. First of all, its results were the intuitively correct ones for those word pairs that had transparent morphological connections (i.e., pairs such as *teach/teacher, dirt/dirty, quiet/quietly*). These pairs were independently rated as being highly similar on both the PS and SS scales and had average MR ratings of 3.95 or above out of a possible 4.00. By the same token, this test also gave the expected results for those other word pairs in which no clear synchronic morphological relationships are intuitive (i.e., pairs such as *dog/puppy, ear/eerie,* and *bash/bashful*). These pairs were rated as having very low PS (the first case) or SS values (the latter two) and had MR means below 1.00. Secondly, and just as importantly, the CF test also gave results that sharply contrasted the SS and MR values for word pairs such as *dog/puppy* and *straw/strawberry,* where the intuitive semantic similarity is high in the first case and low in the second (SS means of 3.74 and 0.92, respectively), but where the MR means for these same words were almost completely reversed (0.95 and 3.20, respectively). These results indicate that the CF test, as intended, was tapping something very different from mere semantic similarity. Both of these

---

[3]A supplementary "recall" test was also used ("Have you ever thought about this before?"), which amounted to a confidence judgment on the original assessment. This test is not discussed here, as its results correlated highly with those from the primary test. (See Derwing, 1976, pp. 50-54, for details.)

findings, then, speak to the critical validity and reliability issues that any useful experimental task must successfully address.

In general, then, the main finding from this study was that both PS and SS strongly influenced MR judgments, as revealed by the CF task, but that, of the two, the semantic factor was the more important or dominant one.

As noted in Derwing and Baker (1986), however, PS and SS were not the only factors that affected MR judgments, as measured primarily by the CF task. More specifically, the following three categories of factors also seemed to play an important role: (1) construction type: the judged morphemic analyzability of some words seemed to be influenced not merely by the phonetic and semantic transparency of its supposed root but also by such factors as the transparency and/or productivity of the supposed affix. (Thus, while the word pairs *wonder/wonderful* and *hand/handle* were rated very much the same with respect to both SS and PS in Derwing's study, the first, with the highly productive affix, received a higher MR score than did the other); (2) orthographic similarity: the pairs *break/breakfast* and *hand/handkerchief* received higher MR ratings than the pair *price/precious,* though all three pairs were similar in terms of phonetic and semantic overlap; (3) subject-specific factors: educational experience, intelligence and even curiosity about language (including knowledge of specific word etymologies, which distorted the MR results in cases like *moon/month* and *holy/Halloween*).

These results were merely suggestive, however, and none, to our knowledge, have ever been systematically followed up in the more than fifteen years since this original work was done. The present chapter attempts to take one of these factors, namely, spelling or orthographic similarity, at least one step further, by exploring in a more systematic way the role that knowledge of spelling might contribute to the MR skill.

Smith's (1987) Exploratory Study with Children

The only prior work known to us that deals with this specific problem is Smith (1987), which attempted to explore the relation between morpheme recognition (MR) and spelling in children in grades 4-7. The study consisted of a spelling production task and a morpheme recognition task.

Procedure

On the spelling task, Smith used 60 pairs of English words, where one member of the pair was the putative "root" of the other "derived" word. The following guidelines were used in selecting words: (1) All word pairs involved spelling similarities that could potentially make the putative morphological relationships clearer than they would be on the basis of phonological and semantic similarities alone (e.g., *cup/cupboard*); (2) All words were common enough that students in grades 4-7 might be reasonably expected to know them (teachers were consulted on this point); and (3) All words selected were ranked from grades 3 to 8 in spelling difficulty on the New Iowa Spelling Scale and the Strothers-Minkler Canadian Word List. This range was chosen to make it likely that there would be both misspellings and correct spellings in the data base.

The final list of word pairs represented varying degrees of orthographic, phonological, and semantic similarity but was limited to a small number of common affixes that were previously determined to be productively controlled by subjects in this age range (see Derwing & Baker, 1979). The list also contained a number of etymological compounds (e.g., *breakfast, cupboard, handkerchief, necklace*) and a few other word pairs having less than obvious (e.g., *cave/cavity, create/creature, price/precious*) or even patently false etymological connections (e.g., *ear/eerie, fry/Friday, table/vegetable,* and *sting/stingy*). The longer or "derived" words in each pair were randomized and dictated to each class. Subjects were 207 students in grades 4 through 7 in two different schools in the Edmonton area. These subjects were asked to attempt the spellings of all words and also to indicate (by means of a check mark) whether they knew the meanings of the words. (The spellings of the roots were elicited as the last step in the MR task, which is briefly described below.)

Subjects and stimuli selected for the MR task were subsets of the subject groups (n=207) and stimulus sets (n=60) just described, based on the primary goal of achieving a rough balance of spellers and non-spellers for each test item. In the final analysis, 24 subjects were chosen from each of the four grades to take the MR test. The final selection of stimuli for the MR test involved two sets of 11 words each: Set 1 for the subjects in grades 4-5 (Group I) and Set 2 for the subjects in grades 6-7 (Group II). Materials are listed in Appendix 1. (Items in overlapping sets are marked by a postposed asterisk.)

In order to assess MR among these child subjects, a new "enhanced" technique was developed, incorporating elements from the two prior experimental investigations of MR (Berko, 1958, and Derwing, 1976) and supplementing them with some new components, some of which we hoped would be of general methodological interest. Thus, in addition to a question modeled on the original form of Derwing's "Comes From" question (Q5 on the test), which provided a candidate source word (e.g., "Do you think the word *teacher* 'comes from' the word *teach*?"), a more rigorous version of this question (Q3) was included which required subjects to provide a suitable source word on their own (e.g., "Does the word *teacher* 'come from' any other word that you can think of?"). A form of Berko's original MR question was also included as Q2 for each item (e.g., "Why is a *teacher* called a *teacher*?"). In addition, all subjects were asked to provide a definition for each derived word and source word (Q1 and Q4, respectively), as a check on whether they really knew the words. Finally, Derwing's "recall question" (cf. n. 4) was also included as Q6. As this was an exploratory investigation, the purpose of multiple questions was to maximize test validity, and to study how well the response patterns to these various questions correlated with one another.

Finally, the directions to the subjects included the two training examples shown in Appendix 2, the first taken to illustrate a supposed clear, uncontroversial case of morphological relatedness (*teach/teacher*), and the second to illustrate a clear case of non-relatedness (*ham/hammer*). At the end of this training, all subjects had concluded that *teach* was related to *teacher* in a way that was of interest in this experiment, and that *ham* was not so related to *hammer* but was merely another word that sounded a lot like it.

Once the examiner was satisfied that each subject understood the task, the testing proceeded with the 11 items in the appropriate stimulus set, which were presented in a different, random order for each subject. Each subject was individually interviewed by the experimenter in a quiet room at school, and all subject responses were recorded. The format of the testing was essentially the same as described in the two examples provided in Appendix 2, with appropriate modifications to accommodate each word pair. At the conclusion of each session the subjects were thanked for their participation and asked not to discuss the task or words with other students. Each MR session lasted about 20 minutes.

Scoring

The individual spellers and misspellers for each stimulus item were defined in terms of a notion of "critical" spelling error. This distinction considered both the spelling of the root and the initial (i.e., pre-MR) spelling of the derived words. If the spelling of the root and the derived word corresponded, the subject was given a score of "S," indicating that the critical spellings were both the *same,* while a score of "D" was assigned to cases where the critical spellings were *different.* Misspellings beyond the root were considered irrelevant to the MR issue under investigation here and were ignored in this classification.

There were two categories of spellings that were coded "S." In the first case, the subject spelled the root *correctly,* and the spelling of the derived word contained all the letters that the derived word and its root had in common. For words like *signal* and *cupboard*, the critical spellings involved the entire root, since for such words the correct spellings of the roots *sign* and *cup* do not vary between the derived forms and the isolated forms. (Only one root was focused on for compounds, usually the first one, as in *cupboard;* with *necklace* it was the second root, *lace,* that was of most interest, as this is the one whose pronunciation varies between its isolated or citation form and its form within the compound.) For the words *knowledge, criminal,* and *decision* the critical spellings involved the first four letters shared in each case with the isolated root words *know, crime,* and *decide* respectively, and for the pair *preside/president* this extended to the first seven letters shared in common. However, for the pair *fable/fabulous* it was just the four shared letters marked by underlining that were taken as critical, as only these letters provided any positive visual information about the commonality of the roots involved. Thus subjects who wrote _cup_/*_cupberd_,[4] _know_/*_knowlge_ and _crime_/*_crimnel_ were all included in the "S" category for purpose of the analysis, as well as those who gave spellings that were correct throughout.

The other spelling pattern that was coded "S" involved _consistently incorrect_ spellings of the putatively shared roots, i.e., cases where a subject misspelled the isolated root word and the root portion of the derived word in the same way. Examples of this type of "S" scoring were *_sighn_/*_sighnal_, *_no_/*_noladge_, and *_polut_/*_polution_. All other misspellings were coded "D."

Under this approach, then, the S-spellers for each word pair were those for whom a shared root morpheme was transparently revealed in the spellings they produced for the two words, while the D-spellers lacked this clue to MR in the spellings they produced. By comparing the performance of S-spellers and D-spellers on the MR task, we were thus in a position to draw some conclusions about the effect of orthographic clues on morpheme identification.

Results

Although a variety of alternative systems were devised by Smith to score the MR data, a "profile" system was used as the starting point for each. In this system, a subject's responses to each item were coded in terms of a six-place profile, with a 1 or 0 supplied for each of the six questions included in the MR test battery. A subject was assigned a score of 1 for every answer indicative of a positive linkage of the derived word with its putative root and a score of 0 for any other response. (The specific criteria used to assess positive responses to each question are indicated in parentheses in Example 1 of Appendix 2.)

An analysis of the full set of response profiles revealed that not all parts of the MR test battery yielded the same amount of useful information. Due to a large number of "I don't know" responses, for example, as well as the common use of paraphrase, very little information was obtained about MR relationships from either the definition question (Q1) or the Berko-type question (Q2), nor did positive responses to the other questions correlate well with positive responses to either of these two. Data from these two questions were thus dropped from all subsequent analyses. Data from Q4, on the other hand, were taken as vital for the validity issue, since only subjects who knew the roots could reasonably be assumed to have any valid morphological intuitions about how those roots might enter into larger morphological constructions. Imposing the constraints of a positive response to Q4 resulted in the loss of a number of subjects' data from subsequent analyses: _preside_/_president_ (all 48 cases were lost, i.e., none of the subjects in Group I claimed to know the root _preside_), _awe_/_awful_ (42 of 48 cases

---

[4]Preposed asterisks are used throughout this chapter to indicate _incorrect_ spellings.

lost), *fable/fabulous* (12 of 48 cases), *draw/drawer* (9 of 96), *lace/necklace* (3 of 48) and *create/creature* (1 of 48). As a result of this situation, the pairs *awe/awful* and *preside/president* were eliminated from this and all subsequent analyses, since, as just noted, virtually no subjects even knew the roots involved.

For the remaining subjects and items, subsequent analyses thus focused on the comparisons of answers to questions Q3, Q5, and Q6. One question concerned the correspondence of responses to Q5 and Q6. In other words, were subjects who thought that the derived word "came from" the proposed root (positive response to Q5) more likely than other subjects to have thought of the relationship before (positive response to Q6)? (There were no subjects who responded negatively to Q5 and positively to Q6.) The responses to these two questions were significantly correlated for about a third of the items on the full test.

Another analysis was also performed that compared the responses to questions Q3 and Q6, where now the issue was whether or not subjects who actually suggested the root on their own were more likely to have thought of the relationship before. Again, the only cases selected for analysis were those where the subjects indicated knowledge of the root (= positive response to Q4). This analysis showed a much stronger relationship than the previous one, as high levels of significance were found for more than half of the items. In other words, positive responses to Q3 better correlated with positive responses to Q6 than did positive responses to Q5. This suggests that the more demanding form of the "Comes From" question (Q3) was somewhat more appropriate for tapping subjects' MR knowledge than was the original one (Q5), which seemed to have a stronger tendency to lead to responses that reflected the learning effect of the task. (Derwing, 1976, also speaks of a "positive bias" effect, which reflects a general tendency to say "Yes" when a specific relationship is proposed to subjects.) For comparative purposes, however, Smith ran separate analyses under both of the following criteria for a positive MR assessment: (1) a positive response to Q5 alone (where subjects accepted the root that was proposed to them) and (2) a positive response to *both* Q3 and Q5 (where subjects both proposed the root on their own and also stated some plausible reason for doing so).

Comparing the results for S-spellers versus D-spellers. Smith (1987) reported two chi-square analyses that compared the proportion of positive versus negative MR assessments between the S and D spellers, one under the Q5 criterion for a positive MR and one under the Q3+Q5 criterion. For the two items *cup/cupboard* (both Group I and Group II subjects) and *draw/drawer* (Group II subjects only), a significant difference was found between the S-spellers and D-spellers, using either criterion for MR. In addition, the pairs *lace/necklace* and *create/creature* show this effect under the Q5 definition (*sign/signal* nearly reaches significance, as well), while *discuss/discussion* and *know/knowledge* show it under Q3 +Q5. For these items it thus appears that some relatively tenuous semantic and phonological connections were significantly enhanced by a common spelling, as indicated by the fact that the spellers were more successful than the non-spellers in recognizing the *cup* in *cupboard,* the *draw* in *drawer,* the *lace* in *necklace,* etc. Note also that for all but one of these items, the spelling of the root is completely contained within the spelling of the derived word. (The only exception is the final E in *create* which was a letter not counted in defining the two spelling categories.) For the remaining items, however, there were no significant differences in MR between the two types of spellers, though a general tendency in favor of the S-spellers was observed throughout.

Discussion

This study complements prior research which showed that speakers do learn some morphological generalizations, based on their exposure to the sound and meaning of related words. This can be most clearly demonstrated in cases where both the phonetic and the semantic similarities between words are transparent and the affixes are regular and highly productive (Derwing, 1976). Beyond such "obvious" cases, however, there is little empirical evidence that the morphological awareness of either the children studied by Smith or the university students tested by Derwing anywhere near approximates the typical linguist's penchant for comprehensive and detailed morphemic analysis. This study produced evidence that many words, such as *fable* and *fabulous,* thought to be synchronically related by many linguists, are thought (at least consciously[5]) to be quite unrelated by ordinary speakers.

It is also clear that the semantic factor is the most important variable in MR, as evidenced by the fact that subjects do not find any relationship at all between pairs like *table/vegetable,* where both phonological and orthographic transparency are relatively high but semantic similarity is obviously very low. However, this study has provided evidence that the semantic connection can be crucially linked to orthographic similarity. If a phonological discrepancy only partially disguises a morphological connection, and if the synchronic meaning of a word bears a meaning that is not too far removed from the meaning of its historical root, literate speakers may still be led to accept the possibility of an MR connection when it is overtly suggested to them by a common spelling. This was evidently the case with the historically related pairs *draw/drawer* and *lace/necklace* in this study, for not only were statistically significant differences in MR found between the S-spellers and the D-spellers for these words, but it was almost always the case that those subjects who scored positively on the MR task were S-spellers (i.e., speakers who spelled the roots in the same way in both their isolated and derived forms). Moreover, to judge from Derwing's (1976)

---

[5]Unfortunately, all of these questions require the making of conscious, analytic judgments on the part of subjects. Tests that involve unconscious, automatic responses (such as a conditioned eye blink or pupillary contraction) also need to be developed in this area.

findings for these word pairs, neither example would seem to provide sufficient semantic similarity for the shared roots to be identified on the basis of natural speech and contextual information alone. (Derwing's SS means for these word pairs were only 2.02 and 1.88, ordinarily well out of the range for common morphemes to be naturally identified.)

A final observation that points to differences in MR performance between the two types of spellers is that, for a number of items, the S-spellers also accounted for many more types of response profiles than did the D-spellers. While these profiles did not necessarily correspond to clear cases of morpheme recognition, they did suggest that the S-spellers at least had different cognitive associations for these items than the D-spellers did.

A NEW EXPERIMENT: SPELLING AND MORPHEME RECOGNITION IN ADULTS

To buttress the findings of Smith's exploratory and largely qualitative study, we replicated the experiment with adults, in order to assess whether the same tendencies observed in the children could also be seen in older subjects. Because we assumed that most of our subjects had acquired the correct spelling for root words, we were interested in determining whether MR was associated with knowledge of how derived words were spelled. Subjects for the new study were 114 undergraduate university students registered in two sections of the introductory linguistics course at the University of Alberta. In order to present a more balanced and controlled set of relationships between spelling and MR, 12 word pairs were selected to represent each of the following four categories: TP, FP, TN, and FN. To illustrate, a T(rue) P(ositive) pair is one in which the spelling suggests that there is a common root shared by the two words and indeed, etymologically at least, there is (e.g., *preside/president*). Though not critical to the experiment, note that we have also assumed that a synchronic morphological connection exists between these words.

By contrast, a F(alse) P(ositive) pair is one where the spelling temptingly suggests that there is a common root when in fact there is etymologically not, and where an appropriate MR test would not be likely to reveal one synchronically (e.g., *pea/pearl*). By the same token, a T(rue) N(egative) pair is one in which the spelling suggests that there is no such shared root and indeed there is not, or so we assumed for the purpose of this taxonomy (e.g., *fact/facsimile*). Finally, a F(alse) N(egative) pair is one in which the spelling, by virtue of at least one difference within the root portions of the words, suggests that there is no shared root when in fact there is, at least etymologically, and where we also presume that one would likely be found in further MR investigations (e.g., *sound/sonic*). Two additional items (not scored) were added to the stimulus set solely for their entertainment value, yielding a total of 50 test items in all. (See Appendix 3 for a full list of practice and test items for this experiment.)

The Modified MR and Spelling Tests

Because the subjects in this case were taking an introductory course in linguistics, the presentation of the MR test was delayed until the students had already been introduced to the basic concepts of word, morpheme, root, and affix. By employing this technical vocabulary, we were able to develop a more efficient MR test that could be group-administered. Subjects were presented with a word pair (e.g., *dirt/dirty* and were asked whether the second word (presented only orally) "contained the same root" as the first (whose spelling was provided on the answer sheet). Subjects responded by marking one of the numbers 1-5 on an optical scoring sheet, corresponding to the following scale: (1) No way (2) Probably not (3) Can't decide (4) Probably and (5) No doubt about it. (Note that the range of possible scores here is from 1-5, rather than from 0-4, as in Derwing's 1976 experiment.) Prior to the actual test, 15 practice items were given and the answers discussed until it was clear that everyone understood the nature of the task.

The spelling test was a standard dictation, with the experimenter taking care that natural, colloquial pronunciations were used (e.g., unstressed vowels were reduced). Subjects were advised to ask for clarification if any of the words were unfamiliar or unrecognized, and two meaning clarifications were made in response to such requests (for the words *medieval* and *pachyderm*); the meaning of the word *hardy* ("strong, tough, able to endure, as in the sentence, 'The hardy plant withstood the frost'") was also provided to all subjects, in order to avoid a possible confusion with its (near-) homonym, *hearty*. Because we felt that the university students we tested would likely be well able to spell most or all of the short "roots" employed in this study, the spelling test was limited to the shorter list of 50 "derived" words (randomly ordered, but presented in the same order to all subjects). As indicated above, however, subjects were provided with the correct spellings of the roots as part of the MR test, in any case, to eliminate this variable as a factor. In order to minimize the possibility that subjects might otherwise draw some connection between their spellings and the MR issue, the spelling test was given the week before the administration of the MR test.

As before, a notion of critical spellings was employed to define the individual "S" and "D" spellers for each of the derived words. For the TP word pairs, the S-spellers were defined by the same criteria as in the prior experiment with children, i.e., both fully correct and only root correct spellings qualified, while a root incorrect spelling did not. Thus, for example, both the spellings *laborotory* and *laboritory* for *laboratory* revealed the same information about the root *labor,* so both were considered correct for our purposes, despite the misspellings of the unstressed vowels. The misspelling *labratory,* however, involved a critical error, as this misspelling tended to obscure somewhat the relationship between this word and its root. Thus any subject who misspelled *laboratory* in this way was defined as a D-speller for that word. The same criteria applied to the FP word group (e.g., *pea/pearl*), although in this case the putative shared root was less semantically transparent, and indeed historically (and no doubt synchronically) incorrect. If spelling similarity is a strong cue to MR, however, we should expect much the same tendency in both of these cases: Although many more subjects overall ought to provide high MR ratings for a TP pair like *sign/signature* than for an FP pair like *heave/heavy*, we would still expect higher MR means from the S-spellers (where the elements of interest are spelled the same) than from the D-spellers (where their spellings differ).

Finally, we may consider the critical spellings for the TN and FN word sets. As the correct spellings of the words (and their shared substrings of interest) now serve to obscure potential morphological relationships, both the fully correct and root correct spellings now serve to define the D-spellers for the items involved. In fact, the only spellings that would yield an S-speller in the TN case would be *misspellings* that made the shared elements appear more similar in writing than they actually are (e.g., such common misspellings as *factsimile, *napsack, *infantesimal* and *midevil*). As noted above, the words in this set were chosen precisely because these were the most common type of misspellings that had been observed for these words.[6] Similarly, in the FN case, it is only critical *mis*spellings of much the same kind (e.g., *spacial, *firey, *turnament, *numerous*, etc.) that serve to enhance the true etymological relationships that in these words are actually rendered more obscure by the correct spellings. (From a morphophonemic point of view, words like *spatial, fiery, tournament*, and *numerous*, etc. are, indeed, badly spelled!)

By defining the S-spellers and the D-spellers in this way, we thus arrive at the following general pre-experimental expectation: If spelling similarity critically affects MR judgments, S-spellers ought to reveal a tendency to give higher MR ratings for *all* word pairs than D-spellers.

Results

The results of the four stimulus categories are summarized in Figure 1, which is based on the 21 items that had at least two subjects in each of the spelling groups. Note that the word pairs in the TP and the FN categories yielded the highest ratings of morphological relatedness overall, which was to be expected from the fact that the word pairs in these two categories were chosen precisely because they were thought to represent cases of true (synchronic) morphological relatedness.

---

[6]All of these misspellings come from Norback and Norback (1974), which was an invaluable aid to stimulus selection for this study.

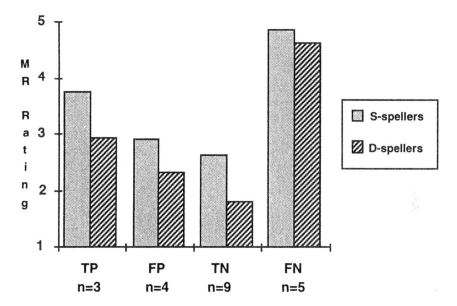

FIGURE 1. MR scores for Same (S) and Different (D) spellers for True (T) and False (F) Positive (P) and Negative (N) derivational relatives.

Even in the FP and TN categories, however, where the word pairs were thought to illustrate cases of likely non-relatedness, and where the mean MR ratings obtained in our experiment were quite low overall, the speakers who spelled the root-like elements of the derived words in the same way as in their isolated forms (i.e., the S-spellers) still tended to give higher morphological relatedness ratings to these word pairs than the subjects who spelled the two forms in a different way (D-spellers).

Table 1 shows the results for each of the 21 individual items for which statistics could be computed. (The rest had counts of 0 or 1 in either the S or D spelling groups.) With three minor exceptions (all involving very small *ns* in one of the spelling categories), S-spellings seem to enhance MR while D-spellings discourage it, and in over half of these cases the result is statistically significant.[7] (Note also that 18 of the 21 *t*-values are positive. Assuming a 50% chance of getting a positive or negative value on each item, this overall result has a .001 probability by a sign test.)

---

[7]This proportion drops to about a third of the items if a Bonferroni adjustment is made to account for the 21 *t* tests performed, taking $p < .10$ as the experiment-wise error. In this situation the probability required for significance reduces from .05 to .002, and the *p* values that remain significant after this adjustment are marked by * in Table 3. To our minds, however, the sign test noted above is the most telling statistic overall.

TABLE 1. *MR Scores for S-spellers vs. D spellers.*

Type	Root	Derived Word	Spelling Group	Count	Mean Rating	S.D.	df	*t*-value	*p* (1-tail)
TP	hand	handkerchief	S	63	3.91	1.43	112	6.643	0.0001*
			D	51	2.14	1.39			
TP	cup	cupboard	S	107	4.26	1.15	112	0.265	n.s.
			D	7	4.14	1.07			
TP	labor	laboratory	S	97	3.08	1.43	112	1.463	n.s.
			D	17	2.53	1.51			
FP	hard	hardy	S	81	4.20	1.21	112	7.251	0.0001*
			D	33	2.24	1.52			
FP	tail	tailor	S	102	2.76	1.49	112	2.282	0.0122
			D	12	1.75	0.87			
FP	gorge	gorgeous	S	108	1.87	1.19	112	-0.597	n.s.
			D	6	2.17	1.17			
FP	furl	furlough	S	102	2.89	1.23	111	-0.743	n.s.
			D	11	3.18	1.17			
TN	cost	caustic	S	36	2.11	1.26	112	3.641	0.0001*
			D	78	1.37	0.87			
TN	infant	infinitesimal	S	2	3.00	1.14	112	0.190	n.s.
			D	112	2.79	1.59			
TN	excel	accelerate	S	26	4.39	1.33	112	6.387	0.0001*
			D	88	2.14	1.64			
TN	lab	lobotomy	S	54	2.88	1.49	112	4.546	0.0001*
			D	60	1.75	1.04			
TN	long	lingerie	S	5	1.60	1.34	112	1.888	0.0308
			D	109	1.13	0.50			
TN	evil	medieval	S	28	3.07	1.41	112	4.111	0.0001*
			D	86	1.94	1.21			
TN	nap	knapsack	S	24	2.71	1.43	112	3.119	0.0012*
			D	90	1.84	1.14			
TN	nut	neutron	S	3	1.33	0.58	112	0.843	n.s.
			D	111	1.11	0.42			
TN	pack	pachyderm	S	18	2.72	1.27	110	1.797	0.0376
			D	94	2.09	1.40			
FN	message	messenger	S	9	5.00	0.00	112	1.383	n.s.
			D	105	4.73	0.58			
FN	proceed	procedure	S	9	5.00	0.00	112	1.647	(0.0512)
			D	105	4.43	1.04			
FN	fire	fiery	S	39	4.87	0.34	112	1.907	0.0296
			D	75	4.56	0.99			
FN	abstain	abstinence	S	3	4.67	0.58	112	-0.584	n.s.
			D	111	4.87	0.58			
FN	space	spatial	S	61	4.82	0.50	112	1.876	0.0317
			D	53	4.57	0.91			

For all five of the items in the FN class, we see evidence of a strong ceiling effect, as MR scores for S-spellers and D-spellers alike are all in the range from 4.43 to the maximum score of 5.00. This would indicate that, for good and poor spellers alike, the high degree of phonetic and semantic similarity between pairs like *message/messenger, proceed/procedure, fire/fiery, abstain/abstinence,* and *space/spatial* is perfectly adequate to indicate the morphological relationships involved, despite small deviations in the spelling.

An analogous floor effect can also be seen for at least two of the four items in the FP set, based on the pairs *tail/tailor* and *gorge/gorgeous,* as well as for the two TN pairs *long/lingerie* and *nut/neutron.* For these items the MR ratings are quite low for S and D spellers alike. This seems to indicate that the suggested morphological relationships between these words are generally regarded as insufficiently plausible on natural phonetic and semantic grounds to be significantly enhanced by accidental spelling similarities.

With few exceptions, the remaining items show a strong positive relationship between morphological and orthographic knowledge. However, only two of these items provide what we consider to be strong support for the specific directionality whereby spelling similarities give rise to morphological identifications. Among the TP set, *hand/handkerchief* shows clear and unambiguous evidence that spelling influences MR. Here the S-spellers and the D-spellers are roughly matched in number, and the former give a relatively high MR rating to this pair of 3.91, while the D-spellers give a mean MR rating of 2.14. Moreover, as with the cases of *draw/drawer* and *lace/necklace* in the first experiment, it seems highly unlikely that the etymological relationship between these words could have been induced by the S-spellers on the basis of the meager phonetic and semantic clues that the spoken form of the word [hǽŋkřčɪf] supplies (cf. Derwing, 1976). Note also that the spelling of the related word *hanky* does not betray its relationship with *hand,* nor is there any apparent tendency for native speakers to misspell this word as **handky* (as evidenced by the fact that this misspelling does not appear in Norback & Norback's collection).

The other item that seems to supply good evidence of spelling as a factor in MR is the FP pair *hard/hardy,* as only the S-spellers (i.e., who spelled the root portion of the derived word correctly) were strongly inclined to accept the idea that the two words *hard* and *hardy* contained the same root. Note that 29 of the 33 D-spellers here spelled the word *hardy* exactly like its homonym *hearty,* even though the meaning of the test word had been clearly explained to them. The misspelling **hearty* in itself constitutes prima facie evidence that no morphological connection has been made by these subjects between this word and the root word *hard.*

However, the bulk of the positive evidence in this study that favors our preexperimental expectation comes from items in the TN stimulus set, where it was critical *mis*spellings of test words that might have provided some impetus for a morphological relatedness judgment. These were word pairs like *cost/caustic* (note the critical misspelling **costic*), *excel/accelerate* (vs. **excel(l)erate*), *lab/lobotomy* (vs. **labotomy*), *evil/medieval* (vs. **midevil*), *nap/knapsack* (vs. **napsack*), and, marginally, *pack/pachyderm* (vs. **packyderm*). In all of these cases S-spellers actually misspelled the words in the ways indicated in parentheses here. This is all well and good for our hypothesis, in principle, except for the fact that for most of these items it seems quite possible that the MR identifications for these word pairs might well have antedated the spellings. In other words, except for the pair *cost/caustic* (for which the MR ratings were very low for both types of spellers, even though the S-spellers still do show a significantly higher score), it is highly plausible in our view that the misspellings of the remaining items in this set might have resulted from a prior identification of a "folk etymology" on purely natural grounds. For example, everyone knows—or at least hopes and believes—that "lobotomies" take place in hospitals or other places very closely associated with "labs," and the "medieval" period is often closely associated with some of the well-documented "evils" of religious excess, etc. Even the meaning of *accelerate* would not seem to be too implausibly removed from the notion of "excelling" (i.e., "doing better than" some norm). In all of these cases, therefore, there seem to be adequate grounds in the sounds and meanings on which to base a positive MR judgment, and spelling errors seem to follow as a natural expectation, at least for subjects who are sensitive to such things. (That the direction of influence can indeed go from the morphological judgment to the spelling is readily attested to by such familiar examples as the common misspelling of the word *pronunciation* as **pronounciation,* an error which preserves the spelling of the second vowel from the isolated root form *pronounce.*[8]) Of course, it is also quite possible that a misspelling like **napsack, *packyderm,* etc. might just as well have its origins in the regular set of sound-spelling correspondences, with the root morpheme judgment (if any) coming afterwards. The point is that almost all of the items in this particular set provide unclear, ambiguous cases, as far as the directionality of influence question is concerned.

In sum, therefore, our findings strongly confirm that knowledge of word spellings and judgments of morphological relatedness are indeed interrelated, though only in the small set of items just noted do we have good evidence that it is spelling that has influenced the relatedness judgments rather than the other way around.

CONCLUSIONS

Both parts of this study have provided some empirical evidence that subjects can and do make use of orthographic information in analyzing words morphologi-

---

[8]Frith (1980), however, presents a fascinating case of good readers but poor spellers who seem almost oblivious to morphological relationships in the way they spell.

cally, although spelling commonalities will not necessarily lead to the perception of a relationship if there is not a reasonably transparent (synchronic) semantic connection to go along with it. In some cases, in fact, like *cup/cupboard, hand/handkerchief, draw/drawer, and lace/necklace,* spelling provides the best—and perhaps the only—good clue to the potential morphological relatedness of the words. Likewise, in cases like *hard/hardy* and *cost/*costic,* the spellings (or misspellings) can evidently incline subjects to "find" shared morphemes that would probably not otherwise have been found. In short, knowledge of spelling (or lack of it) can have a significant effect on the morphological knowledge and intuitions of individual subjects. Though weakened somewhat by the fact that in many other cases of shared spelling and shared morpheme alignments the direction of influence may well be reversed, the conclusion remains that spelling (along with many other educational factors, such as explicit instruction) can and does influence morphological judgments.

One consequence for linguistic theory has already been hinted at in our introduction: If much of what we know about morphology is education- and literacy-derived, we can expect to find rather vast individual differences in "competence" in this area, particularly between highly educated and relatively uneducated speakers. This is precisely what research to date on MR has, in fact, indicated (see McCawley, 1986, in addition to the other references cited on this point). To judge from the relatively few accounts that have explored these matters seriously, the same appears to be true in the fundamental areas of (syntactic) grammaticality judgments (Ross, 1979) and paraphrasing skills (Gleitman & Gleitman, 1970) as well. This has the potential to wreak considerable havoc not only on the "instantaneous" model of language acquisition (cf. n. 1) but also upon the general homogeneity thesis that underlies almost all work in generative grammar (e.g., Chomsky, 1965, p. 3). The potential benefit of recognizing the full extent of individual differences among speakers, as well as the important role that education-based factors play in them, is the development of new theoretical models than are less "ideal" and more "real."

In any event, the study of spelling and all of the other educationally derived aspects of knowledge that affect linguistic competence has been a relatively neglected area. In fact, the developmental course and even the adult limits of morphological decomposition skills in ordinary speakers are not at all well understood, and until they are, linguistic claims based on the unsupported assumptions or professional intuitions of trained linguists will bear little scientific weight. More empirical investigation and more refined methodological tools will be required in order to gain more insight into the sources of speakers' morphological knowledge and to determine the extent to which linguistically naive (i.e., typical) speakers naturally engage in intuitive morphological analysis and the conditions under which it is both successful and unsuccessful.

ACKNOWLEDGMENT

Preparation of this article was supported in part by Social Sciences and Humanities Research Council of Canada Grant #410-91-0249, awarded to the first author.

Thanks to Anne Cutler, Tracey Derwing, Terry Nearey, the editor, and three reviewers for their many very helpful comments and suggestions, not all of which we were wise enough to accept.

REFERENCES

Anderson, S. R. (1992). *A-morphous morphology.* Cambridge: Cambridge University Press.

Berko, J. (1958). The child's learning of English morphology. *Word, 14,* 150-177.

Bloomfield, L. (1933). *Language.* New York: Holt, Rinehart, & Winston.

Carlisle, J. F. (1988). Knowledge of derivational morphology and spelling ability in fourth, sixth, and eighth graders. *Applied Psycholinguistics, 9,* 247-266.

Chomsky, N. (1965). *Aspects of the theory of syntax.* Cambridge, MA: MIT Press.

Chomsky, N., & Halle, M. (1968). *The sound pattern of English.* New York: Harper & Row.

Derwing, B. L. (1973). *Transformational grammar as a theory of language acquisition: A study in the empirical, conceptual and methodological foundations of contemporary linguistics.* Cambridge: Cambridge University Press.

Derwing, B. L. (1976). Morpheme recognition and the learning of rules for derivational morphology. *The Canadian Journal of Linguistics, 21(1),* 38-66.

Derwing, B. L. (1990). Orthographic aspects of linguistic competence. In P. Downing, S. D. Lima, & M. Noonan (Eds.), *The linguistics of literacy* (pp. 193-210). Amsterdam: John Benjamins.

Derwing, B. L., & Baker, W. J. (1979). Recent research on the acquisition of English morphology. In P. Fletcher & M. Garman (Eds.), *Language acquisition: Studies in first language development* (1st ed.) (pp. 209-223). Cambridge: Cambridge University Press.

Derwing, B. L., & Baker, W. J. (1986). Assessing morphological development. In P. Fletcher & M. Garman (Eds.), *Language acquisition: Studies in first language development* (2nd ed.) (pp. 326-338). Cambridge: Cambridge University Press.

Fischer, F. W., Shankweiler D., & Liberman, I. Y. (1985). Spelling proficiency and sensitivity to word structure. *Journal of Memory and Language, 24,* 423-441.

Frith, U. (1980). Unexpected spelling problems. In U. Frith (Ed.), *Cognitive processes in spelling* (pp. 495-515). London: Academic Press.

Gleitman, L. R., & Gleitman, H. (1970). *Phrase and paraphrase: Some innovative uses of language.* New York: Norton.

Jaeger, J. J. (1984). Assessing the psychological reality of the Vowel Shift Rule. *Journal of Psycholinguistic Research, 13,* 13-36.

Leong, C. K. (1989). Productive knowledge of derivational rules in poor readers. *Annals of Dyslexia, 39,* 94-115.

McCawley, J. D. (1986). Today the world, tomorrow phonology. *Phonology Yearbook, 3,* 27-43.

Norback, P., & Norback, C. (1974). *The misspeller's dictionary.* New York: Quadrangle/The New York Times Book Co.

Ross, J. R. (1979). Where's English? In C. J. Fillmore, D. Kempler, & W. S-Y. Wang (Eds.), *Individual differences in language ability and language behavior* (pp. 127-163). New York: Academic Press.

Scinto, L. F. M. (1986). *Written language and psychological development.* Orlando, FL: Academic Press.

Smith, M. L. (1987). *Spelling and morpheme recognition: A methodological study.* Unpublished master's thesis, University of Alberta, Edmonton.

Smith, M. L., & Derwing, B. L. (1987). Spelling and morpheme recognition: An experimental study. In D. Strong-Kraus (Ed.), *Proceedings of the Thirteenth Deseret Language and Linguistics Symposium* (pp. 205-212). Provo, UT: DLLS.

Templeton, S., & Scarborough-Franks, L. (1985). The spelling's the thing: Knowledge of derivational morphology in orthography and phonology among older students. *Applied Psycholinguistics, 6,* 371-390.

APPENDIX 1

STIMULI FOR SMITH'S (1987) EXPERIMENT

Set 1 (Grades 4-5):

awe/awful	cup/cupboard*	lace/necklace
cave/cavity	draw/drawer*	preside/president
create/creature	electric/electricity	sign/signal
crime/criminal	message/messenger*	

Set 2 (Grades 6-7):

cup/cupboard*	draw/drawer*	pollute/pollution
decide/decision	fable/fabulous	price/precious
describe/description	know/knowledge	table/vegetable
discuss/discussion	message/messenger*	

APPENDIX 2

TRAINING EXAMPLES FOR SMITH'S (1987)
MR TEST BATTERY

EXAMPLE 1: TEACH/TEACHER

Q1. (Definition question). "What does the word *teacher* mean to you?" (Does the subject use the "root"?[9] See section on Scoring in main text.)

Q2. (Berko-type question). "Why is a *teacher* called a *teacher?*" (cf. Berko, 1958) (Is the "root" used?)

Q3. (Etymological question). "Does the word *teacher* 'come from' any other word that you know of?" (cf. Derwing, 1976)

A.   If the answer to Q3 was "Yes":

Q4. "Which word? What does this word mean?" (Confirmed by having the subject define the word.)

Q5. "Why do you think so?" (If subjects seemed uncertain or were unable to give a reason here, they were asked to confirm/disconfirm with the following, more direct etymological question: "Do you think that *teacher* 'comes from' the word *teach?*")

Q6. (Recall question) "Did you ever think of this before or did you just think of it now that I asked you about these words?" (cf. Derwing, 1976) (Confirmed by "Yes.")
"Spell *teach.*"[10]
"Spell *teacher.*"

B.   If the answer to Q3 was "No" or "Not sure":

Q4. "Do you know the word *teach?*"

> *1. If the answer to Q4 is "Yes":* "What does it mean?" (Confirmed by having the subject define the word.)
>
> *2. If the answer to Q4 is "No":* Skip Q5 and Q6 and proceed to spelling tasks at end.

---

[9]For example, if a subject were to define *criminal* as "someone who has committed a *crime,*" a 1 would be scored for Q1, while an 0 would be scored for any definition that failed to employ the root overtly, such as "someone who has broken the law."

[10]This is the point at which the spelling of the putative root was elicited. The spelling of the full derived word that follows was included as a double check and to see if the subject's spelling had changed as a result of administering the MR battery of questions. Few differences were noted, but in cases of conflict the first or pre-MR test spelling was taken as criterial for all of the analyses reported here.

Q5. "Do you think that *teacher* 'comes from' the word *teach*?"

> *1. If the answer to Q5 is "Yes":* "Why do you think so?" (Plausible answer sought.)
>
> *2. If the answer to Q5 is "No":* Skip Q6 and proceed to spelling tasks at end.

Q6. (Recall question.) "Did you ever think of this before or did you just think of it now that I asked you about these words?" (Confirmed by "Yes.")
"Spell *teach*."
"Spell *teacher*."

EXAMPLE 2: HAM/HAMMER

The questioning for this item followed the same procedure as in the previous example, but replacing the word *teacher* by *hammer,* and *teach* by *ham.* However, subjects who gave the word *ham* in response to Q4 or answered "Yes" to Q5 were given the following, slightly modified series of questions in lieu of the counterparts shown for Example 1:

1. "What does the word *ham* mean?"
2. "Why do you think the word *hammer* comes from the word *ham?*" (None were able to think of a plausible reason.)
3. "Do you think *ham* is related to *hammer* like *teach* is related to *teacher?*"
4. "Do you think that the word *hammer* 'comes from' the word *ham,* or do you think that *ham* is a different word that sounds the same?"
5. "Did you ever think before that *hammer* came from the word *ham?*"

APPENDIX 3

STIMULI FOR NEW EXPERIMENT

Type	Item No.	Root	Derived Word	Type	Item No.	Root	Derived Word
Practice Items:							
P	1	wild	wilderness	P	8	fame	famous
P	2	bash	bashful	P	9	holy	holiday
P	3	berry	strawberry	P	10	law	lawyer
P	4	dirt	dirty	P	11	dine	dinner
P	5	fry	Friday	P	12	hunger	hungry
P	6	birth	birthday	P	13	wagon	carpenter
P	7	dog	puppy	P	14	teach	teacher
				P	15	oratory	laboratory
Test Items:							
TP	22	preside	president	TN	24	fact	facsimile
TP	49	heal	health	TN	45	cauliflower	broccoli
TP	10	ease	disease	TN	50	cost	caustic
TP	29	hand	handkerchief	TN	37	fad	infidelity
TP	1	break	breakfast	TN	41	infant	infinitesimal
TP	19	sign	signature	TN	44	excel	accelerate
TP	8	awe	awful	TN	26	lab	lobotomy
TP	31	lace	necklace	TN	34	long	lingerie
TP	13	create	creature	TN	35	evil	medieval
TP	43	cup	cupboard	TN	20	nap	knapsack
TP	12	know	acknowledge	TN	6	nut	neutron
TP	40	labor	laboratory	TN	28	pack	pachyderm
FP	15	pea	pearl	FN	11	sound	sonic
FP	21	fame	famish	FN	7	number	numerous
FP	30	hard	hardy	FN	46	moon	month
FP	14	bull	bully	FN	27	message	messenger
FP	47	limb	limber	FN	23	price	precious
FP	38	tail	tailor	FN	39	proceed	procedure
FP	4	mangy	manger	FN	48	fire	fiery
FP	33	grim	grimy	FN	36	abstain	abstinence
FP	25	heave	heavy	FN	5	space	spatial
FP	42	happy	happen	FN	18	spin	spider
FP	16	gorge	gorgeous	FN	9	crown	coronation
FP	3	furl	furlough	FN	2	turn	tournament
TN*	17	sin	syntax	TN*	32	cow	muumuu

*Extra TN items included "for fun" (not scored)

2   Processing the Dynamic Visual-Spatial Morphology of Signed Languages

Karen Emmorey
The Salk Institute for Biological Studies

Language modality (visual-manual vs. aural-oral) may influence grammatical encoding and language processing. Sign language phonology does not rely upon rapid serial distinctions and takes advantage of the visual modality by representing many phonological distinctions simultaneously. In addition, signed languages prefer nonconcatenative morphological processes, in contrast to spoken languages. Several studies investigating lexical processing in American Sign Language (ASL) are summarized in this chapter. These studies suggest the following: (a) ASL signs can be identified earlier than English words, (b) signers tend to identify the base sign prior to the movemental inflection for morphologically complex signs, despite simultaneous articulation, and (c) the internal organization of the ASL lexicon is based in part on morphological relations between lexical items.

INTRODUCTION

Signed languages have evolved within a completely different biological medium, using a different set of articulators and received by another perceptual system. Linguistic structure is expressed by movements of the hands rather than the vocal tract, and this structure must be decoded from a dynamic visual signal rather than an auditory one. Thus, signed languages and spoken languages are restricted by many different articulatory and perceptual requirements. These differing biological constraints may affect language processing and may also influence how grammatical structure is encoded. Given the different processing demands and constraints, signed languages provide unique insight into the possible universal principles of human language processing. In this chapter, I focus on what effects the visual-manual modality might have on morphological and phonological processing, and I discuss aspects of morphological processing that appear to be unique to signed languages.

Although other signed languages are discussed, I focus on American Sign Language (ASL), the language used by deaf people in the United States and parts of Canada. ASL is an autonomous natural language, not derived from English, and is passed down from one generation of deaf people to the next. ASL is one of the most widely studied sign languages, and yet serious linguistic work began only thirty years ago (compared to the hundreds of years of research on English (and the thousands of years of linguistic research on spoken languages in general)). This early work by William Stokoe focused on the phonology of ASL, illustrating that signs were not simply pantomimic gestures but contained non-meaningful sublexical structures that could be combined to create meaningful lexical items (Stokoe, Casterline, & Croneberg, 1965). Figure 1 provides examples of some minimal pairs in ASL. In these examples, signs are contrasted phonologically by handshape, body location, and movement features. Sign language phonology obviously does not involve sound patternings or vocally based features, but many linguists have broadened the term *phonology* to mean the "patterning of the formational units of the expression system of a natural language" and the set of general principles which constrain the organization of these units (Coulter & Anderson, 1993, pg. 5).

Klima and Bellugi (1979) were the first to provide a comprehensive description of the many morphological processes that occur in ASL. Like spoken languages, ASL exhibits inflectional, derivational, and compounding morphological processes. ASL also has a set of noun classifier forms that are embedded in verbs of motion and location; classifier verb constructions perform the same function as prepositional phrases in spoken languages, that is, they express spatial relations and movement. Noun-verb derivations are quite productive in ASL, and examples of ASL inflectional morphology include person and number agreement, subject/object agreement, and around 15 different inflections for distributive and temporal aspect. ASL does not exhibit inflections for verb tense. Although a fair amount is known about the morphological structure of ASL, very little is known about how this structure might be interpreted on-line and what sorts of mechanisms might be required to decode a dynamic visual-spatial linguistic signal.

This chapter focuses only on how deaf signers process the phonology and morphology of ASL. Hanson has shown that ASL signers who are bilingual in English do not recode English into ASL, and the organization of lexical information in English and in ASL is based on language specific principles (Hanson & Feldman, 1989; Hanson & Lichtenstein, 1990). Hanson (this volume;

Hanson & Fowler, 1987) has explored how deaf signers access and represent the phonology and morphology of English given that these subjects do not have access to the auditory modality. In this chapter, we are concerned with how these subjects process and represent their primary language—ASL, a language that is acquired naturally (rather than through instruction) and is accessible to the deaf through the visual modality. First, however, we examine how the visual and auditory modalities might shape the structure of language itself.

THE EFFECTS OF THE VISUAL-SPATIAL MODALITY ON THE LINGUISTIC ENCODING OF MORPHOLOGICAL AND PHONOLOGICAL INFORMATION

Speech perception and production are largely sequential in nature, and this fact has influenced models of auditory word recognition and linguistic analyses of phonological and morphological structure (Kenstowicz & Kisseberth, 1979; Marslen-Wilson, 1987). Until recently linguistic models of spoken language have emphasized the linear ordering of linguistic units: Words are analyzed as *sequences* of phonemes, syllables, or morphemes. In addition, phonotactic and morphotactic rules are most often concerned with the permissible *order* of these linguistic elements within a word; likewise, many phonological and morphological rules are conditioned by the linear arrangement of linguistic elements (e.g., [n] becomes [m] when followed by [b]). With the recent development of feature geometry and autosegmental phonology and morphology, linguistic theory has moved away from an implicit emphasis on the linear structure of words and segments and has focused much more on their nonlinear structure. In these new models, the sequential nature of phonological and morphological structure is captured by reference to a "timing tier" to which autosegmental representations are attached. Nonlinear structures are used to represent the simultaneous nature of groups of phonetic features, to represent syllable hierarchies, and to represent certain morphological structures (e.g., "template" morphology in Semitic languages). The division of phonological structure into linear and nonlinear components has allowed linguistic models to capture significant generalizations about the timing of speech and about how the structure of the vocal tract influences the nature of phonological rules (Clements, 1985; Goldsmith, 1990).

Ironically, while recent phonological models for spoken language have discovered and focused on the nonlinear, simultaneous aspects of speech, models of sign language phonology have recently discovered the importance of *linear* structure to phonological processes and representations (e.g., Liddell & Johnson, 1989). Early work on ASL emphasized that phonological information was primarily articulated simultaneously and argued that, unlike spoken language, sign phonology was organized simultaneously rather than sequentially (Klima & Bellugi, 1979; Stokoe et al., 1965). In these early models, ASL words were phonologically represented as simultaneously organized categories of handshape, place of articulation (body location), and movement. However, Liddell (1984) presented persuasive evidence that ASL phonology and morphology (particularly compounding) contain significant sequential elements. Liddell showed that linear structure was required in order to contrast minimal pairs and to express certain morphological and phonological rules. More recent models of ASL phonology address these findings and attempt to represent both the sequential and the simultaneous properties of sign. Similar to models of oral language phonology, current ASL models propose a linearly arranged timing tier which co-occurs with autosegmental representations of phonological features (see papers in Coulter, 1993).

Differing Articulatory Constraints and Perceptual Capacities

Despite the fact that the grammars of both signed and spoken languages express linguistic distinctions both linearly and through simultaneous structure, these languages differ strongly in their preference for type of grammatical encoding. Signed languages have limited sequential contrasts and permit a greater degree of simultaneous expression compared to spoken languages. For example, the number of linearly arranged phonological segments[1] in monomorphemic words appears to be substantially fewer than the number of segments permitted within monomorphemic words for most spoken languages. Sandler (1989) argues that the majority of ASL words contain only three (or fewer) segments, and many single segment words are also permitted (Perlmutter, 1992). For example, both Perlmutter and Sandler analyze signs such as *candy* or *apple* in Figure 1 as containing a single segment.[2] Fewer segments appear to be possible because a substantial amount of phonological information can be expressed simultaneously (e.g., handshape, body location, hand/arm orientation are all articulated simultaneously). Although this generalization may be tied to how segment is defined within linguistic models, there is nonetheless a clear difference in the speed and number of articulatory gestures which must be mapped onto units of sublexical phonological structure (however this is defined). For example, the articulators for speech (the tongue, lips, jaw) can move quite rapidly, producing easily perceived distinctions on the order of every 50 - 200 ms. In contrast, the major articulators for sign (the hands) move relatively slowly such that the duration of an isolated sign is about 1,000 ms; the duration of an average spoken word is

---

[1]The nature and even the existence of signed segments is still a matter of debate within linguistics (e.g., Liddell, 1993; Wilbur, 1993). For our purposes, segment can be interpreted as a unit of phonological structure below the syllable.

[2]Both Perlmutter and Sandler consider path movement a type of segment in ASL. Signs without path movement such as *apple* or *candy* consist of a single segment, termed a Position segment under Perlmutter's analysis and a Location segment in Sandler's model.

more like 500 ms. If real time language processing has equal timing limits for spoken and signed languages, then there is strong pressure for signed languages to express more distinctions simultaneously.

Signs Contrasting Only in Handshape

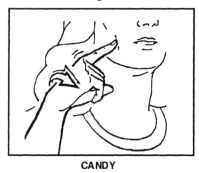
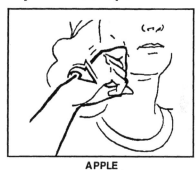

CANDY   APPLE

Signs Contrasting Only in Location

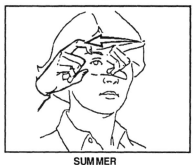

SUMMER   UGLY

Signs Contrasting Only in Movement

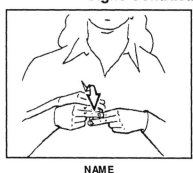
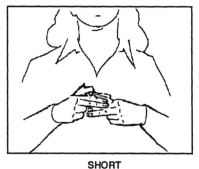

NAME   SHORT

FIGURE 1. Examples of minimal pairs in ASL.

In fact, there is evidence that certain processing limitations are universal. Baddeley has argued that memory span involves an articulatory loop that has a 2-second duration (Baddeley, 1986). Memory span is shorter for items that take longer to rehearse covertly; thus, memory span is inversely related to word length within a given language. For example, Ellis and Hennelly (1980) and Naveh-Benjamin and Ayres (1986) found that speakers of languages that had phonemically complex or multisyllable words for cardinal numbers (e.g., Welsh, Arabic) could not retain as many numbers in short term memory as speakers whose languages had relatively short words for these numbers (e.g., English, Spanish). To the extent that this memory system is involved in normal language processing, the limit on memory span puts pressure on the language system to incorporate as many linguistic distinctions as possible within this time limit. The relatively slow articulators and the limit on processing time may conspire to pressure signed systems to avoid a great reliance on sequentially expressed linguistic distinctions.

The articulatory pressures seem to work in concert with the capacities of the visual and auditory modalities for expressing simultaneous and sequential information. That is, the visual system is well suited for simultaneously perceiving a large amount of information, whereas the auditory system seems particularly suited for perceiving fast temporal distinctions. Thus, both sign and speech have exploited the advantages of their respective modalities. Furthermore, in sign language phonology the actual movement of the articulators does not carry the same type of information that it does for speech. In speech, the acoustic realization of articulatory *transitions* provides the most salient information for phonological processing (Tallal, Miller, & Fitch, 1993). Temporal changes provide strong cues to phoneme identity for both vowels and consonants. In contrast, the identification of phonological structure for sign does not rely as heavily on the transitions of the articulators. Orientation, place of articulation, and hand configuration do not compete and can be observed directly in the signed visual signal. In contrast to speech, movement transitions do not provide essential cues to phonological features, such as place of articulation, because the visual system can perceive these features in parallel.

Sign languages appear to take full advantage of the parallel capacity of the visual system in another way. These languages often express grammatical information simultaneously on the face in co-ordination with the hands. Grammatical facial expressions have a clear onset and offset, and they are co-ordinated with specific parts of the signed sentence. These expressions differ from emotional expressions in their scope, timing, and in the face muscles that are used (Reilly, McIntire, & Bellugi, 1991). Examples of linguistic facial expression include marking for adverbials, topics, WH questions, conditionals, and relative clauses. We don't yet know whether grammatical facial expression is universal for signed languages, but linguistic facial markers have been reported for many different languages (e.g., British Sign Language, Danish Sign Language, Finnish Sign Language, Italian Sign Language).

In sum, the articulatory constraints of the vocal apparatus for speech and the hands and arms for sign conspire with the capacities of the auditory and visual systems to strongly influence how phonological structure is encoded in spoken and signed languages. Spoken languages can exhibit numerous sequential distinctions within a phonological word, whereas signed languages have substantial nonlinear structure in which many phonological distinctions are articulated and perceived in parallel.

Preference for Nonconcatenative Morphology

Another modality-determined effect on grammatical encoding may be the fact that sign languages show a marked preference for nonconcatenative morphological processes, in contrast to spoken languages' preference for affixation. For example, ASL contains only two suffixes, one of which appears to be borrowed[3] from English. Similarly, Sandler has been unable to find any linear affixes in Israeli Sign Language (Sandler, 1993b), and no linear affixes are presented in Kyle and Woll's (1985) description of British Sign Language, although both languages have rich nonconcatenative morphology. Bergman (1982) claims that Swedish Sign Language has neither suffixation nor prefixation but exhibits several types of reduplication and nonconcatenative morphological processes. None of these signed languages are historically related to one another (including American and British Sign Languages). To the extent that they are representative of signed languages in general, the data indicate that linear affixation is rare in signed languages and that simultaneous expression of a base form[4] and its morphological markings is the preferred linguistic encoding.

This pattern of morphological encoding is in contrast to patterns found in spoken languages. For spoken languages, simultaneous affixation (such as template morphology, infixation, or reduplication) is relatively rare in the world's languages (see Bentin & Frost, this volume, for a discussion of nonconcatenative morphology). Cutler, Hawkins, and Gilligan (1985) argue that processing constraints underlie the rarity of morphological processes which alter the phonological integrity of the base form (e.g., infixation which inserts an affix into the middle of a word). Languages avoid processes that disrupt the structural integrity of linguistic units. Hall (1992) also argues that the rarity of nonconcatenative morphology is due to the processing complexity associated with discontinuous elements in general (e.g., center embedding or verbs with

---

[3]Borrowing can occur through Manually Coded English, an invented gesture system used in the education of the deaf in which each English morpheme is given a signed form.

[4]The term "base form" is used in order to be neutral with respect to whether morphological processes are applied to roots or stems.

particles). Discontinuous structure adds to memory load (because an interpretation cannot be immediately assigned), and it may lead to garden path effects if the first element is perceived as a complete form (Frazier, Flores d'Arcais, & Coolen, 1993). Concatenative continuous morphology requires much less computational complexity because of the straightforward mapping between the surface form of a word and its underlying representation (Anderson, 1992). Given these problems, why do signed languages prefer nonconcatenative morphology, and does it pose the same processing challenges that it does for spoken languages?

First, signed languages appear to favor nonconcatenative morphology because, as we have noted, the visual modality affords parallel processing. Moreover, when the linear morphology of a spoken language is transferred to the visual modality, deaf children exposed to this artificial language do not acquire the system and alter it to create simultaneous (spatial) morphological encoding (Supalla, 1991). For example, Manually Coded English (MCE) is an invented language that is sometimes used in the education of deaf children. MCE borrows heavily from the lexicon of ASL, but its inflectional morphology is strictly sequential and based on English morphology. Sam Supalla (1991) has found that children exposed only to MCE modify the inflectional morphology to take advantage of the visual modality. That is, these children produce spatial nonlinear modifications to base verbs and pronominals in order to mark person and case, despite the fact that they were exposed only to linguistic input that produced these distinctions linearly. The children's spatial morphological creations were idiosyncratic, but they were systematic within a child and similar to the grammatical morphology found in signed languages of the world. These results suggest that not only does the visual modality easily afford nonlinear affixation, but visual processing may actually *demand* it.

Secondly, unlike infixation or circumfixation, the morphological processes of ASL (and possibly other signed languages) do not *interrupt* the base form and do not involve discontinuous affixes. Figure 2 illustrates several examples of ASL nonconcatenative morphology. In no case is the base form of the sign actually interrupted by the morphological marking. Discontinuous circumfixation also does not seem to be the proper analysis for these forms. The morphological marking appears to be *superimposed* onto the base form of the verb, and Sandler (1989, 1993a) has analyzed these forms as instances of templatic or autosegmental morphology. Thus, the morphological parsing difficulties that arise from infixation or discontinuous affixation do not seem to be present for ASL.

Before examining how ASL phonological and morphological information might be interpreted during lexical access, I would like to briefly present some data which suggest that differences between the auditory and visual modalities might also influence morphological processing for English.

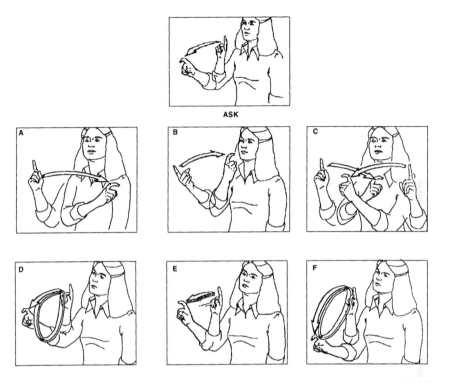

FIGURE 2. Examples of nonconcatenative ASL morphology. Top: base form of ASK; (A) ₁ask₁ 'she asks him'; (B) ₁ask₁st 'she asks me'; (C) ask[reciprocal]; (D) ask [iterative]; (E) ask[habitual]; (F) ask[continual].

Visual and Auditory Modality Effects for English Morphology

Very little research has been concerned specifically with auditory morphological processing in any language. Most research has been conducted with visually presented materials, and we may find that accessing morphologically complex words differs according to the processing constraints of the auditory and visual modalities. The temporal component of auditory language processing may affect how morphological information is interpreted on-line. In fact, following the arguments of Cutler et al. (1985), it is precisely the temporal component of auditory word recognition that creates the linguistic preference for suffixation. For accessing lexical meaning, roots and stems have computational priority such that prefixes delay access to these representations and suffixes do not. Visual word recognition is not tied to serial processing, and recognition of affixal morphemes could proceed in parallel. Readers may be able to identify affixes and base forms simultaneously. Note also that some writing systems require right-to-left scanning (e.g., Hebrew) or even vertical scanning (e.g., Chinese)—indicating that reading and the visual system are not dependent upon a particular temporal order. Later I present some evidence for a difference in morphological processing depending upon mode of presentation (auditory or visual) from an experiment I conducted with English nonwords.

Several studies have reported that visually presented nonwords which contain suffixes (e.g., *corpish*) take longer to reject than unaffixed nonwords (e.g., *garpod*) (Caramazza, Laudanna, & Romani, 1988; Henderson, Wallis, & Knight, 1984; Laudanna & Burani, 1985). According to the Augmented Addressed Morphology (AAM) Model proposed by Caramazza, Laudanna, and colleagues, this result is explained by hypothesizing that nonwords (and new words) are read using a morphological parsing address procedure which accesses an orthographic lexicon containing decomposed roots and affixes. Roots and affixes are represented independently and separately from the whole word (see also Caramazza, Miceli, Silveri, & Laudanna, 1985). Suffixed nonwords take longer to reject because the parser identifies the suffix, which slows rejection time compared to a nonword containing no identifiable morphemes. This model does not assume left-to-right temporal processing (although some models of visual word recognition do hypothesize strict left-to-right processing; see Hudson, this volume).

In contrast to the AAM model, the cohort model of auditory word recognition proposed by Marslen-Wilson and Tyler is highly conditioned by the serial nature of speech. According to the cohort model (and others like it), an acoustic-phonetic representation is sequentially mapped onto lexical entries (see Tyler & Frauenfelder, 1987; Marslen-Wilson, 1987). Lexical candidates which match this initial representation are activated, and as more of a word is heard, activation levels of lexical entries which do not match the incoming acoustic signal are decreased. The sequential matching process continues until only one candidate remains which is consistent with the sensory input. At this point, word recognition can occur. According to the cohort model, English prefixed words and their base forms have separate lexical entries (Tyler, Marslen-Wilson, Rentoul, & Hanney, 1988), but suffixed words do not have entries independent of their base forms (Tyler & Marslen-Wilson, 1986).

The Addressed Morphology model for reading and the cohort model for auditory word recognition differ in the nature of lexical representations and in the temporal constraints on access to the lexicon. I conducted an experiment to investigate potential differences between visual and auditory word recognition with respect to recognizing English suffixes (Emmorey, 1987). In this study, suffixed nonwords were presented both auditorily and visually for lexical decision. The results suggest that suffixes may be recognized in parallel with the base form for visually presented words but serially for auditory presentation. In this experiment, words (monomorphemic, derived, and inflected) were presented along with different types of nonwords for either auditory or visual lexical decision. A cohort type model of lexical access was assumed for auditory recognition, and the nonwords were designed such that they could be distinguished from real words at the same segment. The nonwords formed the following categories: control (*harvame*), suffixed (*garnly*), word-initial (*cagelo*), and pseudowords (*crushly*) (see Appendix).

During auditory word recognition, I hypothesize that no base form should be recognized for control nonwords (*harvame*) or suffixed nonwords (*garnly*), because neither *harv* nor *garn* is a base form. No difference in lexical decision time between *harvame* and *garnly* is predicted because both nonwords can be rejected at the same point—the suffix in *garnly* never gets analyzed as such on-line because no base form has been encountered that would enable access to suffixes stored with the base representation. In contrast, when these two nonword types (control and suffixed) are presented visually, it is predicted that response time will be longer for the suffixed nonword because the suffix can be recognized independently of the base form. Subjects should take longer to reject pseudowords like *crushly* compared to control nonwords for both auditory and visual presentation because both the base form and the suffix can be identified as occurring English morphemes.

The results are presented in Table 1 and support the above predictions. Suffixed nonwords took longer to reject compared to control nonwords for visually presented stimuli but not for auditorily presented stimuli. This finding suggests that suffixes are not identified independently of a base form during auditory processing, unlike reading. Assuming a cohort type model, both control and suffixed nonwords can be rejected at the point where they deviate from stored base forms. The suffix in the nonword is not recognized as a suffix during on-line auditory processing. For both visual and auditory presentation, pseudowords had the longest response times, presumably for the same reason: Both morphemes are recognized, and rejection occurs because of the illegal combination of base form and suffix. Interestingly, word-initial nonwords took longer to reject compared to control nonwords only for visual presentation. Caramazza et al. (1988) also found that visually presented word-initial nonwords took longer to reject in a lexical decision task.

TABLE 1. *Reaction times and error rates for nonwords presented for auditory or visual lexical decision.*

| | NONWORD TYPE | | | |
| | Control | Suffixed | Word Initial | Pseudoword |
Example	*harvame*	*garnly*	*cagelo*	*crushly*
Presentation				
Visual	737 (1)	817** (5*)	772** (3)	922** (21**)
Auditory	946 (2)	970 (4)	958 (1)	1014** (9*)

significantly longer RT or greater error rate than control nonwords ($p < .05$, ** $p < .001$).

They hypothesized that the longer reaction times were due to the fact that the morphological parsing procedure for reading had identified a possible morpheme (the initial root). For auditory lexical decision in the experiment reported here, encountering a possible initial base form did not slow reaction time, suggesting that the base form was not identified during lexical access. One possible explanation may be that prosodic factors obscured the identity of the base form. The syllabification of the base forms within the nonwords may have altered the acoustic form such that it no longer matched the stored lexical representation.[5] If so, then the initial base form would not be activated during lexical access. Such phonological effects did not occur for visually presented stimuli, and the initial word was recognized for these nonwords (slowing rejection time).

The point of presenting these data is to suggest that the modality of language processing may affect how morphology is interpreted for spoken languages as well as for signed languages. It is important to determine what aspects of morphological processing are modality-independent and what aspects are conditioned by perceptual mechanisms. We may find that some aspects of morphological representation are tied to orthographic and phonological lexicons (which in turn access shared semantic and syntactic lexical information). For example, roots and affixes (both prefixes and suffixes) may be stored separately in an orthographic lexicon as hypothesized by the Addressed Morphology Model, whereas in a phonological lexicon, suffixes may be stored with base forms and derivationally prefixed words may have separate lexical entries as hypothesized by Tyler and colleagues. Or we may find no difference in morphological representation, but lexical entries may be accessed differently for reading and listening, and these different access procedures may impact on how morphological structure is recognized. More research is needed comparing auditory and visual recognition of morphologically complex words in order to distinguish between these different possibilities.

MORPHOLOGICAL AND PHONOLOGICAL PROCESSING IN ASL

Compared to our knowledge of the processes involved in lexical access for English (and other spoken languages), we know very little about how lexical access and word recognition occur for a visual-spatial language such as ASL. In this section, I present the results of several gating and lexical decision experiments conducted with ASL. These studies, in conjunction with previous studies of spoken language, provide some indications that processing a signed language involves certain modality-specific factors, but in general they suggest that the basic determinants of word recognition are the same for signed and

---

[5]The majority of word-initial nonwords (10/15) had syllabification patterns that differed from the syllabification of the word in isolation (e.g., *beastig* [bi - stIg] vs. *beast* [bist]).

spoken languages. We examine the speed of lexical identification, the time course of lexical recognition for morphologically complex words, and the unique role of movement in word recognition for ASL.

The Speed of Lexical Identification

In order to track lexical identification through time, Emmorey and Corina (1990) and Grosjean (1981) adapted the gating paradigm for visual presentation of ASL signs. In this task, signs are presented repeatedly, and the length of each presentation is increased by a constant amount (one videoframe or 33 ms in the Emmorey and Corina study); after each presentation subjects report what they thought the stimulus was. These studies found that when presented with gated ASL monomorphemic signs, deaf subjects produced form-based initial responses until a single lexical candidate emerged. Furthermore, both the Grosjean study and the Emmorey and Corina study found that signs were isolated surprisingly rapidly. Although signs are much longer than words, only about 240 ms or 35% of a sign had to be seen before the sign was identified. This is significantly faster than word recognition for English. Grosjean (1980) found that approximately 330 ms or 83% of a word had to be heard before the word could be isolated. There are at least two reasons why signs may be identified earlier than spoken words. First, the nature of the visual signal for sign provides a large amount of lexical information very early such that a lot of phonological information is available simultaneously (or nearly simultaneously). Subjects could identify the place of articulation and orientation of the hand after about 145 ms, and the hand configuration was identified about 30 ms later. The early availability of this phonological information can dramatically narrow the set of lexical candidates for the incoming stimulus.

Second, the phonotactics and morphotactics of a visual language such as ASL may be different than those of speech. In English, many words begin with similar sequences, and listeners can be led down a garden path if a shorter word is embedded at the onset of a longer word—for example, *pan* in *pantomime*. This phenomenon does not commonly occur in ASL. Furthermore, sign initial cohorts seem to be much more limited by phonotactic structure. Unlike English, in which many initial strings have large cohorts (e.g., the strings [kan], [maen], and [skr] are all shared by 30 or more words), ASL has few signs which share an initial phonological shape. This phonotactic structure limits the size of the initial cohort in ASL. The more constrained phonotactics and the early and simultaneous availability of phonological information may conspire to produce numerically and proportionally faster identification times for ASL signs.

The Time Course of Lexical Access

In the gating studies by Emmorey and Corina (1990) and by Grosjean (1981), subjects produced initial responses that shared the place of articulation, hand configuration, and orientation of the target sign but differed in movement. As discussed above, these aspects of a sign can be perceived by the visual system in parallel. In general, when the movement of the sign was identified, the target sign was also identified. This pattern of responses suggests that similar to the speech signal, the visual input signal for sign activates a set of potential word candidates which share some initial phonological features (handshape, location, orientation). This set of candidates narrows as more visual information is presented—until a single sign candidate remains. Clark and Grosjean (1982) showed that sentential context did not affect this basic pattern of lexical recognition, although it reduced the time to isolate a target sign. In this study, gated signs were preceded by a moderately constraining context (semantically and syntactically appropriate) or no context (i.e., in isolation). When a sign was preceded by a constraining context, time to identify the sign was reduced by about 10%.6 Interestingly, context did not affect the time course of recognition for phonological structure. The shape and orientation of the articulators and place of articulation were identified simultaneously, and identification of movement coincided with sign identification.

Emmorey and Corina (1990) conducted a second gating experiment which investigated the time course of recognition for morphologically complex signs. For languages like English which exhibit mostly concatenative morphological processes, recognition of suffixes follows recognition of the base form. Given that ASL generally exhibits nonconcatenative processes in which the morphological inflection is superimposed on a base form, we might expect that the recognition of a morphologically complex form can proceed independently of prior recognition of a base form. In this second study, subjects were presented with monomorphemic and inflected signs that contained similar movements. For the monomorphemic signs, the movement was a nonmeaningful phonological component of the sign, but for the inflected signs, movement was morphological and part of the inflectional template superimposed on the base form. Figure 3 provides examples of two pairs of matched stimuli (the base form of the inflected sign was not presented to subjects but is given in the upper corner for the reader).

The results from this experiment indicated that identification of the base form in fact precedes recognition of the whole inflected form, similar to recognition of suffixed words in spoken languages. In general, subjects did not identify the base form and the inflectional morphology simultaneously. The basic response pattern was to produce a sign with the correct base form (but incorrect inflection), and when the correct inflectional movement was perceived, subjects responded with the correctly inflected sign. The early availability of hand configu-

---

6In this study the amount of a sign that needed to be seen before identification (isolation) was somewhat greater than in the Emmorey and Corina study: 47% with no context and 38% with context.

ration, orientation, and place of articulation information allowed subjects to identify the base prior to the whole inflected form. Inflectional movement is extended over time and is identified after the base form. Thus, although ASL verb roots and movement inflections are articulated simultaneously, they are not perceived simultaneously. Another question of interest was whether degree of simultaneity affected the time course of sign recognition. There were a few signs in this study in which the inflection and the base form were identified simultaneously. For each of these signs, the base form is produced with one hand, but the inflected form is produced with two hands (for an example, see Figure 2c). For these cases, subjects never responded by first identifying the base form and then the inflected form; rather, two-handed phonologically similar signs were produced until the subjects identified the inflected sign. It appears that when non-movemental cues to inflection are present (such as doubling of the hands), the base form and inflection tend to be identified simultaneously. When inflectional information is only signaled by movement, the base form is generally recognized first, and identification of the whole form coincides with identification of the inflectional movement.

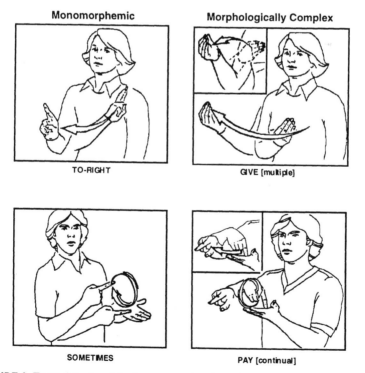

FIGURE 3. Examples of matched monomorphemic and morphologically complex signs from Emmorey and Corina (1990). The base [citation] form of the inflected sign is given in the upper corner for *give* and *pay*.

We also found that morphologically complex signs were identified later than the matched monomorphemic signs in the gating task. The explanation for this difference appears to lie in the nature of phonological movement compared to inflectional movement. Several of the inflected signs had undergone base reduplication (e.g., *pay[continual]* in Figure 3). When inflectional movement involves repetition, subjects must wait for the second repetition in order to identify the reduplicative inflection. In contrast, when monomorphemic signs involve repeated or reduplicated movement, subjects do not have to wait until the second repetition of the movement before they can identify the sign. For example, in the monomorphemic sign *sometimes,* once the circular movement of this sign has been identified, subjects can identify the sign (see Figure 3). Additional repetitions of the circular movement did not change the meaning. However, the verb *pay[continual]* which is articulated very similarly to *sometimes* showed a different response pattern. Subjects first identified the base *pay,* which does not have repeated movement. When subjects recognized that the base verb began to be repeated, they could identify the inflected form of the verb. Therefore, the longer time to identify the morphologically complex signs in a gating task appears to be due in part to differences between phonological and morphological movement.

Interestingly, lexical decision times to these same items did not show significantly longer reaction times for morphologically complex signs compared to monomorphemic signs (Emmorey, unpublished data). Table 2 shows the mean reaction times from 12 deaf native signers (7 of whom also participated in the gating experiment) to the 15 monomorphemic and 15 inflected signs used in the Emmorey and Corina study. Similar to what has been found for spoken languages, morphological complexity does not increase lexical decision time for ASL signs (Cutler, 1983; but see Hudson, this volume). Subjects may take longer to identify morphologically complex signs in the gating task, but when they must indicate whether a form occurs in the lexicon, there is no apparent delay.

TABLE 2. *Reaction times and error rates for ASL signs and nonsigns presented to 12 deaf native signers.*

	SIGN TYPE		
Signs	Monomorphemic 1111 (10)	Inflected 1128 (14)	
Nonsigns	Control 1179 (23)	Inflected 1221 (14)	Pseudosign 1430* (42*)

* significantly longer RT or greater error rate than control nonsigns ($p < .001$).

Table 2 also shows the response times for three types of nonsigns (control, inflected, and pseudosigns) that were presented along with the monomorphemic and complex ASL signs. Control nonsigns were created by changing the phonological shape of a true ASL sign by altering one or more phonological components (e.g., location, handshape, orientation, or movement). For example, *apple* (see Figure 1) was produced in the incorrect location (on the front of the chin) and the incorrect orientation (palm in), thus creating a possible but non-occurring form. Inflected nonsigns were created by producing a "control" nonsign with ASL inflectional morphology; for example, the sign *frog* was produced on the forehead (creating a nonsign) and inflected with the continual. Finally, pseudosigns were created by combining an ASL sign with an illegal inflection; for example, the sign *have* was produced with the durational inflection. Response times for control and inflected nonsigns did not differ, but response times to pseudosigns were significantly longer than either inflected or control nonsigns. This pattern is similar to that found in English for auditory but not visual lexical decision (see Table 1). Similar to suffixed nonwords in the auditory task, ASL signers may have rejected an inflected nonsign when they recognized that the "base form" was not an occurring ASL sign. The "base form" of inflected signs (e.g., *frog* on the forehead) and control nonsigns could be rejected at about the same point (although no cohort analyses were possible for ASL). These results, along with the results from the gating study, suggest that recognition of the base form of many morphologically complex forms in ASL precedes recognition of the inflectional morphology.

The Unique Role of Movement in Word Recognition

In the discussion above, we have seen that movement plays a special role in lexical recognition for ASL. In particular, gating studies have found that the isolation of phonological movement led directly to lexical identification. When subjects identified the movement of a sign, they were able to correctly identify the sign itself. Such a direct correlation between identification of a phonological feature and lexical identification does not occur with English and may not occur for any spoken language. That is, there seems to be no phonological feature or structure, the identification of which leads directly to word recognition. Movement is the most temporally influenced phonological property of sign, and more time is required to resolve it. For speech almost all phonological features have a strong temporal component, and there does not appear to be a single feature that listeners must wait to resolve in order to identify a word. Grosjean (1981; Clark & Grosjean, 1982) has described the ASL pattern of lexical recognition as involving two stages: identification of place of articulation, hand configuration, and orientation; followed by identification of movement. Such a two-stage process does not seem to be present for spoken languages, perhaps because there is no strong division between phonological information arrayed temporally and spatially.

THE ORGANIZATION OF THE ASL LEXICON

Previously, Hanson and Feldman (1989) investigated the lexical organization of ASL using a repetition priming technique. They found that signs were organized based in part on morphological principles. In a sign decision task,[7] Hanson and Feldman observed significant facilitation by repetition among signs that shared the same base morpheme (noun-verb pairs). Repetition priming was not found when signers made lexical decisions to the English translations of these forms which are not morphologically related in English (e.g., *shoot/gun*). Thus, signers represent the morphological structure of ASL and of English separately and independently.

Emmorey (1991) also used a repetition priming technique to investigate the organization of morphologically complex signs in the ASL lexicon. This study compared repetition priming for different types of inflectional morphology, focusing on semantic, phonological, and productivity differences between morphological forms. Two types of morphological inflection were compared: agreement and aspect. Only certain ASL verbs inflect for person and number agreement (Padden, 1983). These verbs are called *agreeing* verbs because their spatial endpoints mark agreement with spatial loci established for the referents of the subject and/or object of the sentence. ASL nominals are associated with loci in signing space, and agreeing verbs are articulated with respect to these spatial loci. Examples of agreement inflection can be found in Figure 2 (a, b, and c). Unlike agreement morphology, which utilizes planes and loci within signing space, aspect morphology is generally expressed by different dynamic movement contours (see Figure 2d, e, and f). Aspect morphology tends to express the temporal features of the verb, whereas agreement morphology identifies the participants in an action.

In the Emmorey (1991) experiments, primes and targets were separated by long lag times (26 - 32 items), and the targets were always the base form of the sign. Primes were either inflected or identical to the base form. The following inflections were studied: *Agreement:* multiple, reciprocal, dual; *Aspect:* habitual, continual. Deaf subjects performed a continuous lexical decision task, and the stimuli consisted of test signs (inflected primes and base form targets), filler signs (inflected and simple), simple nonsigns, and inflected nonsigns. The amount of priming produced by an inflected prime was determined by comparing reaction times to targets preceded by no prime or by a base form prime.

---

[7]Subjects decided whether the ASL sign for an English word presented on the screen was produced with one or two hands.

To investigate the role of phonological structure, I compared repetition priming for ASL morphological processes which produce different phonological effects on the base form of a verb—specifically, the multiple and reciprocal agreement inflections. The multiple is indicated by suffixing a sweeping horizontal arc onto the base form (see Figure 3). In contrast, reciprocal agreement is articulated simultaneously with the base, adds an additional hand to a single-handed sign, and changes the orientation of the hands (see Figure 2c). The spatial phonological change created by the reciprocal inflection appears to be greater than that imposed by the multiple inflection. I hypothesized that if we found different priming strengths for the reciprocal and multiple inflections, it would suggest that morphological cohesion (i.e., the strength of the association between morphologically related forms) is influenced by phonological relatedness in ASL. However, the results showed only a weak effect of phonological relatedness on the degree of morphological priming, suggesting phonological structure is probably not a major determinant of morphological organization for ASL. Similarly, Fowler, Napps, and Feldman (1985) found that English irregular (*heal/health*) and regular (*heal/healer*) morphologically related words showed the same repetition priming effects. Thus, morphological structure in both signed and spoken languages may be represented independently of phonological structure within the lexicon.

To investigate the role of semantics in determining how morphological relations might be represented in ASL, I compared agreement and aspect morphology since they differ in the degree of semantic change that each creates when affixed to a verb (Bybee, 1985). Aspectual morphology is more likely to change the meaning of the verb because it modifies the "internal temporal constituency" of the event or state described by the verb (Comrie, 1976). The function of (person/number) agreement, on the other hand, is simply to index the participants in the state or event described by the verb and leaves intact the inherent meaning of the verb. If the degree of semantic relatedness plays a role in determining the structure of a lexeme entry, then signs inflected with agreement morphology may produce stronger repetition priming compared to signs inflected with aspect morphology, since agreement does not alter the basic meaning of the verb. However, the opposite result was observed: Aspect morphology produced greater facilitation compared to agreement morphology. Thus, semantic distance does not appear to contribute to the amount of facilitation observed for morphologically related forms. The long lag times between prime and target in conjunction with the lack of an effect of either phonological or semantic relatedness suggests that the observed facilitation is due primarily to a morphological relationship (Feldman & Moskovljević, 1987; Henderson, Wallis, & Knight, 1984).

The difference in degree of facilitation produced by ASL aspect and agreement morphology may lie in differences in their morphological productivity which in turn may lead to differences in lexical access and representation. Most verbs in ASL can accept some type of aspect marking depending upon their semantics, but only a subset of ASL verbs are agreeing verbs, and only a subset of those permit the multiple, dual, and reciprocal inflections. In addition, many verbs do not require object agreement even though they are transitive (e.g., *fight, love, eat*)—in fact, these "plain" verbs are ungrammatical if inflected for agreement (Padden, 1983). This characteristic of verb agreement in ASL is quite different from the agreement systems of many spoken languages. Generally, in most inflectional systems verb agreement is pervasive and not limited to a subset of verbs (Bybee, 1985). We can explain the difference in morphological priming between aspect and agreement morphology if *productive* morphologically complex forms are accessed via a decomposed lexical entry, but complex forms created by *less productive* processes are accessed via a whole word representation in the lexicon (see Frauenfelder & Schreuder, 1992, for a description of such dual route models and a discussion of the role of productivity in morphological parsing).

Stronger priming for aspect morphology (specifically the habitual and continual) may be due to repeated activation of the base form within a morphologically decomposed lexical entry. Conversely, weaker priming by agreement morphology (specifically the multiple, reciprocal, and dual) may be due to weaker morphological associations between whole word representations. In the Emmorey (1991) experiments, the target in a prime-target pair was always an uninflected base form, and since an uninflected base form is accessed via the direct (whole word) route, this account hypothesizes that the same base form representation is accessed via both the whole word route and the parsing route. Such an hypothesis is necessary to explain how a "decomposed" base form (i.e., the form accessed when a morphological parse occurs for an inflected form) can prime recognition of the uninflected base form that is accessed directly. In fact, to explain such morphological priming, any dual route model must assume some kind of connection or relation between the base form stored in a decomposed lexical entry and the "whole word" representation corresponding to this same form.

Interestingly, Feldman (1991) observed the opposite result for agreement and aspect morphology in Serbo-Croatian. She found that agreement morphology (specifically person and number agreement) produced greater facilitation than aspect morphology (specifically perfective and imperfective marking). In Serbo-Croatian, aspect morphology is less productive, applying less often, than agreement morphology. Thus, the different distributional properties of these morpheme types in ASL and Serbo-Croatian may explain the differences in priming results (see also Laudanna & Burani, this volume, for a discussion of how the distributional properties of affixes can influence processing). Still to be resolved, however, is how distributional differences between affix types might be built into measures of morphological productivity.

SUMMARY

Signed languages provide unique insight into the biological constraints on human language and its processing. The differing limitations and advantages of the auditory and visual modalities play important roles in shaping the structure of linguistic systems and processing mechanisms. Sign language phonology does not rely upon rapid serial distinctions and takes advantage of the visual modality by representing many phonological distinctions simultaneously. Unlike spoken languages, signed languages prefer nonconcatenative morphological processes, and because of the nature of the visual system, nonconcatenative morphology does not present the same processing challenges that it presents for spoken languages. Language modality may also play an important role for spoken language as well. Evidence has been presented which suggests that morphological structure may be either represented or accessed differently depending upon whether a person is listening or reading. Listening requires temporal processing, whereas reading allows more parallel perception.

Studies of morphological and phonological processing in ASL revealed some modality-specific factors, but in general the basic determinants of word recognition are similar. Gating studies revealed that ASL signs can be identified earlier than English words, in part because of the early and simultaneous availability of phonological information and in part because of the phonotactics of ASL. Furthermore, although ASL inflections and base forms are articulated simultaneously, they are not perceived simultaneously. Generally, signers identify the base form and then the inflectional movement. Both phonological and inflectional movement play a unique role in ASL word recognition. Identification of phonological movement leads directly to word recognition, and there does not seem to be a parallel phonological feature or property that plays the same role in word recognition for spoken languages. Finally, the internal organization of the ASL lexicon is based on morphological relations between lexical items. These relationships do not appear to be determined by phonological or semantic relatedness. The strength of morphological priming (a reflection of morphological structure) may be affected by productivity.

As we understand more about the linguistic structure of signed languages, we will be in a better position to conduct investigations of how this structure is interpreted on-line. For example, understanding the phonetics and phonology of signed languages will enable investigations of how low-level phonetic cues are interpreted visually. Another important avenue of research is how signers process and represent linguistic contrasts that are directly encoded in space itself. Such investigations may also shed light on the relation between (nonlinguistic) spatial cognition and language processing. The dynamic visual-spatial nature of signed languages provides a unique window into language processing and human cognition.

ACKNOWLEDGMENT

This work was supported by NIH grants HD-13249 and DCD 00146. I would like to thank Ursula Bellugi, David Corina, and Edward Klima for many helpful discussions of the issues presented here. Laurie Feldman and Robert Schreuder provided valuable comments on an earlier draft of this chapter. I would also like to thank all of the deaf and hearing subjects who participated in the experiments.

REFERENCES

Anderson, S. R. (1992). *A-morphous morphology.* Cambridge: Cambridge University Press.

Baddeley, A. (1986). *Working memory.* Oxford: Clarendon.

Bergman, B. (1982). Verbs and adjectives: Some morphological processes in Swedish Sign Language. *Forsking on Teckensprak XI* (pp. 22-35), Stockholm University.

Bybee, J. (1985). *Morphology.* Amsterdam: John Benjamins.

Caramazza, A., Miceli, G., Silveri, C., & Laudanna, A. (1985). Reading mechanisms and the organization of the lexicon: Evidence from acquired dyslexia. *Cognitive Neuropsychology, 2(1),* 81-114.

Caramazza, A., Laudanna, A., & Romani, C. (1988). Lexical access and inflectional morphology. *Cognition, 28,* 297-332.

Clements, G. (1985). The geometry of phonological features. *Phonological Yearbook, 2,* 223-52.

Clark, L., & Grosjean, F. (1982). Sign recognition processes in American Sign Language: The effect of context. *Language and Speech, 25(4),* 325-340.

Comrie, B. (1976). *Aspect.* Cambridge: Cambridge University Press.

Coulter, G. R. (Ed.). (1993). *Phonetics and phonology: Current issues in ASL phonology.* San Diego, CA: Academic Press.

Coulter, G. R., & Anderson, S. R. (1993). Introduction. In G. R. Coulter (Ed.), *Phonetics and phonology: Current issues in ASL phonology.* San Diego, CA: Academic Press.

Cutler, A. (1983). Lexical complexity and sentence processing. In G. B. Flores d'Arcais & R. J. Jarvella (Eds.), *The process of language understanding.* New York: Wiley.

Cutler, A., Hawkins, J., & Gilligan, G. (1985). The suffixing preference: A processing explanation. *Linguistics, 23.*

Ellis, N., & Hennelly, R. (1980). A bilingual word-length effect: Implications for intelligence testing and the relative ease of mental calculation in Welsh and English. *British Journal of Psychology, 71,* 43-52.

Emmorey, K. (1987). *Morphological structure and parsing in the lexicon.* Unpublished doctoral dissertation, University of California, Los Angeles.

Emmorey, K. (1991). Repetition priming with aspect and agreement morphology in American Sign Language. *Journal of Psycholinguistic Research, 20(5),* 365-388.

Emmorey, K., & Corina, D. (1990). Lexical recognition in sign language: Effects of phonetic structure and morphology. *Perceptual and Motor Skills, 71,* 1227-1252.

Feldman, L. B. (1991). The contribution of morphology to word recognition. *Psychological Research, 53,* 33-41.

Feldman, L. B., & Moskovljević, J. (1987). Repetition priming is not purely episodic in origin. *Journal of Experimental Psychology: Learning, Memory & Cognition, 13,* 573-581.

Fowler, C., Napps, S., & Feldman, L. B. (1985). Relations among regular and irregular morphologically related words in the lexicon as revealed by repetition priming. *Memory & Cognition, 13(3),* 241-255.

Frauenfelder, U., & Schreuder, R. (1992). Constraining psycholinguistic models of morphological processing and representation: The role of productivity. In G. Booij & J. van Marle (Eds.), *Yearbook of Morphology 1991.* Netherlands: Kluwer Academic Publishers.

Frazier, L., Flores d'Arcais, G. B., & Coolen, R. (1993). Processing discontinuous words: On the interface between lexical and syntactic processing. *Cognition, 47,* 219-249.

Goldsmith, J. (1990). *Autosegmental & metrical phonology.* Cambridge, MA: Basil Blackwell.

Grosjean, F. (1980). Spoken word recognition processes and the gating paradigm. *Perception and Psychophysics, 28,* 267-283.

Grosjean, F. (1981). Sign and word recognition: A first comparison. *Sign Language Studies, 32,* 195-219.

Hall, C. J. (1992). *Morphology and mind: A unified approach to explanation in linguistics.* London: Routledge.

Hanson, V., & Feldman, L. B. (1989). Language specificity in lexical organization: Evidence from deaf signers' lexical organization of American Sign Language and English. *Memory & Cognition, 17(3),* 292-301.

Hanson, V., & Fowler, C.A. (1987). Phonological coding in word reading: Evidence from hearing and deaf readers. *Memory & Cognition, 15(3),* 199-207.

Hanson, V., & Lichtenstein, E. H. (1990). Short-term memory coding by deaf signers: The primary language coding hypothesis reconsidered. *Cognitive Psychology, 22,* 211-224.

Henderson, L., Wallis, J., & Knight, D. (1984). Morphemic structure and lexical access. In H. Bouma & D. Bouwhuis (Eds.), *Attention and performance X: Control of language processes.* Hillsdale, NJ: Lawrence Erlbaum Associates.

Kenstowicz, M., & Kisseberth, C. (1979). *Generative phonology: Description and theory.* New York: Academic Press.

Klima, E. & Bellugi, U. (1979). *The signs of language.* Cambridge, MA: Harvard University Press.

Kyle, J., & Woll, B. (1985). *Sign language: The study of deaf people and their language.* Cambridge, England: Cambridge University Press.

Laudanna, A., & Burani, C. (1985). Address mechanisms to decomposed lexical entries. *Linguistics, 23,* 175-792.

Liddell, S. K. (1993). Holds and positions: Comparing two models of segmentation in ASL. In G. R. Coulter (Ed.), *Phonetics and phonology* (Volume 3, pp. 189-212). New York: Harcourt Brace.

Liddell, S. (1984). THINK and BELIEVE: Sequentiality in American Sign Language. *Language, 60(2),* 372-399.

Liddell, S., & Johnson, R. (1989). American Sign Language: The phonological base. *Sign Language Studies, 64,* 195-277.

Marslen-Wilson, W. (1987). Functional parallelism in spoken word recognition. *Cognition, 25,* 71-102.

Naveh-Benjamin, M., & Ayres, T. (1986). Digit span, reading rate, and linguistic relativity. *The Quarterly Journal of Experimental Psychology, 38A,* 739-751.

Padden, C. (1983). Interaction of morphology and syntax in ASL. *Garland Outstanding Dissertations in Linguistics, Series IV.* New York: Garland.

Perlmutter, D. (1992). Sonority and syllable structure in American Sign Language. *Linguistic Inquiry, 23(3),* 407-442.

Reilly, J. S., McIntire, M., & Bellugi, U. (1991). Baby face: A new perspective on universals in language acquisition. In P. Siple & S. Fischer (Eds.), *Theoretical issues in sign language research: Psychology* (pp. 9-24). Chicago, IL: University of Chicago Press.

Sandler, W. (1989). *Phonological representation of the sign: Linearity and nonlinearity in American Sign Language.* Dordrecht, Holland: Foris Publications.

Sandler, W. (1993a). Linearization of phonological tiers in ASL. In G. R. Coulter (Ed.), *Phonetics and phonology* (Volume 3, pp. 103-129). New York: Harcourt Brace.

Sandler, W. (1993b). Sign language and modularity. *Lingua, 89,* 315-351.

Stokoe, W., Casterline, D., & Croneberg, C. (1965). *A dictionary of American Sign Language on linguistic principles.* Washington, DC: Gallaudet University Press.

Supalla, S. (1991). Manually coded English: The modality question in signed language development. In P. Siple & S. D. Fischer (Eds.), *Theoretical issues in sign language research* (pp. 85-109). Chicago: University of Chicago Press.

Tallal, P., Miller, S., & Fitch R. H. (1993). Neurobiological basis of speech: A case for the preeminence of temporal processing. *Annals of the New York Academy of Sciences, 682,* 27-47.

Tyler, L., & Frauenfelder, U. (1987). The process of spoken word recognition: An introduction. In U. Frauenfelder & L. Tyler (Eds.), *Spoken word recognition*. Cambridge, MA: MIT Press.

Tyler, L., & Marslen-Wilson, W. (1986). The effects of context on the recognition of polymorphemic words. *Journal of Memory and Language, 25(6)*, 741-752.

Tyler, L., Marslen-Wilson, W., Rentoul, J., & Hanney, P. (1988). Continuous and discontinuous access in spoken word-recognition: The role of derivational prefixes. *Journal of Memory and Language, 27*, 368-381.

Wilbur, R. (1993). Syllables and segments: Hold the movement and move the holds! In G. R. Coulter (Ed.), *Phonetics and phonology* (Volume 3, pp. 135-168). New York: Harcourt Brace.

APPENDIX

Control Nonwords		Suffixed Nonwords		Word-Initial		Pseudowords	
pardack	[pardæk]	bermly	[bɚmli]	cagelo	[kejlo]	broodly	[brudli]
sulfack	[sʌlfæk]	garging	[gargiŋ]	cuffack	[kʌfæk]	danking	[deŋkiŋ]
clussig	[klʌsɪg]	tribber	[trɪbɚ]	maplo	[mæplo]	glober	[globɚ]
narrig	[nerɪg]	vermly	[vɚmli]	beastig	[bistɪg]	lacely	[lesli]
grifna	[grɪfna]	fulted	[foltɪd]	drainape	[drenæp]	colted	[koltɪd]
oysko	[oisko]	nephly	[nɛfli]	duskorp	[dʌskorp]	chokely	[čokli]
symbit	[sɪmbɪt]	hundage	[hʌndɪj]	gracelo	[greslo]	guestage	[gɛstʃj]
harvame	[harvem]	garnly	[garnli]	nudgeka	[nujka]	roachly	[ročli]
faska	[fæska]	wobbing	[wabiŋ]	leakma	[likma]	mirthing	[mɚθiŋ]
glistna	[glɪsna}	jargly	[jargli]	clogma	[klagma]	crushly	[krʌsli]
drivna	[drɪvna]	gending	[jɛndiŋ]	fraudig	[fradɪg]	brooming	[brumiŋ]
victope	[vɪktop]	traving	[trævɪŋ]	blobig	[blablg]	creeding	[kridiŋ]
calvape	[kælvep]	fungly	[fʌŋgli]	snapna	[snæpna]	belchly	[bɛlčli]
orgit	[orgɪt]	cassing	[kæsiŋ]	lʌumpack	[lʌmpæk]	harshing	[haršiŋ]
cossote	[kasot]	sarder	[sardɚ]	lagorp	[lægorp]	fuzzer	[fʌzɚ]

3

Where is Morphology and How is it Processed? The Case of Written Word Recognition

Doriana Chialant and Alfonso Caramazza
Cognitive Neuropsychology Lab
Dartmouth College

In this chapter we address the question of how the lexical system encodes morphological information and how it recognizes morphologically complex lexical forms. Although our discussion is restricted to the process of word recognition in the written modality, the theoretical arguments presented are meant to have a more general scope. We argue that neither a whole-word nor a fully decomposed representation and access hypothesis are adequate. They cannot account for linguistic productivity, nor empirical findings such as frequency effects, morphological facilitation and homographic stem inhibition, or the effects of morphological structure in non-word processing. We discuss a model—the Augmented Addressed Morphology model (AAM; Caramazza, Laudanna, & Romani, 1988)—that distinguishes two levels of modality-specific lexical processing: access units and lexical representations. The AAM model postulates two types of access units: whole-word and decomposed forms (stems and affixes). It also assumes that lexical forms are represented as stems for all regularly inflected items and for all forms that may conform to the notions of transparency and similarity on which the model is based. Although this model accounts for morphological productivity as well as for currently available empirical evidence, it is not yet detailed enough to account for sub-regular morphological processes. Although this problem remains to be solved within our proposal as well as within other models of morphological processing, the present model makes some testable predictions about reaction time performance for these problematic cases.

INTRODUCTION

How does our lexical system encode morphological information and how does it recognize or produce morphologically complex lexical forms? Can forms like *walked* and *went* be considered to belong to the same type of morphological process or is the nature of the representation for each of these two lexical forms so distinct as to require different types of processing?

It is uncontroversial that morphological information is part of our linguistic knowledge. Our ability to understand and produce morphologically complex words could not be explained without appealing to knowledge of morphological structure. So for example, we know that a word like *stealer* would mean 'someone who steals' although it is unlikely that we have previously encountered this form. It is our knowledge of the meaning of *steal* and of *-er* that allows us to compute a possible meaning for the word *stealer*. However, it could be argued that knowledge of morphological structure and rules of combination of morphemes are called upon only under specific circumstances. In other words, morphological information must be part of our linguistic knowledge—if we are to account for morphological productivity. However, this does not imply that knowledge of morphological structure is appealed to each time that we comprehend a word, that is, on occasions other than when lexical retrieval fails upon encountering new words.

The debate about the nature of lexical representations and processing remains open. On the one hand, there are proponents of the view that isolated lexical representations do not encode morphological structure and therefore this information is not manipulated in the course of ordinary word recognition and production (e.g., Butterworth, 1983; Lukatela, Gligorijević, Kostić, & Turvey, 1980). On the other hand, there are proponents of the view that lexical representations do encode morphological structure and this information plays a role in word recognition and speech production processes (e.g., Dell, 1986; MacKay, 1976; Taft & Forster, 1975). Intermediate between these two proposals are theories that hold that different types of morphological forms are represented and processed in different ways (e.g., Burani, Salmaso, & Caramazza, 1984; Feldman, in press; Laudanna, Badecker, & Caramazza, 1989; Stanners, Neiser, Harmon, & Hall, 1979; Stemberger & MacWhinney, 1986; Tyler, Marslen-Wilson, & Waksler, 1990). So for example, while derived forms might be accessed and represented as whole words, regularly inflected forms might be accessed and represented on a stem or root base.[1]

---

[1]By *root* of a word we mean the base form of a word which cannot be further analyzed without total loss of the identity of the word. That is, it is that part of the word left when all the affixes are removed. For a morphologically simple word in English the root coincides with the whole word, whereas for a morphologically complex word the root consists of the word stripped of its inflectional and/or derivational affixes. Thus, for both words *dog* and *dogs* the root is *dog*; for the word *untouchables* the root is *touch*. By *stem*

We can reduce the debate about morphology to the following format. Nobody argues that there is no morphological information encoded at some level of the lexical system. For example, the notion of plurality must constitute an independent concept at the lexical semantic level, although it may (or it may not) be represented as an independent morphemic unit at the lexical form level. Furthermore, everybody agrees that morphological information is not relevant at some other levels like, for example, the level at which an input stimulus is visually processed. The debate therefore regards the level at which morphological information becomes relevant, the way this information is encoded, and how it is manipulated during the course of lexical processing. Furthermore, it could be the case that not all morphological information is encoded in the same format and not all of it becomes relevant at the same level of processing.

In this chapter we ask whether different types of morphological knowledge undergo differential processing.

The chapter is organized in three sections. In the first section we review the basic assumptions on which the three theoretically plausible hypotheses about lexical representation of morphologically complex forms rest, that is, the whole word hypothesis, the stem or root based hypothesis, and the third hypothesis which includes aspects of both the preceding ones. In the second section we discuss some empirical findings that are particularly relevant for our discussion. The third section is dedicated to raising questions about specific types of processes and how they might be accomplished by the system. These are issues that remain to be solved, both within our proposal of lexical processing as well as in other proposals that have been advanced in the literature.

Although here we restrict ourselves to the analysis of word recognition processes for words presented in the written modality, the bulk of the *theoretical* arguments presented—although not the specifics of the examples—are meant to be valid for the other modalities (auditory recognition and oral and written production processes). The selection of recognition processes of written words over other types of lexical processes finds its justification in the wider availability of experimental data in this specific area of lexical analysis.

HYPOTHESES ABOUT THE LEXICAL REPRESENTATION AND PROCESSING OF MORPHOLOGICALLY COMPLEX FORMS

By lexical knowledge we mean the information required for the correct identification (or use) of a given lexical form. Two types of information may be

---

of a word we mean that part of the word left when all the inflectional (but not derivational) affixes are removed. Therefore for the words *dog* and *dogs* the stem coincides with the root (*dog*). For a word like *untouchables* the stem is *untouchable*. We are neutral to this distinction for the purposes of the present discussion and we use the term 'base' whenever either interpretation could apply.

distinguished: semantic and formal knowledge. Semantic knowledge refers to the meaning of lexical forms. Formal lexical knowledge consists of the representations of the phonological or orthographic properties of lexical forms. We will use the term "lexical representations" to refer to the representations that carry the information about the formal properties of lexical units in a given modality—auditory/oral and visual/written.

Access to lexical representations is thought to be accomplished by means of lexical access units. Therefore, "access units" are units that mediate between input stimulus and lexical representations. It is generally maintained that lexical access units are sensitive only to superficial aspects of word structure, that is, whether a stimulus matches a whole-word representation and/or can be exhaustively parsed into morphemic units (Caramazza, Laudanna, & Romani, 1988; Tyler et al., 1990). Lexical representations, on the other hand, may take a more abstract form and may also contain, or give access to, all the grammatical information relative to a given lexical unit. For example, while the access unit for a word like *serenity* might be *serenity* or *seren* and *ity,* the lexical representation of *serenity* might be *serene* and *-ity.* That is, the lexical representation might consist of an invariant form that is shared by several lexical items, such as for example *serene* (cf. Tyler et al., 1990).

Different hypotheses of lexical organization hold different views regarding the format and type of information represented by access units and lexical representations. These hypotheses tend to favor one of three logically possible lexical representation systems for morphologically complex forms. Therefore, in the remainder of this section—instead of single specific approaches—we discuss the basic assumptions on which these logically possible positions rest and we consider whether all three positions are indeed tenable accounts of the representation and processing of morphological information. We start by discussing the two extreme and opposite positions—the whole-word representation hypothesis and the fully decomposed representation hypothesis— in order to show why they fail as accounts of representation and processing of morphologically complex forms. The discussion of these positions will be instrumental in highlighting some issues—such as those of productivity and morphological transparency—which are fundamental for every morphologically informed model of lexical processing. It is in the attempt to overcome the difficulties encountered by these two hypotheses that a third position emerges. We conclude that only this third position is a tenable interpretation of a system for the representation and processing of morphologically complex forms.

The Whole-Word Hypothesis

The whole-word representation hypothesis maintains that there is an independent lexical representation for each word of the language. This means that each morphological form of a given unit is fully and independently represented. The mental lexicon is therefore a full list of the lexical forms previously encountered—whether they are morphologically simple or complex. This hypothesis maintains that no morphological structure is encoded at the level of lexical representation of words. Morphological information associated with a given lexical form (e.g., *walked*) would then be part of its semantic information (e.g., the meaning of *walked* is represented by the same features that represent the meaning of *walk* plus the feature of past tense).

It follows that this view also assumes that the morphological structure of words is not processed in the access procedure to lexical information. Recognition of previously encountered words is achieved through a matching procedure between the input stimulus and the lexical representation. If they are identical then the input form can be said to have been identified as a word belonging to our mental lexicon. Under this hypothesis there is no difference in the process that leads to recognition of a morphologically simple or a morphologically complex lexical form. Recognition of the word *walked* is achieved in the same way as recognition of the word *dog,* that is, through a matching procedure. The matching procedure is generally thought to be mediated by lexical access units (cf. Morton, 1979) which are sensitive to the relative frequency of occurrence of words and therefore modulate speed of access to different lexical units (we discuss the relevance of frequency sensitivity of lexical units in the following section).

If a system does not include morphological structure as part of the lexical knowledge, it has to solve the problem of productivity by means of some other mechanism.

There are at least two sides to the productivity problem. One concerns the way the system allows for recognition of new forms. The other concerns the way the system allows for rejection of illegal forms.

The first issue can be resolved by assuming that morphological constituents of words represent independent knowledge in our system. This knowledge would be addressed only when an input form fails to match any lexical form stored in the lexicon. This independent knowledge would therefore include knowledge of the bases and affixes of the language and would allow for the parsing and interpretation of forms like *stealer.*

In order to solve the second problem a further step is required. Suppose that a form like **walkinged* is presented to this system. Parsing into constituents is not sufficient to reject this form as an illegal combination of morphemes. Knowledge of base and affix combinability is needed as well. However, knowledge of the types of affixes and the order they may take in relation to a base is specific to the type of base, as for example the fact that verbs cannot take the affixes that attach to adjectives.[2] Two observations necessarily follow.

---

[2]It is often thought that new forms can be recognized by analogy (cf. Rumelhart & McClelland, 1986; Seidenberg & McClelland, 1989). That is, given an input stimulus like

First, the whole-word model of lexical processing has "solved" the problem of representation and processing of morphologically complex forms by moving it to another component of the system. Within this component the problem of how morphological knowledge is represented and accessed by incoming stimuli reproposes itself.

Second, knowledge represented within a sub-lexical morphological component has to include knowledge specific to particular bases or affixes. This forces the extra-lexical mechanism to resemble the lexical system in that it would have to include information that differentiates among forms that belong to different grammatical classes (so as to rule out forms like *walkest*) and that specifies which affixes a form may take and in what order (so as to rule out forms like *walkinged*). We discuss this issue in greater detail when considering experimental findings obtained with non-word stimuli.

The Fully Decomposed Representation Hypothesis

The fully decomposed representation hypothesis assumes that lexical representations consist of morpheme-sized units. There are two possible interpretations of the morphologically decomposed representation view. On one view, morphemic units consist of roots, derivational affixes, and inflectional affixes independently represented. All morphologically complex words are therefore represented in a fully decomposed format. On the other view, morphemic units consist of stems and inflectional affixes. Therefore, only those morphologically complex forms which present inflectional affixes are represented in a decomposed format.[3]

---

tomber, all the lexical units that share sub-parts of the stimulus would be activated. In particular, all the forms that share the base *tomb* and all the forms that share the ending *-er* would be activated. Through a process of synthesis of the information made available by these units a possible interpretation of the input is provided. However, it is not clear what kind of semantic information would be made available for example by the units sharing the ending *-er*, as different units would carry different types of information (e.g., comparative, nominal, etc.). Furthermore, units sharing other sub-parts of the stimulus, like *tom,* would be activated and would contribute to the interpretation of *tomber.* It is even less clear how and if this system would allow for rejection of illegal forms like *walkinged.*

[3]Under the root-based hypothesis, the functional nature of inflectional and derivational processes is considered to be similar, that is they both pertain to the same level of analysis (that of word structure under some theories, that of syntax under others). Under the stem-based hypothesis inflectional and derivational morphology are considered to be functionally different and therefore relevant at different levels of language processing. Inflectional processes are all those processes that are relevant at the level of the interface between lexical and syntactic processes, whereas derivational processes are those processes (more) relevant at a lexicon internal level. For a review of the theoretical linguistic assumptions on which these two interpretations rest the reader is referred to Anderson (1982) and Scalise (1984).

Both the root and the stem view are compatible with several processing mechanisms for access. One possibility is that access units consist of morphologically decomposed forms. That is, for those morphologically complex forms that are represented in a decomposed format, the input stimulus is going to be parsed into its constituents prior to lexical access. On the decomposed account, the morphological structure of words is detected at an early stage of word recognition and knowledge about this structure is used for the purpose of accessing lexical information.

We consider here the case of inflectional aspects of words as an example, since both the stem and root views assume a decomposed representation format for these forms. The decomposed format of lexical access units is assumed to hold for any given inflectional property of words. However, it is not immediately apparent what type of information is included under the heading of inflectional morphology. Let's consider a very restricted case—that of the formation of the past tense of verbs. All the following forms are in past tense in English: *walked, hit, clapped, sought, went.* Under the decomposed representation hypothesis, all these forms are recognized through the same process of parsing input forms into their morphological constituents. However, each of these cases holds a different relation with its base form.

Even disregarding extreme cases like that of *went -> go,* it is clear that it is impossible to parse the input form in a number of cases. While in the case of a form like *walked* it is straightforward to access the lexical representations *walk* and *-ed,* as the system only needs to identify the morphological boundary (or the morphemic units), other cases, like, for example, *sought -> seek* cannot be handled in the same way. In this case the input form sought needs to be transformed in order to access the lexical representations *seek* and *-ed.* However, the transformation process could not make use of much of the information present in the surface form of the input, as there is no necessary correlation between the orthographic shape of *sought* and the shape of *seek* and *-ed.* For example, while the sequence *ought* is 'rewritten' as *eek* in *seek,* the same sequence is 'rewritten' as *ink* in *think.* Therefore, no general rule could be written to apply to such cases. While an ad hoc solution could be assumed, this would entail the inclusion in the transformation system of processes that apply to single or a small number of cases.

Even more regular cases pose nontrivial problems. For example, it is not clear how the system would handle cases like *clapped -> clap* or *moved -> move.* A simple parse of these forms would result in forms (*clapp+ed or clap+ped* and *mov+ed or move+d*) that do not correspond to morphemes of the language. It is true that a regular process characterizes the past tense formation of verbs ending in a stop, but this process has a purely phonological realization. There is no obvious sense in which orthographic knowledge should encompass phonological features as well, and indeed this would not be a desirable solution to the problem.[4] Resorting to more strictly orthographic factors like the identity of the double consonant letters might seem a viable alternative. However, while the reduction of double consonant letters in base final position to single graphemic units gives the correct result in the case of *clapped,* this generalization would also result in the production of incorrect forms like **cal* for an input form like *called.*

A similar but opposite case is that of forms like *moved.* Although here too a generalization can be found for verbs ending in a voiced labio-dental fricative, this solution relies on phonological and not on orthographic knowledge. Furthermore, a "dumb" parser would produce several incorrect outputs, as for example for the input *revved,* which if treated according to the same generalization would be parsed into **revve* and *-ed.*[5]

However these cases are ultimately going to be solved, the relevant point here is that the hypothesis of fully decomposed lexical access units cannot be maintained. Resorting to phonological knowledge in the case of recognition of orthographic forms creates complex problems without a clear solution, and the adoption of rule-based transformations of the visual input *prior* to lexical access is problematic as well. We return to this issue in the final section of this chapter.

Caramazza's Augmented Addressed Morphology (AAM) Model

Both the whole-word representation and access hypothesis and the fully decomposed representation and access hypothesis encounter non-trivial difficulties. In light of this, we can reasonably ask whether alternative hypotheses that combine the positive features of the whole-word and the decomposed representation accounts would provide a more reasonable theory of lexical organization and processing.

Although several other hypotheses of lexical organization can be entertained (cf. Stemberger & MacWhinney, 1986; Tyler et al., 1990, for spoken production processes) we consider here only one model as a representative example. The hypothesis of lexical processing we discuss is a model that has been proposed in

---

[4]Although in practice phonological and orthographic knowledge influence each other —diacronically in linguistic change and development and syncronically through activation of the whole system (cf. our discussion about sub-lexical routes)—in principle the problem remains of what constitutes a phonological or an orthographic representation. We maintain that they are distinct and independent representations constrained by different principles. We also maintain that phonological and orthographic knowledge constitute functionally independent systems. This position has been maintained and argued for elsewhere and it is not discussed here. The reader is referred to Caramazza (1991) for discussion of this issue.

[5]It is true that an ordering of the two rules would solve this problem. However, the validity of the argument does not depend on whether an ordered set of rules can be defined but on whether it can be properly called upon at this stage of processing, without resorting to an ad hoc solution.

a series of papers by Caramazza and his colleagues (Caramazza et al., 1988; see also Burani & Caramazza, 1987; Burani et al., 1984; Caramazza, Miceli, Silveri, & Laudanna, 1985; Laudanna et al., 1989). One basic assumption of the model is that the system functions in a maximally "transparent" way. That is, it is assumed that processing relies only on information carried explicitly in the surface form of the stimulus. It follows that in the early stages of processing of an orthographic input stimulus the system can only make use of the surface orthographic information provided by the isolated stimulus.

A consequence of having an orthographic surface form guide processing is that all irregular forms (e.g., suppletive forms like the English *go* and *went*) as well as partially irregular forms (e.g., stems which present unpredictable orthographic variations like the Italian *corr-* and *cors-* ("run"[6]) along with predictable orthographic variation of the affix (cf. next section for a discussion of the relevance of these cases) must be represented independently as there is no unambiguous common base form that can be recovered from the input surface form.

Another basic assumption of the model is the idea that similarity plays a crucial role in constraining processing. Thus, the access mechanism is characterized as a parallel activation system where the degree of activation of a stored orthographic representation (lexical unit) is a function of the graphemic similarity between the input letter string and the stored representation (cf. Morton, 1979).

The model also makes the assumption that lexical access to morphologically complex words takes place through whole-word access units for known words and through morpheme-sized access units for unfamiliar morphologically regular words (that is, those cases for which the frequency of the stem is much higher than the frequency of the surface form) or novel words. It follows that for all orthographically transparent forms both whole-word and morpheme-sized access units will be activated, to an extent which is directly proportional to the frequency of the access unit.

The previous assumptions allow for a morphologically decomposed representation for (at least) regularly inflected words; that is, stems and affixes are independent units as long as they are productive units of the language. In this case the morphologically decomposed representations will be accessed by both the whole-word and the decomposed access units. However, access through whole-word units is thought to be faster than access through stems and affixes.

As previously noted, the model is based on the assumption of (orthographic) transparency which entails that access procedures rely on the principle of orthographic similarity. It is therefore crucial to define what we mean by

---

[6]The root *corr-* occurs in all tenses except the participle (and all compounded tenses) and the first person singular and third singular and plural of the simple past tense, in which the root *cors-* occurs instead.

similarity. Specifically, the input unit must satisfy a set of conditions in order to be a valid source of activation for any given lexical unit. First of all, access procedures are sensitive only to the superficial aspects of word structure, that is, whether a stimulus matches a whole word representation and/or whether it can be *exhaustively* parsed into morphemic units. In order to activate an access unit, an input stimulus must not only be orthographically identical to the access unit—that is, constituted by the same letters appearing in the same order as in the access unit—but it must also satisfy conditions related to the distribution of the lexical units in the language. Let's take an example in Italian, a morphologically richer language than English. A suffix like *-ire* will only occur at the end of a word and will never be preceded by a word boundary;[7] that is, it cannot occur in isolation. We can formalize this knowledge in the following way: -ire#.[8] On the other hand, an homographic form like *<ire>* ('anger,' plural), would be represented as: #ire#; that is this form requires flanking by two word boundaries.

Upon presentation of a stimulus like *<partire>*, the access unit -ire# will be activated, whereas the access unit #ire# will not. In fact, the final part of the input unit *<_____ire>* meets all the criteria for activation of the unit -ire#: It overlaps orthographically with this form, and it satisfies its distributional constraints; that is, it is not preceded by a word boundary and it occurs word finally. By contrast, *<_____ire>* does not meet all the criteria for activation of the unit #ire# because, although orthographically it overlaps completely with the unit, it does not satisfy the distributional constraints of this unit; that is, it is not preceded by a word boundary.

A letter string will simultaneously activate all the access units that correspond to parts of the stimulus, with constraints as to word and syllable boundaries. For example, a known word will activate both its whole-word lexical access unit and the units corresponding to the morphemes that comprise the stimulus, if there are any. However, the activation of a whole-word lexical access unit is faster than the activation of the morphemic constituents of the word (cf. Caramazza et al., 1988). Once a lexical entry has been activated, its lexical/grammatical information is made available. This will include information about the combinatory properties of constituent morphemes, grammatical class information, and so forth.

In sum, this model assumes that lexical representations for regularly inflected forms are stored in a morphologically decomposed format. It also assumes that stems and affixes are independently represented and that access procedures contain both decomposed and whole-word representations. Both access units and

---

[7]By "word boundary" we mean, in the case of written word recognition, the fact that each word is flanked by spaces.

[8]With the symbol "-" we mean morpheme boundary and with the symbol "#" we mean word boundary. These formalisms are intended only as a convention to represent some specific knowledge.

lexical representations are modality specific.[9] The access mechanism is clearly constrained by similarity and transparency principles.

Given this theoretical framework, one question that needs to be addressed is the following: In cases other than regularly inflected forms or clearly irregular forms, what is the nature of the lexical representations and how can the relation between inflected (and/or derived) forms and their base be established? In other words, what principles define a form as regular or irregular? Or what determines whether a word is going to be represented as a whole form or decomposed into its constituents?

The distinction may be defined (1) in terms of productivity, with only productive affixes being represented in a decomposed format; (2) in terms of different types of morphological forms, with inflectional and derivational properties of words having a different status; or (3) in terms of frequency, with only frequent forms being represented in a non-decomposed format. More likely, an interaction among several parameters governs the organization of the lexical system (cf. Bybee, 1985, this volume). Each of these aspects of lexical processing is a question worth investigating by itself. However, as this would take us beyond the scope of this chapter, we touch only marginally some of these aspects (e.g., the derivation/inflection distinction) while we spend more time analyzing some others (e.g., the relevance of frequency and the morphological parsability problem) which are more instrumental to the theoretical goal of the present discussion.

In the next section we turn our attention to some experimental results which have provided a partial answer to the question of the nature of lexical representations and processing. We then discuss in further detail some aspects of the processing model we have here summarized.

EMPIRICAL FINDINGS

Root Frequency

Three types of results which bear on the issue of lexical processing of morphologically complex words are discussed in this section: findings about the relevance of the root frequency, the morphological priming effect, and the role of morphological structure in the recognition of morphologically decomposable non-words.

It is well known that the frequency of a word affects the speed with which it is recognized. Several lexical decision studies have reported that words that are more frequent in the language are recognized faster than words with lower

---

[9]This is one of the basic principles of the model outlined here. This position has been defended in several previous papers and it will not be argued for in the present context. The reader is referred to Caramazza, 1988; Caramazza & Hillis, 1990; Caramazza & Miceli, 1990; Rapp & Caramazza, 1990, for a discussion of this issue.

frequency. Taft (1979; see also Burani et al., 1984; Katz, Rexer, & Lukatela, 1991) has extended this basic result by showing that lexical access of inflected words is influenced by the frequency of the root of these words. The frequency of the root is defined as the cumulative frequency of all the words that share that root. The frequency of each whole-word form is called the word or surface frequency. For morphologically complex words the response to a target word is a function of both the frequency of the entire word (surface frequency) and the cumulative frequency of the forms that share a given root (root frequency). So for example, Taft reports that in a lexical decision task it takes less time to recognize a word like *sized* which has a high root frequency and a low surface frequency than it takes to recognize a word like *raked* which has a low root frequency and a comparably low surface frequency.

The fact that the frequency of the root influences recognition times for a form comprising that root has been interpreted as evidence for morphologically decomposed access units and/or lexical representations. In fact, in order to account for the effect of root frequency we have to assume that at some level of lexical processing the input form has been analyzed into its constituents and these constituents have been accessed.[10]

---

[10]In order to account for the root frequency effect within the whole-word representation framework, Lukatela et al. (1980) have proposed for Serbo-Croatian that morphologically related words could be connected to each other in a satellite-like structure. According to this proposal—the satellite-entries hypothesis—each grammatical case of a noun has an individual representation in the lexicon. These representations cluster around the nominative singular which functions as the nucleus and the "embodiment of the noun's frequency" (cf. Lukatela et al., 1980, p. 415). Lexical entries of the different grammatical cases are "organized among themselves and in relation to the nominative singular by a (for now unspecified) principle other than frequency" (p. 417). It is not clear to us how this organization of lexical entries can account for the reported root frequency effect, unless access to the other forms of the satellite occurs via the nucleus. However, if this were the case, then the other satellite representations should not be accessed directly, but only through the activation spreading from the nucleus. In this case, to access a lexical form like *dinara* ('money' genitive singular) we must first access the nominative singular form *dinar* and from there proceed to access *dinara*. However, if the input form is *dinara* how can we proceed to access the form *dinar*? What mechanism would allow selection of this lexical entry that does not exhaustively match an access unit? Furthermore, even if the lexical entry *dinar* could be activated, there would still be the problem of selecting *dinara* as the right inflectional form. That is, once the nuclear form is accessed the information about the exact form of the input is lost—the morpheme *a* of the singular genitive form has been disregarded in the access procedure and what we are left with is now the nuclear form *dinar*. By this account the system cannot decide at this point which lexical form within the paradigm needs to be chosen. The information that the input form was *dinara* and not *dinar* was not preserved. If we allowed for this piece of information to be independently preserved then we would introduce morphological decomposition, which is obviously not an option within this theoretical framework.

Morphological Priming

Priming effects have also been taken as evidence for the role of morphological structure in lexical processing. A number of studies have demonstrated priming of a lexical item by morphologically related words (priming by a base morpheme) (cf. Fowler, Napps, & Feldman, 1985; Murrell & Morton, 1974; Stanners et al., 1979).

Thus, for example, Murrell and Morton (1974) have demonstrated that—in a condition in which the degree of orthographic similarity between morphologically and orthographically related words was controlled—only the prior presentation of a morphologically related word like *cars* and not a merely visually similar word like *card*, affects lexical decision performance for the target word *car*. These results have been interpreted as evidence that the units of activation and/or representation include the morphemic sub-components of a word.

Similar results have been obtained in a series of lexical decision tasks by Laudanna et al. (1989), in a case in which the degree of orthographic similarity was maximally controlled for: the case of homographic stems (e.g., Italian *port-* as in *port-are* 'to carry' and in *port-e* 'doors'). These authors found that, at short lags, only a morphologically related prime, but not a merely orthographically related prime, has a facilitatory effect on recognition of the target word. Thus, they found that lexical decision for stimulus pairs such as *posto* 'place'/*posti* 'places,' which share the stem *post-*, is faster relative to non-morphologically related stem pairs, such as *collo* 'neck'/*colpo* 'blow,' which have the stems *coll-* and *colp-* (see also Stolz & Feldman, this volume).

Furthermore, they also showed that a (morphologically unrelated) homographic stem prime has an inhibitory effect on recognition of a target word. That is, lexical decision for stimulus pairs such as *portare* 'to carry'/*porte* 'doors,' which have homographic stems (*port-*), is delayed relative to non-homographic stem pairs, such as *contare* 'to count'/*corta* 'short,' which have the stems *cont-* and *cort-* respectively. In other words, it takes longer to recognize the target word *porte* 'doors' when it has been preceded by the homographic stem form *portare* 'to carry' than when it has been preceded by a non-homographic root, and it takes a shorter time to recognize the same target word *porte* 'doors' when it has been preceded by the morphologically related word *porta* 'door' than when it has been preceded by a non-related word.

The fact that there is an inhibitory effect for morphologically unrelated but homographic stems suggests that, even though they are orthographically identical, homographic stems *port-* constitute different lexical representations when they combine with different affixes (e.g., *-e* and *-are*). By contrast, the fact that there is a facilitatory effect for morphologically related words suggests that these words do share a lexical representation. That is, facilitation is only obtained when prime and target word share both form and meaning. This arises at the lexical level.

Nonword Structure

Finally, experiments employing nonwords with varying degrees of decompositionality have shown robust effects of morphological structure. It has been found that in lexical decision tasks reaction times to nonword targets vary as a function of the target parsability into morphemes. Taft and Forster (1975, exp. 3) found that lexical decision times to reject nonwords such as *dejuvenate*, formed by a prefix plus a real stem (*-juvenate* < *rejuvenate*) were longer than decision times for nonwords such as *depertoire*, formed by a prefix plus a pseudo-stem (**pertoire* < *repertoire*). However, these findings have been challenged, as the real stem and the pseudo-stem stimuli were not matched for cumulative frequency (cf. Manelis & Tharp, 1977) as well as for the similarity to words (cf. Caramazza et al., 1988). Therefore, the observed difference in reaction times between the two experimental conditions might have simply reflected a difference in stem frequency or degree of "wordness."

In a more recent study by Caramazza et al. (1988) it has been shown that reaction times and/or error rates in lexical decision tasks are significantly affected by morphological complexity even when orthographic similarity to words was controlled and stems were matched for cumulative frequency. Subjects are slower and produce more errors when rejecting nonwords that can be parsed into actual root and affixes (e.g., Italian *cant-evi*; equivalent example in English could be *walk-est*) than when rejecting nonwords that only contain a pseudo-root (Italian *cant-ovi*; English *walk-ost*) or a pseudo-suffix (Italian *canz-evi*; English *wilk-est*) and they perform better still on nonwords that contain no morpheme-like sequences at all (Italian *canz-ovi*; English *wilk-ost*).

This finding cannot be explained in terms of any type of whole-word representation, as the units of processing in this lexical decision task are roots and affixes that cannot stand in isolation. Under the whole-word representation hypothesis, the only feature of an input stimulus that might affect the response is whether it can be identified as a known word or not. Differences in reaction times for different types of nonwords cannot be accounted for, unless it is assumed that their structure is parsed at some stage of the lexical access process.

Perhaps a stronger case for morphological composition in the lexicon is provided by the results of another experiment in Caramazza et al. (1988, exp. 3). In this experiment the authors tested the claim that lexical representations are marked for morphological information that constrains the affixes that an item can take. For example, in Italian, verbs belong to different conjugations and the determination of whether a particular stem+affix combination is legal involves information about both stem and affix type. It follows that both verbs and affixes must be marked for conjugation. In particular, Italian presents a class of partially irregular verbs. Characteristically, these verbs present two stems. One is called "major" and occurs in the infinitive and tenses derived from it. The other is called "minor" and occurs in the participle and tenses derived from it. Usually these stems differ orthographically from each other only locally in a way that is, though, unpredictable (that is, it has to be lexically specified; cf. Bybee, this volume). However, for each form that the stem may take there is a well-defined set of affixes that combines with it in a regular and predictable way. Therefore, even though a regular 2nd conjugation verb would take the past participle suffix *uto* (e.g., *temere/temuto* 'to fear/feared'), whereas an irregular 2nd conjugation verb would take the suffix *o* (e.g., *correre/corso* 'to run/run'; *prendere/preso* 'to take/taken,' etc.), the occurrence of the *o* is totally predictable given the selection of the minor stem (*cors-*). In summary, the verb *correre* 'to run' has two productive stems, *corr-* and *cors-*[11] which participate in predictable inflectional affixation.

The lexical model proposed in Caramazza et al. (1988) assumes that whereas unpredictably irregular inflectional forms are fully listed, predictably irregular forms are represented like fully regular verbs with distinct entries for each of their stems (two in the example in case). Each stem for this type of verb is associated with a separate set of inflectional affixes.

Experiment 3 compared performance in a lexical decision task for nonword stimuli consisting of irregular stems (e.g., *corr/cors* 'run,' infinitive/past participle, 2nd conjugation) associated with either an affix that belongs to the correct conjugation but is not used with irregular stems (e.g., *uto*, which is the regular past participle suffix for the 2nd conjugation and cannot be used with irregular stem), or with an affix that belongs to another conjugation (e.g., *ito,* which is the regular past participle suffix for the 3rd conjugation). For example, the stimulus *corr-uto* consists of a major stem of a predictably irregular second conjugation verb and a second conjugation affix that attaches to regular verbs; the stimulus *cors-uto* is constituted by the other (minor) stem of the same predictably irregular verb and the same second conjugation affix for regular verbs; and the stimulus *corr-ito*[12] is constituted by a 2nd conjugation predictably irregular verb and a 3rd conjugation affix.

In accordance with predictions derived from the model (cf. Caramazza et al., 1988, for details) the longest reaction times and the highest error rate were obtained for stimuli like *corr-uto* and the fastest reaction times and the lowest error rate were obtained for stimuli like *corr-ito* (reaction times had the following pattern: *corruto* > *corsuto* = *corrito*).

---

[11] See footnote 6.

[12]The stimuli actually used for the third experimental condition were verbs of the 3rd conjugation with affixes of the 2nd conjugation. Since it does not make any difference for the point we are making, we simplified the examples by using 2nd conjugation roots for all conditions.

In other words, there is a difference in performance for non-word stimuli that present *different relations* between their stem and their affix. In particular, *corruto* and *corsuto* behave differently. The difference between these two cases cannot be semantic because at that level the two forms are identical except for the feature [+/- past]. The difference cannot be explained on the basis of orthographic similarity either—that is, it is not the case that one type of root has an orthographic shape that is similar to real words while the other type of root does not. In fact, both roots are well represented in the lexicon, so it is not the case that one root is (orthographically) more frequent than the other. Why, then, is *corruto* so much more difficult to reject than *corsuto?* The interpretation would seem to be that *cors-* and *corr-* are marked differently at the lexical representation level. Specifically, the past-tense stem *cors-* is explicitly marked for taking a past-tense ending other than *-uto,* whereas the form *corr* is marked for being an irregular stem which alternates with a minor past-tense stem. Therefore, while *cors-uto* is comprised by two elements that are not conjugation appropriate (within the inflectional paradigm for the minor stem), *corr-uto* is comprised by two elements that are conjugation appropriate and thus constitute a possible word of the language (cf. Caramazza et al., 1988, pp. 318-319). This result strongly suggests that lexical information is represented in terms of the morphological constituents of words.[13]

The model of lexical processing that we have assumed here as our working hypothesis of lexical organization represents a first-pass attempt to account for empirical data currently available.

Within this framework, frequency effects are thought to arise at the level of access units. Whereas whole-word access units are tuned to reflect the surface frequency of words, units the size of morphemes reflect the frequency of occurrence of many words sharing a base form. They will be activated by any stimulus containing that base. In other words, morphemic access units will reflect the frequency of the base morpheme. Because access units send activation to a shared lexical entry, all morphologically related words activate the same morphemic access unit as well as the same lexical entry, and this is how they facilitate each other's recognition.

---

[13]Findings obtained with nonword stimuli in lexical decision tasks have been criticized (cf. Henderson, 1985). That these findings are paradigm-specific can be ruled out by the fact that the same results have been obtained by Laudanna, Cermele, & Caramazza (1992) in a naming task. The criticism has been raised that nonword processing does not resort to mechanisms normally involved in lexical processing but to mechanisms specifically dedicated to novel stimuli. Therefore, findings obtained with nonword stimuli may not be used to infer properties of the lexical system. However, the differences found in reaction times for nonword stimuli with varying degrees of parsability into morphemes find a unitary explanation only under the lexical interpretation. Thus, this interpretation is preferred to the other one.

By contrast, a lexical entry is assumed to send inhibitory activation to homographic stems (cf. Laudanna et al., 1989). As a consequence, a later presentation of an homographic form will result in delayed recognition.

Morpheme-sized access units are also responsible for non-word recognition latencies. If a morphologically decomposable form is presented to the system, only morphemic units will be activated and they will activate their corresponding lexical entries. For example, *walkest* will activate *walk* and *corruto* will activate *corr-* . However, the closer a stimulus resembles a legal lexical form (e.g., **corr-uto*) the slower will be rejection of that form since it will qualify as a lexical item at several stages of the access process and will be discarded only at the moment at which knowledge about affix combinability within a given lexical entry is accessed. Nonwords comprised of morphemic units that activate incompatible sets of lexical knowledge will be discarded at a more peripheral stage of lexical access (e.g., **corr-ito* or **walk-est*). Nonwords comprised of pseudo-morphemic units (e.g., **walk-ost*) will be rejected at the level of access units, as no exhaustive parsing will be possible. These forms will have the shortest latencies in reaction times.

WHAT DOES "SIMILARITY" REALLY MEAN?

The model presented here represents a first attempt to account for the empirical data currently available. A number of issues remain to be solved within the framework of our proposal as well as within alternative explanations of lexical organization.

As already noted, the notion of similarity plays a crucial role in the access procedure, and the way it is defined within the presented model poses several constraints on the type of stimuli that can activate a given lexical entry. It also poses constraints on which units may be represented in a morphologically decomposed form and which may not.

The proposed hypothesis of lexical representation allows, on the one hand, for decomposed representation of regularly inflected words and, on the other hand, for whole-word representations for suppletive or irregular forms.[14]

---

[14]Several dimensions may play a role in lexical organization. A main distinction could be drawn between inflectional and derivational processes (cf. Feldman, in press; Laudanna, Badecker, & Caramazza, 1992; Miceli & Caramazza, 1988). Inflectional processes might be called upon each time that we understand or produce a sentence, but derivational processes might be called upon only when we have to manipulate particular lexical forms. Within these two main classes of morphological processes—inflectional and derivational—progressively more fine-grained distinction can be made. Another relevant feature is that of transparency. Lexical forms that present different degrees of semantic and/or formal transparency might be represented in different ways. It is clear that in the case of semantic opacity decomposition is not possible nor relevant, because the meaning of the input form cannot be recovered from the meanings of the parts. The issue of decompositionality therefore concerns only forms that present different degrees

For reasons of expository simplicity we have chosen to restrict our discussion to inflected forms. Let's consider again the case of the past tense form of verbs. Let's assume that lexical representations are morphologically decomposed only to the extent that the base form can be unequivocally derived from the orthographic form of the input stimulus.

Under this assumption the correspondence between *went* and *go+ed* or between *sought* and *seek+ed* can be made at the semantic level but not at the orthographic or word-form level.

This implies that such irregular cases require whole word representations that can be directly accessed from the surface form through a matching procedure. That is, *sought* would access the lexical representation *sought* and not the lexical representations *seek* and *ed*. At the semantic level the representation *sought* and the representation *seek* would share all relevant features except that of tense.

By contrast, regularly inflected forms like *walked* will be represented in a decomposed format. An input stimulus like *walked* will therefore activate the access units *walk* and *-ed* as well as *walked*; however, both access units, *walk* and *walked* will access the same lexical entry.

The problematic cases are those that fall between these two extremes—that is, regular past tense forms like *moved* and *clapped*. The problem posed by these forms is special in as much as the orthographic alteration of the base form is a regular process which extends to new forms. In other words, although we could simply conclude that all forms that are not exhaustively parsable are represented as whole words, in so doing we propose a solution that goes against one of the basic features of the model—the fact that it has to account for productivity. This solution would then constitute a failure to capture a generalization about past tense formation of English. The problem we want to solve is therefore the following: How does the system recognize forms like *clapped* and *moved* the first time it encounters them?

Upon presentation of input forms like *clapped* or *moved* the system may activate whatever is possible, that is, the access units *clap* and *-ed* or the access units *move* but not *-ed* (or *-ed* but not *move*). At this point there are two possibilities.

The system fails to recognize *clapped* or *moved* as past tenses of their base forms, as the input is not exhaustively parsable. These forms may then be read sub-lexically. Only after appealing to the phonological code—under which these forms are truly regular—the system will make the connection between past tense forms and their bases.

Alternatively, as these past tense formation processes are productive, there may be a specific procedure to deal with them. In the case of *clapped,* after activation of the access units *clap* and *-ed* the input procedure is left with a

---

of formal transparency within the realm of semantically transparent lexical forms (see Schreuder & Baayen, this volume).

stranded <p>. Then the system may check whether this element is identical to the preceding one. If so, the input fits the restrictions on the process of doubling. Recognition of the past tense *clapped* would then occur by establishing connections between the access units *clap* and *-ed* and the corresponding lexical representations. In the case of *moved* the system needs to decide where to assign the grapheme <e>—to the stem or to the affix. However, since the past tense formation process is productive, we can suppose that the system allows for allographic variation, thus encoding both *-ed* and *-d* as access units. However, the allograph *-d* would be fully activated only under specific conditions.

Although purely hypothetical, these proposals make some testable predictions. If the first time the system has to recognize a form like *clapped* it has to proceed through activation of the access units *clap* and *-ed,* then we would expect that a form like *claped* would also be accepted as the past tense of *clap.* Similarly, if the first time the system has to recognize a form like *moved* it has to proceed through activation of the access units *move* and *-d,* then we would expect that a form like *moveed* would also be accepted as the past tense of *move.* Thus, we can ask whether in a lexical decision task, subjects would reject nonwords with a structure like *claped* or *moveed* as easily as they would reject nonwords with a structure like *rakked* or *rakd.* As data are currently lacking to answer this question, the problem remains open.

CONCLUSIONS

In this chapter we have dealt with the question of how the lexical system encodes morphological information and how it recognizes morphologically complex lexical forms. We have argued that neither a whole-word access and representation hypothesis nor a fully decomposed access and representation hypothesis is tenable, and that only a system that includes features of both can account for language specific features like productivity and affix combinability as well as for the experimental evidence currently available.

We have also argued that fine-grained distinctions within the realm of morphology not only can be drawn in principle but also follow as a consequence of the way lexical knowledge is organized. We maintain that morphological decompositionality is the result of both semantic and formal decompositionality. Therefore morphological information cannot only be regarded as part of the semantic representation of a lexical item but is also encoded along with the formal properties of the lexical unit at the lexical representation level.

We have discussed a model that postulates two types of access units: whole-word and decomposed forms (stems and affixes). The model also assumes that lexical forms are represented as stems for all regularly inflected items and for all forms that may conform to the notions of transparency and similarity on which the model is based.

We have also shown that although this model accounts for the empirical evidence currently available (such as frequency effects, morphological priming, homographic stem inhibition, and morphologically complex nonword processing) in its current formulation it is not detailed enough to account for specific sub-regular morphological processes. This latter problem remains to be solved within our proposal as well as within other models of morphological processing.

ACKNOWLEDGMENT

The preparation of this chapter and the research reported here was supported in part by NIH grant DC00366 to Dartmouth College. We would like to thank Joan Bybee, Laurie Feldman, Leonard Katz, and another anonymous referee for their helpful comments on an earlier version of this paper.

REFERENCES

Anderson, S. (1982). Where is morphology? *Linguistic Inquiry, 13*, 571-612.

Burani, C., & Caramazza, A. (1987). Representation and processing of derived words. *Language and Cognitive Processes, 2/3,4*, 217-227.

Burani, C., Salmaso, D., & Caramazza, A. (1984). Morphological structure and lexical access. *Visible Language, XVIII, 4*, 342-352.

Butterworth, B. (1983). Lexical representation. In B. Butterworth (Ed.), *Language production, Vol. 1*. London: Academic Press.

Bybee, J. L. (1985). *Morphology*. Amsterdam: John Benjamins.

Caramazza, A., (1991). *Issues in reading, writing and speaking: A neuropsychological perspective*. Dordrecht: Kluwer.

Caramazza, A. (1988). Some aspects of language processing revealed through the analysis of acquired aphasia: The lexical system. *Annual Review of Neuroscience, 11*, 395-421.

Caramazza, A., & Hillis, A. (1990). Where do semantic errors come from? *Cortex, 26*, 95-122.

Caramazza, A., Laudanna, A., & Romani, C. (1988). Lexical access and inflectional morphology. *Cognition, 28*, 297-332.

Caramazza, A., & Miceli, G. (1990). The structure of the lexicon: Functional architecture and lexical representation. In J. L. Nespoulous & P. Villiard (Eds.), *Morphology, phonology, and aphasia*. New York: Springer Verlag.

Caramazza, A., Miceli, G., Silveri, M. C., & Laudanna, A. (1985). Reading mechanisms and the organization of the lexicon: Evidence from acquired dyslexia. *Cognitive Neuropsychology, 2*, 81-114.

Dell, G. S. (1986). A spreading-activation theory of retrieval in sentence production. *Psychological Review, 93/3*, 283-321.

Feldman, L. B. (in press). Beyond orthography and phonology: Differences between inflections and derivations. *Journal of Memory and Language.*

Fowler, C. A., Napps, S. E., & Feldman, L. B. (1985). Relations among regular and irregular morphologically related words in the lexicon as revealed by repetition priming. *Memory & Cognition, 13,* 241-255.

Henderson, L. (1985). Toward a psychology of morphemes. In A. Ellis (Ed.), *Progress in the psychology of language.* Hillsdale, NJ: Lawrence Erlbaum Associates.

Katz, L., Rexer, K., & Lukatela, G. (1991). The processing of inflected words. *Psychological Research, 53,* 25-32.

Laudanna, A., Badecker, W., & Caramazza, A. (1989). Priming homographic stems. *Journal of Memory and Language, 28,* 531-546.

Laudanna, A., Badecker, W., & Caramazza, A. (1992). Processing inflectional and derivational morphology. *Journal of Memory and Language, 31,* 333-348.

Laudanna, A., Cermele, A., & Caramazza, A. (1992, September). *Morphological representations and reading.* Paper presented at the Fifth Conference of the European Society for Cognitive Psychology, Paris.

Lukatela, G., Gligorijević, B., Kostić, A., & Turvey, M. T. (1980). Representation of inflected nouns in the internal lexicon. *Memory and Cognition, 8,* 415-423.

MacKay, D. (1976). On the retrieval and lexical structure of verbs. *Journal of Verbal Learning and Verbal Behavior, 15,* 169-182.

Manelis, L., & Tharp, D. A. (1977). The processing of affixed words. *Memory & Cognition, 5/6,* 690-695.

Miceli, G., & Caramazza, A. (1988). Dissociation of inflectional and derivational morphology. *Brain and Language, 35,* 24-65.

Morton, J. (1979) Word recognition. In J. Morton & J. Marshall (Eds.). *Psycholinguistics 2: Structures and processes.* Cambridge, MA: MIT Press.

Murrell, G. A., & Morton, J. (1974). Word recognition and morphemic structure. *Journal of Experimental Psychology, 102,* 963-968.

Rapp, B., & Caramazza, A. (1990). Lexical deficits. In M. Sarno (Ed.), *Acquired aphasias.* Orlando: Academic Press.

Rumelhart, D. E., & McClelland, J. L. (1986). On learning the past tense of English verbs. In J. L. McClelland & D. E. Rumelhart (Eds.), *Parallel distributed processing: Exploration in the microstructure of cognition, Vol. 1.* Cambridge, MA: MIT Press.

Scalise, S. (1984). *Generative morphology.* Dordrecht: Foris.

Seidenberg, M., & McClelland J. L. (1989). A distributed developmental model of word recognition and naming. *Psychological Review, 96/4,* 523-568.

Stanners, R. F., Neiser, J. J., Harmon, W. P., & Hall, R. (1979). Morphological structure and its effects on visual word recognition. *Journal of Verbal Learning and Verbal Behavior, 8,* 399-412.

Stemberger, J. P., & MacWhinney, B. (1986). Frequency and the lexical storage of regularly inflected forms. *Memory & Cognition, 14,* 17-26.

Taft, M. (1979). Recognition of affixed words and the word frequency effect. *Memory & Cognition, 7,* 263-272.

Taft, M., & Forster, K. I. (1975). Lexical storage and retrieval of prefixed words. *Journal of Verbal Learning and Verbal Behavior, 14,* 638-647.

Tyler, L. K., Marslen-Wilson, W., & Waksler, R. (1993). The representation and access of derived words. In G. T. M. Altmann & R. C. Shillcock (Eds.), *Cognitive models of speech processing: The Sperlonga Meeting II.* Hillsdale, NJ: Lawrence Erlbaum Associates.

PART 2

Semantic Issues in Morphological Processing

4

Case Morphology and Thematic Role in Word Recognition

Leonard Katz, Karl Rexer,[*] and Mira Peter
University of Connecticut
Haskins Laboratories

This chapter discusses the effects of thematic role (semantic role) on word processing. One of the two languages studied was Serbian,[1] in which thematic role is tied to a word's case-inflection morphology. The other language was English, which depends on other mechanisms (such as word order and prepositions) to express thematic role. The data in both languages showed that a target word's recognition was slowed by ambiguity in the word's thematic role. This ambiguity effect can account for the fact that, in case-inflected languages like Serbian, there is faster recognition of a word in its nominative case form than in one of its oblique case forms; the nominative case has far fewer thematic role interpretations than other cases and is, therefore, the least ambiguous. The effect of role ambiguity was contrasted with the effect of ambiguity in lexical semantics (polysemy). In contrast to the effect of thematic role ambiguity, polysemy does not slow word recognition and, in fact, tends to speed it. This suggests different processing loci for thematic and semantic ambiguity and is consistent with a modular view of syntactic processing.

---

[*]Now at College of the Holy Cross and Haskins Laboratories.
[1]Serbian refers to the language spoken in Serbia. In papers published before the former Yugoslavia split, we referred to the language as Serbo-Croatian.

INTRODUCTION

This chapter presents experimental evidence on the processing of thematic role. Thematic role (also called semantic role and functional role) is an idea that provides a theoretical bridge between inflectional descriptions of grammatical case and semantics. It works by describing the valency of predicates, as in the following two sentences, *He jumped through the window* and *He recuperated through walking*. In both sentences, the verbs subcategorize for a subject and a prepositional phrase. However, the semantic functions of the two prepositional phrases differ. The thematic roles of the noun in the first sentence and the gerund in the second characterize the ways that they take part in the events denoted by their verbs. Thus, the word *window* takes part by fulfilling the role of *location* denoted by the verb *jump*. The idea of source and destination *locations* are implicit in the verb's meaning. In the second sentence, the word *walking* fulfills the role of *instrument* that is denoted by its verb. In a theoretical description of each verb, one would have to include a listing of these and other thematic roles that are permitted for its arguments. Such a list would contain the roles of *agent* and *location* as permissible roles for the arguments of *jump* and the roles of *patient* and *instrument* as permissible roles for the arguments of *recuperate*.

In languages that have case inflection morphology, there is covariation between case and thematic role. A word's thematic role in a sentence is in part conveyed by its case. Consider Serbian, a heavily inflected Slavic language of the Balkan Peninsula. There are seven cases in Serbian and, together, they convey roles such as *agent, experiencer, instrument, possessor*, etc., with each role being assigned to one case. However, the number of roles, perhaps in excess of 75, is much greater than the number of cases. Within each inflected case there are several different possible roles, thus creating an ambiguity for the listener/reader as to which role was intended by the speaker. This ambiguity is normally resolved by the verb context for the noun; the role of the word *tears* is *location* in the sentence, *He looked through his tears,* but it is *instrument* in the sentence *He recuperated through his tears.* In Serbian, the two sentences are *Gledao je kroz plač* and *Ozdravio je kroz plač.* Note that in Serbian, as in English, the phrase "through (his) tears" is identical in both sentences (*kroz plač*). The grammatical case of *plac* ('tears') is accusative in both sentences; however, the themes of the word differ because of the different verbs: *to look through* denotes a locative function while *to recuperate through* denotes an instrumental function.

Obviously, listeners are able to arrive at the correct interpretations for the different roles played by *tears* in the two sentences. But is there a cost to the processing system in dealing with the initial ambiguity in the noun itself—with the fact that the noun's thematic role must be resolved? This is the major question we explore in this study. In English and in Serbian, the prepositional phrase has not only the two possible interpretations of *location* and *instrument* but additional ones besides. Does this multiplicity of possible themes influence the processing load? It seems plausible to conjecture that the greater the number of possible themes for a noun (ceteris paribus), the greater the processing effort needed to resolve the thematic ambiguity. A second source of uncertainty exists. In a lexical decision task, the subject does not know, typically, the case of the noun that will be presented. There are seven possible cases that have different natural frequencies of occurrence in normal speech or print. Thus, uncertainty about which case form will be presented precedes the uncertainty of thematic role for the particular case form after it is identified. Both uncertainties contribute to thematic role ambiguity. An appropriate unit of this aggregate uncertainty is the information-theoretic index of number of bits of information carried by a noun, as determined by the frequency of occurrence of its case form together with the number of thematic roles which are possible for that case form.

The lexical decision task is a useful way to study the processing demands created by ambiguity in syntactic role because it removes the verb context and presents words or phrases in isolation. By presenting a noun or prepositional phrase without a verb, the noun's thematic ambiguity is maximized. Because it is known that some inflected forms (i.e., some cases) have a greater number of possible thematic roles, we should find their greater thematic ambiguity leading to slower word recognition for nouns with those inflections.

Consider an example of two cases with different numbers of possible roles. The nominative case has few and the genitive case has many; thus, these two cases differ in their potential for thematic role ambiguity. An experiment by A. Kostić (1991; see also A. Kostić, this volume) studied recognition of the same word stem in its different case-inflected forms. His results indicated, as we have been suggesting, that the more thematically ambiguous a word's case was, the slower subjects were to recognize the word in that form as compared to other inflected forms of the same noun. We use Kostić's analysis as a point of departure for the experiments in the present paper. In contrast to Kostić, who studied the effect of ambiguity by observing the correlation between the role ambiguity for a particular case form and speed of word recognition, we manipulated role ambiguity experimentally by varying the noun's phrasal context.

The present research was designed, in part, to address some shortcomings of Kostić's approach. In his chapter in this volume, Kostić presents a formulation, based on information theory, which predicts the reaction time to recognize a noun as a function of its ambiguity, i.e., as a function of that noun's case frequency and its number of alternative thematic roles. He validates the information-theory model by assessing the goodness-of-fit of word recognition latencies to target word ambiguity, as measured in number of bits. He demonstrates that the fitted curves are linear with high correlations. There are two kinds of concerns with this approach. First, there is a theoretical inconsistency in that the relative frequency of case forms are taken into account but the relative frequencies of each case's thematic roles are not. For Kostić, if a case form has, say, 50 forms, all of these are considered to be of equal likelihood of occurrence, an assumption that is surely false. Yet to ignore the relative frequencies of roles is to obscure the information carried by each role and, therefore, to miscalculate the information load of the case form to which it belongs.

A second concern with Kostić's formulation is that the RT function observed in each experiment is based on only three to five points. (This is a nearly inescapable problem; there are only seven noun cases in all.) Therefore, although the correlations that Kostić obtained are nearly perfect, there are few degrees of freedom involved in determining the best-fitting regression line and, therefore, high correlations would be expected even if the true relationship were not precisely linear. The fact that these fitted functions are statistically significant is not particularly important, as we show below. A more serious problem with the formulation, however, is that fact that the slope of the linear function (of RT to bits) it describes is found to change strongly from one experiment to the next. That is, the estimation of the information load that is said to characterize a particular case form changes from one experiment to another. This inconsistency alone suggests that Kostić's formulation is incomplete.

Moreover, it is well known that quite different theories (based on very different premises) can generate near-identical quantitative predictions; similarity between models is strongest when summary statistics (like group RT functions) are predicted. In order to differentiate among competing models, more detailed data need to be explained. These lessons were learned by the mathematical modelers in psychology in the 1960's (of whom, the senior author was one). For example, it was common for quite different models of paired-associates learning to predict nearly identical group learning curves. A one-element model might make the same general predictions as a stimulus-sampling model, even though the psychological assumptions behind each were very different. However, the various models could usually be discriminated successfully when finer details were predicted, such as distributions of individual learning curves or runs of correct and incorrect responses (cf. Katz, 1966). The universally accepted technique in assessing a model's validity is to compare it with models of equal plausibility. The comparison takes place via goodness-of-fit statistics (such as Chi-Square, or the approach used by Kostić, R-Square). The statistical evidence in favor of goodness-of-fit that is acceptable is evidence that a particular model fits the data better than the alternative models. In contrast, testing only a single model and showing that it has a good fit to the data is not traditionally viewed as strong evidence.

Another way to validate a model is to find independent experimental support for its psychological assumptions. This validation process would buttress the claim of the information-theoretic model of thematic role. Its psychological premises need to be assessed directly, outside of the model itself. The bottom line is that it is not enough to fit curves to general group behavior in order to assess a quantitative model.

In addition to studying the effects of role ambiguity, we also studied the effects of a second kind of ambiguity: semantic ambiguity (i.e., polysemy). The comparison is of interest because the former is morphological in origin while the latter is semantic; the first type of ambiguity is the property of an inflected grammatical case that generalizes to all words that include it, while the second, polysemy, is the specific property of a given lexical item. As we show below, there is reason to expect that these two kinds of ambiguity will have different effects on word recognition.

Two of our experiments use the lexical decision task, a task in which the subject is presented with a string of letters and is required to decide as quickly as possible if the string is a real word or not. Because the lexical search itself and all subsequent processing are under time pressure, we hoped to stress the processing system, thereby finding effects of the word's thematic ambiguity. But based on requirements of the task, one may ask why we expected a lexical decision task to show effects of *postlexical* processing; it may seem that the task informs us only about processing up to the moment that a word is identified in the mental lexicon and not beyond that point. That the effects we are looking for must be postlexical is obvious: Logically, ambiguity of case function in Serbian cannot arise until *after* a word is recognized. This follows from the facts that identification of the noun's case (and therefore, its thematic ambiguity) depends on first knowing its gender (i.e., its syntactic declension). But information about gender is necessarily lexical; it cannot, in general, be identified by a word's case marking because, in many instances, the same suffix indicates different cases for different genders. For example, the form *čoveka* (*čovek+a*) is the genitive and accusative form for 'man'; the form *žena* (*žen+a*), which has the same suffix inflection as *čoveka*, is the nominative for 'woman.' Thus, any interpretation of the inflectional suffix must *follow* lexical identification of the stem. Therefore, if the lexical decision task is not sensitive to processing after lexical identification, it would be inappropriate to use it to study the processing of thematic ambiguity, which must occur later. However, there is much evidence that the lexical decision task is affected by postlexical as well as by prelexical processing. In spite of its name, the lexical decision task is understood to include more than just the recognition that the target stimulus is (or is not) in the subject's mental lexicon; it also includes postlexical processing of contextual information, as priming studies have shown (Colombo & Williams, 1990; Neely & Keefe, 1989).

For generality, we studied thematic role ambiguity in two languages: Serbian and English. The two languages make for an interesting contrast. The former is a heavily inflected language while the latter is only moderately inflected. Semantic roles for nouns are expressed in Serbian largely through the morphological mechanism of inflection (along with some use of prepositions), while English depends on word order and a much larger reliance on prepositions to achieve the same goal.

Finally, we sought independent support for the psychological reality of the concept of thematic role itself. We focused on certain roles, such as *instrument, location,* etc. In order to assess, in an independent way, the psychological validity of these categories of semantic role, we studied subjective judgments of role in Experiment 1 (in Serbian) and in Experiment 3 (in English). The investigations of the effects on word recognition of thematic role ambiguity were carried out in Experiment 2 (Serbian) and Experiment 4 (English).

EXPERIMENTS IN SERBIAN

The Serbian language has been a rich source of evidence about the processing of morphology. This heavily inflected language's system of noun case inflection has received much attention from researchers over the past decade (e.g., Lukatela, Feldman, Turvey, Carello, & Katz, 1989; Lukatela, Gligorijević, A. Kostić, & Turvey, 1980). The purpose of a case inflection system is to constrain the functional (thematic) role played by a noun or adjective. For example, in the Serbian sentence, *Jede kašikom* ('He eats with a spoon'), the idea of the spoon's instrumentality is signaled by the inflectional suffix *-om*, the ending for the instrumental case. This contrasts with examples in which the same stem is in the accusative case: *Jede kašiku* ('He eats the spoon') or the nominative case: *Jede kašika* ('The spoon eats'). (In these latter sentences, the meaning may be unusual or nonsensical but they are both grammatically correct sentences). Moreover, each case has more than one possible thematic role: In addition to expressing instrumentality, the instrumental case can function to express accompaniment ('The fork goes with the spoon') or can function to express attribute, as well as other roles, some of which are specific to use with a particular preposition. As an example of the different number of possible roles associated with each case, the nominative case has only four while the accusative case has more than thirty (Dj. Kostić, 1961). A. Kostić (1989) was the first to point out that for words presented in isolation, the various case forms of a stem differ in their degree of role uncertainty.

It seemed to us likely that, in natural discourse, some processing resources must be expended by a listener/reader in order to resolve thematic role ambiguity by means of the available context. Congruent with this account are the reaction time differences due to case, a result first reported by Lukatela et al. (1980). Their lexical decision experiment showed that the nominative case form of an isolated word was recognized faster than the same word stem in any of its other cases (e.g., genitive, dative, etc.). For example, a noun is recognized substantially faster in its nominative case than in its genitive case. It is clear that the effect is not related to differences in the frequency of use of each case; the nominative and genitive cases have roughly the same frequency. The different recognition times occur even though the stem's semantic content is, of course, the same for all of its cases.[2] This reaction time advantage for the nominative has since been replicated under a variety of conditions (e.g., for print, speech, plurals, and all genders) and is quite robust (Feldman & Fowler, 1987; Katz, Boyce, Goldstein, & Lukatela, 1987; A. Kostić & Katz, 1987).

A word in the nominative case can take on the following themes: *subject* (*Hell is feared by the wicked*), *agent* (*Hell burns the wicked*), *predication* (War is *hell*), or *exclamation* (*Hell!*). Of these, the *subject* and *agent* roles are by far the most frequent, making the nominative very nearly a two theme case. In contrast to the nominative, the genitive case can take on more than 30 themes, such as *possession* (The toy *of the child* is blue), *partitive* (Give me some *of the cheese*), the object of certain verbs (I am afraid *of the cheese*), with certain prepositions such as *except* (No access except *for children*), etc. The different number of functions for the nominative and genitive cases (and for the other five cases as well) offers a possible explanation for the differences in lexical decision speed, an explanation that is in accord with a straightforward application of information theory (A. Kostić, 1991): Words presented in the nominative case yield faster recognition times because they have fewer alternative thematic functions to resolve; they carry a smaller information load. Of course this explanation depends on the assumption that thematic role *must* be resolved before a lexical decision response can be made—that a determination of theme is obligatory. Such an assumption is consistent with our data and the data of Kostić (1991, this volume), but it needs to be established independently as well.

The interpretation of nominative case superiority that we have just presented differs from that given by Lukatela et al. (1980). They saw it as a reflection of the primacy of the nominative case in the mental organization of morphological information. Their "satellite model" characterized the set of inflected case forms as a star-shaped network in which a word in its nominative form is the hub and the words representing its other case forms are satellites connected to the hub. In their model, when any word is perceived, the nominative form is always activated. The nominative form is the "citation" form and carries the main semantic content of the cluster. The other case forms are collectively termed, by convention, the "oblique" forms.

Burani (in press) offered a similar explanation for the primacy of the nominative case form. She pointed out that the nominative form is (1) a form from which the oblique inflected forms can be productively generated, and (2)

---

[2]Neither can the difference can be ascribed to orthographic or phonological differences between the nominative and the other cases. For example, the suffix inflection of a feminine noun in the nominative case is the letter *-a,* which is identical to the genitive case inflection for a masculine noun. The suffix *-a* is not sufficient to determine the case without the additional knowledge of the noun stem's declension. Declension membership is essentially arbitrary and this additional information must be learned, word by word, along with the lexeme's semantic meaning.

the form that is typically unmarked and therefore more natural. However, we may question Burani's first point. Logically, any of the case forms can be the basis for generating all the other forms. Thus, the citation form explanation is an arbitrary one; logically, the recognition process could be organized as a hierarchically structured search with any one of the case forms at the top. With regard to Burani's second point, it might be argued in her support that the nominative case is more natural because its primary themes—*subject* and *agent*—are more central to cognition (beyond language itself) than the other thematic roles. However, this notion, can also be challenged; heavily inflected languages like Serbian typically have a free word order, so that the word in the nominative case often does not precede the rest of its phrase. If the nominative case word were more important to the process of creating a structural description (i.e., in creating logical form or a mental model), it could be expected to always be the first item that was communicated. Although the absence of morphological marking may indicate that the nominative form is more "natural," the cause of that naturalness may be the ease of communicating the nominative's small number of thematic alternatives rather than the particular meaning or content of those functions. Alternatively, even if one considers the nominative form to be more cognitively important, one might view the fact that it has acquired fewer functions as the processing system's way of insuring that perception of the nominative is facilitated, relative to the other case forms. In this view, the focus of the explanation is on the nominative case's reduced information load (its fewer roles) relative to the loads of the oblique cases.

Thus, there are two alternative explanations of the nominative case's superiority in recognition. The question of which is the correct one goes beyond the Serbian noun system itself and addresses, more generally, a fundamental question about the nature of morphosyntactic organization: To what extent can morphosyntactic organization be reduced to principles of information theory, that is to say, to principles that are not uniquely linguistic? Do we explain the superiority of the nominative case in word recognition by its smaller ambiguity (smaller information load)? Or, is its superiority due, instead, to a special grammatical relation with the other cases, i.e., the possibility that, as Burani suggests, it has a special status as the citation form from which the other forms derive? We should note, however, that in the latter explanation, there is no independent rationale for nominative case superiority. It is, in fact, a circular explanation: Citation form is the form that is fastest and any form that is the fastest is the citation form. In contrast, in the information theoretic explanation, the differences between cases are rationalized as differences that occur in the process of resolving different degrees of thematic ambiguity. In the process of word recognition, all inflectional case forms can be accessed with equal ease; the differences between them emerge only in post-access processing when their theme must be resolved. This explanation is based on a general information theoretic principle of resource-limited processing: When a response requires a choice among alternatives, the more alternatives there are, the slower the response will be.

Experiment 1

The first experiment attacks the question of the psychological reality of the concept of thematic function. The notion of thematic role has been defined in previous work solely by means of rational analysis—that is to say, by linguistic intuition. A more empirical justification is needed. For example, it seems to the linguist, via introspection, that only the functions of *subject, agent, predication,* and *exclamation* are expressed by the nominative case in Serbian. The linguist, after arriving at this hypothesis, tests the idea's discriminant validity by looking for instances in which other case forms express one of the same functions; finding none, the idea receives support. Convergent validity is assessed by finding instances in which one of the putative themes is expressed by the nominative. But no such empirical test is given to the discriminant validity of the four themes hypothesized to be distinct functions. Although the linguist is able to draw a distinction among the four themes, that is no guarantee that the four have distinct psychological existences in the mental processing that goes on in language comprehension and production. What is needed is more objective proof that people who are not linguists perceive the same putative roles as the linguist. The test that is needed is one that determines if there is agreement between linguists and nonlinguists on when a case form in two different sentences express a single theme and when they express two different themes. In short, we need to demonstrate that a set of specific themes have convergent and discriminant validity.

The thematic roles of the various cases that we used were culled from linguistic analyses reported by Dj. Kostić (1961). We asked subjects to judge the similarity between two prepositional phrases in sentential context; in all of them, the same preposition was used in both phrases. For some sentence pairs, the phrase expressed the same putative theme in both sentences; in other pairs, the phrase expressed putatively different themes. A representative sample of roles (those studied in our subsequent Experiment 2) was studied. If there is psychological validity to the notion of thematic role, subjects should be able to distinguish reliably between two different themes when they are putatively different even though both phrases use exactly the same preposition. Likewise, similarity of function between two phrases using the same preposition should also be perceived when they are thematically identical. Because the same preposition is used in all comparisons, there is no overt cue to similarity or difference.

Method and Design

Subjects were high school students in Belgrade. All were native speakers of Serbian. Like secondary school students in most countries, they were not trained to be highly analytic about language. There were 197 students divided into three instructional conditions (described later). Seventy participated in Instructional Condition 1, 63 in Condition 2, and 64 in Condition 3.

Twenty-six pairs of sentences were created from 30 individual sentences. Sentence length varied from three to six words. Each sentence contained one prepositional phrase consisting of a preposition and a single accusative noun; the preposition was underlined.

In each sentence pair, the comparable phrases used the same preposition. The thematic similarity or dissimilarity between the two sentences was subtle: The words in both sentences were always different (except for the preposition) even when the roles for the nouns were the same. Twelve of the sentence pairs contained the preposition *kroz* and 12 contained the preposition *uz*; both prepositions are associated with three potential thematic roles. Each sentence was paired once with three others. The prepositions in one pair of sentences expressed the same role; for the other two pairings the other two thematic roles associated with that preposition were paired. Finally, the preposition *niz*, which has only one function, was included in two same-function sentence pairs. Thus, there were 26 sentence pairs, half of which were same-theme sentence pairs and half were different-theme pairs. Table 1 presents examples of same-theme and different-theme sentence pairs. See Experiment 2 for English translations of the thematic roles for the other prepositions.

All subjects saw the same list of 26 sentence pairs. The sentence pairs were distributed on three printed pages such that no sentence was repeated on the same page. There were three different orderings of the three pages. The subjects were tested in small groups. The initial instructions asked them to read each sentence pair and "decide whether the underlined prepositions in the two sentences were used in the same way or not." Subjects wrote the appropriate initial letter for "same" or "different" in the blank space between the two sentences.

TABLE 1. *Experiment 1. Examples of sentence pairs with same or different thematic roles for an accusative case prepositional phrase.*

SAME ROLE	
Spatial	Spatial
(1) Gledao je *kroz suze.* 'He will look *through tears.*'	(2) Baciće se *kroz prozor.* 'He will jump *through the window.*'

DIFFERENT ROLE	
Spatial	Instrumental
(1) Baciće se *kroz prozor.* 'He will jump *through the window.*'	(2) Ozdraviće *kroz šetnju.* 'He will recuperate *through walking.*'

Three different kinds of instructions were used. In Instruction Condition 1, subjects were given an example: a single sentence written on a blackboard; the preposition in the sentence was underlined. In Instruction Condition 2, the experimenter wrote a pair of same-function sentences on the blackboard, using a preposition different from the experimental list prepositions. The experimenter stated that the underlined prepositions in the example sentences had the same "idea" but did not provide additional explanation. In Instruction Condition 3, subjects were also given two same-function sentences, but in this case the preposition used was identical to one used in the experimental list they were about to see (the preposition *kroz*). In each condition, after instructing the subjects, the experimenter erased the examples from the blackboard before the subjects began work on their printed list of sentence pairs. Each session lasted about 30 minutes.

Results and Discussion

Figure 1 presents hits and false alarms. A hit was a "same" response when the two prepositional phrases had the same thematic role; a false alarm was a "same" response when the two phrases had different themes. The figure summarizes the data for each of the three instruction conditions. An analysis of variance was performed on the number of hits and false alarms for each subject. The difference between hits and false alarms was highly significant, $F(1,194) = 2,819$, $MS_e = 2.55$, $p < .001$, as might be expected by inspection of Figure 1.

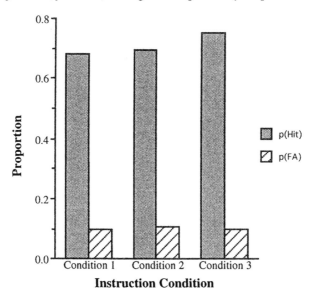

FIGURE 1. Proportion of Hits and False Alarms in judging Serbian prepositional phrase pairs to be equivalent in thematic role. Results are given for each instruction condition.

The mean number of hits was 9.88 (82%), and the mean ratio of hits to false alarms was 7.38:1.

The difference between hits and false alarms varied slightly, but significantly, with instruction condition: $F(2,194) = 3.75$, $MS_e = 2.55$, $p < .03$. There was a greater superiority in hit rate for Instruction Condition 3, in which the preposition in the example had been the same as one of the prepositions used in the test itself.

Thus, the results of Experiment 1 show clearly that even secondary school students can discriminate accurately among different functional meanings of accusative case nouns. Having established, with this experiment, a plausible case for the psychological reality of differences in thematic role, we have a reasonable basis for the next experiment in which we study whether the act of recognizing a word is affected by the *number* of different thematic roles that the word's case can assume.

Experiment 2

In order to study whether thematic role ambiguity affects word recognition, we used a primed lexical decision paradigm. Based on A. Kostić's work (1991) we expected that increased role ambiguity would affect word recognition by slowing it; the greater the ambiguity, the greater the slowing. This expectation is in line, of course, with standard information theory which states that information load increases as the number of alternative states at each processing stage increases. However, a word's thematic role can affect reaction time only if resolving thematic status is something that is *necessary* for the word recognition process—and logically, at least, there is no reason to insist that word recognition include obligatory comprehension of the word's functional status. Logically, a subject need only recognize the string of letters as something in his or her lexicon and neither its thematic function nor any other lexical or syntactic characteristics need take part in the lexical decision. Yet Kostić's data seemed to require the explanation that his subjects did, in fact, process thematic role obligatorily in recognizing the word. However, Kostić's study did not test, directly, the conjecture that it was thematic ambiguity and not some correlate that was responsible for the pattern of word recognition speeds he observed. In the present experiment, we test this notion directly by presenting the target word either in isolation (i.e., ambiguously) or in a thematically disambiguating context. If thematic ambiguity is the reason that word recognition is slow, we would expect word recognition time to be faster when we constrain the context to be unambiguous.

A related question concerns the distinction between morphological processing and semantic processing. We wished to determine whether any thematic role effects we found could be labeled as a product of morphosyntactic processing. One way of strengthening the argument that thematic role effects are morphosyntactic in nature is to demonstrate that they are not semantic in origin, that they are qualitatively different from the effects of semantic ambiguity.

Polysemy is a useful semantic variable in this regard because it, like functional ambiguity, can be viewed as a kind of uncertainty: Words with many meanings are more lexically ambiguous when presented in isolation. Therefore, according to information theory, polysemy might be thought to be subject to the same dynamics as thematic uncertainty. However, there has been considerable evidence that polysemy affects word recognition speed in the *opposite* direction of thematic uncertainty. Jastrzembski (1981) and Millis and Burton (1989) demonstrated that isolated polysemous words are recognized *faster* than words with a single meaning. From the fact that responses are not slowed, it seems likely that the locus of the polysemy effect is prior to a stage when the word's several meanings collide. Perhaps the lexical decision response is initiated as soon as any one of a word's meanings is accessed; having more meanings may offer a greater likelihood that one of them is rapidly activated. Alternatively, all of the meanings may be activated creating a homogeneous aggregate "buzz" of activation that quickly biases a subject to decide that this high level of activity means that the target stimulus is a word. This latter explanation is consistent with evidence that a word's multiple semantic representations all become activated during word recognition. Consequences of such multiple activations have been detected within 200 ms of word onset, although only the contextually appropriate meaning remains active after that time (cf. Seidenberg, Tanenhaus, Leiman, & Bienkowski, 1982; Swinney, 1979, 1982). The explanation that lexical decisions are biased toward a "word" response by an aggregate but diffuse number of activations is also consistent with research by Pugh, Rexer, and Katz (submitted) and Pugh, Rexer, Peter, and Katz (1994) on the effects of a word's orthographic neighborhood (i.e., words that are spelled similarly to the target word) on its recognition.

Lexical and syntactic ambiguity were conjoined factorially in the present experiment. Lexical ambiguity was manipulated by selecting sets of monosemous and polysemous nouns, controlled for length and frequency of usage. Thematic ambiguity was manipulated by presenting some words in the nominative case (low ambiguity) and some in the accusative (high ambiguity). These words were preceded by a neutral "prime" (asterisks). As we stated above, the nominative case form is functionally less ambiguous than the accusative because the former has only four possible roles while the latter has more than 30 (Dj. Kostić, 1961).

In this experiment we used feminine nouns because it is in only that declension that the accusative case is unambiguously accusative. This was important since this case was the object of the experimental priming manipulation. However, the choice of feminine nouns necessarily presented us with a confounded nominative case form: The same form that is feminine nominative is also feminine plural genitive, so any noun with that form is necessarily ambiguous with regard to case. Nevertheless, we continue to call that form "nominative," partly for the sake of convenience and partly because to do so does not impinge on the use we are making of that form experimentally. Its function, experimentally, is to provide a low-information load noun form against which to gauge the effect on word recognition time of recognizing an accusative form when it has high information load (unprimed by a preposition) versus when it has low information load (primed by a preposition).

In a low information load condition, accusative case nouns were preceded by a preposition prime that reduced their number of possible roles to a single one, removing the accusative target's thematic ambiguity. In this situation, responses to the accusative case form were predicted to be about as fast as responses to the nominative because the disambiguating preposition should make the accusative case noun even less ambiguous than the nominative. Thus, among the three experimental conditions there were effectively only two levels of thematic uncertainty: low ambiguity for both neutral-primed nominatives and preposition-primed accusatives and high ambiguity for neutral-primed accusatives.[3] In line with our discussion above, we predicted that lexical decisions would become faster with increasing *lexical* ambiguity (from monosemy to polysemy) but would get slower with increasing *thematic* ambiguity (from one or a few roles to many). Finally, a finding that the two ambiguity effects do not interact would be consistent with the hypothesis that they have different loci of origin.

Method and Design

Sixty first year university students from Belgrade University participated as part of their course requirements. All were native speakers of Serbian.

Target word stimuli were selected from an initial set of 400 feminine nouns, four, five, or six letters in length. For control purposes, the stimuli were evaluated, subjectively, for number of semantic meanings and frequency of use. First, 5 university-educated native speakers of Serbian generated, from memory, all the alternative semantic meanings they could think of for each noun. From these, two large subsets were culled in which there was consensus by the judges that a word had either only a single meaning (e.g., *reka*—'river') or more than one meaning (e.g., *ploča*—'phonograph record,' 'desk,' 'tombstone'). These words were also checked against a dictionary of common usage. The two subsets were then presented to 100 Belgrade secondary school students who judged each noun for familiarity. Each noun was rated on a scale from 1 ("I have never heard of this word and I do not know what it means") through 4 ("I am very familiar with this word and use it sometimes") and 5 ("I am very familiar with this word and use it very often"). Only nouns that were rated in categories 4 or 5 by at least 85% of the sample were selected for use in the lexical decision experiment.

---

[3]It is ungrammatical (and not meaningful) to prime a nominative case noun with a preposition.

Three common prepositions were chosen as primes for the accusative case nouns: *kroz* ('through'), *uz* ('up'), and *niz* ('down'). These are never used in the language with any other case. The first two prepositions, used in combination with a noun, can each express three different thematic roles, while the third can express only one. The three thematic roles conveyed by the preposition *kroz* can be translated, roughly, as follows: (1) through distance, from one side to another, as in 'throughout the woods' (*kroz šumu*); (2) through time, as in 'in two days' (*kroz dva dana*);[4] and (3) by means of, as in 'through (hard) work' (*kroz rad*). The preposition *uz* can indicate (1) direction up, as in 'up the stairs' (*uz stepenice*); (2) next to, as in 'next to the house' (*uz kuću*); and (3) accompaniment, as in 'along with the salad' (*uz salatu*). The preposition *niz* can convey only the single thematic role 'down,' as in 'down the stairs' (*niz stepenice*). Table 2 illustrates the range of functional ambiguity for two nominative case nouns, their accusative case forms, and their accusative case forms within a prepositional phrase. The isolated accusative case form has high thematic role ambiguity while the other two conditions have little or none.

TABLE 2. *The design of Experiment 2, with stimulus examples. The noun target was preceded by either asterisks or a preposition.*

CONDITION

Number of Thematic Roles:	Nominative[5] Four	Accusative 10 or more	Preposition + Accusative One role
Monosemous:	* reka river	* reku ... river	kroz reku through the river
Polysemous:	* ploča record desk stone	* ploču ... record ... desk ... stone	kroz ploču through the record through the desk through the stone

[4]In expressions involving number, the appropriate inflection is determined in a complex manner. Linguists consider these inflections to be vestiges of an ancient declension. In none of these, however, can the inflection be confused with the standard nominative singular inflection used in the present experiment.

[5]By ignoring the fact that the feminine genitive plural has the same inflection as the nominative singular, we assume that our subjects' processing strategy involved only singular forms; most forms in the experiment were unambiguously singular and the rest were the ambiguous nominative-singular/genitive-plural form, which were likely to be interpreted as nominative. Also, because the nominative form is so much more frequent than the other, the informational value for the inflection is dominated by the nominative's frequency. Thus, even if the plural form is considered, the ordinal relationships noted in Table 2 still hold.

Each word appeared three times in the master stimulus set. One appearance consisted of the noun in the nominative case preceded by a neutral "prime" (3 asterisks): *** -*reka*. A second appearance consisted of the same word in the accusative case: *** -*reku*. A third appearance consisted of the accusative case form preceded by one of the prepositions: *kroz* -*reku*. Each preposition was paired with only one noun, but across stimuli, all prepositions occurred equally often.

A comparable set of pseudowords was generated by changing the initial letter of comparable four-, five-, or six-letter words in a manner consistent with Serbian phonotactic constraints. All stimuli were presented in uppercase letters.

Three experimental stimulus lists were constructed from the master list. Each subject saw only one list. A given stem appeared only once in each list, either in the nominative or accusative case preceded by a neutral prime or in the accusative case preceded by a preposition. Thus, the thematic ambiguity associated with words based on the same stem was counterbalanced across lists. Each list contained all of the monosemous and polysemous words and contained 90 words and 90 pseudowords. Of the 90 words, there were 15 in each combination of semantic and thematic ambiguity. There were 36 practice trials.

As stated earlier, the nominative form is the same as the genitive plural form. However, the latter is much less frequent in language use and, in the experiment itself, there was no support for an interpretation of the stimulus as a plural; all of the stimuli that were unambiguous with regard to case (66%) were singular and, of those that were ambiguous with regard to number, 73% of the time in language use, the usage is singular. We continue to call the ambiguous form "nominative," but it should be noted that a more precise description is that the form has an information load that is low but not quite as low as a "pure" nominative because the genitive plural has a large number of thematic roles.

Each trial began with a brief auditory signal followed by a 500 ms fixation point that appeared in the center of the computer screen. One hundred ms after the offset of the fixation point, a target (with preposition) appeared one line below. The target stimulus remained on the screen until the subject responded, up to a maximum of 1400 ms. From time to time, following a trial (randomly, averaging every 10 trials), the subject was asked by a message on the screen to report aloud the target stimuli. These check trials ensured that the subject attended to the preposition as well as to the target.

Results and Discussion

The factors of the analyses were Preposition (*kroz, uz, niz*), Polysemy (one meaning, more than one), and Condition (Nominative, Accusative, Preposition + Accusative). Condition corresponded to thematic ambiguity as follows: ambiguity was low (and roughly equal) for Nominative and Preposition + Accusative but high for Accusative alone. Figure 2 presents the mean RT by Polysemy and

Condition. RT was faster when the target word had more than one meaning. In addition, words presented in the accusative case without a constraining preposition (i.e., high functional ambiguity) were recognized more slowly than words in the nominative case or words in the accusative case that were preceded by a preposition. These results are consistent with a number of other studies that have found that not only is the nominative case form recognized faster than the accusative but is, in fact recognized faster than any of the oblique case forms (e.g., A. Kostić, 1991; A. Kostić & Katz, 1987; Lukatela, Gligorijević, Kostić, & Turvey, 1980). These findings are extended, however, by our principal finding: that priming an accusative noun, and thereby reducing its thematic uncertainty, reduced response times to approximately that of the nominative. Recall that the nominative form is also the form of the genitive plural. Thus, because the nominative form has its information load increased by the many low frequency functions of the genitive case plural, the information of the primed accusative and therefore RT, should be even lower than the accusative in isolation. Inspection of Figure 2 suggests that this is so.

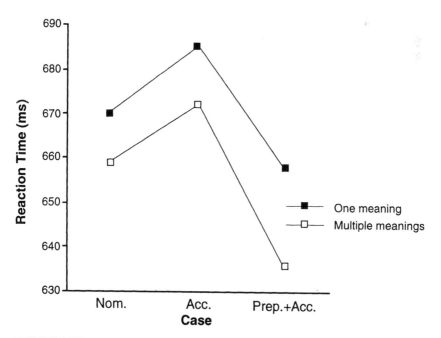

FIGURE 2. RT to Serbian monosemous and polysemous words with few thematic roles (Nominative), many roles (Accusative), and one role (Preposition + Accusative).

These trends were supported by the analyses of variance of RT (error rates were low and not informative). In the subjects analysis, Condition was significant: $F(2,100) = 26.21$, $MS_e = 2,728$, $p < .001$. Polysemy was also significant: $F(1,50) = 17.34$, $MS_e = 2,904$, $p < .001$. The same effects in the items analysis were: Condition, $F(2,168) = 5.90$, $MS_e = 3,631$, $p < .003$, and Polysemy, $F(1,84) = 3.33$, $MS_e = 4,907$, $p < .07$.

Some arguments against our interpretation still remain. For example, it might be argued that the common finding that the oblique case forms, such as the accusative, are recognized more slowly is not because they have more possible thematic roles than the nominative but rather because the particular roles they represent are more "difficult" to process. The argument is that it is the *quality* of the roles that affects RT, not the number of roles, per se. That argument seems weak to us because it has been found that recognition speed for all of the cases order themselves exactly as predicted by the number of roles they represent (see A. Kostić, 1991). For this argument, the fact that the number of the roles covaries with the quality of the roles would have to be merely accidental. But such a correlation strikes us as implausible; a case form that is used to process a difficult function should, more naturally, be designed to carry *fewer* functions, not more, so as not to burden that case with a double load of not only more roles but more difficult ones as well. It seems inefficient for language to evolve a given case form that is heavily burdened by many roles each of which is of the greatest processing difficulty. In fact, it is the reverse that seems more plausible: The case form with the least ambiguity (the nominative) might carry few roles because those few require the most processing activity. Nevertheless, we make no claim about qualitative processing distinctions among the various kinds of roles; we have explored here only the mechanism of number.

The results of Experiment 2 were essentially as predicted. They support the claim that a target's thematic ambiguity slows lexical decision time but polysemy does not: If anything, semantic ambiguity facilitates reaction time. In addition, consistent with the two ambiguity effects being at different stages of the word recognition process, no interaction was found between Polysemy and Condition.

EXPERIMENTS IN ENGLISH

The purpose of the two English experiments was to examine a language whose morphological structure is substantially different from Serbian in order to generalize the ambiguity effects found in that language. In Experiment 3, our intention was similar to that of Experiment 1: to assess the psychological reality of our linguistic descriptions of thematic ambiguity. In Experiment 4, we examined the effects of polysemy and thematic uncertainty on lexical decision, as we did for Serbian in Experiment 2.

A comparison of polysemy across languages is straightforward; all languages have words with more than one meaning. However, the comparison between English and Serbian with regard to thematic ambiguity is a little more complicated. The kinds of noun case roles we examined in Serbian are sometimes conveyed in English in a similar way and sometimes in a different way. For example, the possessive function conveyed by the inflected Serbian form *coveka* can be expressed in English by the inflected form, *the man's,* or by the prepositional phrase, *of the man*. However, with the exception of the possessive, there is no inflection for English nouns comparable to Serbian case (only inflection for number). For purposes of comparison, we needed a way to study both the effects of polysemy and the effects of thematic ambiguity in a primed lexical decision paradigm. We focused on prepositional phrases as the appropriate counterpart to case inflections in English. Fillmore (1968) suggested that prepositions in English are selected on the basis of structural features that are exactly analogous to those that determine particular case forms in case-inflected languages.

Experiment 3

Central to the logic of the experimental design for Experiment 3 is the assumption that some prepositions carry a higher thematic information load. That is, a noun following certain prepositions will have more possible thematic roles than that a noun following other prepositions. In Experiment 3, like Experiment 1, we sought to establish the psychological reality of the definition of thematic role which was to be the basis for a subsequent experimental test of ambiguity. In Experiment 3 we attempted to provide independent evidence that English-speaking subjects can accurately and reliably perceive distinctions and similarities between prepositional phrases based on their thematic functions. Experiment 3 had two parts: Both had the same goal but differed in method. In Experiment 3a, subjects were required to sort 21 prepositional phrases (presented in sentential contexts) into three equivalence classes without the aid of examples of any of the classes. In Experiment 3b, subjects sorted 25 phrases into five functional classes after viewing examples of each of the five classes. Here, subjects had to choose which of the five types of examples a given test phrase was most similar to.

Method and Design

Experiment 3a. Twenty-two native English speaking undergraduates at the University of Connecticut were presented with sentences containing one of three thematically different kinds of prepositional phrases. The phrases were underlined and all used the same preposition, *with.* The phrases conveyed either (1) manner, as in 'The tired man spoke *with detachment* about the accident,' (2) instrument, as in 'I carried water *with an old bucket,*' or (3) accompaniment, as in

'Potatoes *with gravy* is my cook's specialty.' Subjects were given 21 randomly ordered sentences printed on one page; 7 sentences used each function. Subjects were asked to sort the sentences into three groups of seven "on the basis of how their underlined phrases were used." Subjects indicated group membership by writing the number 1, 2, or 3 next to each sentence, assigning the same number to each sentence they perceived as belonging in the same group.

Experiment 3b. Nineteen subjects were given a sorting task with materials and directions similar to those used in Experiment 3a. However, Experiment 3b contained 25 sentences: five sentences with prepositional phrases expressing each of five thematic categories. Again, only the preposition *with* was used. The functional categories were (1) manner, (2) instrument, and (3) accompaniment— as in Experiment 3a—with the addition of (4) description, as in "The comedian *with the lamp shade* was the funniest," and (5) ingredient, as in "Candles *with bees-wax* smell nice." In another departure from Experiment 3a, subjects were given two example sentences for each of the five thematic categories. The categories of the examples were identified only by number.

Results

Experiment 3a. The sentences were numbered for analysis so that the sentences with the *manner, instrument,* and *accompaniment* phrases were given the codes 1 to 7, 8 to 14, and 15 to 21, respectively. Subjects' responses were pooled into a proximity matrix. For each pair of sentences in the set of 21, the matrix recorded the number of times subjects classified them both in the same group. The complete-link hierarchical clustering procedure was applied to the proximity data (Milligan & Cooper, 1987). Figure 3 (top) presents the dendrogram summarizing the agglomerative sequence and the distance, alpha, between joined clusters. Sentences/clusters that were reliably perceived as more similar have smaller alphas. A variety of stopping rules were applied (Milligan & Cooper, 1985) which indicated that a three-cluster solution best represented the structure in the proximity data. Examination of the three cluster solution also revealed that 18 of the 21 sentences clustered into the hypothesized groups of *manner, instrument,* and *accompaniment.* The three sentences that subjects misclassified (marked by asterisks in Figure 3) were also the last sentences to be joined to their clusters by the procedure. This indicates that there was little intersubject agreement about group membership, which suggests they were perceived to be least like the other sentences in their respective groups.

Experiment 3b. The sentences were numbered so that the sentences with the *manner, description, instrument, accompaniment,* and *ingredient* phrases were coded 1 to 5, 6 to 10, 11 to 15, 16 to 20, and 21 to 25, respectively. A complete-link hierarchical clustering procedure was run. The resulting dendrogram is presented in Figure 3 (bottom). The stopping rules indicated a five-cluster solution revealing that subjects' classifications again resembled the proposed thematic groupings very closely. Only 2 of the 25 sentences were misclassified by the subjects, and again the clustering procedure showed these sentences to be the ones least like the other sentences in their groups.

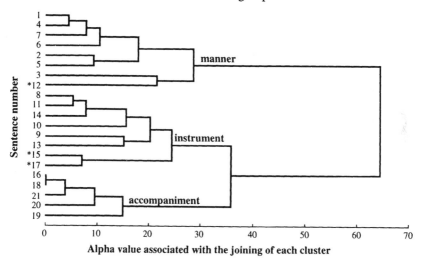

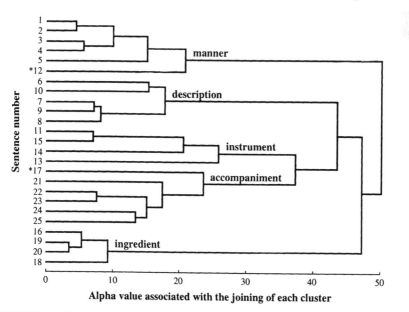

FIGURE 3. Cluster dendograms for English thematic role three category sort (top) and five category sort (bottom). See text for description. Only the sentences with asterisks were incorrectly grouped.

Discussion

The results of both parts of Experiment 3 indicate that subjects can discriminate different thematic uses of the preposition *with* accurately and can, as well, accurately identify phrases that do not differ. The results demonstrate divergent and convergent validity for the concept of prepositional phrase thematic role. The results of Experiment 3 show that English-speaking subjects, like their Serbian-speaking counterparts, appear (within the bounds of this study) capable of accurately perceiving thematic role.

Experiment 4

In Experiment 2, we demonstrated that polysemous Serbian nouns are recognized faster than nouns with only one meaning. This finding was consistent with earlier studies of English nouns that also showed a subtle but stable facilitative effect of polysemy (Millis & Burton, 1989). In the present experiment, Experiment 4a, we looked for such a polysemy effect on English prepositions. Some prepositions have relatively few meanings while others have many. If the polysemy effect generalizes to prepositions, then prepositions with many meanings should be recognized faster in a lexical decision task than prepositions with few.

Most of a preposition's meanings (but not necessarily all) are indications of thematic role. Thematic role is determined in part by the governing verb, but this verb may subcategorize for certain prepositions, and these prepositions, in turn, will constrain the possible thematic roles of the nouns they modify. In a second experiment, Experiment 4b, we studied the effect of the ambiguity projected by the preposition on the prepositional phrase itself. As in Experiment 2, the recognition of the noun in the phrase should be slowed in thematically ambiguous prepositional contexts. Thus, we wished to see if the same prepositions that show *facilitative* effects of polysemy—that are recognized faster when presented in isolation—would also produce an *inhibitory* effect on the nouns they modify. Assuming that the subject cannot avoid comprehending the prepositional phrase (during the process of recognizing the noun), then thematic ambiguity in the phrase should slow the lexical decision response to the noun. The specific predictions were, first: In Experiment 4a, prepositions in isolation that are associated with many thematic meanings will be recognized faster; second, in Experiment 4b, nouns preceded by such prepositions (i.e., nouns in thematically ambiguous prepositional phrases) will be recognized more slowly. Thus, it is the preposition that proximally determines the noun's thematic ambiguity by determining the number of possible roles for the noun.

Method and Design

Forty-two University of Connecticut undergraduates, all native English speakers, participated in Experiment 4 to fulfill a course requirement. Experiment 4a consisted of a simple lexical decision task with 22 prepositions and 22 pseudowords presented in a different random order to each subject. The words' frequencies (Kučera & Francis, 1967) ranged from 11 to 26,149. Polysemy was operationalized as the number of definitions given in a standard desk dictionary (Funk & Wagnalls, 1964). The words' number of meanings ranged from 2 to 32, but not all of these were prepositional meanings. For example, the word *onto* has not only a prepositional sense (e.g., "Put the sticker *onto* the window") but also a verbal sense (e.g., "I'm *onto* you," meaning "I'm aware of what you're doing"). The preposition *over* has, in addition to its prepositional meaning, an intensifier meaning, as in, "I'll think the matter *over*." The number of specifically prepositional meanings ranged from 1 to 23. (There was a high correlation between total number and number of preposition-only meanings, $r = .86$.) Pseudowords were created that matched the words for length and general orthotactic familiarity.

Experiment 4b employed a primed lexical decision paradigm. The 22 prepositions used in Experiment 4a, together with the word *the* served as primes (e.g., *beneath the*). Twelve concrete nouns (five or six letters in length) served as targets; their frequencies of occurrence in printed American English were approximately equal: Kučera and Francis mean = 26.68, $SD = 4.77$. Eighty-eight pseudowords, matched to the nouns for length and general orthotactic familiarity, were created. Each preposition prime was paired with four different word targets and four different pseudoword targets, yielding 176 trials. Each noun appeared either 7 or 8 times in the list, each time with a different preposition; each pseudoword appeared only once.

Procedure. In Experiment 4a each subject viewed the entire list of prime-target pairs in a different random order. Thus, there were usually several trials between repetitions of the same preposition; when it reappeared, it preceded a different noun. Stimuli were presented on a Macintosh computer screen. Each trial began with a fixation point for 400 ms, followed by a 32 ms blank, followed by the target preposition or pseudoword. The target remained on the screen until a response occurred or the time-out period of 1,400 ms expired. The intertrial interval was 1,400 ms. There were 10 practice trials and 44 experimental trials.

Following Experiment 4a each subject participated in a portion of Experiment 3. This experiment was described previously. Experiment 3 took approximately 20 minutes. Each subject then participated in Experiment 4b. In Experiment 4b a 400 ms fixation point was followed by a 32 ms blank, which was followed, in turn, by the prime (e.g., *beneath the*) for 400 ms. The prime was presented to the left of the screen's vertical midline. At the offset of the prime, the target noun (e.g., *fruit*) appeared to the right of the midline for up to 1,400 ms, as in Experiment 4a. There were 10 practice trials and 176 experimental trials.

Results and Discussion

Experiment 4a. For the simple lexical decision experiment, each subject's data consisted of a reaction time to each of the 22 prepositions and 22 pseudowords. The average error rate was 6.4%. For each subject, the partial correlation between the RTs to words and the number of meanings was calculated with log Kučera and Francis frequency partialled out. The resulting correlations were aggregated over subjects and a mean partial correlation was calculated for the group of subjects. Two mean correlations were obtained, one based on the total number of meanings for each stimulus and the other on only the number of specifically prepositional meanings for each stimulus. Because the stimuli occurred in isolation, there was no context to limit a stimulus exclusively to its prepositional meanings, and it seemed likely that the total number of meanings—both the dominant prepositional meanings and the secondary nonprepositional meanings—would affect the recognition process. That is, the recognition process ought to be sensitive to overall polysemy but insensitive to the syntactic class of the information carried by the stimulus (i.e., whether the meaning was prepositional or not).

The results supported this notion. Although the total number of meanings and the preposition-only number of meanings were both significantly related to RT (as predicted, prepositions with greater polysemy were recognized faster), the relation was stronger by far for the total number of meanings. For the partial correlation between recognition RT and total meanings was $-.189$, $t(38) = 5.33$, $p < .001$. But for number of preposition-only meanings, the mean partial correlation was lower (mean $r = -.087$, $t(38) = 2.49$, $p < .02$). The difference between the two mean correlations was significant, indicating that total number of meanings was a better indicator of polysemy (mean difference $= .101$, $t(38) = 3.62$, $p < .001$). Note that, although the average correlation of .189 is low, it is a quite conservative statistic—a partial correlation with the effect of word frequency removed. Because word frequency is itself strongly correlated with number of meanings, by partialing out frequency we are, in effect, removing all of the polysemy effect that is correlated with it. Thus, the remaining polysemy effect represents only its minimum contribution to word recognition latency and is quite conservative. It should be noted further that the t test on the difference of the partial correlations is a strong test of the effect of polysemy on RT. Although a simple null hypothesis predicts mean correlations of zero for both, a more complex hypothesis might predict that some unknown artifact could increase each subject's correlation in the same direction (either positive or negative), thereby producing a spurious but sizable correlation. But both the correlation based on total number of meanings and the correlation based on preposition meanings alone reflect the same RTs to the same stimulus words and, therefore, both correlations would be affected by a confound in exactly the same way. The fact that they produce results that are significantly different counters any such artifactual explanation of the facilitative effect of polysemy.

Experiment 4b. It had been predicted that the greater the thematic uncertainty of the preposition prime, the slower RT would be to the target noun that follows it because the noun's thematic role would be more ambiguous. Thus, preposition primes that are associated with more potential thematic roles should produce slower target noun recognitions. Mean RTs for each subject were calculated over each of the 22 sets of four noun targets that had been primed by a given preposition. Only correct responses were included; error rate was 2.7%. For each subject, the 22 mean RTs were correlated with the number of meanings for the corresponding prepositions; as before, these were partial correlations in which frequency was partialled out. As in Experiment 4a, separate correlations were calculated for the total number of the prime's meanings and for the number of preposition-only meanings. In contrast to Experiment 4a, in which the polysemy effect predominated, it was expected in Experiment 4b that it should be the number of specifically *prepositional* function meanings, rather than the more general total number of meanings, that should determine lexical decision RT.

The results supported this expectation. The partial correlations between RT and total number of meanings and between RT and number of preposition-only meanings were calculated for each subject, and then each was averaged over subjects. For the total number of meanings, mean partial $r = .049$, not significantly different from zero. In contrast, for the partial correlation between recognition RT and number of preposition-only meanings, mean $r = .090$, $t(41) = 2.68$, $p < .01$. Note that, unlike the correlations in Experiment 4a, this one is positive, indicating that the greater the number of (prepositional) meanings of the prime (and, therefore, the greater the thematic ambiguity of the phrase), the slower word recognition was. In addition, the difference between all the meanings correlation and the preposition-only meanings correlation was significant (mean difference = .041, $t(41) = 2.18$, $p < .04$). Although the mean partial correlation between target recognition RT and thematic ambiguity is small, it is consistent over subjects and indicates that RT to a target word was slowed when the word's role within the prepositional phrase was more ambiguous. As with the statistical test of the correlation difference in Experiment 4a, this difference also is not attributable to the particular stimulus characteristics of the noun targets.

GENERAL DISCUSSION

An aim of the present work was to study the processing consequences of thematic role ambiguity and to contrast thematic role ambiguity with semantic ambiguity. For generality, we studied two languages, Serbian and English. The two languages have some differences (as well as similarities) in the ways that thematic role is expressed. In Serbian, inflectional morphology plays a major part in constraining thematic role through the relation between case inflection and role: Some cases convey a greater number of possible thematic roles than others. In English, word order provides the syntactic information provided by case in Serbian. In spite of these differences, both languages behaved similarly with regard to ambiguity in thematic role as well as with regard to ambiguity in word meaning (polysemy). Lexical decisions were facilitated by increased polysemy. In contrast, thematic role ambiguity strongly slowed lexical decisions.

As ancillary experiments, we had also provided experimental support, by means of non-speeded choice paradigms, for the psychological reality of the particular categories of thematic role that formed the basis for our theoretical analysis of thematic role ambiguity. In order to claim that RT had been slowed because subjects had been uncertain as to which of several possible thematic roles were intended by an isolated Serbian noun in a particular case or by an English noun in a prepositional phrase, we had to show that subjects can actually differentiate the various roles. By demonstrating the psychological reality of several roles, we bolstered the likelihood that the results of thematic ambiguity manipulations in the lexical decision experiments were, in fact, due to the perceived ambiguity in the thematic roles of the target words.

The effect of thematic ambiguity that we demonstrated may, perhaps, be similar to a general comprehension effect, like that reported by Colombo and Williams (1990). That is, the process by which case thematic role or prepositional thematic role is resolved may be no different than the presumably high level cognitive processing that uses non-syntactic pragmatic knowledge and other world knowledge to understand a message in ordinary discourse.

On the other hand, it may be that the processing of thematic role is not the same as a general comprehension process. There is some evidence to suggest that certain kinds of syntactic information, at least, are processed independently of semantics. Gurjanov, Lukatela, Moskovljević, Savić, and Turvey (1985) and Katz et al. (1987) demonstrated that a pseudonoun (a nonword stem with a legitimate inflection) will show an effect of nominative case superiority: It is more quickly rejected as a word when it has an unmistakably nominative case inflection than when it carries another case's inflection. This is an example of a syntactic effect in the apparent absence of semantic content. Note that the nominative case inflection does not make the pseudoword seem more "wordlike"—a characteristic that would slow down its rejection instead of speeding it; instead, nonword responses are faster when the nonword is in the nominative case. Moreover, if a pseudonoun is primed by an adjective that agrees with it inflectionally (in case and number), it is also rejected faster. The inflections on the adjective and noun/pseudonoun are not identical, in general; therefore, the priming effect is not a simple form repetition effect but is truly syntactic in nature. These results suggest that the language system evaluates the morphological information carried by the suffix inflection independently from the semantic information carried by the word stem. Thus, there is some reason to consider the possibility that not only the inflectional message itself but also its implications for thematic role may be processed in a different manner than the semantics of the stem. In the introduction to our Serbian experiments, we discussed the satellite model of inflectional organization. This model was proposed in order to explain the well-known phenomenon that words are recognized fastest in their nominative case form. Various explanations based on the physical characteristics of the word (e.g., its orthographic or phonologic characteristics) or its frequency of occurrence have been ruled out (Katz et al., 1987; Katz, Rexer, & Lukatela, 1991); the phenomenon seems to be caused purely by the cognitive syntactic meaning carried by the word.

Lukatela and his associates (e.g., Lukatela, Gligorijević, Kostić, & Turvey, 1980) proposed that the superiority of the nominative case reflected its central position in lexical organization: the satellite model. The present results suggest a different explanation of nominative case superiority. In line with the theoretical insight and data presented by A. Kostić (1989, 1991, this volume), we suggest that isolated words in the nominative case are recognized faster because they have fewer alternative thematic roles. Words in the nominative case are faster because there are fewer thematic alternatives to choose among.

ACKNOWLEDGMENT

This research was supported by National Institute of Child Health and Human Development Grant HD–01994 and by a grant from the University of Connecticut Research Foundation. For the seminal idea that case thematic ambiguity affects word recognition, we are indebted to Aleksandar Kostić. Georgije Lukatela's generous assistance in the planning of the Serbian experiments was crucial.

REFERENCES

Burani, C. (in press). The lexical representation of prefixed words: Data from production tasks. In F. Keifer (Ed.), *The interface between morphology and syntax.* Amsterdam: John Benjamins.

Colombo, L., & Williams, J. (1990). Effects of word- and sentence-level contexts upon word recognition. *Memory & Cognition, 18,* 153-163.

Feldman, L. B., & Fowler, C. (1987). The inflected noun system in Serbian: Lexical representation of morphological structure. *Memory & Cognition, 15(1),* 1-12.

Fillmore, C. (1968). The case for case. In E. Bach & R. T. Harms (Eds.), *Universal in Linguistic Theory.* New York: Holt, Reinhart and Winston.

Funk & Wagnalls Company. (1964). *Standard Desk Dictionary.* New York.

Gurjanov, M., Lukatela, G., Moskovljević, J., Savić, M., & Turvey, M. T. (1985). Grammatical priming of inflected nouns by inflected adjectives. *Cognition, 19,* 55-71.

Jastrzembski, J. (1981). Multiple meanings, number of related meanings, frequency of occurrence, and the lexicon. *Cognitive Psychology, 13,* 278-305.

Katz, L. (1966). Amount of reward and relative frequency of amount of reward in paired-associated learning. *Canadian Journal of Psychology, 20,* 136-142.

Katz, L., Boyce, S., Goldstein, L., & Lukatela, G. (1987). Grammatical information effects in auditory word recognition. *Cognition, 25,* 235-263.

Katz, L., Rexer, K., & Lukatela, G. (1991). The processing of inflected words. *Psychological Research, 53,* 25-32.

Kostić, A. (1989). *A new approach to isolated word recognition.* Paper presented at the European Psychological Association Workshop on Word and Sentence Recognition, Zadar, Yugoslavia.

Kostić, A. (1991). An informational approach to the processing of inflectional morphology: Standard data reconsidered. *Psychological Research, 53,* 62-70.

Kostić, A., & Katz, L. (1987). Processing differences between nouns, adjectives, and verbs. *Psychological Research, 49,* 229-236.

Kostić, Dj. (1961). Syntactic roles of cases in Serbian. Technical Report. Institute of Experimental Phonetics and Speech Pathology, Belgrade.

Kučera, H., & Francis, W. N. (1967). *Computational analysis of present-day American English.* Providence, RI: Brown University Press.

Lukatela, G., Feldman, L. B., Turvey, M. T., Carello, C., & Katz, L. (1989). Context effects in bi-alphabetical word perception. *Journal of Memory and Language, 28,* 214-236.

Lukatela, G., Gligorijević, B., Kostić, A., & Turvey, M. T. (1980). Representation of inflected nouns in the internal lexicon. *Memory & Cognition, 8,* 415-423.

Milligan, G. W., & Cooper, M. C. (1985). An examination of procedures for determining the number of clusters in a data set. *Psychometrika, 50,* 159-179.

Milligan, G. W., & Cooper, M. C. (1987). Methodology review: Clustering methods. *Applied Psychological Measurement, 11,* 329-354.

Millis, M. L., & Burton, S. B. (1989). The effect of polysemy on lexical decision time: Now you see it, now you don't. *Memory & Cognition, 17,* 141-147.

Neely, J. H., & Keefe, D. E. (1989). Semantic context effects on visual word processing: A hybrid prospective/retrospective processing theory. In G. H. Bower (Ed.), *The psychology of learning and motivation: Advances in research and theory* (Vol. 24). New York: Academic Press.

Pugh, K. R., Rexer, K., & Katz, L. (submitted). Effects of orthographic neighborhood distribution in visual word recognition.

Pugh, K. R., Rexer, K., Peter, M., & Katz, L. (1994). Neighborhood effects in visual word recognition: Effects of letter delay and nonword context difficulty. *Journal of Experimental Psychology: Learning, Memory, and Cognition.*

Seidenberg, M. S., Tanenhaus, M. K., Leiman, J. L., & Bienkowski, M. (1982). Automatic access of ambiguous words in context: Some limitations of knowledge-based processing. *Cognitive Psychology, 14,* 489-537.

Swinney, D. A. (1979). Lexical access during sentence comprehension: (Re)consideration of context effects. *Journal of Verbal Learning & Verbal Behavior, 18,* 645-679.

Swinney, D. A. (1982). The structure and time-course of information interaction during speech comprehension: Lexical segmentation, access, and interpretation. In J. Mehler, E. C. T. Walker, & M. Garrett (Eds.), *Perspectives on mental representation.* Hillsdale, NJ: Lawrence Erlbaum Associates.

5   The Role of Orthographic and Semantic Transparency of the Base Morpheme in Morphological Processing

Jennifer A. Stolz and Laurie Beth Feldman*
The University at Albany, SUNY
*Also Haskins Laboratories

In this chapter we describe some evidence for morphological processing in visual word recognition. Orthographically similar words with and without a common morpheme are compared in a variety of experimental tasks in order to examine the role of the morpheme. In addition, morphological formations whose base morphemes retain their spelling (and pronunciations) under affixation (transparent base) and morphological formations whose base morphemes change their spelling (and pronunciations) under affixation (opaque base) are compared in order to probe the role of orthographic (and phonological) similarity in morphological processing. The present approach focuses on patterns of activation between words that share a base morpheme or have similar orthographic form and examine how those patterns change over time. Results indicate that even when the components of a word are not easily decomposed either orthographically, phonologically, or semantically, skilled readers still demonstrate sensitivity to component morphological structure. It is concluded that similarity based on orthography (and phonology) or on associative semantics alone cannot account for morphological effects and that the time course for the orthographic and semantic dimensions of morphological relatedness are different.

INTRODUCTION

Morphemes are central to language processing, because they are the bases for the formation of new words and for a word's fit into the syntactic frame of a sentence. However, theoretical accounts of the psychological processes that underlie word recognition often minimize the role of the morpheme which, according to some theorists (e.g., Aronoff, 1976), is an abstract linguistic unit. These accounts tend to explain apparent effects of morphological structure as reflecting, instead, orthographic and phonological patterning of letter units, with or without semantic similarity. For example, Seidenberg (1987) has suggested that patterns of high and low probability of transitions among sequences of letters can account for syllabic or even morphological effects because transitional probabilities of letter sequences that straddle a syllabic or morphological boundary tend to be low (bigram troughs) relative to probabilities of sequences within a syllabic or morphological unit. Similarly, much of the effort in current connectionist modeling of morphology (e.g., Rumelhart & McClelland, 1986) represents an attempt to account for the recognition or production of words in terms of orthographic patterning without invoking morphological rules.

In this chapter we describe some evidence for morphological processing in visual word recognition. Much of the original work examining the role of morphology focused on units for lexical access (Taft, 1985, 1991; but see Taft & Zhu, this volume) and has been reviewed elsewhere (Henderson, 1985). Other work (e.g., Lukatela, Carello, & Turvey, 1987) has explored issues of representation of regular and irregular morphologically complex words presented in isolation. Regular and irregular morphologically complex words differ with respect to the transparency of their bases, and this has implications for processing. Morphological formations whose base morphemes retain their pronunciations (and spelling) under affixation are phonologically (and orthographically) transparent. Morphological formations whose base morphemes change their pronunciations (and spelling) under affixation are phonologically (and orthographically) opaque. Only morphological processing of transparent bases can be easily described in terms of rules that append (or remove) affixes to (from) bases. Consequently, comparisons of transparent and opaque forms speak to how morphological structure is represented in the lexicon. Some researchers (e.g., Chialant & Caramazza, this volume) have posited different mechanisms for regular and irregular formations. Others (e.g., Fowler et al., 1985; Marslen-Wilson, Tyler, Waksler, & Older, 1994) have posited a single mechanism. The present study examines this issue by including both transparent and opaque base morphemes.

A second focus of investigations of morphological processing differentiates shared morphology from phonological and orthographic overlap in the absence of morphological similarity. Experiments vary the type of similarity that context words share with a target and the temporal relations between them. Rather than examining morphological access units or morphologically complex words presented in isolation, the present approach focuses on patterns of activation between words that share a base morpheme and how that pattern changes over time. In the first section, effects due to a shared morpheme and effects due to phonological and orthographic similarity are differentiated. In the second section, effects of sharing a base morpheme are differentiated from effects due to semantic similarity between words, and in the third section new evidence for analysis of a word's morphological components is described. The studies of morphology described in the first two sections contrast long- and short-term priming manipulations. The studies in the third section use a new task that combines elements of both perception and production.

DO MORPHOLOGICAL EFFECTS REQUIRE ORTHOGRAPHIC/PHONOLOGICAL TRANSPARENCY?

In concatenative languages such as English, morphological formation generally entails the addition of affixes either before or after a base morpheme. Words that share a base morpheme but differ in terms of their affixes are morphological relatives. It is well documented that presentation of a word in the lexical decision task produces long-term facilitation for morphological relatives as compared to first presentations of the same word (prime). This facilitation has been obtained in experiments conducted in English (Feldman, 1992; Fowler, Napps, & Feldman, 1985, Stanners, Neiser, Hernon, & Hall, 1979), in Italian (Laudanna & Burani, 1986), and in Serbo-Croatian (Feldman & Andjelković, 1992; Feldman & Fowler, 1987). Facilitation due to repetition of a morpheme is robust in that it is obtained even when the repetition is separated from the first occurrence by as many as 50 intervening items. However, in concatenative languages, insofar as the base morpheme tends to remain intact because affixes are added either before or after it, morphologically-related words tend to share phonological and orthographic structure as well as a morpheme. The goal of the first series of experiments reported here was to determine whether phonological and orthographic overlap between prime and target is sufficient to account for patterns of facilitation seen for morphological relatives and whether a shared morpheme must be transparent to produce facilitation.

Strong evidence against an orthographic interpretation of facilitation in repetition priming comes from the finding in Serbian[1] that equivalent facilitation is obtained for targets preceded by morphologically related primes, whether the prime is printed in an alphabet different from or the same as the target. That is, NOGOM facilitated the target NOGA no more strongly than did its Cyrillic transliteration НОГОМ (Feldman, 1992; Feldman & Moskovljević, 1987). However, because the transcriptions are of the same phonological entity (word), this finding does not rule out a phonological account of facilitation.

---

[1]Serbian refers to the language spoken in Serbia. In papers published before the former Yugoslavia split, we referred to the language as Serbo-Croatian.

There are, however, some data to suggest that morphological facilitation is not sensitive to phonological similarity either. Equivalent facilitation has been observed for morphological relatives in which both prime and target are pronounced similarly (e.g., *healer-heal*) and in which the prime and target are pronounced differently (e.g., *health-heal*) (Fowler et al., 1985). This finding indicates that across primes and targets, transparent *phonology* contributes little or nothing over and above a shared morpheme. Similar results have been reported when the base morpheme of morphological relatives differs in spelling as well as pronunciation (e.g., *decision-decide*) both in English (Fowler et al., 1985) and in Serbian (Feldman & Moskovljević, 1987).

Compelling evidence for interpreting facilitation as morphological derives from the comparison of morphological relatives with transparent and opaque base morphemes. A simple rule-based interpretation of morphological processing may be appropriate for transparent forms, but it is often claimed that phonological complexity makes it unlikely to apply for opaque forms. For example, the rules to derive *decision* from it base *decide* are more complex than the rules to derive *management* from the base morpheme *manage*. The basic argument is that if similar results are observed regardless of transparency, then it is unlikely that different mechanisms or styles of representation in the lexicon underlie processing of regular and irregular formations.

A second source of evidence that a shared abstract morpheme rather than phonological/orthographic similarity between prime and target alone underlies morphological facilitation comes from the differing effects of phonological/orthographic overlap with and without morphological relatedness. Studies that included an orthographic control have shown that facilitation is not obtained for morphologically unrelated but orthographically similar items when prime and target are separated by a long lag (Hanson & Wilkenfeld, 1985; Napps, 1989; Napps & Fowler, 1987).

When no items intervene between the presentation of the prime and the target, the pattern exhibited by orthographically related prime-target pairs without a shared morpheme and orthographically related prime-target pairs with a shared morpheme are distinct. Typically, whether orthographically similar items are displayed in close succession or at lags of many intervening items, responses to targets are *facilitated* when preceded by morphological relatives (Feldman & Andjelković, 1992; Forster, Davis, Schoknecht, & Carter, 1987; Grainger, Colé, & Segui, 1991). In contrast, orthographically related (but morphologically unrelated) control primes generally have no effect on target response when there is at least one intervening item. However, when primes immediately precede targets, *inhibition* is often obtained for these prime-target pairs relative to a control condition (Feldman & Andjelković, 1991; Grainger, 1990; Grainger, Colé, & Segui, 1991; Grainger, O'Regan, Jacobs, & Segui, 1989; Segui & Grainger, 1991). Inhibition for orthographically related but morphologically unrelated prime-target pairs is greatest when the prime has a *lower frequency* than the target and precedes the target with a stimulus onset asynchrony (SOA) of 300 ms and no mask (Segui& Grainger, 1991). Orthographic inhibition has been attributed to processing that occurs during prime identification. Grainger has argued that when subjects identify a prime (e.g., *char,* which is French for 'wagon'), its orthographic neighbors (words that share all but one letter) are activated as possible candidates in a frequency-ordered search and are subsequently rejected as incorrect. The rejected candidates are then suppressed. If the subsequently presented target is one of the higher frequency rejected prime candidates (e.g., *chat,* which is French for 'cat'), recognition will be impaired. Similarly, morphologically unrelated pairs such as *portare* and *porte* in Italian (which have different but homographic stems, specifically *port* meaning 'to carry' and 'doors,' respectively), yielded slower lexical decision times relative to control pairs such as *collo* and *colpo* which have different stems (*coll-* and *colp-,* respectively; Laudanna, Badecker, & Caramazza, 1989). Indeed, because morphologically unrelated homographic stems and control prime-target pairs were not matched on position and degree of orthographic overlap, inhibition such as that described by Grainger may underlie Laudanna et al.'s (1989) observation that when two words are presented simultaneously and subjects make lexical decisions to the pair, words formed from homographic morphemes produce *inhibition* relative to orthographic controls.

In summary, a compelling condition for interpreting facilitation in terms of a shared morpheme rather than phonological or orthographic overlap is the inclusion of a morphologically unrelated (control) condition where control items and morphologically related items are matched for phonological/orthographic overlap. If the morphologically unrelated primes influence recognition of the target differently from morphologically related primes, then there is evidence of morphological processing. Unfortunately, many repetition priming studies have not included this control condition.

In the remainder of this section we describe two experiments of our own that provide additional evidence that neither orthographic/phonological overlap nor phonological/orthographic transparency of the base morpheme is necessary to account for the effects of morphological relatedness. (Note that no attempt to differentiate phonological and orthographic dimensions is included in the present discussion. Materials were equated with respect to both dimensions, and only morphological relatedness was manipulated.) Experiment 1 was a repetition priming experiment using the lexical decision task and English materials presented at long lags. Experiment 2 was a short-term priming experiment using the lexical decision task and the same English materials.

In Experiment 1 we sought to replicate, within the same experiment, the differential effects of repetition on orthographically related items with and without a shared morpheme by including prime-target pairs that were either identical (e.g., *mark-mark*), morphologically related (e.g., *marked-mark*), or orthographically related (e.g., *market-mark*). In addition to orthographically transparent items, the use of English materials allows for a comparison with a second type of items whose spelling and pronunciations change across repetitions in the morphologically related (e.g., *repetition-repeat*) as well as the orthographically related (e.g., *repent-repeat*) conditions. Because orthographically opaque words have stems that undergo change when affixed, any interaction between type of prime and the transparency variable would speak to the role of (phonological and) orthographic transparency of the base morpheme in morphological processing. Following Grainger (1990), for each pair primes were of lower frequency than their target.

Morphological relatives in the opaque condition tended to be more similar in length than were morphological relatives in the transparent condition. Items were constructed such that for both the transparent and opaque conditions, the orthographically related and morphologically related primes were matched in terms of orthographic and phonological overlap with the target. Specifically, the proportion of graphemes the prime shared with its respective target (defined as the number of shared graphemes divided by the number of graphemes in the target) averaged .69 and .68 for the transparent items in the morphological and orthographic conditions, respectively, and .65 and .67 for the opaque items. Likewise, the morphological and orthographic primes shared average proportions of .68 and .66 phonemes respectively with the target for the transparent items and .59 and .60 for the opaque items. Because they are matched on orthographic and phonological similarity, any differences obtained between the morphologically and orthographically related prime-target pairs cannot be attributed to differing degrees of orthographic and/or phonologic overlap between the morphologically and orthographically related prime-target pairs.

Two sets of pseudoword repetitions were also constructed by taking a meaningless base and adding the same real affixes as were used on the words. The pseudoword repetitions were made similar to the word repetitions such that identity repetitions (e.g., *darp-darp*), "morphologically related" (e.g., *darps-darp*), and orthographically related (e.g., *darpet-darp*) pairs were constructed for both the transparent and opaque conditions.

For both words and pseudowords, all prime-target pairs were separated by lags of between 7 and 13 intervening items with an average of 10. Three experimental lists were constructed so that across lists the position of the target was held constant and each target occurred in each of the identity repetition, morphologically related, and orthographically related conditions. Each list contained both transparent and opaque base morphemes in prime-target pairs and all three prime-target relations. Fifty-four native English speakers from the University at Albany served as subjects and were instructed to make a lexical decision to each letter string.

The results of Experiment 1 are summarized in Table 1. (Unless otherwise indicated, for this and the following experiments only effects that were significant with both subject and items as random variables are reported.) The effect of prime type (identity, morphological, and orthographic) did not differ for the opaque and transparent items. Because orthographic/phonological transparency does not influence the patterns of effects seen for morphologically related items at long lags, the representation of shared morphemes must be sufficiently abstract to encompass allomorphic variation for irregulars. Further discussion is therefore based on the means of each of the priming conditions collapsed over the transparency variable. Facilitation was assessed by subtracting reaction times to targets preceded by primes from reaction times for the same targets on their first presentation (No Prime). Reaction times were significantly faster (52 ms) to identity repetitions than to first presentations. Significant facilitation (27 ms) was also obtained for morphologically related prime-target pairs, replicating the robust morphological priming effect found at long lags in previous experiments. In contrast, nonsignificant facilitation (12 ms) was obtained for orthographically related prime-target pairs that were matched in degree of orthographic and phonological overlap to the morphologically related pairs.

TABLE 1. *Target latencies and error rates for identity, morphological, orthographic, and no prime conditions in the lexical decision task at long lags in Experiment 1.*

			TYPE OF PRIME		
		Identity	Morphological	Orthographic	No Prime
BASE MORPHEME					
Transparent					
prime		mark	marked	market	mark
target		mark	mark	mark	
RT		526	542	563	574
%E		9.5	9.5	9.2	9.4
	Facilitation	48	32	11	
	Facilitation	-0.1	-0.1	0.2	
Opaque					
prime		repeat	repetition	repent	repeat
target		repeat	repeat	repeat	
RT		530	563	573	587
%E		9.0	9.0	9.1	9.2
	Facilitation	57	24	14	
	Facilitation	0.2	0.2	0.1	
Combined					
RT		528	553	568	580
%E		9.5	9.4	9.2	9.2
	Facilitation	52	27	12	
	Facilitation	-0.3	-0.2	0	

In summary, in order to observe effects of morphological relatedness at long lags it is not necessary that the base morpheme retain the same form over successive presentations. The facilitatory effects of a morphologically related prime on responses to a target following it at a lag of several intervening items does not require a transparent orthographic and/or phonologic base morpheme. Moreover, similar spelling and pronunciation in the absence of a shared morpheme is not sufficient to produce any effect. Words that have similar orthographic and phonological forms but do not share a base morpheme do not significantly influence each other at long lags.

Experiments 2a and 2b were conducted to examine, at a short lag, the effects of repeating a transparent morpheme or of repeating similar orthographic forms and to contrast these findings with those from the long lag procedure of Experiment 1. Orthographically related prime-target pairs with and without a shared base morpheme and presented at short lags were compared. Materials were the same as in Experiment 1 except that an unrelated prime condition (e.g., *tack-mark*) replaced the identity condition and provided a neutral baseline. Primes were presented for 250 ms and were followed by a 50 ms blank screen and then by a target whose presentation terminated when the subject responded or when 2,000 ms elapsed, whichever occurred first. Subjects were 55 native English-speaking students from the University at Albany. They were instructed to make a lexical decision on the second item in each pair.

The results of Experiment 2a are summarized in Table 2. Response times to transparent targets following morphologically related primes were significantly faster (27 ms) than to the same targets preceded by unrelated primes, replicating the robust morphological facilitation effect seen in other experiments. In contrast, responses to targets preceded by orthographically related control primes were significantly *inhibited* (-49 ms) relative to responses in the unrelated prime condition. Response times to opaque targets following morphologically related primes were not significantly faster (-7 ms) than to the same targets preceded by unrelated primes. This outcome does not replicate the robust morphological facilitation seen in the first experiment. Responses to targets preceded by orthographically related control primes were significantly *inhibited* (-38 ms) relative to responses in the unrelated prime condition. Failure to observe facilitation for morphological relatives with an opaque base morpheme was not anticipated based on the results observed at long lags. One plausible account is that when length was preserved, as it was for the majority of opaque bases, facilitation due to morphological relatedness was offset by inhibition from orthographic similarity. This interpretation was examined in a subsequent experiment.

In Experiment 2b opaque materials were formed from the same base morpheme as in the previous experiments except that targets were altered so that the lengths of the prime and the target were not identical in the morphological relatedness condition (e.g., *slung-slings*). Results are summarized in Table 3.

TABLE 2. *Target latencies and error rates for targets following unrelated, morphological, and orthographic primes in the lexical decision task with a short lag in Experiment 2a.*

| | | TYPE OF PRIME | |
	Unrelated	Morphological	Orthographic
BASE MORPHEME			
Transparent			
prime	tack	marked	market
target	mark	mark	mark
RT	656	629	705
%E	9.1	9.0	8.6
Facilitation		27	-49
Facilitation		0.1	0.5
Opaque			
RT	655	662	693
%E	8.9	8.5	8.6
Facilitation		-7	-38
Facilitation		0.4	0.3

TABLE 3. *Target latencies and error rates for targets following unrelated, morphological, and orthographic primes in the lexical decision task with a short lag in Experiment 2b.*

| | | TYPE OF PRIME | |
	Unrelated	Morphological	Orthographic
BASE MORPHEME			
Transparent			
prime	tack	marked	market
target	mark	mark	mark
RT	619	563	630
%E	9.0	8.8	8.5
Facilitation		56	-11
Facilitation		0.2	0.5
Opaque			
prime	scrap	slung	slang
target	slings	slings	slings
RT	652	617	653
%E	8.9	9.2	8.6
Facilitation		35	-1
Facilitation		-0.3	0.3

Response times to targets with opaque bases following morphologically related primes were significantly faster (35 ms) than to the same targets preceded by unrelated primes. This patterns replicates the robust effect of morphological facilitation observed in Experiment 1 and for targets with transparent bases in Experiment 2a. However, responses to targets preceded by orthographically related control primes were not significantly inhibited (-1 ms) relative to responses in the unrelated prime condition. Because word length is correlated with neighborhood density and perhaps with other variables as well, it is not possible to explain the absence of inhibitory orthographic effects at this time.

Although all the details are not yet elaborated, Experiment 2 demonstrates a dissociation at a short lag between the effects of orthographic similarity of primes and targets with and without morphologic relatedness. Orthographically related but morphologically unrelated primes tend to inhibit. Words with a shared morpheme tend to facilitate, although the effect is less reliable with opaque bases than with transparent ones. In essence, morphological effects at short lags may be sensitive to phonological and/or orthographic overlap or to another associated variable.

Taken together, the results of Experiments 1 and 2 reinforce the claim that morphological effects are qualitatively different from orthographic/phonologic effects and cannot to be accounted for by the same mechanism. Orthographic effects appear to be restricted to short lag presentation conditions, and they retard target recognition, at least under the present conditions. Morphological effects appear both at long and at short lags and tend to speed target recognition. Furthermore, because morphological effects have been observed at short and at long lags for transparent as well as opaque base morphemes, it is unlikely that transparency of the base morpheme alone determines the mechanism by which morphologically complex words are processed.

DO MORPHOLOGICAL EFFECTS REQUIRE SHARED SEMANTICS?

Morphologically related words share a base morpheme; these units are meaningful. It follows that in addition to being orthographically and/or phonologically related, two words that are morphologically related tend to have similar meanings. It is possible, therefore, that facilitatory effects obtained when morphologically related primes precede targets could reflect the semantic similarity between prime and target. The facilitatory effects of semantically associated primes on responses to targets has received considerable attention in the literature (see Neely's 1991 review). However, much less is known about the role of semantics in the facilitation of morphologically related primes on responses to targets. It is therefore important to differentiate the contribution of a shared morpheme from that of semantic association (Lupker, 1984) when discussing evidence for morphological processing. It should be noted that the semantic relationship shared by prime-target pairs in the typical semantic priming study is generally an associative relationship defined on the whole word. However, the following discussion of previously reported experiments and of our own recently completed experiment includes varying types of semantic relationships between prime and target.

In a repetition priming study with English materials, Feldman and Stotko (unpublished, cited in Feldman, 1992) examined the contribution of semantics over and above shared morphology to visual word recognition by contrasting the effects on target recognition (e.g., *create*) of an identity repetition with the effects of both a semantically transparent relative (e.g., *creation*) and a semantically opaque relative (e.g., *creature*). In a pilot experiment, 40 subjects rated the overall similarity of meaning between prime and target words. Triples consisting of a target and two morphological relatives, one of which was distant and one of which was close in meaning to the target, were created. Subjects made lexical decisions to targets preceded at long lags by morphologically related words that were either "close" or "distant" semantic relatives of the target. Whereas robust facilitation was obtained for identity repetitions (+93 ms), smaller effects (+33 ms) were obtained for all morphologically related items. The degree of facilitation did not vary according to whether the morphologically related prime was a close relative (+36 ms) or a distant relative (+30 ms) of the target. This outcome suggested that semantic transparency defined by the degree of semantic similarity between morphologically complex prime and target does not affect the magnitude of facilitation at long lags.

A study conducted with Hebrew materials contrasted facilitation from associatively related and morphologically related primes at long lags and zero lags (Bentin & Feldman, 1990). Targets were preceded by primes that were related only morphologically, only semantically, or both morphologically and semantically. In this study, words that were related both semantically and morphologically tended to have semantically transparent bases. For example, in Hebrew, the words for *library* and *librarian* share both a semantic and a morphological relationship (transparent), whereas the words for *library* and *number* share only a morpheme (opaque). The results indicated that whereas the magnitude of facilitation from morphologically related primes did not vary statistically across lag (i.e., +17 ms for lag 0 vs. +19 ms for lag 15), semantically related primes produced facilitation only in the no lag condition (i.e., +43 ms for lag 0 vs. -5 ms for lag 15). With respect to the present discussion of semantic transparency, at lag 0, facilitation was greater for the morphological plus semantic condition (+47 ms) and for the semantic condition (+43 ms) than for the morphological condition (+17 ms), whereas at lag 15 (statistically) equivalent facilitation was obtained for the semantic plus morphological condition (+23 ms) and the morphological condition (+19 ms). In summary, semantic and morphological facilitation effects are differentially affected by the lag between presentation of the prime and the target. Moreover, semantic transparency contributes over and above morphological relatedness only when relatives are presented in close temporal succession (see also Marslen-Wilson et al., 1994).

Taken collectively, the results summarized here suggest that the semantic contribution of the base morpheme to each morphologically complex form is temporally limited. Specifically, Feldman and Stotko (cited in Feldman, 1992) demonstrated that the degree of semantic overlap between morphologically related prime and target has no effect on the magnitude of facilitation obtained at long lags. Bentin and Feldman (1990) observed equivalent morphological facilitation for more and less semantically transparent morphological relatives at long lags. Effects of semantic transparency were evident only at short lags. In conclusion, the effects of semantic transparency of the base morpheme on word recognition are distinct from the whole word effects of associative relatedness. They differ with respect to units (morpheme vs. whole word) and temporal domain. Accordingly, they should be understood in terms of different mechanisms. Finally, the effects of semantic transparency are not general enough to account for morphological effects that persist at long lags. The remainder of this section discusses a recently-completed experiment that uses the short-term priming paradigm to investigate conditions under which the semantics of a word's morphological components do influence word recognition.

It is well documented that the component morphological structure of isolated pseudowords affects recognition processes. Specifically, decision latencies to Italian pseudowords composed of two real morphemes in an illegal combination (e.g., formations such as English *walken*) differ from latencies to pseudowords composed of one real and one "pseudo" morpheme (e.g., *valken*) or to two "pseudo" morphemes (Caramazza, Laudanna, & Romani, 1988; Chialant & Caramazza, this volume). Experiment 3 investigated whether or not the component structure of a pseudoword affects lexical decision responses to a word target that follows it. The pseudoword primes were formed from a morphologically simple word (e.g., *steal*) that was a semantic associate of the target (e.g., *thief*) and primes immediately preceded targets. The base morphemes (simple words) were transformed into pseudowords by the addition of affixes according to two criteria that varied in compositionality. The addition of the affix in the compositional prime condition yielded a pseudoword by illegal combination of base morpheme with an agentive affix (e.g., *er*). The affixes (e.g., *en*) used in the control condition were inappropriate for that form of the morphologically simple word (e.g., *steal*) although they were appropriate for that form class and, in fact, for another form of that verb (e.g., *stole*). The compositional and control affixes were matched in orthographic and phonologic structure (i.e., *er* vs. *en*). Finally, the two components of the compositional pseudoword prime were at least partially comparable in meaning to the target. For example, *stealer* is not a real word and, in fact, its coinage is "blocked" (Aronoff, 1976) by the existence of the target *thief*. Processing of the primes was assessed by examining their effects on processing of the target word. Because the pseudoword primes in the two conditions use the same base morpheme and have affixes equated along phonologic and orthographic dimensions, differences in reaction times to the targets were expected only to the degree that subjects access information about *both* the base morpheme and the affix, that is, the full composition of the pseudoword prime.

Two stimulus lists were constructed such that across the lists each target item was preceded by both types of primes. A set of pseudoword-prime, pseudoword-target pairs were also constructed to be similar to the pseudoword-prime, word-target experimental pairs. Primes were presented for 250 ms and were followed by a 50 ms blank screen. Targets were then presented for 1,500 ms or until the subject responded. A total of 30 native English-speaking University at Albany undergraduates participated. They were instructed to press the "yes" key if *one* of the two items presented was a properly spelled English word and to press the "no" key if *both* of the two items presented were pseudowords.

The results indicated that subjects are sensitive to the morphological composition of pseudoword primes. Responses to targets (e.g., *thief*) were significantly facilitated (+18 ms) when preceded by compositional primes (e.g., *stealer*, 638 ms) relative to control primes (e.g., *stealen*, 656 ms). Error rates for the two conditions were 9.5% and 10.0%, respectively, and did not differ statistically. Because the two prime types were equated in degree of semantic association to the target item, these results suggest that (1) morphemic structure of pseudowords primes can influence processing of a successive word target, and (2) subjects are sensitive to the meaning of both morphological components in bimorphemic pseudoword primes.

DOES MORPHOLOGICAL PROCESSING REFLECT COMPONENT STRUCTURE?

The results from the lexical decision task provide evidence that morphological effects in visual word recognition are not necessarily tied to orthographic or phonological transparency or to word level semantics and that subjects are sensitive to the morphological composition of the words they read. However, some of the most compelling evidence for morphological processing comes from patterns of errors in language production. More specifically, the disruptions that occur during spontaneous speech and the manner in which morphemic segments get recombined into novel sequences during spontaneous speech production suggest that morphemic units also play an important role in the production of language (Dell, 1986; Fromkin, 1973; Stemberger, 1985).

The segment shifting task provides a way to simulate, in the lab, the errors made during spontaneous speech (Feldman, 1992; Feldman & Fowler, 1987; Feldman, Frost, & Pnini, in press). In this task, subjects are instructed to separate a designated segment from a source word, to shift the segment onto a target word, and to name the new result aloud as rapidly as possible. Shifting times for morphologically complex words such as *brighten* (when presented with *bright*) are compared when the shifted segment (viz., *en*) comes from a morphemically complex word (e.g., *harden*) or from a morphemically simple (e.g., *garden*) source word.

The rationale underlying the segment shifting manipulation is the observation that the morphemic composition of many words cannot be determined without lexical information. In the absence of a word context, the morphemic status of many sequences of letters is indeterminate. In the presence of a word context, some sequences may but need not be morphemic, and it is necessary to consult the lexicon to make this determination. Consider the status of final sequence *en* in words such as *garden* and *harden*. *Garden* is morphologically simple. *Harden* is morphologically complex in that the sequence *en* forms a morpheme which is affixed to the base morpheme *hard*. In short, whether or not *en* is a morpheme depends on the particular word to which it is affixed such that morphemic processing in this task cannot be confined to specification of units for accessing the lexicon.

Recent work by Laudanna and Burani in Italian (this volume; Burani & Laudanna, 1992) and by Schreuder and Baayen in Dutch (1994) has suggested that the distributional characteristics of letter sequences that form affixes is nevertheless important in determining how morphemes are processed. Although the measures vary from laboratory to laboratory (e.g., some are type-based, others are token-based), generally the reliability with which a particular letter sequence functions as a morphemic affix influences processing. Common to most measures is an index of the number of words in which a letter sequence functions morphemically. This index can be further translated into a salience measure by forming a ratio of morphemic to nonmorphemic instances (Laudanna & Burani, this volume) or into a morpheme ratio which takes the total number of occurrences of that sequence into consideration. In this sense, these indices can be interpreted as measures of how reliably a letter sequence functions as an affix. As a first approximation for English, the *Capricorn Rhyming Dictionary* (Redfield, 1965) provides estimates of the number of word types which end in a particular morpheme and of the total number of words (without proper nouns and archaic terms) that end in that letter sequence.

Ambiguity of morphological status was exploited in a fifth experiment in order to probe morphological processing. In our experiment, stimuli consisted of pairs of English words including a morphologically complex word composed of a base morpheme and a morphological suffix and a morphologically simple control word composed of only one morpheme. The control word ended with the same sequence of letters that functioned morphemically in its corresponding complex word. In this way, the boundary between stationary and shifted portions was controlled for phonemic and syllabic structure. Two experimental lists were constructed such that across lists both types of source words preceded the target.

Both inflectional (e.g., *winning*) and derivational (e.g., *harden*) morphemically complex forms were included, and performance on complex items was compared to performance on their phonemically matched but morphologically simple counterparts (e.g., *inning* and *garden*, respectively).

Morphological affixes included 11 pairs with *er* including both inflectional (e.g., *colder*) and derivational (e.g., *swimmer*) functions; six pairs with *en* which also included inflectional (e.g., *driven*) and derivational (e.g., *soften*) functions; six pairs each with *ing* which is ambiguous as to morphological type (e.g., *writing*); and six with *est* (e.g., *neatest*) and *y* (e.g., *lacy*). In addition, there were two pairs with *al* (e.g., *rental*), and one each with *ic* (e.g., *scenic*), *ster* (e.g., *mobster*), and *or* (e.g., *sculptor*). The morpheme counts (total number of word types listed in *Capricorn Rhyming Dictionary*) and ratios (count divided by total number of entries in *Capricorn Rhyming Dictionary*) for these affixes are summarized in Table 4. Target words were selected so that the affixation of the ending never necessitated a spelling or a pronunciation change to the base morpheme of the target. Source and target words were phonologically and semantically unrelated. An experimental triad consisted of the target to which the designated segment was shifted, a morphologically complex source word, and a morphologically simple control word.

Subjects were 46 native English-speaking undergraduates. Source words such as *harden* or *garden* appeared on the computer screen and after 750 ms, the *en* was highlighted. The target word (e.g., *bright*) then appeared below the source word and a clock started (see Figure 1). Subjects were instructed to strip the highlighted part of the source word and to attach it to the target word and name the new word as rapidly and as accurately as possible. The source and target words remained visible for 1,500 ms and then a blank screen returned.

TABLE 4. *Number of morphemic entries, total number of entries, and ratio of morphemic to total number of entries for the affixes used in Experiment 5.*

		COUNT	
	Morpheme	Total Count	Ratio
AFFIX			
AL	14	96	.15
EN	35	108	.32
ER	50	353	.14
EST	21	99	.21
IC	34	152	.22
ING	74	263	.28
OR	25	110	.23
STER	5	11	.45
Y	0	41	.0

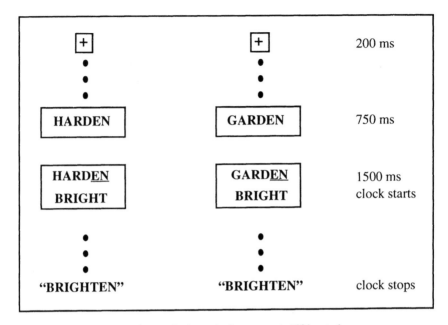

FIGURE 1. Presentation format for items in the segment shifting task.

Means in the morphologically complex (e.g., *harden*) and morphologically simple (e.g., *garden*) conditions were 583 ms and 598 ms respectively. Shifting latencies were significantly faster (+15 ms) to targets formed with a morphemic ending than to targets formed with a nonmorphemic ending. Error rates were 8% for both the morphologically complex and morphologically simple conditions. Accordingly no formal analysis of the error data was carried out.

Shifting latencies indicated that skilled readers are sensitive to a word's morphological structure. Interestingly, morphologically complex source words produced faster shifting latencies than simple source words even though the words in the complex condition had lower average frequency than the words in the morphologically simple condition (see also Frauenfelder & Schreuder, 1991). Because the requisite response was equated over the morphologically complex and simple experimental conditions, this outcome cannot merely reflect the phonological relationship between target word (e.g., *bright*) and what subjects produced (e.g., *brighten*). Furthermore, source words were selected so that several letters close to the shifted portion, along with the shifted portion itself, represented the same phonemes. It is therefore unlikely that this outcome reflects phonological factors or sequential orthographic probabilities.

Subsequent analyses looked at the difference in shifting times for targets formed from morphemically complex and morphemically simple source words as a function of the frequency of target and source words and of reliability of the affix. The mean difference in shifting time for targets from morphemically complex and morphemically simple source words was significantly correlated with number of morphemic words listed, $r = .33$, $p < .05$, and with the ratio of morphemic to total number of entries, $r = .39$, $p < .05$. The mean difference in shifting latencies was not correlated with the surface frequency of either the morphemically complex or the morphemically simple source word, $r = -.19$, $p > .10$ and $r = -.23$, $p > .10$, respectively. Finally the difference was not correlated with the cumulative type frequency of words formed from the base of the morphologically complex source word.

Although the processing locus of the segment shifting effect has not yet been specified, it is evident that either the morphological structure of source words is analyzed and decomposed into stem and affix in the course of segmenting the designated segment or that the produced utterance is built up from available morphological constituents of the target and the "affix" from the source word. These are not mutually exclusive alternatives. Interestingly, the effect reflects the morphemic reliability of the final letters of a source word rather than its surface frequency or the frequency of its base morpheme.

CONCLUSION

We have reviewed a sample of the existing evidence and provided some new support from a series of our own experiments that morphology plays a distinct role in visual word recognition. It has been shown that: (1) The effects of morphologically related primes on targets are qualitatively different from the effects of orthographic/phonologic similarity alone; (2) Morphologically related word primes that differed from their targets in semantic transparency and were presented at long lags did not differentially affect processing of the target, although semantically transparent base morphemes may have influenced morphological processing at short lags; (3) The morphologic components of pseudoword primes matched in degree of associative relatedness to targets and presented at short lags influence processing of the targets; (4) Finally, a new task that combines aspects of perception and production provides further evidence for the psychological reality of morphological components at a locus that cannot be prelexical but does reflect distributional characteristics of the affix.

The present data, consistent with the findings of others, suggest that the semantic and orthographic dimensions are essential aspects of printed word recognition and, further, that any model that purports to be a complete model of morphological processing needs to account for the time course of information provided by both orthographic and semantic characteristics of the base morpheme. In a semantically analytic model (Schreuder & Baayen, this volume) the meaning of morphologically complex but semantically transparent (compositional) forms is computed by way of activational feedback between form-derived (i.e., access) and semantic levels of representation. In an orthographically analytic model (e.g., Chialant & Caramazza, this volume), representations of regular items are represented in decomposed form, such that morphological information is represented as orthographic properties of the lexical entry. The logic underlying the present study holds orthographic similarity constant and varies morphological similarity to examine the effects of shared meaning based on a common morpheme. Then it holds morphology constant and varies orthographic similarity to examine the role of orthographic transparency. By design, this experimental logic is not optimal if the essence of the morpheme is defined by a complex covariation between these two dimensions over sets of words. Nevertheless, the evidence summarized in the present chapter suggests that similarity based on orthography and phonology or on associative semantics alone cannot account for morphological effects. When the components of a word are not easily decomposed either orthographically, phonologically, or semantically, skilled readers can still demonstrate sensitivity to component morphological structure. Moreover, any contribution of the orthographic and semantic dimensions to morphological relatedness are complex. In summary, any account of morphology must encompass time varying patterns among morphologically related words including those with only abstract similarity.

ACKNOWLEDGMENT

The research reported here was conducted at The University of Delaware and at The University at Albany and was supported by funds from National Institute of Child Health and Human Development Grant HD-01994 to Haskins Laboratories. We thank Carol Fowler, Jacqueline Larabee, and Jim Neely for comments on an earlier draft, and Tammy Boyd, Elizabeth Megathlin, and Suzanne Polastri for running subjects.

REFERENCES

Aronoff, M. (1976). *Word formation in generative grammar.* Cambridge, MA: MIT Press.

Bentin, S., & Feldman, L. B. (1990). The contribution of morphological and semantic relatedness to repetition priming at short and long lags: Evidence from Hebrew. *Quarterly Journal of Experimental Psychology, 42,* 693-711.

Burani, C., & Laudanna, A. (1992). Units of representation for derived words in the lexicon. In R. Frost & L. Katz (Eds.), *Orthography, phonology, morphology and meaning: An overview.* Amsterdam: Elsevier.

Caramazza, A., Laudanna, A., & Romani, C. (1988). Lexical access and inflectional morphology. *Cognition, 28,* 297-332.

Dell, G. S. (1986). A spreading-activation theory of retrieval in sentence production. *Psychological Review, 93,* 283-321.

Feldman, L. B. (1992). Morphological relationships revealed through the repetition priming task. In M. Noonan, P. Downing, & S. Lima (Eds.), *Linguistics and literacy* (pp. 239-254). Amsterdam: John Benjamins.

Feldman, L. B. (1993). Bi-alphabetism and the design of the reading mechanism. In D. M. Willows, R. S. Kruk, & E. Corcos (Eds.), *Visual processes in reading and reading disabilities* (pp. 237-261). Hillsdale, NJ: Lawrence Erlbaum Associates.

Feldman, L. B., & Andjelković, D. (1992). Morphological analysis in word recognition. In L. Katz & R. Frost (Eds.), *Orthography, phonology, morphology, and meaning: An overview.* (pp. 343-360). Amsterdam: Elsevier.

Feldman, L. B., & Bentin, S. (1994). Morphological analysis of disrupted morphemes: Evidence from Hebrew. *Quarterly Journal of Experimental Psychology, 47,* 407-435.

Feldman, L. B., & Fowler, C. A. (1987). The inflected noun system in Serbo-Croatian: Lexical representation of morphological structure. *Memory & Cognition, 15,* 1-12.

Feldman, L. B., Frost, R., & Pnini, T. (in press). Decomposing words into constituent morphemes: Evidence from English and Hebrew. *Journal of Experimental Psychology: Learning, Memory, & Cognition.*

Feldman, L. B., & Moskovljević, J. (1987). Repetition priming is not purely episodic in origin. *Journal of Experimental Psychology: Learning, Memory, & Cognition, 13,* 573-581.

Forster, K. I., Davis, C., Schoknecht, C., & Carter, R. (1987). Masked priming with graphemically related forms: Repetition or partial activation? *Quarterly Journal of Experimental Psychology, 39,* 211-251.

Fowler, C. A., Napps, S. E., & Feldman, L. B. (1985). Relations among regular and irregular morphologically related words in the lexicon as revealed by repetition priming. *Memory & Cognition, 13,* 241-255.

Frauenfelder, U. H., & Schreuder, R. (1992). Constraining psycholinguistic models of morphological processing: The role of productivity. In G. E. Booij & J. van Marle (Eds.), *Yearbook of Morphology, 1991* (pp. 165-183). Dordrecht: Kluwer.

Fromkin, V. A. (1973). Introduction. In V. A. Fromkin (Ed.), *Speech errors as linguistic evidence.* (pp. 11-45). The Hague: Mouton

Grainger, J. (1990). Word frequency and neighborhood frequency effects in lexical decision and naming. *Journal of Memory and Language, 29,* 228-244.

Grainger, J., Colé, P., & Segui, J. (1991). Masked morphological priming in visual word recognition. *Journal of Memory and Language, 30,* 370-384.

Grainger, J., O'Regan, J. K., Jacobs, A. M., & Segui, J. (1989). On the role of competing word units in visual word recognition: The neighborhood frequency effect. *Perception & Psychophysics, 45,* 189-195.

Hanson, V. L., & Wilkenfeld, D. (1985). Morphophonology and lexical organization in deaf readers. *Language and speech, 28,* 269-280.

Henderson, L. (1985). Toward a psychology of morphemes. In A. Ellis (Ed.), *Progress in the psychology of language.* Hillsdale, NJ: Lawrence Erlbaum Associates.

Laudanna, A., Badecker, W., & Caramazza, A. (1989). Priming homographic stems. *Journal of Memory & Language, 28,* 531-546.

Laudanna, A., & Burani, C. (1986). Effetti di ripetizione e priming su forme morfologicamente collegate. *Giornale Italiano di Psicologia, 13,* 123-139.

Lukatela, G., Carello, C., & Turvey, M. T. (1987). Lexical representation of regular and irregular inflected nouns. *Language and Cognitive Processes, 2 (1),* 1-17.

Lupker, S. J. (1984). Semantic priming without association: A second look. *Journal of Verbal Learning and Verbal Behavior, 23,* 709-733.

Marslen-Wilson, W., Tyler, L. K., Waksler, R., & Older, L. (1994). Morphology and meaning in the English lexicon. *Psychological Review, 101,* 3-33.

Napps, S. E. (1989). Morphemic relationships in the lexicon: Are they distinct from semantic and formal relationships? *Memory & Cognition, 17,* 729-739.

Napps, S. E., & Fowler, C. A. (1987). Formal relationships among words and the organization of the mental lexicon. *Journal of Psycholinguistic Research, 16,* 257-272.

Neely, J. H. (1991). Semantic priming effects in visual word recognition. A selective review of current findings and theories. In D. Besner & G. Humphreys (Eds.), *Basic processes in reading: Visual word recognition.* Hillsdale, NJ: Lawrence Erlbaum Associates.

Redfield, B. G. (1965). *Capricorn Rhyming Dictionary.* New York: Capricorn Books.

Rumelhart, D. E., & McClelland, J. L. (1986). On learning the past tense of English verbs. In J. L. McClelland & D. E. Rumelhart (Eds.), *Parallel Distributed Processing: Exploration in the microstructure of cognition, Vol 1.* Cambridge, MA: MIT Press.

Schreuder, R., & Baayen, R. H. (1994). Prefix stripping re-revisited. *Journal of Memory and Language, 33,* 357-375.

Seidenberg, M. S. (1987). Sublexical structures in visual word recognition: Access units or orthographic redundancy? In M. Coltheart (Ed.), *Attention & Performance, XII* (pp. 245-263). Hillsdale, NJ: Lawrence Erlbaum Associates.

Segui, J. & Grainger, J. (1990). Priming word recognition with orthographic neighbors: Effects of relative prime-target frequency. *Journal of Experimental Psychology: Human Perception and Performance, 16,* 65-76.

Stemberger, J. P. (1985). An interactive activation model of language production. In A. Ellis (Ed.), *Progress in the psychology of language.* (Vol. 1, pp. 143-186). Hillsdale, NJ: Lawrence Erlbaum Associates.

Stanners, R. F., Neiser, J. J., Hernon, W. P., & Hall, R. (1979). Memory representation for morphologically related words. *Journal of Verbal Learning and Verbal Behavior, 18,* 399-412.

Taft, M. (1985). The decoding of words in lexical access: A review of the morphographic approach. In D. Besner, T. G. Waller, & G. E. MacKinnon (Eds.), *Reading research: Advances in theory and practice, Vol V.* New York: Academic Press.

Taft, M. (1991). *Reading and the mental lexicon.* Hillsdale, NJ: Lawrence Erlbaum Associates.

6 Modeling Morphological Processing

Robert Schreuder[†] and R. Harald Baayen[‡]
†Interfaculty Research Unit for Language and Speech
‡Max-Planck-Institut für Psycholinguistik

We present a model in which the crucial function of morphological processing is seen as calculating meaning. The process by which meaning is obtained from form is analyzed in terms of a hybrid architecture in which symbolic computations are carried out on representations that have become available through spreading activation. We introduce a mechanism of activation feedback from the semantic and syntactic representations to so-called concept nodes and from these concept nodes to form-based access representations. This allows the model to become tuned to the requirements imposed on the recognition system by the language specific structural and distributional characteristics of the morphological system to which it is exposed. The model is compared with other models proposed in the literature.

1. INTRODUCTION

This chapter presents an attempt to come to grips with a broad range of complexities characterizing the processing of morphologically complex words. Building on earlier work by Frauenfelder and Schreuder (1992), we outline an abstract model of morphological processing that explicitly takes into account a large number of interacting factors that are often ignored in existing models. This model is perhaps best considered as a meta-model aimed at describing the characteristics that language-specific models of morphological processing should possess. In contrast to models that limit the role of morphology to the access of morphological constituents (as in many models in computational linguistics and psycholinguistics), our approach is based on the conviction that the role of morphology is essentially one of computing (new) meaning. Hence the architecture of our model reflects—to our mind—the central role of semantic computation, even though the exact mechanisms and representations involved cannot but remain underspecified. Our chapter is structured as follows. Section 2 introduces the empirical facts that any model of morphological processing should take into account. Section 3 presents a detailed description of our meta-model, and section 4 considers some developmental aspects of the model. In section 5, we sketch how the model takes into account the various empirical facts discussed in section 2. Finally, section 6 compares our meta-model with other models that have been put forward in the literature.

2. EMPIRICAL DATA

Models of morphological processing should be constrained by experimental and distributional facts. In this paper we consider only those well-known experimental results that have been extensively replicated and where some consensus has been obtained: cumulative root frequency effects (e.g., Taft & Forster, 1976), clearer and stronger effects for inflectional morphology compared to derivation (e.g., Feldman, in press; McQueen & Cutler, in press), and stronger effects for semantically transparent complex words compared to semantically opaque complex words (e.g., Marslen-Wilson, Tyler, Waksler, & Older, 1994). Other empirical data concern the distributional properties of words in a given language. Models should reflect the ability of the reader/listener to process unfamiliar regular complex words (the productivity constraint; see, e.g., Baayen, 1992, 1993; Frauenfelder & Schreuder, 1992). Models should also take into account that the phonological form of some affixes may be linked with different meanings (affixal homophony, e.g., English -er as in *walker* versus *greater*). Models should also reflect the possibility that extensive pseudo-prefixation (*re-* in *reach* versus *react*) may affect morphological processing (see, e.g., Laudanna & Burani, this volume; Schreuder & Baayen, 1994). Finally, the structural properties of languages differ widely, leading to substantial differences in the extent of morphological complexity and to the frequencies of morphologically complex words (see, e.g., Baayen, 1992).[1] Such differences may substantially affect the way in which the mental lexicon develops. Ideally, a

---

[1]For an extensive overview of the various experimental and distributional factors that should be considered when modeling the role of morphology, see Baayen and Schreuder (in press).

single underlying mechanism of morphological processing and representation should explain different ways of handling morphology.

3. A META-MODEL FOR MORPHOLOGICAL PROCESSING

3.1 General Assumptions

The model we are proposing is a spreading activation model combined with a mechanism for carrying out symbolic computations on representations that have become available through activation. Symbolic computations are required for the modeling of the parsing process, which we conceive of as consisting of three different but related stages. The first stage, segmentation, concerns the mapping of the speech input onto form-based access representations of full as well as bound forms (affixes, bound stems). Prosodic information, resyllabification, stress shifts, tone sandhi, and other phonological mutations may complicate this mapping operation. The second stage, licensing, involves checking whether representations that have become co-active can be integrated on the basis of their subcategorization properties. The third stage, combination, deals with the computation of the lexical representation of the complex word from the lexical (syntactic and semantic) representations of its constituents, given that this integration has been licensed.

In addition to the assumption that the parsing process can be analyzed into these three stages, we make two other assumptions. First, any language has complex words, the meanings of which are not functions of the meanings of the constituent parts. Since the non-compositional readings of such words cannot be generated by rule, we assume that these words have their own lexical representations at various levels. Second, we assume that frequency effects are autonomous in the sense that any word leaves a memory trace, irrespective of its morphological properties. Thus we do not exclude that, due to repeated exposure, fully regular complex words (including inflections) may develop their own lexical representations (see Pinker, 1991).

3.2 General Outline of the Model

We first globally trace the processing of morphologically complex words from initial access to the final delivery to postlexical processing systems. At the initial stages of word recognition, the speech signal is transformed into an intermediate access representation that will often contain more than one word. This intermediate access representation has to be mapped onto the access representations proper, as shown in Figure 1. Such 'lexical' access representations may be present for full complex forms, for stems, whether bound or free, for affixes, and for clitics. They contain modality-specific form information that is normalized both with respect to the inherent variability in the speech signal and with respect to the variability caused by phonological processes such as vowel harmony and various kinds of assimilation processes. Each access representation has its own activation level.

The mechanism by which the intermediate access representations are accessed differ substantially for the auditory and the visual modality (see also Emmorey, this volume, for a discussion of sign language representations). In the auditory modality, some strategy capitalizing on prosodic cues in the intermediate access representation along the lines of Cutler and Norris (1988) may be exploited to solve the sentence segmentation problem. Moreover, some cohort-like mechanism might mediate access to the access representations involved. In the visual modality, the mapping from the intermediate access representation onto the access representations proper is probably more straightforward, thanks to the space characters between words.

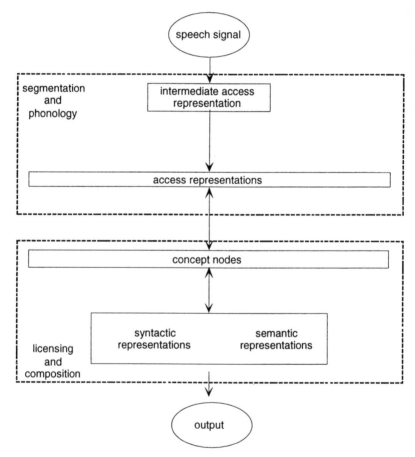

FIGURE 1. General outline of a model of morphological processing.

The speed with which an access representation may become active is determined not only by its resting activation level but also by the complexity of the mapping operation from the intermediate access representations onto the access representations proper. Complex words with affixes triggering phonological mutations that cause the surface form of the base to differ substantially from its underlying, 'normalized' form will take longer to segment than words that are phonologically transparent with respect to their constituents. Similarly, we hypothesize that local and relatively shallow phonological changes (e.g., vowel harmony in Turkish) will require less computational effort than phonological changes in the stem triggered by later occurring suffixes (cf. Sproat, 1992, pp. 191-192). Given that morphological operations (subtractive morphology, reduplication, non-concatenative morphology) are sometimes brought about by phonological operations on words (see Stemberger, this volume), the computational complexity of this mapping operation should not be underestimated (see Baayen & Schreuder, in press). What we assume here is that a complex word is in principle able to activate the access representations of its constituent morphemes and its full form representation, if present.

Each access representation is connected with in general one but sometimes more than one lexical representation. A lexical representation consists of a concept node that in turn is connected with syntactic and semantic representations. Thus the mapping of the access representations onto the relevant syntactic and semantic representations is mediated by the concept nodes.

Both concept nodes and access representations may receive activation feedback from higher levels. This is represented in Figure 1 by means of double-headed arrows. It follows that the activation level of a concept node is a function not only of direct excitation by some access representation but also of the feedback from the semantic and syntactic representations that will often have been activated by other words sharing syntactic and semantic properties.

The feedback from the concept nodes to their access representations ensures that frequently processed complex words will eventually be recognized on the basis of their full forms rather than on the basis of their constituents (see section 3.4.2 for detailed discussion). Crucially, the extent to which an access representation may benefit from activation feedback is a function not only of the amount of feedback it receives but also of its own activation level at that moment. This ensures that the system is tuned in such a way that only those access representations that have led to the activation of concept nodes will benefit. Otherwise, hearing the word *doctor* frequently would cause semantically related words such as *nurse* and *stethoscope* to receive high activation levels for their access representations, which would lead to an unattested high frequency status for low-frequency words such as *stethoscope*. In sum, the activation level of an access representation is a function of the frequency of occurrence of its activator and of the amount of feedback it receives from the concept nodes with which it is associated.

Finally, the output of the lexicon is what we have called a lexical representation, that is, a concept node and its associated syntactic and semantic representations. In the simplest case, that in which a monomorphemic word is processed, one concept node with its associated syntactic and semantic information is delivered to higher-order processing systems. At the other extreme, novel complex forms require the invocation of procedural lexical knowledge, no appropriate lexical representation being available. The dotted box labeled 'licensing and composition' refers to the mechanisms operating on simultaneously activated concept nodes and their associated syntactic and semantic representations. Its function is to create on the fly a new lexical representation that can be delivered to the syntax.

In what follows we consider various aspects of this model in some more detail. Section 3.3 focuses on how the mapping of form onto meaning is accomplished. Section 3.4 outlines the flow of activation feedback from the semantic and syntactic representations to the concept nodes and from these concept nodes to the access representations. Finally, section 3.5 illustrates the role of licensing by means of an example of a multiply complex word.

3.3 Mapping Form onto Meaning

The concept nodes play a crucial role in the mapping of form onto meaning. Section 3.3.1 briefly describes some of their properties. Section 3.3.2 outlines how the concept nodes and their associated syntactic and semantic representations are exploited at the licensing and composition stages.

3.3.1 Concept Nodes

Concept nodes are linked with syntactic and semantic representations. The syntactic representations specify their combinatorial properties (subcategorization, word class, argument structure, etc.). The semantic representations specify various meaning aspects. Concepts need not receive explicit lexical form, there being concepts for which we have no words (the so-called lexical gaps; see Schreuder & Flores d'Arcais, 1989). In the present model, the concept nodes are those concepts that receive verbal expression in the language at the form level. Hence, each concept node in our model is linked with at least one access representation.

Sufficiently activated concept nodes are copied into a short term memory, where stacking and structure-building operations can be carried out, if required. In this way we ensure that long-range dependencies (see section 3.4) and hierarchically structured complex words can be handled adequately. Similarly, words in which the same affix occurs more than once, such as *ununinterrupted,* can be analyzed correctly only if the two instances of *un-* are assigned separate (individual) representations rather than a single, strongly activated representation.

3.3.2. Computing Meanings

Once concept nodes have been activated, it must be determined whether the syntactic representations license their combination. As soon as it has been ascertained that combination can proceed, the meaning of the complex whole has to be computed. There is substantial variability in the complexity of the composition process. We first discuss the simple case of processing a plural inflection. Then, we consider how a reasonably transparent derived word is handled and following this, we trace how the meaning of a derivational neologism would be arrived at. Finally, we briefly discuss the relation between inflection and derivation.

Generally, inflectional processes require the simplest kind of computation. Consider the system depicted in Figure 2, which has access representations for the singular Dutch form *boek,* 'book,' the plural form *boeken,* and the plural affix *-en.* Let BOOK denote the set of representations that are connected to the concept node of *boek,* and let PLURAL be the set of representations linked with the concept node of the plural. Assuming for reasons of expositional simplicity that the singular is unmarked for number, the representation of the plural *boeken* can be analyzed as the union of the two sets of representations, BOOK ∪ PLURAL. Hence it is sufficient for the access representation of *boeken* to have connections with the concept nodes BOOK and PLURAL. The joint activation of these concept nodes and their associated representations will lead to the correct set of activated representations for the plural *boeken.* Note that no concept node for the plural *boeken,* 'books,' is necessary. This ties in nicely with the well-known fact that changes in the meaning of a word are immediately inherited by its inflectional variants. For instance, any change in the meaning of *boek* in Figure 2 carries over to the interpretation of the plural *boeken.* If *boeken* were to have its own concept node, ancillary mechanisms would be required to effect the change in meaning for the plural.

It is important to observe that in the case of *boeken* the composition process is trivial, consisting simply in the union of the relevant sets of representations. In fact, we propose the following hypothesis for the necessary and sufficient conditions under which a concept node is created:

> Concept nodes are only added to the lexicon when the meaning of a complex word cannot be obtained as a union of the representational sets of the constituent elements.

Consequently,

1. Forms receive their own concept nodes when they are not fully transparent semantically, and
2. Any process requiring computation (i.e., operations on the representational sets other than a simple union) will result in the establishment of a new concept node.

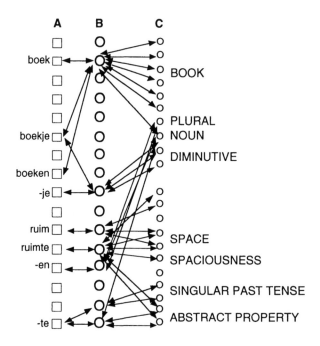

FIGURE 2. Access representations (layer A); concept nodes (layer B); semantic and syntactic nodes (layer C); and their connections for the Dutch noun *boek*, 'book,' the adjective *ruim*, 'spacious,' and related inflected and derived complex forms.

Consider, for instance, the processing of the derived noun *ruim+te*, 'space,' derived from the adjective *ruim*, 'spacious,' by affixation of the derivational suffix *-te* (historically related to English *-th* in *warmth*). Focusing first on the semantic representations of *ruimte*, we find that the concept node of *ruimte* is connected with a number of meaning representations that does not fully overlap with those connected with the concept node of *ruim*. *Ruimte* has technical readings that *ruim* lacks (see Figure 2). Inclusion of a new node is the way in which the absence of full compositionality is handled. Because the meaning of *ruimte* cannot be obtained from the meanings of its constituents alone, we posit a separate concept node for *ruimte*. When *ruimte* is encountered, its access representation will activate this concept node, which in turn will activate the correct set of semantic representations.

Now consider the processing of a novel transparent derivation (neologism) say, *slonzigheid*, 'frumpishness.' Initially, there is no access representation, nor is a concept node available. Let's assume, however, that access representations for *slonzig* ('frumpish') and *-heid* ('-ness') are present and become active on hearing *slonzigheid*. These access representations in turn activate the concept nodes of *slonzig* and *-heid*, and these in their turn activate their associated syntactic and semantic representations. At this point (t_1 in Figure 3) two different syntactic representations for word category status (N and A) are simultaneously activated. A simple union of these representations is not possible. However, the combination of the adjective with the suffix is licensed on the basis of the subcategorization information that is also activated by the concept node of *-heid*. Hence the adjective and the suffix can be combined. The word category node of *slonzig* should be deactivated and that of *-heid* should remain active.[2] How the semantic reading of the complex whole is arrived at must remain underspecified given the limited knowledge of lexical semantics in current (psycho)linguistic theories. The main point we want to make here is that the resulting configuration of activated syntactic and semantic representations is not the result of the simple union of representations as in the case of the plural *boeken*.

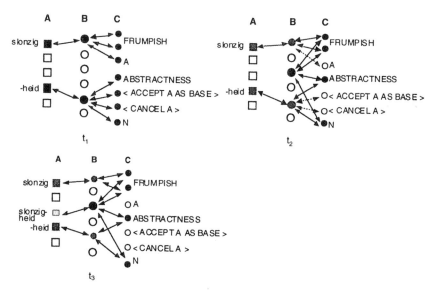

FIGURE 3. Three time steps in the processing of the neologism *slonzigheid*, 'frumpishness': Access representations (A); concept nodes (B); semantic and syntactic nodes (C). Degrees of shading reflect activation levels.

---

[2]In other words, we view the subcategorization information of *-heid* as an instruction for the composition process to unify the syntactic and semantic representations of the affix with those of its base, along the lines of the unification algorithm proposed by Ritchie, Pulman, Black, and Russel (1987).

The result of the composition process is a set of activated syntactic and semantic representations linked with a new concept node (t_2). This concept node with its associated representations is passed on to further processing systems. The newly created concept node is also linked with the memory trace of its full form in the access system (t_3). The initial representational strength of a new concept node may well be a function of the amount of computational effort required by the combinatorial processes. Once created, the new representation will be subject to decay of activation over time in the same way as already existing representations. If not encountered sufficiently often, new representations will fade from memory.

We have discussed examples of how inflected and derived words are processed. Note that the degree of computational complexity is not by definition determined by whether the complex word is an inflected form or whether it is a derived form or a compound. Consider the Dutch diminutive suffix -je in boekje, 'small book,' a derivational affix that determines the gender of the complex word and hence can be analyzed as its morphological head. Nevertheless, the computations involved are extremely simple when compared to deverbal nominalizations in which operations on argument structure are required. For -je, the associated computational costs may well be so low that the new concept node will have a very weak initial activation level. Hence it will fade from memory while its full form access representation may remain linked to the concept nodes of its base and affix. This situation is depicted in Figure 2, where diminutives are processed in a similar way to inflections. Thus the difference between inflection and derivation is not a principled one in our model (see also Bybee, this volume; McQueen & Cutler, in press). It is not their linguistic status but the complexity of the semantic and syntactic operations involved that determines how complex words are processed and represented.

3.4 Activation Feedback

We have proposed a model in which activation flows from the access representations via the concept nodes to the semantic and syntactic level. We now turn to consider the effects of activation feedback from the semantic and syntactic level to the concept nodes (section 3.4.1) and from the concept nodes to the access representations (section 3.4.2). The feedback of activation is initiated once the concept nodes on which the recognition system has converged have been passed on to the postlexical processing system. An assumption crucial to the theory developed here is that a semantically transparent relation between a complex word and its constituents can be modeled as a substantial overlap between the set of (semantic) representations of the complex word and the sets of representations of its constituents. This assumption follows from the way in which we assume that semantic information is stored, namely only once, the links with the concept nodes serving as the means for distinguishing and addressing concepts.

Note that morphological relations in the mental lexicon in general can be understood along these lines. Rather than expressing morphological relations in terms of a spatial metaphor ('morphologically related words are stored together'), our model expresses directly the crucial role of shared semantic and syntactic properties that bring words together in morphological families.

3.4.1 Feedback to the Concept Nodes

Once a concept node has activated a number of semantic and syntactic representations, some activation will flow back to the concept node level. In general, it is not only the activating concept node that will receive such feedback but also concept nodes that are connected to subsets of these representations. This is illustrated in Figure 4 for the semi-transparent derivation *groente,* 'vegetable,' and the fully transparent derivation *trotsheid,* 'pride.'

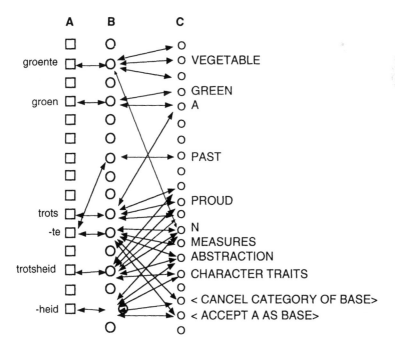

FIGURE 4. Connections for semantically semi-transparent *groente,* 'vegetable' and fully transparent *trotsheid,* 'pride.' Access representations (A); concept nodes (B); semantic and syntactic nodes (C).

First consider *groente*, literally 'greenth,' built from the adjective *groen*, 'green,' and the abstract noun-forming suffix *-te*. The meaning of *groente*, 'edible herbacious plant,' cannot be obtained from the meaning of *groen* and that of the abstract noun forming suffix *-te*, even though it is possible, albeit a posteriori, to trace why the base *groen* has been used.[3] This implies that when *groente* has been processed, hardly any activation from the semantic representations of *groente* will flow back to *groen*, there being almost no connections between the concept node of *groen* and the semantic and syntactic representations linked to *groente*. Similarly, activating the concept node of *groen* will not affect the concept node of *groente*.

Next consider the situation in which a transparent derivation is processed. Suppose that in Figure 4 the concept node of *trotsheid* has become active. This concept will activate several semantic representations that in turn will, through activation feedback, activate not only the concept node of *trotsheid* itself but also to some extent the concept node of its base *trots*, given the large number of shared semantic representations. Similarly, the concept node of *-heid* will receive activation feedback from *trotsheid*. Comparing this state of affairs with *groente*, we find that relatively little activation will flow back from *groente* to its base *groen* and the suffix *-te*. Thus the activation level of the concept node of an affix is a function of the number of semantically transparent formations in which that affix occurs and of the frequencies of those formations.

3.4.2. Feedback to the Access Representations

Active concept nodes similarly allow activation to flow back to the access representations. As discussed in section 3.2, the extent to which a given amount of activation feedback affects the activation level of an access representation is proportional to that representation's current activation level. For a semantically transparent formation such as *trotsheid* (Figure 4), it is the concept node of the complex whole that receives the most activation feedback from the semantic and syntactic representations. Hence the access representation of *trotsheid* will receive more activation feedback than the access representations of its constituents, *trots* and *-heid*. Repeated exposure to *trotsheid* will therefore allow the access representation of *trotsheid* to play an increasingly important role in word recognition. Frauenfelder and Schreuder (1992) postulated an ad hoc mechanism to ensure that their whole-word address route would benefit from repeated exposure to a greater extent than their parsing route; the desirable property that whole-word-based access should take place for frequently occurring forms is an emerging property in the present model.

---

[3]For native speakers of Dutch, the relation between *groen* and *groente* is similar to that between *disease* and *ease* in English. In both cases, it is impossible to predict the meaning of the whole on the basis of its parts.

3.5 Processing Multiply Complex Words

As an example of the way in which the model proposed here handles slightly less trivial complex words, we now consider how a word such as *onwerkbaar*, 'unworkable,' is processed. Note that the meaning of *onwerkbaar* cannot be

$$[_A on[_A [_V werk][_A baar]]]$$

obtained by a simple linear algorithm that operates on successively available representations of the constituent morphemes: *on-* is not subcategorized for combination with verbs. As a first approximation of how long-distance dependencies may be solved—a problem that has received very little attention in psycholinguistic models—we propose the following sequence of events. For ease of exposition, we consider the case that *onwerkbaar* is encountered for the very first time, that *werkbaar* has not been encountered before either, and that representations for its constituent morphemes are already available. We consider the state of the model at five different moments. Initially, at t_1, the access representations of *on-* and *werk* have activated the corresponding concept nodes and their associated semantic and syntactic representations. The licensing mechanism detects that *on-* cannot combine with *werk, on-* being subcategorized for adjectives but not for verbs. Hence the lexical representations of *on-* and *werk* are kept active. At time step t_2, the representations of *-baar* have also become active. This is shown in the left panel of Figure 5. At the next step, the combination of *werk* and *-baar* is licensed, allowing the meaning of *werkbaar* to be calculated and assigned to a new concept node. This entails that the only word category information that remains active is the adjectival status of the new concept node. Similarly, various other semantic and syntactic representations have to be activated or deactivated, as sketched in Figure 5. The system is not allowed to output *werkbaar* to the postlexical processing system because the concept node of *on-* is activating a syntactic representation requiring computational integration with an adjective. But now (at t_4) the combination of *on-* with the lexical representation of *werkbaar* is licensed, so that a concept node can be constructed for *onwerkbaar* as a whole, as shown in the right-hand panel of Figure 5. Note that a number of semantic and syntactic representations that were originally active are no longer so (dotted arrows). We assume that there is no feedback from these representations to the concept nodes. Since there are no more syntactic representations active that contain instructions for further compositional processing, the newly created concept node and its associated representations can be passed on to further processing systems. Furthermore, the new concept node is connected with its memory trace in the access system. We realize that the present unification-based processing mechanism needs to be worked out in far more detail. Nevertheless, a mechanism of this kind is required if psychological models of word recognition are to do more than just identify constituent morphemes.

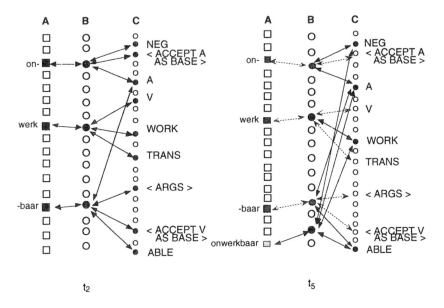

FIGURE 5. Processing long-distance dependencies. Two time slices in the processing of a neologism with long-distance dependencies (*onwerkbaar*, 'unworkable'). Access representations (A); concept nodes (B); semantic and syntactic nodes (C).

4. DIACHRONIC ASPECTS: THE ACQUISITION OF AFFIXAL REPRESENTATIONS

Until now we have assumed the existence in the mental lexicon of representations for affixes of various kinds. The question with which we are concerned now is how such representations are acquired and how the acquisition process influences the development of representations over time. At present very little is known about the precise mechanisms that lead to the setting up of lexical representations of bound forms (see Taft & Zhu, this volume). Nevertheless, it is possible to sketch some of the characteristics of what we call the affix discovery procedure and the constraints under which it operates.

We base our discussion on the classical structuralist notion of the morphological category, defined as a set of words which systematically share form and meaning properties. It is the task of the affix discovery procedure to monitor the expanding mental lexicon for correspondences between form and meaning. This is a two-stage process. First, the system has to detect patterns of co-activations of (developing) semantic representations. If a particular pattern occurs often enough, a concept node is created for this pattern. Once a concept node has been created, a corresponding representation at the access level can begin to develop. For instance, we assume that the child masters the concept of plurality relatively early. Then the pattern of co-activation between a particular subpattern in the access representations (the plural ending *-en,* for instance) and a particular concept node (that of the plurality concept) is noted. This is illustrated in Figure 6. The left-hand panel shows the system after having created a concept node for the plural. Notice that the access representations of plurals such as *honden* ('dogs') and *stoelen* ('chairs') are at this stage linked to concept nodes of their own, in contrast to the organization of the adult system (displayed in Figure 2 where *-en* has its own concept mode).

Following the installation of the concept node for plurality, access representations with the final ending *-en* will activate the concept of plurality by the mechanism of activation feedback. The resulting pattern of co-activation will be detected at some moment in time and will lead to the installation of an affixal access representation that will receive a connection with the concept node for plurality. This is shown in the right-hand panel of Figure 6. Let's assume that the child is already familiar with the word *paard,* 'horse.' Also assume that he/she has not yet heard its plural form, *paarden.* Upon hearing this plural form, the access representations of its stem *paard* and the plural *-en* will be activated, resulting in the activation of the corresponding concept nodes and their associated lexical representations. As argued previously, composition amounts to the simple union of the activated lexical representations. Hence no separate concept node is set up. On the other hand, the complex form will leave a memory trace in the form of a weakly activated access representation connected with the concept nodes of its constituents.

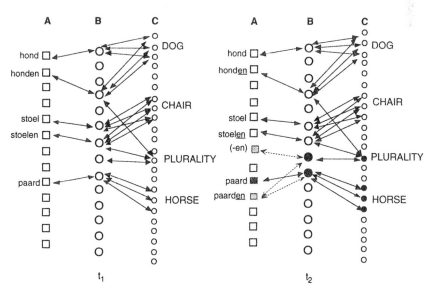

FIGURE 6. Two time slices in the development of representations for the Dutch plural affix *-en.* Access representations (A); concept nodes (B); semantic and syntactic nodes (C).

Most derivational processes are far more complex than the simple example of the plural in Dutch suggests. There are at least six different factors which are relevant to the model: conceptual complexity, semantic transparency, phonological transparency, the complexity of the word formation operations, pseudo-affixation, and affixal homonymy. We discuss each of these factors in turn.

First consider the role of conceptual complexity. Some derivational processes require a fairly high level of abstraction. For instance, children will acquire the concept of plurality well before they have grasped the abstract concepts underlying deadjectival suffixes such as English -ness and -ity. Hence we predict that plural morphology will be mastered before morphology requiring higher levels of abstractness.

The semantic transparency of a morphological category also plays an important role. We predict that transparent affixes are acquired before semantically less transparent or even opaque affixes. Similarly, representations for bound stems will develop only for those cases where the bound stem occurs in a semantically compositional formation. Thus relatively transparent bound stems such as -gress in ingress, egress, progress will be represented, in contrast to opaque stems such as -mit in remit, permit, admit (see Taft & Zhu, this volume).

The phonological transparency of a morphological category is similarly relevant. Affixes that appear in different forms, such as the Dutch diminutive suffix, which has five allomorphs, -je, -tje, -etje, -kje, and -pje, may take longer to discover than an affix with a single phonological form, such as -heid ('-ness').

Furthermore, the complexity of the semantic operations to be carried out may play a role. For instance, deverbal nominalization (destruction) is computationally more complex than deadjectival nominalization (weakness). In the case of deverbal word formation, the argument structure of the base has to be integrated in the lexical conceptual structure of the affix (cf. Jackendoff, 1990). For much of deadjectival and denominal word formation, the computations are more simple, no argument structure being involved. Again we predict that such differences will be reflected in the age of acquisition.

Also consider the issue of pseudo-affixation. Large numbers of words with pseudo-affixes render the discovery of form and meaning correspondences more difficult and will slow down acquisition. Hence, such affixes will develop relatively low activation levels. For instance, depending on one's definition of pseudo-prefixation, 50%-90% of all word tokens in the Cobuild corpus (Sinclair, 1987) beginning with the orthographical or phonological string be- turn out not to begin with the English prefix be-. Similar results are obtained for un-, re-, de-, and en-. In Dutch, the percentages are slightly lower (15%-30%) for a similar set of affixes (Schreuder & Baayen, 1994). Such a state of affairs may render the detection of form-meaning correspondences extremely difficult and has been observed to have empirical consequences for on-line lexical processing (see Burani & Laudanna, this volume).

Finally, it may happen that one and the same affix has two different and un-related meanings. In the present model, two homonymic affixes will share one access representation but will have different concept nodes. For instance, the Dutch derivational suffix -te (ruim-te, 'space'; see Figures 2 and 4) has an inflectional homonym that indicates the singular past tense (werk-te, 'worked'). Because inflectional -te is far more frequent in the language as well as more transparent, the abstract reading of deadjectival -te has to be "discovered" in competition with another, far more dominant pattern of form-meaning corre-spondences. Again we predict a late discovery for the less dominant reading of homophonic affixes.

Summing up, it is clear that the "discovery" of an affix is determined by a large number of often interacting factors. We predict that each of these factors may influence the age at which a certain affix is mastered as well as the way in which the adult system represents it. Suppose that two affixes occur with equal numbers of tokens and types in the language but that one of the two is discovered late due to a combination of the factors discussed above. By the time that the latter affix has been installed, the former will already have developed well-established representations. Hence the more regular affix will be characterized by higher activation levels. One may expect that for the more highly activated affix composition will play the more substantial role. Note that this implies that whether compositional processes are involved in the recognition of complex forms within a given language is not an all-or-nothing question. Within one and the same language, some affixes might play a very minor role in word recognition while others are critically involved. Across languages, it is also the case that the overall role of morphology may be crucial (Turkish) or relatively minor (English, Dutch).

5. EXPLAINING EMPIRICAL FACTS

We now turn to discuss the way in which the present model accounts for the empirical facts discussed in section 2. Frequency effects are explained by introducing frequency sensitivity at two levels, that of the access representations and that of the concept nodes. For instance, since both thinking and thinker activate the concept node THINK, it is at the concept node that repeated exposures to words sharing a stem accumulate. The so-called cumulative stem frequency effect is accounted for in this way. Word frequency effects are handled in terms of the activation levels of the access representations.

We have observed (section 3.3) that the effects of inflectional morphology are generally easier to observe experimentally than are effects of derivational morphology. This follows directly from the central role accorded to semantic transparency. Stronger experimental effects for semantically transparent complex words are explicitly modeled in terms of how activation flows back from the semantic and syntactic level to the concept nodes and from the concept nodes to the access representations. In addition, we have claimed that lower degrees of transparency are correlated with a later age of acquisition and hence lower activation levels.

As required, the model also meets the productivity constraint (section 3.5). On encountering a novel complex form, the system computes its meaning, leaving a memory trace in the form of a concept node connected to an access representation for the complex form. Because the new representations are subject to decay over time, they may disappear. To remain in the lexicon a new word must be encountered frequently. Thus the model describes a system that adjusts itself dynamically over time; it assimilates new words as they come along and drops them from the lexicon upon lack of exposure.

How affixal homonymy is handled was discussed in detail in section 4 (see also Figure 2), as was the issue of pseudo-prefixation.

We have suggested that it is desirable for a meta-model to describe a single underlying mechanism of morphological representation and processing irrespective of what language to which it is exposed. At the same time, the particular language input will determine essential properties of the systems. In a language such as Turkish, characterized by a rich and extremely transparent morphology, the lexical frequency distributions will be dominated by very large numbers of low frequency complex words. In such distributions high frequency complex words will be relatively rare. In contrast, the relatively poor morphology of a language such as English or Dutch gives rise to frequency distributions with high frequencies of occurrence for many morphologically complex words (Baayen, 1992). In other words, the many morphologically complex words in Turkish will on average have a low frequency of use, whereas in English or Dutch substantially smaller numbers of complex types are, on average, used far more frequently.

These different distributional properties have important consequences for the way in which the processing system will develop over time. When the system is exposed to a language with a relatively simple morphology, large numbers of full form access representations will develop. In the case of fully transparent complex words which require minimal computation, the development of full form access representations obviates the need for segmentation at the form level. For these transparent words, rule-based computation is involved only for the licensing and composition stages of the parsing process. When the processing system is exposed to a language with a rich morphology, however, full form access representations are less likely to be established due to the lower frequencies of occurrence of complex forms. Hence segmentation will be carried out more often.

Likewise, languages differ substantially with respect to the semantic transparency of their affixes. In languages such as Dutch or English, for instance, derivational morphology is characterized by the presence of many semi-transparent affixes.[4] Words with semi-transparent affixes have on average high frequencies of occurrence. Consequently, they have their own concept nodes in addition to their access representations so that the licensing and composition stages of the parsing process can be bypassed along with the initial segmentation. Note that the concept nodes of semi-transparent affixes will have relatively low activation levels in the absence of substantial semantic activation feedback, however. In Turkish, by contrast, most of the morphology is transparent. Hence there will be relatively few concept nodes for complex forms and many well-developed concept nodes for bases and affixes, because these concept nodes continuously receive support from semantic feedback.

6. GENERAL DISCUSSION

The reader will have observed that the model presented here shares a number of properties with other models that have been proposed in the literature. To our mind each of these models captures essential insights about the issues involved. Our model can be seen as an attempt to integrate these insights into a common framework. It is instructive to discuss in some detail which aspects of our model have been incorporated into other models. We focus on the way in which the three stages of the parsing process (i.e., segmentation into affix and stems, licensing based on appropriateness of morpheme combinations, and composition based on semantic and syntactic properties of the constituents) are modeled. Furthermore, we discuss how these models treat meaning in complex words.

Table 1 summarizes Butterworth's (1983) Full Listing model, Pinker's (1991) purely rule based model,[5] Taft and Forster's (1975) prefix-stripping model, Taft's (1991) interactive activation model, Caramazza, Laudanna, and Romani's (1988) Augmented Addressed Morphology (AAM) model, Frauenfelder and Schreuder's (1992) Morphological Race Model (MRM), and the present (meta) model as they pertain to the processing of previously encountered complex words. The models of Butterworth and Pinker represent ends of the continuum. According to Butterworth, parsing plays no role at all, while Pinker argues that at the segmentation and composition stages, parsing is always involved in the recognition of regularly inflected words. The prefix-stripping model is similar in spirit to that of Butterworth, in that initial morphological segmentation is carried out with the aim of speeding access to stored meanings. (But see Schreuder & Baayen, 1994, who show that prefix stripping along the lines of Taft & Forster,

---

[4]For example, English -ity has a lower degree of semantic transparency than its paradigmatic rival -ness (Aronoff, 1976). In the frequency domain, however, -ity shows up with higher token frequencies than -ness (see Baayen & Lieber, 1991). For an extensive analysis of the semi-transparency of a number of Dutch prefixes, the reader is referred to Lieber and Baayen (in press).

[5]Pinker's (1991) model is actually a model of language production. His basic assumptions, however, carry over to models of word recognition.

1975, actually slows down the search efficiency of a serial search model.) Taft's (1991) interactive activation model similarly focuses on segmentation issues. Letter nodes activate subword units. These activate morphological units, which in turn connect to (localized) semantic units. No licensing and composition takes place. Segmentation is introduced to account for various experimental data, but its role in the process of word recognition is not specified.

The AAM model is similar to the meta-model proposed here. However, there are two important differences. First, the AAM model strictly distinguishes between novel complex words and complex words that have been encountered before. The latter kind is always processed via its own access representation. Only novel complex words require segmentation at the access level. To our mind, such a rigid distinction between what has and what has not been encountered before is somewhat artificial. The frequency distributions of productive affixes are characterized by large numbers of types occurring once only, even in fairly large text corpora (Baayen, 1992, 1993; Baayen & Lieber, 1991). If representations are subject to decay over time, such words are not likely to have full-fledged access representations. A second important difference concerns the effect of frequency of occurrence on lexical representations. Burani and Caramazza (1987) suggest that frequently occurring, fully transparent words have their own lexical representations. In our model this issue crucially depends on semantic transparency. Fully transparent words require minimal computation and do not acquire independent concept nodes. While we assume that high-frequency transparent complex words have their own access representations, we share Pinker's (1991) intuition that rule-based composition applies to such transparent forms. Note, however, that as computational complexity increases, complex words tend to receive their own concept nodes even though they may be fully regular.

TABLE 1. *Components of models for lexical processing.*

	PARSING			STORAGE OF MEANING
	segmentation	licensing	composition	
Butterworth	-	-	-	+
Taft & Forster	+	-	-	+
Taft	+	-	-	+
AAM	-	+/-	+/-	+/-
MRM	+	+	+	+/-
meta model	+/-	+/-	+/-	+/-

The Morphological Race Model is, as suggested by its name, a dual route model in which two independent access routes operate in parallel. On encountering a morphologically complex word an attempt at parsing is initiated for the whole word in combination with an attempt at direct look-up. Access representations, whether for monomorphemic or morphologically complex words or affixes, are all linked to their own independent and fully specified meaning representation. Any word with a frequency of occurrence high enough to have an access representation is assumed to have a meaning representation as well. Consequently, it can be recognized directly on the basis of its full form alone. Alternatively, parsing is assumed to proceed on the basis of activated meaning representations of stems and affixes. The speed with which the parser is able to compute a meaning is a function of the resting activation levels of the relevant access representations and of the semantic transparency of their combination. The phonological and semantic transparency of a word, its surface frequency, and the frequencies of other morphologically related complex words determine whether the direct route or the parsing route will be the first to deliver the required meaning to the postlexical processing system. At this point, the lexical system is purported to increase slightly the activation levels of the access representations employed by the winning route. Positive feedback is introduced into the system to ensure that productive affixes will obtain higher resting activation levels than unproductive affixes, even though the latter may appear in more word tokens than the former (see Baayen, 1992, 1993; Frauenfelder & Schreuder, 1992).

The MRM is not without its share of problematic properties. Perhaps its most unsatisfactory aspect is that the mechanism of selective positive feedback is not a natural property of the processing system. In addition, it is unclear in what way the speed of the parsing route should be constrained as a function of the transparency of the input. In the present model, an explicit treatment of the role of semantics has enabled us to handle the role of transparency in a more principled way.

Finally note that the present model is not a dual route model in which recognition is mediated by two independent and noninteracting access mechanisms. In our model, the two access mechanisms interactively converge on the desired meaning representations. The complexity of the interaction is such that without knowledge of a word's frequency and transparency, no prediction can be made about the relative contributions of the two mechanisms.

Interestingly, most of the models make similar predictions to the present model with respect to particular *subsets* of words. Butterworth's (1983) full listing model and Caramazza et al.'s (1988) AAM model claim that high frequency inflected words and large numbers of derivationally complex words are processed by direct look-up at the level of the access representations. In our model, depending on the complexity and transparency of the morphological processes involved, access representations may become connected to concept nodes of their own. Pinker's (1991) position describes how fully regularly inflected words as well as low frequency derivationally complex forms and neologisms are handled at the levels of concept nodes and semantic and syntactic representations, namely, on the basis of procedural lexical knowledge.

There is one important model that we have not yet discussed, namely, Bybee's 'network' model (Bybee, 1985, 1988, this volume), In contrast to all other models discussed here, Bybee's model does not distinguish between rules and representations. Morphological processing is mediated by the multiple connections between complex words in a lexical network. We would like to stress the relevance of the insights Bybee accounts for by means of her connection model. The main difference between her model and the one outlined here resides in the way in which the links expressing similarities and relations between words are implemented. We have opted for a strict separation of form and meaning properties of words into separate levels of representations rather than having both form and meaning links between lexical nodes. In addition, our semantic and syntactic nodes mediate semantic and syntactic relations between words—there are no direct links between our concept nodes. We hope that this architecture captures the same generalizations that Bybee's model accounts for, while remaining computationally tractable. These differences are direct consequences of the constraints imposed on a lexical model once various aspects of lexical processing, notably the time course of lexical access as well as developmental issues, are taken into account.

Finally, note that we have not attempted to design a model that accounts for the many—often controversial—experimental results one may find in the literature. Confining ourselves to a number of basic results, we have outlined a dynamic system that adapts itself to the structural and distributional properties of the language to which it is exposed. Undoubtedly, the present model will have to be modified in various ways as our knowledge of human lexical processing increases. What we hope to have shown is that it is essential to trace the full path from the incoming speech signal to the semantic system if the role of morphology in lexical processing is to be understood.

ACKNOWLEDGMENT

Both authors have contributed equally to the present chapter. We are indebted to Uli Frauenfelder, Laurie Feldman, and Marcus Taft for helpful suggestions and comments.

REFERENCES

Aronoff, M. (1976). *Word formation in generative grammar.* Cambridge, MA: MIT Press.

Baayen, R. H. (1992). Quantitative aspects of morphological productivity. In G. E. Booij & J. van Marle (Eds.), *Yearbook of morphology 1991* (pp. 109-149). Dordrecht: Kluwer.

Baayen, R. H. (1993). On frequency, transparency and productivity. In G. E. Booij & J. van Marle (Eds.), *Yearbook of morphology 1991* (pp. 227-254). Dordrecht: Kluwer.

Baayen, R. H., & Lieber, R. (1991). Productivity and English derivation: A corpus-based study. *Linguistics, 29,* 801-843.

Baayen, R. H., & Schreuder, R. (in press). Modeling the processing of morphologically complex words. In A. Dijkstra & K. de Smedt (Eds.), *Computational psycholinguistics: Symbolic and subsymbolic models of language processing.* Hemel Hempstead: Harvester Wheatsheaf: Simon and Schuster International Group.

Burani, C., & Caramazza, A. (1987). Representation and processing of derived words. *Language and Cognitive Processes, 2,* 217-227.

Butterworth, B. (1983). Lexical representation. In Butterworth, B. (Ed.), *Language production (Vol. II): Development, writing and other language processes* (pp. 257-294). London: Academic Press.

Bybee, J. L. (1985). *Morphology: A study of the relation between meaning and form.* Amsterdam: John Benjamins.

Bybee, J. L. (1988). Morphology as lexical organization. In M. Hammond & M. Noonan (Eds.), *Theoretical morphology: Approaches in modern linguistics* (pp. 119-141). London: Academic Press.

Caramazza, A., Laudanna, A., & Romani, C. (1988). Lexical access and inflectional morphology. *Cognition, 28,* 297-332.

Cutler, A., & Norris, D. G. (1988). The role of strong syllables in segmentation for lexical access. *Journal of Experimental Psychology: Human Perception and Performance, 14,* 113-121.

Feldman, L. (in press). Beyond orthography and phonology: Differences between inflections and derivation. *Journal of Memory and Learning.*

Frauenfelder, U. H., & Schreuder, R. (1992). Constraining psycholinguistic models of morphological processing and representation: The role of productivity. In G. E. Booij & J. van Marle (Eds.), *Yearbook of morphology 1991* (pp. 165-183). Dordrecht: Kluwer.

Jackendoff, R. (1990). *Semantic structures.* Cambridge, MA: MIT Press.

Lieber, R., & Baayen, R. H. (in press). Verbal prefixes in Dutch: A study in lexical conceptual structure. In G. E. Booij & J. van Marle (Eds.), *Yearbook of Morphology 1993.* Dordrecht: Kluwer.

Marslen-Wilson, W., Tyler, L. K., Waksler, R., & Older, L. (1994). Morphology and meaning in the English mental lexicon. *Psychological Review, 101,* 3-33.

McQueen, J., & Cutler, A. (in press). Morphology in word recognition. In A. M. Zwicky & A. Spencer (Eds.), *The handbook of morphology.* Oxford: Basil Blackwell.

Pinker, S. (1991). Rules of language. *Science, 253,* 530-535.

Ritchie, G., Pulman, S., Black, A., & Russel, G. (1987). A computational framework for lexical description. *Computational Linguistics 13,* 290-307.

Schreuder, R., & Baayen, R. H. (1994). Prefix-stripping re-revisited. *Journal of Memory and Language, 33,* 357-375.

Schreuder, R., & Flores d'Arcais, G. B. (1989). Psycholinguistic issues in the lexical representation of meaning. In W. Marslen-Wilson (Ed.), *Lexical representation and process* (pp. 409-436). Cambridge, MA: MIT Press.

Sinclair, J. M. (Ed.) (1987). *Looking up: An account of the cobuild project in lexical computing.* London: Collins.

Sproat, R. (1992). *Morphology and computation.* Cambridge, MA: MIT Press.

Taft, M. (1991). *Reading and the mental lexicon.* Hillsdale, NJ: Lawrence Erlbaum Associates.

Taft, M., & Forster, K. I. (1975). Lexical storage and retrieval of prefixed words. *Journal of Verbal Learning and Verbal Behavior, 14,* 638-647.

Taft, M., & Forster, K. I. (1976). Lexical storage and retrieval of polymorphemic and polysyllabic words. *Journal of Verbal Learning and Verbal Behavior, 15,* 607-620.

PART 3

Phonological Issues in Morphological Processing

7 The Role of Phonology and Orthography in Morphological Awareness

Anne E. Fowler* and Isabelle Y. Liberman†
*Bryn Mawr College and Haskins Laboratories
†Haskins Laboratories

This chapter explores the interdependence of morphological, phonological, and orthographic knowledge in 48 children 7.5 to 9.5 years of age. To examine the role of phonological complexity, we employed a morphology production task, modeled after Carlisle (1987, 1988) involving six common derivational suffixes presented with base forms that were either phonologically deformed by the suffix (PhonComplex, e.g., *five/fifth*) or phonologically unchanged (PhonNeutral, e.g., *four/fourth*). Reading and spelling skills were significantly correlated with overall performance on the morphology task, even after controlling for shared variance due to age and vocabulary knowledge. However, reader group differences were most pronounced in the PhonComplex condition, suggesting that problems that are apparently morphological are exacerbated by phonological deficits known to exist in poor readers. Reading-level comparisons of older poor readers and younger average readers matched on reading skill yielded no differences in morphology production; this leaves open the question of whether morphological weaknesses hamper reading acquisition or whether experience with the orthography promotes morphological sensitivity.

†Isabelle Y. Liberman died before this paper was written but after having invested considerable energy and interest in guiding the design and execution of this study and in interpreting our preliminary results; these results were first presented at the American Educational Research Association in Boston in 1990.

Recent accounts of reading acquisition and reading disability have focused on the now impressive body of evidence linking reading problems to limited *phonological awareness*. The strong association between reading and phonological awareness has been observed for a variety of alphabetic orthographies and transcends individual differences in IQ, vocabulary knowledge, chronological age, or even reading experience; the association holds from kindergarten to adulthood and across a diverse set of measures (Adams, 1990; Liberman, Shankweiler, & Liberman, 1989; Pratt & Brady, 1988; Rack, Snowling & Olson, 1992; Stanovich, 1988). Still other research indicates that phoneme awareness is a necessary, though not sufficient, component of normal reading acquisition (e.g., Gough & Tunmer, 1986; Juel, 1988).

Although phonological awareness requires metalinguistic insight, a growing body of evidence suggests that individual differences in achieving phoneme awareness stem less from a general lack of metacognitive skill than from the weak phonological foundation upon which phoneme awareness must be erected. In addition to difficulty in gaining explicit access to the phonological units of the language, poor readers also display subtle but consistent deficits in the ability to retain information in a phonological store (Brady, 1991; Shankweiler, Liberman, Mark, Fowler, & Fischer, 1979; Stone, 1992; Torgesen, 1978, 1991), to identify spoken words embedded in noise (Brady, Shankweiler, & Mann, 1983), to accurately produce tongue twisters (Rapala & Brady, 1990), and to rapidly retrieve the accurate phonological labels for pictured objects (Catts, 1986; Katz, 1986; Wolf, 1991). These abilities are compromised not only in school-aged poor readers but also in kindergarten children who later become poor readers (Mann & Liberman, 1984; Share, Jorm, MacLean, & Matthews, 1984). On the basis of this evidence, several investigators have proposed that reading disability stems from a fundamental *phonological deficit* (Brady, 1991; Liberman et al., 1989; Stanovich, 1990; Wagner & Torgesen, 1987). According to this hypothesis, the language problems associated with reading are specific to the phonological domain, though these may have ramifications throughout the language system (e.g., Crain & Shankweiler, 1988; Shankweiler & Crain, 1986).

Morphology, in contrast to phonology, has received considerably less attention in studies of both reading acquisition and reading disability. And yet, because English orthography represents both phonology and morphology, one would expect that an explicit awareness of both levels of language structure should be required for reading and spelling success. Consistent with this, there is evidence that children and adolescents who have reading and spelling problems have marked difficulty with morpheme awareness tasks, even after apparently having achieved phoneme awareness. In the present chapter, we explore whether the morphological insensitivity found in poor readers implicates both phonological and morphological weaknesses within the language system. As an alternative to that account, we consider how individual differences in morphological awareness might arise from more basic deficits at the phonological level.

BACKGROUND

Why Morphological Awareness Should Prove Important for Reading and Spelling

There are reasons to expect that an awareness of morphemes should be an important component in reading success. First, a large body of research indicates that English vocabulary, and the vocabulary of schoolbooks and schoolchildren in particular, is morphemically complex. Not only do many multimorphemic words exceed what can be read in a single fixation (Elbro, 1989), but plausibility alone suggests that the 80,000 word vocabulary acquired by the average high school graduate could not possibly have been learned one word at a time (Miller & Gildea, 1987). Rather, Nagy and Anderson (1984) estimate that 60% of the new words acquired by school-aged children are morphologically complex with relatively transparent morphological structures, such that the meanings of the parts give sufficient information to make a good guess at the meaning of the whole words (knowing *dog* and *house* should lead to a good guess at the meaning of *doghouse*). They estimate that, "For every word a child learns, there are an average of one to three additional related words that should also be understandable to the child, the exact number depending on how well the child is able to utilize context and morphology to induce meaning" (Nagy & Anderson, 1984, p. 304; see also White, Power, & White, 1989).

There is psycholinguistic evidence that morphemically complex words are in fact treated in an analytic fashion by skilled readers. For example, lexical decision responses to low frequency complex words are facilitated when the cumulative frequency of the stem is high, including its appearance in both inflectionally and derivationally related forms (e.g., Colé, Beauvillain, & Segui, 1989; Katz, Rexer, & Lukatela, 1991; Kelliher & Henderson, 1992; Nagy, Anderson, Schommer, Scott, & Stallman, 1989). Similarly, in repetition priming tasks looking at the pattern of facilitation between prime and target as an index of morphological processing, unaffixed words are primed by inflected and derived relatives, but not by words that are unrelated and similar in form (Feldman & Bentin, 1994; Fowler, Napps, & Feldman, 1985; Napps, 1989).

The second reason to fairly expect that morphological awareness may be important for reading acquisition is the fact that young children bring to the task of reading a developing knowledge of derivational and inflectional morphology that is at least implicit. For example, in children aged 5, 7, and 9 years of age, Gordon (1989) found that a high stem frequency facilitated the recognition of low-frequency suffixed words using an untimed lexical decision task with auditorily presented words. Other evidence for productive morphology in young children derives from their creative word formation, as *cooker* to refer to 'one who cooks' or *fix-man* to mean 'mechanic' (Bowerman, 1982; Clark & Berman, 1984, 1987; Clark & Hecht, 1982); from the ability to acquire new complex forms (Clark & Cohen, 1984); and from children's interpretation of novel word forms (Clark & Berman, 1987; Naigles, Gleitman, & Gleitman, in press; Naigles, Fowler, & Helm, 1992).

The third, and for our purposes most significant, reason that morphological awareness should facilitate reading and spelling is that many orthographic conventions in English cannot be explained by a straightforward phonemic approach but are entirely sensible from a morphological perspective. According to a recent review of the world's writing systems (DeFrancis, 1989), English occupies a position midway between the frankly phonemic endpoints epitomized by Italian or Finnish and the more nearly (though by no means entirely) morphologic endpoints represented by Chinese or Korean. The English orthography is morphophonemic, bound by phonemic constraints, but sufficiently removed from phonemic transcription that a single spelling of a morpheme can transcend differences arising from regional dialects, historical change, and morphological variation (Chomsky & Halle, 1968; Liberman, 1992; Liberman, Liberman, Mattingly, & Shankweiler, 1980; Mattingly, 1992). In English, distinctive spellings often serve to disambiguate different morphemes with identical phonological shapes, as in *threw* versus *through.* Conversely, common morphemes are often represented with identical spellings despite distinct phonological structures, as in *electric/electricity* or *heal/health.* If a reader does not appreciate the past tense marker as a morphemic entity, it would be hard to appreciate why the three different pronunciations of *-ed* illustrated in *asked, begged,* and *pleaded* should be represented with a single spelling (Rubin, 1991). Similarly, it should be much easier to remember why *electricity* and *plasticity* are spelled with a 'c' rather than an 's' if the morphophonemic status of the 'c' is appreciated. In short, as will be obvious to anyone who has tried to convey the idiosyncrasies of English orthography to the novice reader, phoneme awareness alone will not suffice.

There are then at least three reasons that morphological knowledge might make a unique and important contribution to reading success, separate from that provided by phoneme awareness. But is there sufficient variability in morphological awareness to bear importantly on reading success? Although it will be argued that morpheme awareness is more natural than phoneme awareness, not all of morphology is equally straightforward. At one extreme are such (phonologically) obvious pairs as *agree/agreeable*, which should pose little difficulty to the poor reader whose difficulties are exclusively phonological. In direct contrast, morphological relationships that involve a phonological change of the stem, as in *respond/responsible*, may prove especially elusive to the phonologically insensitive child.

Why Morphological Awareness Might be Easy to Attain

For all of the reasons that it is difficult to segment speech into isolable phonemes, there are complementary reasons to expect that morpheme awareness might be more easily achieved. First, whereas phonemes distinguish *between* meaningful elements (e.g., p/b distinguishes *pat* from *bat)*, morphemes are themselves meaningful, thereby increasing their salience. Thus, *electric* and *electricity* share a common meaningful unit in a way that *pat* and *bat* do not. Second, phonemes cannot, generally, be produced in isolation, as in the case of the first and last phoneme of *pat*. Rather, for important reasons of efficiency, they are coarticulated in time (A. Liberman, 1989, 1992). In contrast, morphemes are more typically isolable, even when abstract, as in the suffix of *plasticity*. Third, it is argued that the morpheme is a more "natural" cut on the language. For example, whereas the alphabetic orthography based on the phoneme was invented once, and moreover, only by accident (Faber, 1992; Gleitman & Rozin, 1977; Mattingly, 1992), there are several independently evolved writing systems that turn on the morpheme (see DeFrancis, 1989). Further evidence that morphology may be "more natural" derives from the observation that both preschoolers and illiterate adults can handle linguistic tasks at the syllable or morpheme level (these are often confounded), at a point where they continue to fail at phoneme awareness (Gleitman & Rozin, 1977; Morais, Cary, Alegria, & Bertelson, 1979; Read, Zhang, Nie, & Ding, 1986; Rozin, Poritsky, & Sotsky, 1971). For these reasons, one might expect that children would display considerably more sensitivity to morphemes than to phonemes; they may recognize that *motor* and *motorcycle* are related, even as they fail to notice the common element in *meat* and *motorcycle.*

Interestingly, for all the evidence speaking to the morphological complexity of both spoken and written English, and for all the plausible reasons why morphological awareness might be readily achieved, explicit awareness of English morphology is by no means guaranteed and varies within and among even the most sophisticated users of the language (e.g., Freyd & Baron, 1982; Gleitman & Gleitman, 1969; Mattingly, 1992). According to these investigators, although both the meaning and the phonological structure of the two morphemes in *blackboard* are clear, the word is generally acquired as a lexical item separate from *black* and *board,* and only in a flash of insight does the speaker realize that it is componential in its meaning (delayed, no doubt, by the move toward green blackboards). Similarly, most of us know the meaning of *health* and the meaning of *heal,* but arguably few have ever stopped to note the morphological association between these two words. Individual differences in skill are apparent not only for derivational morphology, where both the meaning and phonological relationship between the parts and the whole can be obscure, but, depending on the task, also for inflectional morphology, in which there is a consistent relationship between form and meaning (e.g., Berko, 1958).

The picture we have drawn is complex. First, we have suggested that morpheme awareness, like phoneme awareness, should play an important role in learning to read and spell. Then, after pointing out critical ways in which morpheme awareness should be free from the very obstacles that so regularly impede phoneme awareness, we noted that individuals nonetheless vary in how morphologically analytic they are. Is this variation important for reading? And if so, does this imply that the phonological deficit hypothesis, as presently conceived, is too narrow in its scope? Would it necessarily follow that the metalinguistic deficits of disabled readers extend beyond the phonological domain?

One possibility is that variance in morphological awareness is specifically associated with reading only when the child must appreciate morphemic identity across phonologically distinct items (as in *heal/health*). Although awareness at the morpheme level alone may suffice to recognize the *true* in *truly* or the *teach* in *teacher*, attention must be given to phoneme level alternations (morphophonemes) to fully master the intricacies of English derivational morphology. For example it would be helpful to recognize (even implicitly) that vowels in English receive one pronunciation (the long vowel) when fully stressed (e.g., *invi̲te, coura̲geous*) and another (the short vowel) when receiving secondary stress (e.g., *invi̲tation, coura̲ge*). Similarly, an astute observer may note that a morpheme ending in final /k/ regularly goes to /s/ when followed by the morpheme /ity/; the single grapheme c̲ encodes this regularity (e.g., *electri̲c/electri̲city, plasti̲c/plasti̲city, eccentri̲c/eccentri̲city*, etc.). We consider it important to distinguish morpheme awareness that does and does not require attention to the (morpho)phonemic level. If poor readers experience difficulty *only* at the morphophonemic level, that would argue against a general linguistic deficit and would be entirely consistent with the phonological deficit account. Before introducing our own study bearing on these questions, we should examine several studies implicating an association between morpheme awareness and a child's ability to read and spell and consider the factors that may be responsible for the findings obtained.

Morphological Awareness and Reading: The Evidence to Date

Although the number of studies is not large, three lines of evidence converge on the suggestion that poor readers have special difficulty in analyzing morphologically complex forms. First, in clinical report, it has often been noted that the writing of poor readers is marked by errors in expressing—or a failure to express—grammatical and derivational morphemes, as in "It is protecting familyhood of which I am a strong belief" (Shaughnessy, 1977, cited in Tyler & Nagy, in press, p. 75). (For supporting evidence see Anderson, 1982; Cicci, 1980; Duques, 1989; and Myklebust, 1973; see Rubin, 1991, for a review). Similarly, clinical studies also suggest that poor readers have particular difficulty in reading aloud closed class morphemes such as inflectional suffixes (e.g., Henderson & Shores, 1982). These findings would seem to suggest a global insensitivity to the internal structure of the word.

Secondly, experimental studies have replicated the kinds of errors reported by clinicians and have provided follow-up analyses of these errors. These studies suggest that morphological errors in spelling cannot readily be ascribed to difficulties with letter-sound correspondences alone. For one thing, morphological problems persist even after phoneme-grapheme correspondences have been learned. For example, Carlisle (1987) reports that dyslexic ninth graders typically failed to note the relationship between *magic* and *magician* while producing phonemically acceptable errors such as *magition, magishion,* or *magishan.* In her study, the dyslexic students were significantly more apt to spell derived words without regard for morphemic structure than were normal readers in the fourth grade. Similarly, Hanson, Shankweiler, and Fischer (1983) found that reading-disabled adolescents spelled phonemically transparent words such as *plastic* or *splinter* just as well as their normal readers of the same age. Group differences were most pronounced in the spelling of words which required sensitivity to morphophonemic structure (as in *condemn/condemnation*) or systematic orthographic conventions (e.g., *heroes* or *galleries*). (See also Fischer, Shankweiler, & Liberman, 1985, and Templeton & Scarborough-Franks, 1985). It might be noted that although each of these experimental studies speaks to an insensitivity to morphophonemic patterns, it is difficult from these examples alone to determine whether the problem is morphemic as well as phonemic.

A third line of evidence suggests that the morphological limitations of poor readers are evident not only in reading and writing but also in metalinguistic tasks involving spoken words. For example, it has long been observed that poor readers of all ages are less able than good readers to produce the appropriate morphological suffix on nonsense words, using measures modeled after Berko's (1958) *wug/wugs* task (*this is a wug/here are two ____/wugs*) (Brittain, 1970; Doehring, Trites, Patel, & Fiedorowicz, 1981; Vogel, 1975, 1983; Wiig, Semel, & Crouse, 1973). Two studies suggest that there may be a direct link between performance on these tasks and the ability to express morphological knowledge in reading and writing. Elbro (1989), working with dyslexic ninth graders, found a strong correlation between the number of errors made in reading inflectional endings aloud and the ability to add inflectional suffixes in a Berko-type task. Rubin (1988, 1991), studying second graders, found a close association between frequency of attempts to represent the past tense form in spelling and the ability to apply the past tense rule in a Berko-type task. Beyond their difficulties with inflections, the adolescents studied by Elbro (1989) also had great difficulty in reversing elements of compound words (*mailbox* to *boxmail*) and counting the number of words (especially functors) in sentences read aloud to them. And Carlisle (1988) found poor readers in the fourth, sixth, and eighth grade were less adept than good readers at producing morphologically derived and base forms in an orally presented sentence completion task (e.g., *Magician. I really enjoy ____/magic*). In that case, performance was highly related to the ability to accurately spell the same set of words.

There is, then, general agreement that poor readers of all ages experience difficulty in reading, spelling, and explicitly analyzing morphologically complex forms involving either inflectional or derivational morphemes. Although firm conclusions regarding whether and how these two kinds of grammatical knowledge differ in their association with reading await further study (e.g., Feldman & Andjelković, 1990), the evidence suggests that both present difficulty for the poor reader. We now explore the underpinnings of the association between derivational morphology and reading. Are poor readers generally insensitive to language structure of any kind? Does poor reading itself impede morphological awareness? Can both morphological insensitivity and poor reading be interpreted as a simple function of generally limited intelligence or vocabulary knowledge? Finally, is morphological insensitivity exacerbated by phonological demands? Although several factors almost certainly bear on the association between morphology and reading, here we consider them one at a time.

Potential Explanations for Deficits in Morphological Awareness

General intellectual factors. Historically, the study of reading disability has focused on its purest manifestation, among children who are normal in all other aspects of intelligence. To disentangle what other aspects of cognitive function go with specific reading disability, groups of poor readers are typically matched with good readers on some measure of general intelligence, such as a standardized vocabulary test. Even after intellectual differences are controlled for, phonological difficulties remain significantly associated with reading difficulty. More recent studies indicate a tight association between phonological skill and reading even in individuals of low normal (e.g., Stanovich, 1991) or subnormal intelligence (Fowler, in press; Fowler, Doherty, & Boynton, 1993), and even when accompanied by other learning disabilities such as Attention Deficit Disorder or math disability (Fletcher et al., 1994).

In principle, it is also possible to separate morphological awareness from more general intellectual skill, as demonstrated by Freyd and Baron (1982), who found that eighth grade students of average intelligence were less able to use morphological rules productively than highly intelligent sixth graders despite the fact that the two groups were matched on raw vocabulary scores. However, few studies of morphology and reading to date have controlled for individual differences in vocabulary or other intellectual factors. Therefore, it is often hard to know whether reading-related problems with morphological tasks derive from a failure to understand the task or even a lack of familiarity with the words being analyzed.

The role of written language in acquiring morphological insights. It may be that individual differences in morphological awareness are the result of weak reading skills, rather than the source. Given the number of morphologically complex items introduced through printed language (Miller & Gildea, 1987; Nagy & Anderson, 1984; White et al., 1989), this proves to be a question of central importance. Is it the ability to extract the regularities from spoken language that distinguishes good readers from poor readers? Or does the deficit arise primarily from a failure to acquire the orthographic lexicon that provides important clues to morphology? It is often argued that many of the linguistic regularities we accept as part of English are discernible most readily, or perhaps *only*, through a study of the written language (e.g., Derwing & Baker, 1977, 1979; Liberman et al., 1980). C. Chomsky (1970, p. 17) suggests that "the sound system that corresponds to the orthography may itself be a late intellectual product" and that "the process of internalization...is no doubt facilitated in many cases by an awareness of how words are spelled" (p. 298). Moskowitz (1973) goes so far as to argue that the ability of older students to pronounce derived words, including the accurate application of the vowel shift rule, depends not on the observed occurrences of these words in spoken language but rather on an exposure to the words through reading. In sum, it may be that morphophonemic representations are more fully specified only after an introduction to literacy (see Mattingly, 1992, for a discussion).

To investigate the role of the orthography in accounting for children's facility with complex derivational morphology, Templeton (1979) asked good spellers in grades 6, 8, and 10 to produce derived forms from base forms; what varied was whether the base forms were presented to the subjects orally or in writing. All subjects were more likely to pronounce the derived words correctly when the base forms were written rather than spoken. In a follow-up study, this time asking both good and poor readers in the 6th and 10th grade to pronounce and spell derived forms given a nonsense stem and ending (e.g., *tivine* and *ity*), Templeton and Scarborough-Franks (1985) replicated the original finding, also finding that correct spelling of derived forms exceeded correct pronunciation in all groups. From this result, they reasoned that knowledge of vowel alternation patterns is mastered in writing prior to its productive usage in the spoken language. They concluded that the "primary source of an individual's knowledge of many processes of derivational morphology in English...is the orthographic rather than the phonological system" (p. 372).

Only two investigators (Carlisle, 1987; Elbro, 1989) explicitly tested whether poor readers have morphological deficits when compared to younger normally developing readers matched on orthographic knowledge; the results varied as a function of the task. On the one hand, Carlisle (1987) found no differences between learning-disabled ninth graders and reading-level matched sixth graders with regard to knowledge of derivational morphology as assessed through an oral sentence completion task. Similarly, Elbro (1989) found that severely dyslexic adolescents were no worse than reading-level matched second and third graders on either the Berko task or in their ability to synthesize two morphemes into a word (*good + ness = goodness*). On the other hand, Carlisle's adolescents were significantly *behind* the reading level controls when asked to *spell* morphologically complex words. And Elbro's adolescents were significantly behind the reading-level controls in their ability to reverse elements of compound words, to count the words in sentences read aloud to them, or to produce whole words containing target morphemes (e.g., *overwhelm*, given *whelm*).

These latter results leave open the possibility that morphological weaknesses may not be a matter of limited orthographic knowledge alone. Indeed, it would seem that Carlisle's (1987) results directly contradict those of Templeton and Scarborough-Franks (1985); in her subjects, spoken knowledge exceeded written knowledge. Similarly, lack of exposure to the orthography does not explain why second graders studied by Rubin (1991) were unable to represent in any form even the most productive inflectional morphemes. And finally, lack of orthographic knowledge cannot explain why children who are better able to explain the meaning of *bee-grass* or *grass-bee* at 5 or 6 years of age become the better readers in subsequent years (Torneus, 1987, cited in Elbro, 1989). More reading-level comparisons are needed to determine whether poor readers simply lack the orthographic base on which so much derivational knowledge seems to depend or whether they are truly less able to glean the generalizations necessary to appreciate the complex morphophonemic structure of English.

A general linguistic—or metalinguistic—deficit. It is, perhaps, most commonly assumed that poor readers lack morphological awareness because they have a general metalinguistic deficit—an insensitivity to language structure that includes not only phonology but also morphology and syntax. According to this view, the child who experiences difficulty with phoneme awareness and reading might also prove less able to explicate sentence level regularities or to consciously attend to the morphological structure of words (e.g., Freyd & Baron, 1982; Siegel & Ryan, 1988; Tunmer & Bowey, 1984; Tunmer, Herriman, & Nesdale, 1988). This account is specifically metalinguistic, rather than metacognitive, to account for the fact that poor readers do not necessarily do less well on nonlinguistic measures. The problem is considered *meta*linguistic, rather than linguistic, because in most cases, poor readers lacking awareness of a particular structure do have tacit linguistic knowledge of that form (e.g., Fowler, 1988). For example, Smith-Lock (1991) confirmed that poor readers in second grade omit far more inflectional endings than good readers in a written task, but the same inflections were applied appropriately in an oral language elicitation task. These results suggest that it may be explicit awareness rather than an underlying language deficiency that creates problems with metalinguistic tasks such as the Berko task and which apparently leads to the omission of morphemes in written language. In the next section, we review how an investigation of morphological awareness might distinguish between a general metalinguistic deficit and a specific phonological deficit.

Distinguishing morphological weaknesses from phonological weaknesses. As hinted earlier, despite what was originally presented as a sharp distinction between phonological and morphological structure, in truth the distinctions between phoneme and morpheme awareness are often blurred. Insensitivity to both phonemes and morphemes may stem from a single underlying phonological deficit, as in a failure to recognize the alternation between /k/ and /s/ in *electric/electricity*. If we are to argue that poor readers have a global insensitivity to language structure, then we should be able to demonstrate that they have difficulties not only when they must appreciate the morphemic identity of two phonologically distinct elements (as in *courage/courageous*), they should also lag behind good readers in analyzing complex morphological items that involve a straightforward concatenation of morphemes with constant phonological shape (as in *danger/dangerous*).

Further potential for confounding morphological and phonological factors derives from the fact that measures used to assess morphology make major demands on the very phonological processes that are known to stress the poor reader. For example, in naming tasks, poor readers are less rapid and accurate in their search for the phonological shape of a particular word, even when that word is within their receptive vocabulary. And yet, the ability to come up with a name is exactly what is called for when subjects are asked to come up with a word that contains the morpheme *whelm* (Elbro, 1989) or for the correct word to complete a sentence (Carlisle, 1987, 1988). In addition, it could be argued that the ability to convert *mailbox* to *boxmail* in Elbro's research may stress working memory; the words have to be held in a phonological store for the manipulation.

Prior research suggests that children who have difficulties in learning to read also have difficulty in explicitly stating and/or applying those rules that govern English morphology. In the present study, we wish to explore further the basis for the association between morphological awareness and reading and spelling. In the present study, we wish both to control for knowledge of spoken vocabulary and to take into careful consideration the actual content and nature of the tasks being presented to the young children. It is our expectation that those tasks which most stress the phonological system (those involving morphophonemic shifts) will be most strongly associated with reading. The pattern of performance should help distinguish between general metalinguistic and specific phonological accounts of reading disability.

EXPERIMENT 1

The present study examined the relation between knowledge of derivational morphology and facility with reading and spelling in 48 schoolchildren between 7.5 and 9.5 years of age. As a starting point, we expected to replicate prior research with older children reporting an association between morphological awareness and reading skill. We expected too that the relationship could not be explained as a simple function of differences in general receptive vocabulary. We went on to address two further questions of theoretical interest: (1) Is the association between morphological awareness and reading mediated by joint demands on phonological awareness, or do less-skilled readers lack metalinguistic insight even where awareness of phoneme-level units is not required? (2) Can an association between morphological awareness and reading skill be explained as a function of children's acquired knowledge of the written language, with its cues to morphological structures?

To address the impact of phonological complexity on morphological knowledge, we capitalized on the fact that the association between some derivationally
related word pairs (e.g., *four/fourth*) is phonologically transparent or "neutral"
("PhonNeutral"), whereas the association between other pairs (e.g., *five/fifth*) is
phonologically more opaque ("PhonComplex"). By design, word frequency and
choice of suffix remained constant across these two levels of phonological
complexity. In analyses involving all subjects, we anticipated that performance
would be generally superior in the PhonNeutral over the PhonComplex condition and that reading would be more strongly associated with PhonComplex
performance than PhonNeutral performance. In comparisons of subgroups of
good and poor readers matched on age and vocabulary, we were especially interested in whether there would be a group by condition interaction, hypothesizing that the less skilled readers would be relatively more affected by the
PhonComplex condition than more skilled readers. If reading-related differences
were evident *only* in the PhonComplex condition, this would be consistent with
arguments that poor readers' problems are fundamentally phonological and do
not extend to other parts of the language system except insofar as phonological
processes are implicated. Alternatively, if differences emerge even with
PhonNeutral items, a broader language deficit may be implicated.

To address the potential impact of orthographic knowledge on morphology,
we constructed a *reading-level match* such that the oldest poor readers in our
sample were compared on morphological awareness with younger children
matched on current reading level and receptive vocabulary standard score. If
much of the association between reading and morphological awareness stems
from (rather than contributes to) the acquisition of written language skills, then
these two groups should not differ. Alternatively, if morphological awareness (or
the abilities that underlie it) develops relatively independently of written
language, then it may turn out that children who come to reading slowly
continue to display an insensitivity to morphology even relative to younger
"faster" readers reading at the same level.

Our design allowed us to explore two additional questions. First, because
subjects were asked to produce Derived Targets given a base form and Base
Targets from a derived form, we could explore the relative difficulty of these
two tasks and ask whether performance on one is more related to reading than
performance on the other. Although we expected that the Derived Target task
would be generally more difficult than the Base Target task, we did not
anticipate an interaction between task and reading group. A second additional
question concerned whether reading or spelling would be more strongly
associated with morphological knowledge. Although there are strong theoretical
reasons for spelling to be especially related to morphology in more advanced
stages of literacy, we expected there would be considerable overlap between
these two abilities at the reading levels under study.

Method

Subjects

Forty-eight children were selected to represent the full range of reading ability in a working-class town in southern New England. Half of the children were selected to fall within 7.5 and 8.5 years of age, and half between 8.5 and 9.8 years. At each of these two age levels, we selected eight children at each of three reading levels: below average ("Low"), average ("Mid"), and above average ("High"); these children were selected from the second (n=14), third (n=25), or fourth grade (n=9) in one of several public schools. There were eight children in each cell. "Low readers" included but were not restricted to children who had been diagnosed learning disabled by the school and were receiving aid in a Resource Room. Reading ability, defined as relative for the purpose of this study, was initially based on teacher referral and was later confirmed on the basis of performance on the Word Attack and Word Recognition measures from the Woodcock Johnson Psycho-Educational Battery (Woodcock & Johnson, 1977). Within each age level, and cutting across reading levels, groups were matched as nearly as possible on age, sex, and verbal IQ (here, estimated by standard scores on the Peabody Picture Vocabulary Test-Revised, PPVT-R, Dunn & Dunn, 1981). All subjects were native speakers of English, achieved standard scores above 80 on the PPVT-R, and were free of gross neurological, sensory, or language impairment.[1] (Refer to Table 1 for further information on the overall subject pool.)

Materials

Standardized measures of vocabulary, reading, and spelling. To assess receptive vocabulary, we relied on the Peabody Picture Vocabulary Test-Revised (Dunn & Dunn, 1981) in which subjects select which of four pictures corresponds to an orally presented label. To assess reading, we included two subtests from the Woodcock-Johnson Psycho-Educational Battery (Woodcock, 1977): a test of word recognition (WJ13: Letter-Word Identification) and a nonsense word decoding task (WJ14: Word Attack). Because it has been suggested that spelling may be even more dependent than reading on morphological knowledge, we also included a spelling measure, here the Test of Written Spelling (Larsen & Hammill, 1976).[2]

---

[1]The measures introduced in this study were developed as part of an extensive battery of language and nonlanguage measures for a large scale dyslexia study being conducted by a collaborative team of researchers from Haskins Laboratory and the Yale University Medical School (Fletcher et al., 1994; Shaywitz et al., 1991). The subjects' ages and exclusionary criteria were those of the subtyping study.

[2]The Test of Written Spelling includes separate subscores for orthographically regular words and orthographically irregular words; this subdivision is of potential interest in light of an earlier suggestion that phonological knowledge alone would be sufficient for orthographically regular words, whereas morphological knowledge should also be

TABLE 1. *Characteristics of all subjects participating in the study.*

| | AGE AND READING-ABILITY LEVELS | | | | | | | |
| | Younger | | | Older | | | Total | |
	Low	Mid	High	Low	Mid	High	*M*	*SD*
n	8	8	8	8	8	8		
Age in months	96.3	98.6	97.4	110.4	110.0	108.5	103.5	7.7
PPVT-R standard score	99.6	100.6	104.6	94.8	102.4	113.5	102.5	12.2
Word Recognition raw score	22.8	32.8	36.0	30.8	34.1	38.3	32.4	5.5
standard score	98.3	116.4	124.6	98.8	107.5	120.5	111.0	12.3
Pseudoword Decoding raw score	4.6	11.8	17.8	9.0	13.2	20.3	12.8	5.9
standard score	91.5	107.8	117.5	94.4	102.5	116.3	105.0	12.6
Test of Written Spelling raw score	15.6	28.0	31.3	25.6	39.0	46.8	31.0	12.0

Test of Morphological Production (MorphProd). To examine morphological awareness, we relied on a procedure patterned after that devised by Carlisle (1987, 1988) but adapted to our younger subject population to include both more familiar vocabulary items and shorter sentence frames. (In our version, there was no written component and the condition of orthographic change was eliminated.) As presented in Table 2, the measure tested knowledge of six common suffixes, each occurring three times with a base form that underwent phonological change (PhonComplex, as in *five/fifth*) and three times with a phonologically unaltered base form (PhonNeutral, e.g. *four/fourth*). An important feature of our design was the use of identical suffixes in both the PhonNeutral and the PhonComplex condition. All items were selected on the basis of word frequency to be appropriate for elementary schoolchildren (minimum Standard Frequency Index, SFI, of 42, overall mean SFI of 54.5); word frequency was calculated following Carroll, Davies, and Richman (1971) and was carefully matched across the phonological conditions.

---

necessary to spell irregular items. In this study of readers in the primary grades, the two forms were virtually identical in terms of their association with other measures; hence we present just the total spelling score.

TABLE 2. *Design of Morphology Study, including examples and average Standard Frequency Index* for each category (3 pairs per cell).*

| SUFFIX | CONDITION | | | |
| | PhonNeutral | | PhonComplex | |
	Base	Derived	Base	Derived
-ous	danger	dangerous	courage	courageous
	53.1	51.9	53.4	48.1
-y	shine	shiny	anger	angry
	53.6	56.5	53.5	54.8
-th	four	fourth	five	fifth
	64.6	55.1	63.4	55.4
-able/ible	agree	agreeable	respond	responsible
	56.9	45.7	53.7	48.4
-ation	examine	examination	combine	combination
	57.9	50.6	56.1	52.6
-tion/sion	suggest	suggestion	decide	decision
	56.1	56.5	56.7	53.2
overall SFI	57.0	52.7	56.1	52.0

*SFI of 50 = 1 token per 100,000 printed words, (Carroll, Davies, & Richman, 1971).

There were two tasks: Children had to produce the Derived target given the base form (e.g., *Four. The big racehorse came in* _____), and Base targets given the derived form (e.g., *Fourth. When he counted the puppies, there were* _____). For each task, 36 different sentences were constructed, varying between four and seven words in length. In order that no child receive both the base and derived form of a related word pair, two forms of the test were constructed; these forms were closely matched in all respects and were presented to an equivalent number of boys and girls reading at each of the three reading levels. The sentences were read aloud by a female native speaker of English and recorded on audiotape using high-quality equipment.

So that all children would derive some success over the course of testing, and to identify any children who could not understand the task at all, we included three additional wordpairs with the suffix *-er* (e.g., *teacher, dancer, driver*). Productive use of this suffix has been observed by 4 years of age (e.g., Clark & Hecht, 1982); we therefore anticipated that all children would succeed on these items.

Procedure

All measures were administered to the subjects on an individual basis in a quiet room. The standardized measures were given in the first session, lasting 20-25 minutes; the Test of MorphProd was presented in the second session, taking 12 minutes. The Derived production task was presented first, preceded by training involving practice and feedback using three highly productive suffixes not occurring in the actual testing (*help/helpful, happy/happiness, sudden/suddenly*). Training and testing for Base production followed immediately after completion of the Derived task. The experimental stimuli were presented over headsets, using a high quality tape recorder. Two weeks later, 20 of the students were given the same form of the Test of MorphProd to measure test-retest reliability.

Results

Analyses Involving the Total Sample

Overall performance for all subjects as a function of task and condition is presented in Table 3. As anticipated, repeated-measures ANOVAs yielded a main effect of task, $F(1,47) = 159$, $p < .0001$; children were significantly more adept at producing Base forms when given Derived forms than at generating Derived forms from the Base. There was also a main effect of condition, $F(1,47) = 77.24$, $p < .0001$, with children responding more accurately with PhonNeutral items than with PhonComplex items. Finally, there was a significant interaction between task and condition, $F(1,47) = 5.31$, $p < .05$, which indicated that generating PhonComplex Derived forms was especially demanding. As seen in Table 3, all subjects achieved a near perfect score on the *-er* items; this demonstrates that the task itself was well within the grasp of this age group. Combining performance across all tasks and conditions, Total scores ranged from 57% to 95% correct (mean = 70.5% ; s.d. = 11.9). Test-retest reliability on the Test of Morphological Production ranged from .76 (for Derived targets) to .80 (for Base Targets).

TABLE 3. *Performance on the Test of Morphological Production as a function of task and condition (n = 48).*

TASK	-er items	CONDITION PhonNeutral	PhonComplex	Overall
Base target				
% correct	99.3	86.8	73.6	81.0
S.D.	4.8	11.8	22.3	13.0
Derived target				
% correct	95.8	62.5	41.0	58.1
S.D.	11.1	16.8	20.9	14.5
Overall				
% correct	97.6	74.7	57.3	70.5
S.D.	6.9	11.9	18.3	11.9

As evident in Table 4, Total scores on MorphProd were significantly correlated with age, vocabulary, reading, and spelling, as were the individual subtests. Partial correlations, controlling for both age and vocabulary, also yielded significant correlations between MorphProd and the three reading and spelling measures. Although each of the morphology subtests was also significantly related to reading and spelling, one subtest (producing the Base Target when given a PhonComplex Derived form) appeared to have more predictive power than the other three. Indeed, this subtest alone, with just 9 items, was as highly correlated with reading as is the Total MorphProd score with 42 items. This was confirmed in stepwise multiple regression analyses which showed that reading was best predicted by the Base-PhonComplex task (explaining 42% and 34% of the variance in word recognition and pseudoword decoding, respectively); only the Derived-PhonComplex task made a small but significant further contribution to either of the reading measures (5.8% to pseudoword decoding). This pattern differed slightly when predicting variance in spelling. For spelling, it was the Derived task of the PhonComplex condition that proved to be the single most significant predictor, explaining 34% of the variance; further significant contributions were made by both the Base-PhonComplex subtest (14%) and age (7%).

TABLE 4. *Correlations between descriptive measures and performance on morphological production (n = 48).*

	TOTAL SCORE	BASE PRODUCTION		DERIVED PRODUCTION	
		Phon Neutral	Phon Complex	Phon Neutral	Phon Complex
Predictor variables					
Age	.38**	.18	.24	.36*	.37*
Vocabulary	.59**	.43**	.43**	.43**	.54***
Word Recognition	.68***	.48***	.65***	.47***	.46**
Pseudoword Decoding	.64***	.40**	.58***	.44**	.47***
Spelling	.71***	.45**	.58***	.51***	.59***
Partial correlations, controlling for age and vocabulary					
Word Recognition	.56**	.35*	.56**	.32*	.25
Pseudoword Decoding	.59**	.29*	.51**	.35*	.36*
Spelling	.53**	.30*	.44**	.30*	.35*

*p < .05
**p < .01
***p < .001

The importance of the Base-PhonComplex subtest was further explored via hierarchic regression analyses in which we varied the point at which Base-PhonComplex was entered into the equation. The results, in this case using Word Recognition as the dependent variable, are presented in Table 5. Age and vocabulary were always entered first (Steps 1 and 2); the R-squared change value estimates the additional percentage of variance explained by a given step after previous steps have been entered. This table shows that when the Base-PhonComplex subtest is entered as Step 4, after either the other Base subtest or the other PhonComplex subtest, it explains a significant amount of additional variance in reading (15 to 20%). In contrast, when the Base-PhonComplex subtest is entered as Step 3 in the equation, no other subtest explains any additional variance in reading. Finally, if each of the other subtests are entered into the equation first (as Steps 3 through 5), the Base-PhonComplex subtest still proves to be highly significant, explaining a further 12% of the variance in reading. The pattern is much the same when predicting pseudoword decoding instead of word recognition; when the Base-PhonComplex subtest is entered last, after all other factors, it explains an additional 10% of the variance, $F(1, 41) = 7.04$, $p < .05$. As was evident in the multiple regression analysis, the results varied somewhat for spelling. The Base-PhonComplex subtest did explain variance after all other subtests were entered, $F(1, 41) = 4.04$, $p = .06$, but the levels were much reduced (R-squared is 4% as compared to 10 or 12%).

TABLE 5. *Results of hierarchical regression analyses predicting word recognition from subtests of morphological production, after entering age and vocabulary.*

	R	R^2	R^2 change	p level for R^2 change
Step 1. Age	0.146	0.021	0.021	n.s.
Step 2. Vocabulary	0.475	0.225	0.204	$F(1,45) = 11.67**$
Step 3. Base - PhonNeutral	0.568	0.322	0.097	$F(1,44) = 6.30*$
Step 4. Base - PhonComplex	0.693	0.480	0.158	$F(1,43) = 13.07**$
Step 3. Derived - PhonComplex	0.525	0.276	0.051	n.s.
Step 4. Base - PhonComplex	0.692	0.479	0.202	$F(1,43) = 16.67**$
Step 3. Base - PhonComplex	0.685	0.469	0.244	$F(1,44) = 15.84**$
Step 4. Base - PhonNeutral	0.693	0.480	0.011	n.s.
Step 4. Derived - PhonComplex	0.692	0.479	0.010	n.s.
Steps 3-5. All other subtests	0.617	0.381	0.156	$F(5,42) = 5.17**$
Step 6. Base - PhonComplex	0.707	0.500	0.119	$F(1,41) = 9.76**$

   *$p < .05$
   **$p < .01$

Reading Group Comparison Matched on Age and IQ

Although the regression analyses allow us to look at patterns of correlations, they do not allow us to test directly for an interaction between phonological complexity and reading group, following up on the hypothesis that poor readers are especially hampered in the PhonComplex condition. To test for this interaction, we analyzed the performance of two groups of children (n=10 per group), chosen from the larger group to vary markedly on reading ability but matching in chronological age and receptive vocabulary. Assignment to one of these reader groups required a consistent score on word recognition, word attack, and teacher evaluation. (See Table 6 for descriptive statistics and results.)

The results were submitted to a 2(group) × 2(condition) × 2(task) repeated measures ANOVA. As in the larger group, the children overall performed significantly better on Base Targets than on the Derived Targets, $F(1,18) = 65.3$, $p < .001$, and on PhonNeutral items compared to the PhonComplex items, $F(1,18) = 96.1$, $p < .0001$. In addition, there was also a significant main effect of group, with more-skilled readers exceeding less-skilled readers in Total MorphProd scores, $F(1,18) = 4.9$, $p < .05$). Although there was no interaction between group and task, there was, as predicted, a significant interaction between phonological complexity and group, $F(2,36) = 6.5$, $p < .01$. As indicated in t tests, the skilled readers had an advantage on both tasks in the PhonComplex condition; in contrast, there were virtually no group difference for either task in the PhonNeutral condition. The lack of reader group effect cannot be readily attributed to ceiling effects, for the Derived production task was very difficult for all subjects. The results clearly support the hypothesis that poorer readers are disproportionately affected by the phonologically complex items relative to better readers. The results are less clear regarding whether poor readers have any special difficulties at all with morphology when phonological factors are not implicated; they suggest tentatively that the poor readers' difficulties are restricted to the phonological level.

Reading-level Comparisons of Older and Younger Children

The final set of analyses addressed the possibility that reading-related variation in MorphProd may derive from, rather than contribute to, a child's current reading level. Because the more-skilled readers in the previous analysis could read and spell more words than the less-skilled readers, it is possible that greater morphological awareness could stem from that more extensive knowledge base. In the present analysis, therefore, we compared groups of older and younger readers who were equivalent in current levels of reading and spelling knowledge but differed in the apparent ease/speed with which they had attained current levels, as indexed by standard scores on normative reading measures (refer to Table 7 for descriptive statistics and results). Younger and older readers were equivalent on PPVT-R standard score.

No significant differences in MorphProd distinguished the older readers from younger readers matched on reading attainment. Although the lack of a significant difference could mean that weak morphological skills hindered further reading development, it could also indicate that reading and spelling knowledge contributed to morphological skill.

TABLE 6. *Comparison of skilled and less skilled readers matched on age and vocabulary level.*

	Less skilled		More skilled		
	READER GROUP				
	$n = 10$		$n = 10$		
	M	(SD)	M	(SD)	t test, df = 18
Matching variables					
Age (years; months)	8;8	(0;7)	8;6	(0;8)	n.s.
Grade	2.8	(.74)	2.9	(.74)	n.s.
PPVT-R standard score	102.7	(10.4)	102.8	(9.8)	n.s.
Distinguishing variables					
Word Recognition (WJ 13)					
raw score	28.5	(6.2)	36.7	(2.1)	-3.99***
standard score	102.6	(9.9)	122.4	(6.1)	-5.39***
grade equivalent	3.0		6.1		
Pseudoword Decoding (WJ 14)					
raw score	7.8	(4.4)	19.4	(3.4)	-6.55***
standard score	94.6	(11.6)	118.2	(7.2)	-5.46***
grade equivalent	2.8		12.9		
Test of Written Spelling (TWS)					
Predictable	19.0	(6.7)	26.4	(5.9)	-2.63*
Unpredictable	6.0	(5.1)	13.0	(5.9)	-2.85**
Total	25.0	(11.2)	39.4	(11.2)	-2.88**
Percentage correct on morphological subtests					
Base Targets					
PhonNeutral	90.0	(6.31)	90.0	(8.2)	n.s.
PhonComplex	64.4	(19.44)	86.7	(15.53)	-2.82**
Derived Targets					
PhonNeutral	61.1	(19.07)	65.6	(20.59)	n.s.
PhonComplex	31.1	(22.11)	53.3	(23.89)	-2.16*

*$p < .05$
**$p < .01$
***$p < .001$

TABLE 7. *Comparisons of older "less skilled" readers and younger "more skilled" readers matched on reading level.*

	COMPARISON GROUP		
	Younger	Older	
	$n = 10$	$n = 10$	
	M (SD)	M (SD)	F test, df=1,20
Matching variables			
Word recognition - raw score	33.1 (2.8)	32.4 (2.8)	n.s.
Pseudoword decoding - raw	14.3 (3.8)	10.8 (3.9)	4.38*
Vocabulary - standard score	99.5 (8.9)	96.9 (9.9)	n.s.
Test of Written Spelling -raw	31.3 (9.1)	30.2 (10.5)	n.s.
Distinguishing variables			
Age (years; months)	8;2 (0;5)	9;5 (0;4)	48.78***
Grade	2.6 (0.5)	3.5 (0.5)	13.97**
Word recognition - std score	116.7 (8.2)	102.2 (8.3)	17.17***
Pseudoword decoding - std	111.5 (7.4)	97.1 (9.7)	15.22***
Percentage correct on MorphProd subtests			
Base Targets			
PhonNeutral	86.9 (4.5)	86.9 (8.3)	n.s.
PhonComplex	76.7 (16.1)	69.7 (18.7)	n.s.
Derived Targets			
PhonNeutral	58.6 (15.8)	61.6 (31.5)	n.s.
PhonComplcx	37.3 (15.1)	37.3 (20.7)	n.s.

*$p < .05$
**$p < .01$
***$p < .001$

Discussion

The present chapter explored knowledge of derivational morphology and its relationship to reading and spelling in schoolchildren aged 7.5 to 9.5 years. Confirming the results of prior studies with older children, we too found a strong association between reading skill and morphological knowledge, here assessed by overall performance on a Test of Morphological Production. An important goal of the present research was to probe the basis of that association, determining which aspects of morphology were the most troublesome for children with difficulty in learning to read. Although reading scores were correlated with all of the morphology subtests after controlling for age and vocabulary knowledge, reading was most strongly related to performance in the Base-PhonComplex condition, in which the task was to extract the base form (e.g., *courage*) from a morphophonemically complex derived form (e.g., *courageous).* A further goal was to explore the direction of the relation between morphology and reading. Our results are consistent with the view that sensitivity to derivational morphology may stem, in part, from experience with written language.

Vocabulary and Morphological Awareness

In the present study, comparisons of selected good and poor readers matched on age and vocabulary indicate that at least some differences in morphological awareness are specifically related to reading skill. This association was also confirmed with the larger sample of subjects. In that case, there remained a significant association between morphology and reading after covarying for age and vocabulary. These results confirm similar findings in the few other studies that controlled for vocabulary knowledge (e.g., Carlisle, 1988; Elbro, 1989; Templeton & Scarborough-Franks, 1985). It is, however, important to note that vocabulary knowledge was also strongly related to performance on all morphological subtests. Differences in vocabulary knowledge between successful and unsuccessful readers must be taken into account in designing and interpreting studies focusing on morphology. In the present sample, age, per se, was not importantly related to morphological knowledge.

Morphological versus Phonological Awareness

Of particular interest is the question of whether poor readers had a basic deficit in both morphological and phonological awareness. We argued that if, for some children, morphophonemic changes may mask the morphological relationship between two lexical items (e.g., *courage/courageous*), this could be construed as a problem deriving from a weakness at the phonological level. Convincing evidence for a morphological insensitivity over and above a phonological insensitivity would require that poor readers display less analytic insight even on morphologically complex items that are phonemically straightforward (*danger/dangerous*). In the present study, performance in the PhonNeutral condition was only weakly related to reading in the full sample, and no differences were evident in the IQ- and age-matched comparisons of more and less skilled readers. The fact that performance in the PhonComplex condition was so much more strongly related to reading provides additional support for the position that phonologically demanding tasks tax the poor reader unduly, much more so than can be explained by either vocabulary knowledge or general metalinguistic factors. Our results clearly suggest that phonological problems are paramount for children with reading difficulty, whereas general linguistic awareness is more weakly implicated, if at all.

The results of the present research, then, are largely consistent with the view, supported by Liberman et al. (1989) and Stanovich (1990), that the primary language weakness associated with early reading difficulty is phonological. But our results must be reconciled with other studies as well. Although both Torneus (1987) and Mahoney and Mann (1992) found hints in their data to suggest a role for deficiencies in morphological awareness distinct from deficiencies in phonological awareness, we are struck by some recent findings by Carlisle and Nomanbhoy (1993) that are entirely consistent with the present results. In that study, whereas phonological awareness predicted 33% of the variance in first grade reading skill, morphological awareness accounted for just 4% of the additional variance. In short, if morphology does play a separate role from phonology, and in that case it was significant, it is a small role indeed. What still requires further explanation is the separate question of sensitivity to inflectional morphology and grammatical functors; these areas have been implicated in both second graders (Rubin, 1991) and severely dyslexic adolescents (Elbro, 1989). Of course, given the low phonological salience of grammatical markers, this difficulty too may be ultimately phonological at base.

Generating Derived versus Base Forms

As expected, children found generating Derived forms from the base more demanding than extracting the Base from the derived form. Unexpectedly, however, it was the Base generation task that was more strongly related to reading difficulty. Because this result was not predicted and has no clear precedent in prior research, confirmation should be sought before reaching firm conclusions. In the meantime, we offer two speculations. One possibility is that the Base generation task can be accomplished with only a general awareness of linguistic regularities, whereas the Derived generation task depends more on knowledge of individual lexical items. It is the first rather than the second kind of knowledge that has been specifically associated with reading.

There is some support for a dissociation between the identification of base and derived forms from other research paradigms. For example, in priming tasks, it appears that morphological facilitation generally derives from a contribution from the stem, not from the suffix. Whereas the stem appears to provide lexical information and be central to accessing tasks, proper use of the affix appears to depend on syntactic and semantic constraints determined by lexical idiosyncrasies and sentence context. Consistent with this, even high school-aged normal readers typically show little productive knowledge of derivational suffixes (Freyd & Baron, 1982; Wysocki & Jenkins, 1987; see Tyler & Nagy, 1990, for a good discussion and review).

A second reason that the Base generation task might be more strongly associated with reading might have to do with the requirements of the reading task. In that connection, it is interesting to note that spelling is best predicted by the Derived task. Reading is a task more akin to analyzing than assembling complex words, whereas spelling, like the Derived task, is more generative in nature, involving the production of meaningful constructions from base elements.

Morphology and Reading versus Morphology and Spelling

Although the strong association between Base form generation and reading clearly invites further exploration, it should be kept in mind that reading and spelling overlapped considerably in their association with morphology, as indeed they should. Both reading and spelling were significantly correlated with all subtests of morphology, even after partialling out the effects of age and vocabulary. And, when any one literacy measure was entered into a multiple regression analysis predicting performance on a morphological measure, no other literacy measure contributed significant further variance. These results suggest that at the early stages of literacy, these particular reading and spelling measures are roughly equivalent with regard to their association with morphology. On the other hand, the subtle differences we did observe may be consistent with suggestions by other researchers that the two measures may diverge in interesting ways as the child develops and/or when comparable stimuli are used in reading, spelling, and morphology measures (e.g., Carlisle, 1987, 1988; Shankweiler & Lundquist, 1992).

The Influence of Written Language on the Acquisition of Derivational Morphology

Our final question concerned the role of experience with written language in shaping children's knowledge of derivational morphology. In the present study, we found that good and poor readers matched on actual reading knowledge obtained nearly identical scores on the Test of Morphological Production, suggesting it may be acquired reading skill rather than more basic phonological/linguistic ability that determines much of our knowledge of derivational morphology. Although both are probably implicated, these results are consistent with the often expressed view that orthographic knowledge is a powerful source of information regarding derivational morphological relationships. They are also consistent with the argument that morphophonemic regularities may best be acquired through written rather than spoken language (e.g., Templeton & Scarborough-Franks, 1985).

The contrast between morpheme awareness and phoneme awareness is striking with regard to how they fare in comparisons of good and poor readers matched on reading level. In this and other studies of derivational morphology (Carlisle, 1989), younger good readers have no obvious advantage over older poor readers. In contrast, in studies of phoneme awareness, younger good readers are consistently superior to older poor readers matched on reading level (e.g., Bradley & Bryant, 1978; Fowler, 1990). Whereas phoneme awareness and the other phonological abilities associated with it are likely causal factors in learning to read, it is less likely that a lack of awareness of derivational morphology contributes independently to early reading difficulties.

CONCLUSIONS

Have we then demonstrated that morphological awareness is yet another area of weakness for the poor reader? On a practical level, our answer is certainly Yes. Poor readers were shown to experience considerable difficulty not only at the phonological level but with detecting morphological relationships as well, particularly when these relationships are phonologically complex. This insensitivity surely limits the ability to extract the meaning of novel, morphologically complex items while reading, further compounding the poor reader's difficulties. Consistent with the "Matthew effects" hypothesis suggesting that specific disabilities at the beginning stages of reading lead to a wide spectrum of educational handicaps later on (Stanovich, 1986), our results indicate the young poor reader is at special risk for later morphological problems on at least two counts. First, the poor reader is all too likely to read less often and less accurately and thereby miss out on this crucial source of input provided by orthographic knowledge. Second, even when the input is provided, the poor reader, as a consequence of weak phonological skills, may fail to note the association between two words whose relation is phonologically complex.

On the other hand, we have not conclusively demonstrated that an insensitivity to derivational morphology observed in our poor readers constitutes a separate deficit over and above well-documented limitations in receptive vocabulary, orthographic knowledge, and phonological sensitivity, all of which proved to affect morphological production. In other words, we still lack solid evidence that the deficits of the poor reader extend beyond what is already implicated in the phonological deficit hypothesis. Rather, on the basis of these results, the pattern of deficits unique to the poor reader continues to be overwhelmingly phonological at base but far-reaching in consequence.

We stress the fact that the poor readers were clearly able to appreciate morphological relationships in at least the PhonNeutral condition. This should be seen as good news: first, because words with neutral suffixes constitute the bulk of printed school matter that is morphologically complex (White et al., 1989); and second, because reference to PhonNeutral relationships can provide a ready entry point for discussions of less transparent relationships. Similarly, the possibility that orthographic knowledge may be crucial in acquiring derivational relationships may be regarded as an opportunity. Building on this fact, teachers should be encouraged to take every opportunity to emphasize spelling in instructing children about derivational relationships among words. Further, given the important role of morphological awareness in acquiring new vocabulary during the school years, it would seem especially important that the weaker readers receive explicit instruction in derivational facts that the better readers may be gleaning spontaneously through the orthography.

ACKNOWLEDGMENT

We would like to acknowledge the assistance of J. Carlisle in designing the stimuli and of S. M. Labrecque in collecting the data. We thank S. Bentin, J. Carlisle, L. B. Feldman, A. M. Liberman, and especially D. Shankweiler for their helpful comments on an earlier draft of this chapter, and H. Scarborough and V. Seitz for sharing their statistical expertise. We are also grateful to the students and staff of the Overbrook, D. C. Moore, and Deer Run Elementary Schools of East Haven, Connecticut for their generous sharing of time and space to allow this study to be done.

This research was supported by a grant from National Institute of Child Health and Human Development, #HD-21888, subcontracted to Haskins Laboratories from Yale University; it was completed with the aid of a Science Scholar Award to the first author from the National Down Syndrome Society and Program Project Grant HD-01994 awarded by the National Institute of Child Health and Human Development.

REFERENCES

Adams, M. J. (1990). *Beginning to read: Thinking and learning about print.* Cambridge, MA: MIT Press.

Anderson, P. L. (1982). A preliminary study of syntax in the written expression of learning disabled children. *Journal of Learning Disabilities, 15,* 359-362.

Berko, J. (1958). The child's learning of English morphology. *Word, 14,* 150-177.

Bowerman, M. (1982). Reorganizational processes in lexical and syntactic development. In E. Wanner & L. R. Gleitman (Eds.), *Language acquisition: The state of the art.* Cambridge: Cambridge University Press.

Bradley, L., & Bryant, P. (1978). Deficits in auditory organisation as a possible cause of reading backwardness. *Nature, 271,* 746-747.

Brady, S. A. (1991). The role of working memory in reading disability. In S. A. Brady & D. P. Shankweiler (Eds.), *Phonological processes in literacy* (pp. 129-151). Hillsdale, NJ: Lawrence Erlbaum Associates.

Brady, S. A., Shankweiler, D., & Mann, V. A. (1983). Speech perception and memory coding in relation to reading ability. *Journal of Experimental Child Psychology, 35,* 345-367.

Brittain, M. (1970). Inflectional performance and early reading achievement. *Reading Research Quarterly, 6,* 34-38.

Carlisle, J. (1987). The use of morphological knowledge in spelling derived forms by learning-disabled and normal students. *Annals of Dyslexia, 37,* 90-108.

Carlisle, J. (1988). Knowledge of derivational morphology and spelling ability in fourth, sixth and eighth graders. *Applied Psycholinguistics, 9,* 247-266.

Carlisle, J. F., & Nomanbhoy, D. M. (1993). Phonological and morphological awareness in first graders. *Applied Psycholinguistics, 14.*

Carroll, J. B., Davies, P., & Richman, B. (1971). *Word frequency book.* New York: American Heritage.

Catts, H. (1986). Speech production/phonological deficits in reading-disordered children. *Journal of Learning Disabilities, 19,* 504-508.

Chomsky, C. (1970). Reading, writing, and phonology. *Harvard Educational Review, 40,* 287-309.

Chomsky, N., & Halle, M. (1968). *The sound pattern of English.* New York: Harper & Row.

Cicci, R. (1980). Written language disorders. *Bulletin of the Orton Society, 30,* 240-251.

Clark, E., & Berman, R. (1984). Structure and use in the acquisition of word formation. *Language, 60,* 542-591.

Clark, E., & Berman, R. (1987). Types of linguistic knowledge: Interpreting and producing compound nouns. *Journal of Child Language, 14,* 547-567.

Clark, E. V., & Cohen, S. R. (1984). Productivity and memory for newly formed words. *Journal of Child Language, 11,* 611-623.

Clark, E. V., & Hecht, B. F. (1982). Learning to coin agent and instrument nouns. *Cognition, 12,* 1-24.

Colé, P., Beauvillain, C., & Segui, J. (1989). On the representation and processing of prefixed and suffixed derived words: A differential frequency effect. *Journal of Memory and Language, 28,* 1-13.

Crain, S., & Shankweiler, D. (1988). Syntactic complexity and reading acquisition. In A. Davidson & G. Green (Eds.), *Linguistic complexity and text comprehension: Readability issues reconsidered.* Hillsdale, NJ: Lawrence Erlbaum Associates.

DeFrancis, J. (1989). *Visible speech: The diverse oneness of writing systems.* Honolulu: University of Hawaii Press.

Derwing, B., & Baker, W. (1977). The psychological basis for morphological rules. In J. McNamara (Ed.), *Language learning and thought.* New York: Academic Press.

Derwing, B., & Baker, W. (1979). Recent research on the acquisition of English morphology. In P. Fletcher & M. Garman (Eds.), *Language acquisition.* Cambridge: Cambridge University Press.

Doehring, D., Trites, R., Patel, P., & Fiedorowicz, C. (1981). *Reading disabilities: The interaction of reading, language and neuropsychological deficits.* New York: Academic Press.

Dunn, L., & Dunn, L. (1981). *Peabody Picture Vocabulary Test-Revised.* Circle Pines, MN: American Guidance Service.

Duques, S. (1989). Grammatical deficiencies in writing: An investigation of learning disabled college students. *Reading and Writing, 2,* 1-17.

Elbro, C. (1989). Morphological awareness in dyslexia. In C. von Euler (Ed.), *Wenner-Gren International Symposium Series: Brain and Reading.* Hampshire, England: Macmillan.

Faber, A. (1992). Phonemic segmentation as epiphenomenon: Evidence from the history of alphabetic writing. In P. Downing, S. Lima, & M. Noonan (Eds.), *Language and literacy: Papers from the symposium* (pp. 111-134). Amsterdam: John Benjamins.

Feldman, L. B., & Andjelković, D. (1992). Morphological analysis in word recognition. In L. Katz & R. Frost (Eds.), *Orthography, phonology, morphology, and meaning: An overview.* Hillsdale, NJ: Lawrence Erlbaum Associates.

Feldman, L. B., & Bentin, S. (1994). Morphological analysis of disrupted morphemes: Evidence from Hebrew. *Quarterly Journal of Experimental Psychology, 47,* 407-435.

Fischer, F. W., Shankweiler, D., & Liberman, I. Y. (1985). Spelling proficiency and sensitivity to word structure. *Journal of Memory and Language, 24,* 282-295.

Fletcher, J. M., Shaywitz, S. E., Shankweiler, D. P., Katz, L., Liberman, I. Y., Francis, D. J., Stuebing, K. K., Fowler, A., & Shaywitz, B. A. (1994). Cognitive profiles of reading disability: Comparisons of discrepancy and low achievement definitions. *Journal of Educational Psychology, 86(1),* 6-23.

Fowler, A. (1988). Grammaticality judgments and reading skill in grade 2. *Annals of Dyslexia, 38,* 73-94.

Fowler, A. (1990). Factors contributing to performance on phoneme awareness tasks in school-aged children. *Haskins Laboratories Status Report on Speech Research, 103/104,* 137-152.

Fowler, A., Doherty, B., & Boynton, L. (1993). *Phonological limits on reading in young adults with Down syndrome.* Paper presented at the Third International Conference on Child Language, Trieste.

Fowler, C., Napps, S., & Feldman, L. B. (1985). Relations among regular and irregular morphologically related words in the lexicon as revealed by repetition priming. *Memory & Cognition, 13,* 241-255.

Freyd, P., & Baron, J. (1982). ndividual differences in acquisition of derivational morphology. *Journal of Verbal Learning and Verbal Behavior, 21,* 282-295.

Gleitman, L. R., & Gleitman, H. (1969). *Phrase and paraphrase: Some innovative uses of language.* New York: Norton.

Gleitman, L. R., & Rozin, P. (1977). The structure and acquisition of reading: Relation between orthography and the structured language. In A. S. Reber & D. L. Scarborough (Eds.), *Toward a psychology of reading* (pp. 1-53). Hillsdale, NJ: Lawrence Erlbaum Associates.

Gordon, P. (1989). Levels of affixation in the acquisition of English morphology. *Journal of Memory and Language, 28,* 519-530.

Gough, P. B., & Tunmer, W. E. (1986). Decoding, reading, and reading disability. *Remedial and Special Education, 7,* 6-10.

Hanson, V. L., Shankweiler, D., & Fischer, F. W. (1983). Determinants of spelling ability in deaf and hearing adults: Access to linguistic structure. *Cognition, 14,* 323-344.

Henderson, A. J., & Shores, R. E. (1982). How learning disabled student's failure to attend to suffixes affects their oral reading performance. *Journal of Learning Disabilities, 15,* 178-182.

Juel, C. (1988). Learning to read and write: A longitudinal study of 54 children from first through fourth grades. *Journal of Educational Psychology, 80,* 437-447.

Katz, L., Rexer, K., & Lukatela, G. (1991). The processing of inflected words. *Psychological Research, 53,* 25-32.

Katz, R. (1986). Phonological deficiencies in children with reading disability: Evidence from an object naming task. *Cognition, 22,* 225-257.

Larsen, S. C., & Hammill, D. (1976). *Test of Written Spelling.* Austin, TX: Pro-Ed.

Liberman, A. M. (1989). Reading is hard just because listening is easy. In C. von Euler (Ed.), *Wenner-Gren International Symposium Series: Brain and reading.* New York: Macmillan.

Liberman, A. M. (1992). The relation of speech to reading and writing. In R. Frost & L. Katz (Eds.), *Orthography, phonology, morphology, and meaning* (pp. 167-178). Amsterdam: Elsevier.

Liberman, I. Y., Liberman, A. M., Mattingly, I. G., & Shankweiler, D. (1980). Orthography and the beginning reader. In J. Kavanaugh & R. Venezky (Eds.), *Orthography, reading and dyslexia.* Baltimore: MD: University Park Press.

Liberman, I. Y., Shankweiler, D., & Liberman, A. M. (1989). The alphabetic principle and learning to read. In D. Shankweiler & I. Y. Liberman (Eds.), *Phonology and reading disability* (pp. 1-34). Ann Arbor, MI: University of Michigan Press.

Mahoney, D. L., & Mann, V. A. (1992). Using children's humor to clarify the relationship between linguistic awareness and early reading ability. *Cognition, 45,* 163-186.

Mann, V. A., & Liberman, I. Y. (1984). Phonological awareness and verbal short-term memory: Can they presage early reading problems? *Journal of Learning Disabilities, 17,* 592-599.

Mattingly, I. G. (1992). Linguistic awareness and orthographic form. In R. Frost & L. Katz (Eds.), *Orthography, phonology, morphology and meaning* (pp. 11-26). Amsterdam: Elsevier.

Miller, G., & Gildea, P. (1987). How children learn words. *Scientific American, 257,* 94-99.

Morais, J., Cary, L., Alegria, J., & Bertelson, P. (1979). Does awareness of speech as a sequence of phones arise spontaneously? *Cognition, 7,* 323-331.

Moskowitz, B. (1973). On the status of vowel shift in English. In T. Moore (Ed.), *Cognitive development and the acquisition of language.* New York: Academic Press.

Myklebust, H. (1973). *Development and disorders of written language: Studies of normal and exceptional children.* New York: Grune & Stratton.

Nagy, W., & Anderson, R. C. (1984). How many words are there in printed school English? *Reading Research Quarterly, 19,* 304-330.

Nagy, W., Anderson, R. C., Schommer, M., Scott, J. A., & Stallman, A. C. (1989). Morphological families in the lexicon. *Reading Research Quarterly, 24,* 262-282.

Naigles, L., Fowler, A., & Helm, A. (1992). Developmental shifts in the construction of verb meaning. *Cognitive Development, 7,* 403-427.

Naigles, L., Gleitman, L., & Gleitman, L. (1992). Children acquire word meaning components from syntactic evidence. In E. Dromi (Ed.), *Language and cognition: A developmental perspective.* Norwood, NJ: Ablex.

Napps, S. E. (1989). Morphemic relations in the lexicon: Are they distinct from semantic and formal relationships? *Memory & Cognition, 17,* 729-739.

Pratt, A. C., & Brady, S. (1988). Relation of phonological awareness to reading disability in children and adults. *Journal of Educational Psychology, 80,* 319-323.

Rack, J. P., Snowling, M. J., & Olson, R. K. (1992). The nonword reading deficit in developmental dyslexia: A review. *Reading Research Quarterly, 27,* 29-53.

Rapala, M. M., & Brady, S. (1990). Reading ability and short-term memory: The role of phonological processing. *Reading and Writing: An Interdisciplinary Journal, 2,* 1-25.

Read, C., Zhang, Y., Nie, H., & Ding, B. (1986). The ability to manipulate speech sounds depends on knowing alphabetic reading. *Cognition, 24,* 31-44.

Rozin, P., Poritsky, S., & Sotsky, R. (1971). American children with reading problems can easily learn to read English represented by Chinese characters. *Science, 171,* 1264-1267.

Rubin, H. (1988). Morphological knowledge and early writing ability. *Language and Speech, 31,* 337-355.

Rubin, H. (1991). Morphological knowledge and writing ability. In R. M. Joshi (Ed.), *Written language disorders* (pp. 43-69). Boston: Kluwer Academic Publishers.

Shankweiler, D., & Crain, S. (1986). Language mechanisms and reading disorder: A modular approach. *Cognition, 24,* 139-168.

Shankweiler, D., Liberman, I. Y., Mark, L. S., Fowler, C. A., & Fischer, F. W. (1979). The speech code and learning to read. *Journal of Experimental Psychology: Human Learning and Memory, 5,* 531-545.

Shankweiler, D., & Lundquist, E. (1992).On the relations between learning to spell and learning to read. In R. Frost & L. Katz (Eds.), *Orthography, phonology, morphology and meaning* (pp. 179-192). Amsterdam: Elsevier.

Share, D., Jorm, A., MacLean, R., & Matthews, R. (1984). Sources of individual differences in reading acquisition. *Journal of Educational Psychology, 76,* 1309-1324.

Shaughnessy, M. (1977). *Errors and expectations.* New York: Oxford University Press.

Shaywitz, B. A., Shaywitz, S. E., Liberman, I. Y., Fletcher, J. M., Shankweiler, D. P., Duncan, J., Katz, L., Liberman, A., Francis, D., Dreyer, L., Crain, S., Brady, S., Fowler, A., Kier, L., Rosenfield, N., Gore, J., & Makuch, R. (1991). Neurolinguistic and biological mechanisms in dyslexia. In D. D. Duane & D. B. Gray (Eds.), *The reading brain: The biological basis of dyslexia* (pp. 27-52). Parkton, MD: York Press.

Siegel, L. S., & Ryan, E. B. (1988). Development of grammatical sensitivity, phonological, and short-term memory skills in normally achieving and learning disabled children. *Developmental Psychology, 24,* 28-37.

Smith-Lock, K. M. (1991). Errors of inflection in the writing of normal and poor readers. *Language and Speech, 34,* 341-350.

Stanovich, K. E. (1986). Matthew effects in reading: Some consequences of individual differences in the acquisition of literacy. *Reading Research Quarterly, 21,* 360-407.

Stanovich, K. E. (1988). The right and wrong places to look for the cognitive locus of reading disability. *Annals of Dyslexia, 38,* 154-180.

Stanovich, K. E. (1990). Explaining the differences between dyslexic and the garden variety poor reader: The phonological-core variable-difference model. In J. K. Torgesen (Ed.), *Cognitive and behavioral characteristics of children with learning disabilities.* Austin, TX: Pro-Ed.

Stanovich, K. E. (1991). Discrepancy definitions of reading disability: Has intelligence definitions led us astray? *Reading Research Quarterly, 21,* 7-29.

Stone, B. (1992). *Speech production abilities in children with differential reading skill: A chronological and reading-age comparison.* Unpublished doctoral dissertation, University of Rhode Island.

Templeton, S. (1979). Spelling first, sound later: The relationship between orthography and higher order phonological knowledge in older students. *Research in the Teaching of English, 13,* 255-264.

Templeton, S., & Scarborough-Franks, L. (1985). The spelling's the thing: Knowledge of derivational morphology in orthography and phonology among older students. *Applied Psycholinguistics, 6,* 371-390.

Torgesen, J. K. (1978). Performance of reading disabled children on serial memory tasks: A review. *Reading Research Quarterly, 19,* 57-87.

Torgesen, J. K. (1991). Cross-age consistency in phonological processing. In S. A. Brady & D. P. Shankweiler (Eds.), *The role of working memory in reading disability* (pp. 187-193). Hillsdale, NJ: Lawrence Erlbaum Associates.

Torneus, M. (1987). *The importance of metaphonological and metamorphological abilities for different phases of reading development.* Paper presented at The Third World Congress of Dyslexia, Crete.

Tunmer, W. E., & Bowey, J. A. (1984). Metalinguistic awareness and reading acquisition. In W. E. Tunmer, C. Pratt, & M. L. Herriman (Eds.), *Metalinguistic awareness in children* (pp. 144-168). The Hague: Mouton.

Tunmer, W. E., Herriman, M. L., & Nesdale, A. R. (1988). Metalinguistic abilities and beginning reading. *Reading Research Quarterly, 23,* 134-158.

Tyler, A., & Nagy, W. (1989). The acquisition of English derivational morphology. *Journal of Memory and Language, 28,* 649-667.

Tyler, A., & Nagy, W. (1990). Use of derivational morphology during reading. *Cognition, 36,* 17-34.

Vogel, S. (1975). *Syntactic abilities in normal and dyslexic children.* Baltimore, MD: University Park Press.

Vogel, S. (1983). A qualitative analysis of morphological development in learning disabled and achieving children. *Journal of Learning Disabilities, 16,* 416-420.

Wagner, R. K., & Torgesen, J. K. (1987). The nature of phonological processing and its causal role in the acquisition of reading skills. *Psychological Bulletin, 101,* 192-212.

White, T. G., Power, M. A., & White, S. (1989). Morphological analysis: Implications for teaching and understanding vocabulary growth. *Reading Research Quarterly, 24,* 283-304.

Wiig, E., Semel, E., & Crouse, M. (1973). The use of morphology by high-risk and learning-disabled children. *Journal of Learning Disabilities, 6,* 457-465.

Wolf, M. (1991). Naming speed and reading: The contribution of the cognitive neurosciences. *Reading Research Quarterly, 26(2),* 123-141.

Woodcock, R. W., & Johnson, M. B. (1977). *Woodcock-Johnson Psycho-Educational Battery. (Part Two: Tests of Achievement).* Boston: Teaching Resources.

Wysocki, K., & Jenkins, J. (1987). Deriving word meanings through morphological generalization. *Reading Research Quarterly, 22,* 66-81.

8 Morphological Awareness and Early Reading Achievement

Joanne F. Carlisle
Northwestern University

This chapter discusses the development of morphological awareness in the early school years, providing a rationale for the view that linguistic awareness in this language domain might be centrally related to the acquisition of reading skills. A longitudinal study of children in kindergarten through second grade is reported; it was dsesigned to investigate whether 1) morphological awareness made a unique contribution to the prediction of second-grade reading achievement, beyond that of language knowledge, 2) the growth of morphological awareness was significant between kindergarten and first grade, and 3) first graders' performance on phonological and morphological awareness tasks accounted for significant portions of the variance on the second-grade reading tests (word analysis and comprehension). The findings suggest that kindergartners had trouble with a morphological awareness task, demonstrating relatively little explicit awareness of the morphemic structure of words; first graders performed significantly better on this task. First-graders' performance on morphological and phonological awareness tasks accounted for a significant portion of the variance on second-grade word analysis and reading comprehension tests; a morphological production task was the strongest predictor of reading comprehension, while a phonological awareness task was the strongest predictor of word analysis. Thus, morphological awareness, like phonological awareness, appears to be significantly related to reading achievement in the early school years. Questions are raised for future study of the development of morphological awareness as it relates to early reading achievement.

INTRODUCTION

The period in which children are beginning their formal schooling (kindergarten and first grade) is of particular interest to those researchers seeking to understand metalinguistic development. Many children begin moving from an implicit to a more explicit awareness of language use and language structures in this period. The timing of this shift may be important to the successful acquisition of reading skills because reading and writing activities are thought to require explicit awareness, or metalinguistic functioning.

The purpose of this chapter is to discuss the development of linguistic awareness in one particular area, morphology, in the period from kindergarten to second grade. Of all areas of metalinguistic development, children's awareness of and ability to manipulate the morphemic structure of words has received the least attention. In a recently published book, Gombert (1992) offers a comprehensive discussion of metalinguistic development; while he includes separate chapters on different language areas, there is no chapter on morphological awareness. Despite the neglect by researchers, it is possible that morphological awareness is quite relevant to the acquisition of reading and spelling capabilities in these early school years. Morphological awareness entails phonological, semantic, and syntactic knowledge and so would seem to draw on the kinds of linguistic knowledge used in various written language activities, such as word reading, reading comprehension, or spelling. In the first part of the chapter a conceptual framework for the development of morphological awareness is presented and pertinent literature is reviewed. The second part of the chapter presents a longitudinal study designed to investigate aspects of the morphological awareness of children in kindergarten, first grade, and second grade. On the basis of the results, further studies of the development of morphological awareness and its relationship to the acquisition of reading proficiency are recommended.

CONCEPTUAL FRAMEWORK AND LITERATURE REVIEW

Language Development and Metalinguistic Awareness

Metalinguistic awareness, the ability to make language forms opaque and attend to them in and for themselves, is a special kind of language performance, one which makes special cognitive demands, and seems less easily and less universally acquired than the language performance of speaking and listening (Cazden, 1976, p. 603).

The research literature continues to reflect differences of opinion as to the relationship of language knowledge and metalinguistic development. One view is that metalinguistic capabilities develop as a natural outgrowth of language learning, becoming gradually more evident as children gain linguistic competence (Clark, 1978). Critics of this view (e.g., Gombert, 1992; Tunmer & Herriman, 1984) remark that some of the early childhood language behaviors that are considered metalinguistic (e.g., self-corrections) involve an *intuitive* grasp of appropriate language use, often tied to familiar contexts. They see metalinguistic behavior as characterized by more intentional or conscious manipulation of language, often observed in decontextualized language tasks.

Some researchers see children's linguistic awareness as developing in stages or phases; these may be linked to their cognitive development and to their exposure to facilitating experiences (e.g., instruction in reading). Based on the work of Leontev, Andresen, and Slobin, Valtin (1984) has proposed three stages of language awareness: 1) unconscious awareness or automatic use of language, 2) actual awareness, and 3) conscious awareness. Of particular concern to those interested in kindergartners and first graders is the transition from actual awareness to conscious awareness. Actual awareness implies that children are "increasingly able to abstract the language from the action and the meaning context and to think about some of the properties of the form of the language" (p. 214), but knowledge of language units is still implicit. Spontaneous creative manipulation of language and answers to interviews suggest that children are able to think about some aspects of language. Conscious awareness, on the other hand, implies that children can "deliberately focus on and manipulate linguistic units" (p. 215); children's knowledge of language units is more explicit. Valtin believes that conscious awareness is dependent on instruction and that reading and writing enhance conscious awareness. (See Gombert, 1992, for a similar theory of metalinguistic development.)

Metalinguistic Tasks and Written Language Activities

Gleitman and Rozin (1977) have argued that explicit awareness of the structure of the language is particularly related to learning to read: "Learning to read requires a rather explicit and conscious discovery and building from what one already knows implicitly for the sake of speech: the structure of one's language and, particularly, the sound structure of one's language" (p. 3). Awareness of the sound structure of the language and an ability to manipulate sounds in words appear to facilitate children's mastery of the alphabetic code; for this reason, phonemic awareness may be the aspect of metalinguistic development that is most closely related to early achievement in reading and spelling (Bradley & Bryant, 1983; Liberman et al., 1989). Somewhat similarly, Mattingly (1984) has argued that it is *access* to one's knowledge of the structure of the language that is the central feature of linguistic awareness, insofar as it is related to learning to read. He reminds us that English orthography generally preserves the identity of the morphemes, even in the face of semantic and phonetic variation (e.g., *heal, health,* and *healthy*). Appreciation of or access to the morphophonemic structure of words greatly facilitates the process of reading and spelling.

These arguments focus our attention on phonological and morphological awareness as important links to the reading process. Of all aspects of metalinguistics, phonological awareness has unquestionably received the most attention, presumably because it is related to children's learning of the alphabetic principle. The premise explored in this chapter is that morphological awareness is also closely linked to the process of learning to read. It draws on phonological knowledge, but it is also integrally related to other aspects of children's language knowledge and awareness, including syntax and semantics. In fact, because it draws on various aspects of linguistic knowledge, morphological awareness may provide a more general index of metalinguistic capability than any one of these areas considered alone.

The relationship of metalinguistic capabilities in language domains other than morphology and early reading achievement has been investigated. Tunmer, Herriman, and Nesdale (1988) used tasks of phonological awareness (tapping out the number of phonemes in nonword syllables), syntactic awareness (correcting sentences with word-order errors), and pragmatic awareness (judging stories told by a puppet, some with intersentential inconsistencies). The children were followed from the beginning of first grade through second grade. The researchers found that children's metalinguistic performance, collectively, contributed differently to performance on different reading tasks (word reading and comprehension). At the end of second grade, the standardized beta weight was a nonsignificant .15 when metalinguistic ability was used to predict reading comprehension but a significant .23 when pseudoword decoding was predicted. Thus, the three metalinguistic tests together were more related to decoding than to comprehension in the second-grade year. The influence of each metalinguistic task was not considered separately. It may be apparent from the results of this study that the choice of language domains used in linguistic awareness tasks and the aspect of reading assessed (i.e., word reading or comprehension) can affect the outcome of studies of the relationship between metalinguistic development and reading.

Some researchers have suggested that in the early school years, language knowledge, not metalinguistic awareness, is the important link to reading achievement. Bowey and Patel (1988) gave first graders tests of phonemic awareness and syntactic awareness but found that they did not significantly add to the prediction of reading achievement (using measures of word reading and reading comprehension) when general language effects (here measured by receptive vocabulary and sentence imitation tasks) were statistically controlled. While the particular tasks selected by these researchers may have influenced this outcome, the results suggest that in first grade explicit awareness of language structures and use may not be sufficiently developed to emerge as significant predictors of reading achievement.

Morphological Awareness and Learning to Read and Spell

Several researchers have looked at morphological awareness in relation to reading or spelling achievement in the early school years. Rubin (1988) investigated awareness of morphological structure in spelling inflected forms among kindergartners and first graders. She found that first graders with poor morphological knowledge omitted more inflectional morphemes in spelling and were less able to identify base morphemes in spoken words than kindergartners and first graders with higher levels of implicit morphological knowledge. In a second study, Rubin, Patterson, and Kantor (1991) investigated the morphological knowledge in spoken and written language of second graders, learning disabled children, and adults with literacy problems. They found that the ability to apply morphological rules and to analyze the morphemic structure of words was highly related to the accuracy with which the subjects represented morphologically complex words in their written language. These researchers analyzed performance on the Berry-Talbott Exploratory Test of Grammar, which taps implicit understanding of morphology, and on a morpheme analysis task, involving explicit awareness of the structure of the word. This task ("Is there a smaller word in ___ that means something like ___?") enabled them to compare oral and spelling performances on one- and two-morpheme words such as *list* and *kissed*. The groups' performance on the implicit task closely paralleled their performance on the explicit tasks, but their performance on the explicit task was more closely related to written language achievement.

Brittain (1970) found a significant relationship, independent of intelligence, between inflectional performance and reading achievement for first and second graders. She used Berko's (1958) test of morphology, which assessed the children's ability to complete sentence stems by adding the correct morphological ending to a nonsense word. She interpreted their ability to produce the correct inflectional endings for nonsense words in sentence contexts as indicating semantic knowledge (e.g., signaling of number) and grammatical information (i.e., marking of form class); both of these are important for successful reading comprehension.

Other researchers have investigated the relation of morphological knowledge and reading achievement for older students. Feldman and Andjelković (1992) gave a sentence completion task involving different types of morphologically complex words and a phoneme deletion task to 7- and 8-year-old children who were native speakers of Serbo-Croatian. The correlation between phoneme deletion and use of inflections was .37, while the correlation of phoneme deletion and use of derivations was .52; further analyses indicated that these relationships could not be explained by general intelligence or vocabulary knowledge. Although the researchers did not assess reading ability, they remind us that metalinguistic skill is claimed to be the single most important factor in learning to read. While phonological awareness is the aspect of metalinguistics most closely associated with reading acquisition, they suggest that awareness of linguistic units above the level of the phoneme may significantly contribute to reading skill. Ben-Dror and her colleagues (1992) investigated the phonological, morphological, and semantic awareness of fifth graders with and without reading disabilities. Their results indicated that morphological awareness significantly distinguished the reading disabled and nondisabled students; semantic and phonological awareness also distinguished these groups, but not as strongly. Other studies involving older students (Fischer, Shankweiler, & Liberman, 1985; Leong, 1989; Templeton & Scarborough-Franks, 1985; Wysocki & Jenkins, 1987) have also provided evidence that awareness of the morphological structure of words is related to reading or spelling achievement.

In certain respects, we know little about the importance of morphological awareness to the initial stages of learning to read. It is not clear, for instance, whether morphological awareness begins to emerge before children learn to read and write or is dependent upon exposure to written language activities. In part, this question might be addressed by first assessing morphological awareness early in the kindergarten year, when few children can read, and then tracking the development of morphological awareness as they learn to read. Another consideration is the relationship of phonological and morphological awareness. Phonological awareness is related to success in learning to read; what is not known is whether morphological awareness has a somewhat different relationship to early reading achievement because it entails semantic and syntactic as well as phonological knowledge.

Morphological Knowledge in the Early School Years

Morphological awareness focuses on children's conscious awareness of the morphemic structure of words and their ability to reflect on and manipulate that structure. Clearly, the extent of a child's morphological awareness is limited by his/her morphological knowledge. Thus, an important aspect of the assessment of morphological awareness is the determination of the morphological knowledge that has been acquired by children at a certain age.

In the period when children are beginning to read and write (kindergarten and first grade), they are typically in the final stages of mastering the inflections (Berko, 1958; Brown, 1973; Clay, 1982; de Villiers & de Villiers, 1973). They are also learning derivational principles, as is evident from their spontaneous inventions of words that are ruleful in nature (e.g., the addition of the adjectival suffix -y to make words like yucky) and their use of productive forms such as the -er agentive (Clark & Cohen, 1984). Clark has provided examples of preschool children who have invented words like winder (describing a machine for making ice cream) or flyable (1982, p. 390).

Children in kindergarten and first grade are primarily learning derived forms that are phonetically and semantically transparent (i.e., the base word is clearly represented in the derived form), productive, and close in meaning (e.g., *bake* and *baker*). In learning both inflections and derivations, they are learning ruleful relations and systematic phonological variation (e.g., the allomorphs of the plural, /s/, /z/, or /ez/). MacWhinney (1978) has given the example of the problem the child faces in learning the morphological structure of *wives*; the child not only must master the plural allomorphs but also must identify phonological variants of the base morpheme, *wife* and *wive*.

Phonological relations between base and derived forms are more varied in form and less systematic for derivations than for inflections (e.g., the shift from *divide* to *division* entails shortening of the second vowel, while the shift from *invade* to *invasion* does not). The more complex phonological shifts from base to derived forms appear to be beyond the grasp of most children as they begin school. Jones (1991) found that first-grade children were aware of the relation of surface representations and underlying forms of some morphologically complex words. When asked to delete a segment and then to explain the meaning of the remaining word, they were able to perform quite accurately on compounds and relatively transparent derived forms (e.g., *eight* in *eighth*), but they were much less able to respond correctly to words requiring more complex phonological changes (e.g., *pressure* or *natural*). While young school-age children are learning derivational principles that involve transparent structure and semantic relations, the more complex morphological relations, those that are less transparent semantically and that involve phonological shifts, are learned later, beginning somewhat before the fourth grade (Carlisle, 1988; Tyler & Nagy, 1989).

In assessing the morphological knowledge of young school-age children, we might consider including not only inflections but also derivations, despite their limited knowledge of these forms. Using only inflections may limit our view of the extensiveness of the children's knowledge of morphological relations. Furthermore, derivations might turn out to be better predictors of reading achievement than inflections because they involve understanding of phonological relations, syntactic roles, and semantic relations. Derived forms constitute an increasingly large portion of the new words children learn over the school years, and the extensiveness of their vocabulary is related to their reading achievement (Anderson & Freebody, 1985; Anglin, 1993; Nagy & Anderson, 1984).

The Transition from Implicit to Explicit Awareness

Assessment of children's developing morphological awareness in kindergarten and first grade focuses on the transition from implicit, intuitive awareness of the morphemic structure of words to a more explicit awareness. We should not confuse children's use of morphemically complex words with their awareness of the morphemic structure of those words. Varying degrees of awareness become evident, for example, when children are asked to explain the meaning of morphemically complex words (see Anglin, 1993). To understand the transition from implicit to explicit awareness, we need to focus on behaviors that might signal this shift and the tasks that might provide evidence of explicit awareness.

Van Kleeck (1982) has suggested the following order of difficulty for tasks used to assess language awareness: spontaneous performance, elicited comprehension, evaluation, correction, and explication. It is not clear from this ranking which tasks are likely to indicate that children have explicit awareness of language structures. One problem is that different researchers have different views about what behaviors signal explicit or metalinguistic awareness. Goodman (1986) has inferred metalinguistic awareness from children's overt statements showing analysis of language (e.g., remarking on classmates' names that begin with the same sound or letter). Gombert (1992) has indicated that we may not be able to infer conscious awareness from spontaneous statements children make about language or language use. In fact, he has said that the major problem faced by researchers investigating metalinguistic awareness is determining the conscious character of a mental activity.

One way to assess children's explicit awareness is to use tasks with detailed instructions that require them to analyze language (e.g., manipulate or judge language use). A danger with this approach is that such highly directed tasks may overestimate children's metalinguistic capabilities because they require children to examine and think about language in ways they might not, left to their own devices. Another danger may be in using tasks that are too sophisticated for young children. Clark (1978) has described various studies in which children ages 5 through 8 were able to judge, correct, or produce different language structures. However, complex instructions and abstract or unfamiliar tasks may pose problems for children who are just beginning to develop an explicit awareness of the structure of words.

An additional issue is whether the tasks present words to the child in isolation or in sentence contexts. Some of the researchers who have investigated morphological awareness have used decontextualized tasks, asking children about words in a straightforward manner (Derwing, 1976; Jones, 1991; Rubin, 1988); others have provided sentence contexts, with an explicit request to judge or manipulate a part of the sentence (Feldman & Andjelković, 1992; Fowler & Liberman, this volume). Direct questions about words seem to require children to treat language as an object of thought; however, sentence contexts may be needed to assess awareness of the structure, function, and meaning of morphologically complex words. Tasks that require the manipulation of words or sentences may tap some level of explicit awareness, as they are likely to indicate whether children can analyze and use language in non-automatic ways.

Tracking children's movement from implicit to explicit awareness may be important to our understanding of children's developing morphological awareness in relation to reading achievement. The problem that remains is how to achieve this goal.

A LONGITUDINAL STUDY OF MORPHOLOGICAL AWARENESS

The present study describes a longitudinal investigation of the morphological awareness of kindergarten through second-grade children. It entailed assessment of aspects of their language knowledge, metalinguistic development (phonological awareness and morphological awareness), and performance on different reading tasks (word analysis and reading comprehension). It included the following research questions:

1) Does performance on a morphological awareness task and language knowledge subtests administered in kindergarten significantly account for performance on reading tasks (word analysis and reading comprehension) in second grade? Morphological awareness in kindergarten was expected to be a weak predictor of second-grade reading achievement when considered in conjunction with language knowledge (performance on tests of vocabulary and grammar) because kindergartners are likely to have limited explicit awareness of morphological relations. Thus, it was anticipated that language knowledge would account for more of the variance on second-grade reading tests than would morphological awareness.

2) Are there significant changes in morphological awareness between kindergarten and first grade? This question was designed to assess the growth of morphological awareness between kindergarten and first grade; the expectation was that the children would do significantly better on the morphological awareness task in first grade than in kindergarten.

3) To what extent does performance on tasks of morphological and phonological awareness in the first grade account for variance in reading tasks in the second grade? Do these linguistic awareness tasks account for different portions of the variance in different reading tasks (i.e., phonetic analysis of words and comprehension of short passages)? It seemed likely that morphological awareness would be a stronger predictor of second-grade reading comprehension than would phonological awareness, whereas phonological awareness was likely to be a stronger predictor of word analysis performance. The reading comprehension test presumably tapped various linguistic capabilities, including semantics and syntactics, as did the tests of morphological awareness. On the other hand, the word analysis task required the child to analyze the sound structure of words, thus drawing upon some of the knowledge presumably required by the phonological awareness task.

Description of the Children

In the first year of the study the children were in regular kindergarten classes in an urban school system in western Massachusetts. School personnel had administered screening tests to determine the children's proficiency in English and to identify children with potential learning difficulties. No children with known disabilities were included. Initially, 154 students (81 boys and 73 girls) participated in the study (average age 67.2 months, 4.7 SD). The attrition rate over the 2-year period was very large, presumably because of depressed economic conditions in the area. By second grade only 85 of the original group of students could be located in the school system; one of these was in special education and was not included in the data analysis.

Standardized and Experimental Tests

Different tests were administered to the children in different years of the study, as Table 1 shows.

In the fall of the kindergarten and first grade years, the children were tested individually by trained assistants; each testing session lasted about one-half hour. In the spring of the second grade, the children were tested in small groups. Both the researcher and one research assistant were present; the testing session lasted about an hour.

Language knowledge. The Test of Language Development (TOLD) (Hammill & Newcomer, 1982)—the Picture Vocabulary (PV) subtest (a receptive vocabulary measure)—and the Grammatic Completion (GC) subtest (a task of elicited responses assessing grammatical and morphological knowledge) was administered to the children in the fall of the kindergarten year. The purpose was to assess children's language knowledge in two areas that are thought to be related to morphological learning, vocabulary and grammar.

Morphological awareness. Two tasks (one receptive language and one expressive language) were used; each is described.

TABLE 1. *Tests administered in the kindergarten, first-grade, and second-grade years.*

Kindergarten	First Grade	Second Grade
TOLD PV	TAAS	SDRT RC
TOLD GC	Production	SDRT PA
Morph. Production	Morph. Judgment-Revised	
Morph. Judgment		

a) The Morphological Production task (henceforth called Production): This expressive-language task involved producing the correct form of a word (a morphologically complex form) to complete a sentence. The children were given a base word and a sentence with the last word missing; they were asked to finish the sentence with a form of the word they had been given initially (e.g., *Farm. My uncle is a ____.* The expected response was *farmer.*) About one third of the responses were inflected forms, about one third were derived forms with transparent relations (e.g., *drive* and *driver*), and about one third were derived forms that underwent phonological changes (e.g., *explode* and *explosion*). An attempt was made to use only words familiar to elementary school children (see Carlisle & Nomanbhoy, 1993). The task was administered in the fall of the kindergarten and first-grade years.

b) The Morphological Judgment task: This receptive-language task (henceforth Judgment) required the children to judge possible morphological relations. The task, as it was administered in the kindergarten year, was patterned after a test of morphological knowledge developed by Derwing (1976), on which subjects were asked whether one word came from another (e.g., "Do you think the word *fabulous* comes from the word *fable*? Have you ever thought about this before?"). Although efforts were made to use words familiar to young children (e.g., *corner* and *corn*), the task turned out to be very difficult for the kindergartners; the error rate was high, and patterns of guessing were found on a number of the children's test protocols. Data from this task are not presented in this report. The Judgment task was revised for administration to the first graders. This version (Judgment-Revised) entailed judging orally presented sentences as to whether they were correct or incorrect statements of agentive or instrumental relations (e.g., *A person who teaches is a teacher* versus *A person who makes dolls is a dollar*). Thus, some items were morphologically related, and some were not. The children were asked whether each sentence made sense or was silly. A picture-identification vocabulary test was used to determine whether the children knew the words on this task; only the items containing words they had identified correctly were used in scoring their performance on Judgment-Revised (see Carlisle & Nomanbhoy, 1993, for further discussion).

Phonological awareness. Rosner's Test of Auditory Analysis Skills (TAAS) (Rosner, 1975) is a test of phonological awareness that requires children to make a new word, having deleted a specified element (e.g., "Say *meat*. Now say it again, but don't say /m/"). The trial items and the first few test items involve deletion of a morpheme in a compound word or a syllable in a two-syllable word. The remaining items involve omitting a phoneme, first in the initial position, then at the end of the word, and finally from consonant blends at the start of the word. This test was administered to the children in the fall of the first grade.

Standardized tests of reading. The children were given two subtests of the Stanford Diagnostic Reading Test (SDRT), Red Level, Form G (Karlsen, Madden, & Gardner, 1984), the Reading Comprehension (RC) and Phonetic Analysis (PA) subtests, in the spring of the second grade. The Phonetic Analysis subtest required the child to pick the word from a choice of four that had a specified sound (e.g., "Look at box 4. You see a picture of a sock. Fill in the space next to the letter that stands for the beginning sound of *sock*."). The Reading Comprehension subtest involves picking correct answers to questions following a short passage or completing sentences by choosing the best answer.

Linguistic and Metalinguistic Contributions to Reading Achievement

The first question addressed by this study was whether performance on the kindergarten language knowledge tests (TOLD PV and GC) and the morphological awareness task (Production) would significantly predict second-grade reading achievement on the SDRT subtests, Reading Comprehension and Phonetic Analysis. It was expected that performance on the Production task might not add to the predictive power of the language knowledge performance because kindergartners might have little awareness of morphological relations. This question was answered on the basis of the performance of the 84 second graders who took the SDRT achievement subtests.

Preliminary analyses indicated that the correlations of the language knowledge tests and the Production task were significant (.48 for TOLD GC and Production and .47 for TOLD PV and Production). A stepwise multiple regression analysis was completed to determine the amount of variance in reading comprehension accounted for by TOLD PV, TOLD GC, and Production. These variables accounted for 23% of the variance in reading comprehension, $F(2,78) = 11.693$, $p < .001$. More importantly, however, the Production task did not account for a significant portion of the variance. A second stepwise regression analysis was completed with Phonetic Analysis as the dependent variable. The TOLD subtests and Production accounted for 21% of the variance in Phonetic Analysis, $F(3,77) = 9.634$, $p < .001$. All three tests entered the equation, but the Production task added a nonsignificant 1% to the amount of variance accounted for by the TOLD subtests. Thus, in the kindergarten year, performance on a morphological awareness task (i.e., Production) did not add to the prediction of second-grade reading achievement beyond that of the language knowledge tests. These results are like those of Bowey and Patel (1988); in both cases, language knowledge was a significant but modest predictor of reading achievement, and the children's metalinguistic awareness was not sufficiently developed to make a significant independent contribution beyond that of language knowledge.

Growth of Morphological Awareness between Kindergarten and First Grade

The second question addressed by this study was whether children's morphological awareness, as assessed by the Production task, improved significantly from the fall of the kindergarten to the fall of the first-grade year. The results, based on the 115 first graders who took the test in both years, confirmed the expectation that the first graders would perform significantly better on this task, $t(114) = 9.46$ $p < .001$. On the whole, the kindergartners did not do very well on the Production task. They performed better on the inflected forms (36.5%, 20.5 SD) than the transparent derived forms (22.8%, 16.2 SD). Few children could give correct answers to the test items that required phonological-change derived forms (1.9%, 9.4 SD). The first graders were more adept at producing the correct morphologically complex words: inflected forms, 61.1% (18.5 SD); derived transparent forms, 40.9% (17.5 SD); and phonological-change derived forms, 11.2% (16.9 SD).

Many of the kindergartners had trouble with the Production task. Their performance on items that required producing inflected forms (e.g., *Jacket. Millie has three* _____) was surprisingly poor, especially because the results of other studies (e.g., Berko, 1958; Brown 1973) have indicated that kindergartners are generally quite accurate in forming regular plurals (and other inflections). We might infer that it was the metalinguistic task that posed problems for them. The first graders did not appear to have the same kind of difficulty with the Production task. Not only did they do better on the task overall, but also the correlation of performance on the Production task and reading comprehension was stronger in first grade (.55) than in kindergarten (.33). Perhaps the process of learning to read brought about improvement in their word analysis capabilities.

Domains of Metalinguistic Awareness and Reading Achievement

The third set of research questions concerned the relationship between performance on morphological and phonological awareness tasks administered in the fall of the first grade and performances on the second-grade reading tests, SDRT Reading Comprehension and Phonetic Analysis. The issue was whether morphological awareness (Production and Judgment-Revised) was a better predictor of Reading Comprehension than phonological awareness (TAAS) and whether phonological awareness was more highly related to performance on Phonetic Analysis than morphological awareness. The analysis was based on the performance of the 84 second graders who took the reading achievement subtests (SDRT).

Pearson correlations, shown in Table 2, indicated a moderate positive relationship between each of these linguistic awareness tasks and the reading achievement tests. The Judgment task had a weaker relation with the reading tests than Production or TAAS had.

Two standard multiple regression analyses were completed. First, the first graders' performance on the phonological and morphological awareness tasks were used to predict second-grade Reading Comprehension performance. This analysis yielded a significant equation, $F(3,78) = 13.35$, $p < .001$, and showed that the three metalinguistic tasks accounted for 34% of the variance in Reading Comprehension. As Table 3 shows, only the first-grade Production scores contributed significantly. Partial correlations were examined to determine the unique contribution of the each independent variable; each accounted for a very modest percent of the variance: TAAS, 3%; Judgment-Revised, 3%; and Production, 10%. Because the unique contributions are so small, it can be inferred that most of the variance was shared by the metalinguistic tasks.

TABLE 2. *Correlations of variables in the first- and second-grade year.*

Variable	TAAS	PROD.	JUDG	SDRT PA	SDRT RC
TAAS	--				
PROD	.52	--			
JUDG	.30	.55	--		
SDRT PA	.50	.50	.32	--	
SDRT RC	.41	.55	.42	.77	--

Note: All significant, $p < .01$.

TABLE 3. *Contributions of the Test of Auditory Analysis Skills (TAAS), Judgment-Revised (JUDG), and Production (PROD), administered in the first grade, to SDRT Reading Comprehension (RDG COMP) and Phonetic Analysis (PHON ANAL), administered in the second grade.*

Variable	Beta	t	p level
RDG COMP			
PROD	.366	2.99	.004
TAAS	.175	1.64	.105
JUDG	.164	1.49	.140
PHON ANAL			
TAAS	.328	3.009	.004
PROD	.300	2.417	.018
JUDG	.060	0.540	.581

A second regression analysis was completed with the Phonetic Analysis subtest as the dependent variable; the resulting equation was significant, $F(3,77) = 12.88$, $p < .001$, and showed that the three metalinguistic tasks accounted for 33% of the variance on the Phonetic Analysis subtest. As Table 3 shows, TAAS contributed most significantly, but Production made a significant contribution as well. Again, partial correlations indicated that the unique contribution of each was modest: TAAS, 10%; Production, 7%; and Judgment, .3%. Here, too, the metalinguistic tasks together accounted for a significant amount of the variance on the Phonetic Analysis test.

The results of these regression analyses support several of the expectations described in the first part of this chapter. One was that morphological awareness might be more strongly related to reading comprehension than phonological awareness. As the values in Table 3 show, the first graders' performance on the

Production task contributed more to the prediction of second-grade Reading Comprehension than did performance on TAAS, the phonological awareness task. A second expectation was that morphological and phonological awareness might be closely related. Analysis of the partial correlations indicates that the metalinguistic tasks share influences on reading activities. To some extent, the morphological and phonological awareness tasks (particularly Production and TAAS) may have tapped similar metalinguistic capabilities.

Two additional findings are of particular interest. One is that performance on both phonological and morphological awareness tasks (specifically, Production) accounted significantly for variance on the word analysis task. Why morphological awareness contributed significantly is not clear, since the word analysis test employed monomorphemic words and focused on the identification of letter-sound correspondences. The second is that performance on the Production task was more related to reading achievement than was performance on the Judgment task. The results of the regression analyses suggest that the task of judging word relations was not an effective way to assess children's morphological awareness, insofar as it related to the children's second-grade reading achievement.

ISSUES FOR FURTHER STUDY

Morphological Awareness and Phonological Awareness

A premise that guided the present study was that the ability to analyze the internal structure of words is centrally related to reading achievement (Gleitman & Rozin, 1977; Liberman et al., 1989). This ability was presumed to be part of children's growing morphological as well as phonological awareness (Mattingly, 1984). In fact, a second premise was that phonological knowledge and morphological awareness are related in important ways. As was discussed earlier, phonological processing plays a vital role in morphological learning. For example, in the age range examined in this study, children are learning the categorical relations of allomorphs and systematic phonological shifts that appear when morphemes are used in different combinations (e.g., Jones, 1991). It was expected that few of the kindergartners and first graders would show awareness of the morphological structure of words that involve complex phonological relations between base and derived forms. While almost no kindergartners gave correct responses on the test sentences requiring derived forms with phonological shifts (e.g., *easy* and *easily*), follow-up comparison of the kindergartners' and first graders' performances indicated significant improvement on not only the transparent but also the opaque derived forms. Evidently, awareness of complex phonological relations is beginning to develop in the early school years.

The development of phonological and morphological awareness may be reciprocal. An ability to manipulate the sound segments of words may facilitate the development of morphological awareness. Morphological awareness may foster growth in phonological awareness as children learn to appreciate systematic variations that occur in morphologically related words. Nonetheless, morphological awareness, as it was tested here, is apparently not just a reflection of phonological awareness. One bit of evidence to support this claim is that performance on both tasks separately accounted for significant portions of the variance on the word analysis task. The results of the present study suggest that awareness of word structure at both the level of the phoneme and morpheme is related to reading acquisition.

The link between phonological awareness and morphological awareness is complex and needs to be more fully explored even in the early school years. Systematic comparisons of the awareness of phonological and morphological structure of different types of words, following the examples set by Rubin (1988) and Jones (1991), would be revealing, particularly if the children were tested before and as they learn to read and spell.

Tasks and the Problem of Inferring Explicit Awareness

As was discussed earlier, because reading achievement is believed to be associated with explicit linguistic awareness, researchers face the problem of defining the behaviors that signal explicit awareness. Even though many types of experimental measures have been used to assess metalinguistic functioning, the suitability of different tasks for assessing morphological awareness should be explored. In addition, researchers need to consider the appropriateness of tasks for young children, the degree of explicitness of the instructions, and the suitability of specific tasks for the type of language knowledge that is being investigated.

The tasks used in the present study were chosen because they are manageable for young children (Clark, 1978; Van Kleeck, 1982). These included a receptive language task (Judgment) and an expressive language task (Production). Because it was important to assess children's awareness of the syntactic, semantic, and phonological characteristics of morphemically complex words, the Production task was designed to use sentence contexts. Initially (kindergarten year), following the example set by Derwing (1976), Rubin (1987), and Jones (1991), the Judgment task was a decontextualized one (e.g., "Does *corner* come from *corn?*"). Because the kindergartners had extreme difficulty with this task, the decision was made to revise the task so that judgments were made on word pairs used in sentences (see discussion of this issue in Derwing, Smith, & Wiebe, this volume). Thus, in first grade, both morphological awareness tasks used sentence contexts. Because these tasks required judging or completing sentences, they may have tapped implicit, intuitive knowledge; on the other hand, because the children's attention was directed toward analysis of the sentences (i.e., to judge or to manipulate words), some level of explicit awareness was probably involved. The significant improvement of the children's performance on the Production task between kindergarten and first grade may be an indication that the children are in a transition from implicit to explicit morphological awareness in these years.

The results of the present study showed that although there was a significant correlation between performance on Production and Judgment-Revised (.55), performance on the Production task was more predictive of reading achievement (both word analysis and comprehension) than performance on Judgment-Revised. Other researchers have also found production tasks to be more closely related to reading achievement than judgment tasks (see Fowler, 1988). One reason is that children are more likely to attend to the task completely when they have to give a form of a word that fits a sentence than when they can give a "yes" or "no" response. An alternative consideration, however, is that the Production task required the children to analyze and manipulate the sound structure of words. Of course, the task also required attention to the syntax and meaning of the sentences, and it may be for this reason that it was a more powerful predictor of reading comprehension than either the Judgment task or the phonological awareness task. In short, the Production task appears to offer a promising way to assess the varying aspects of language knowledge that are part of morphological awareness.

It would be helpful if future studies of morphological awareness included orderly comparisons of different tasks of morphological awareness. Aspects of morphological knowledge and the response requirements of the tasks might be systematically varied. In addition, to get around the problem of children's unfamiliarity with contrived tasks, specific tasks might be taught to children and their performance on them tracked over time, possibly varying the particular words or the type of morphological relations used.

Morphological Awareness and Learning to Read

The results of the present study indicate that there is a relationship between morphological awareness and reading achievement in the early school years. Previous studies have reported a similar relationship for older students (e.g., Leong, 1989). Morphological awareness may be particularly important for older students because morphological decomposition and problem-solving provide one way to understand and learn the large number of derived words used in the books they read (Nagy & Anderson, 1984). Yet it appears that even as children are gaining basic reading skills in first and second grade, there is a relationship between their sensitivity to the morphological structure of words and their reading achievement.

Many questions about this relationship need to be answered. For instance, how many morphologically complex words are children apt to encounter in their reading by the end of second grade? If future studies show that the number is very small, we might infer that it is a general ability to analyze linguistic structures, not specifically morphological awareness, that is the basis for the strong relationship to early reading achievement. Another question involves the nature of the reading instruction. The first and second graders in the present study were given reading instruction through a traditional basal reading series. Might the results have been different if the children were in a school system that stressed phonics instruction or in one that used literature as the basis for reading instruction? The answers to such questions will further our understanding of the importance of emerging morphological awareness to reading achievement.

The work reported herein suggests that morphological awareness, like phonological awareness, may bear a privileged relation to reading achievement in the early school years. As noted earlier, uncovering the nature of the association between phonological and morphological awareness is a particularly important area for future study. The results of the present study depend on correlational analyses, which are inadequate for investigating possible causal links. Case studies of young children with deficits in phonological and morphological awareness might provide evidence of the relation of the two, developmentally, as well as specific information about the difficulties such children have learning to read and spell. Future studies might also ask whether children with deficiencies in morphological awareness respond differentially to different treatments, along the lines of the work on phonological awareness of Bradley and Bryant (1983). Certainly, the answers to these and other questions will bring us closer to the goal of understanding how early morphological awareness contributes to the process of learning to read.

ACKNOWLEDGMENT

Gail Furman provided invaluable support and collaboration, coordinating the project for the school system. Joyce Morisette, Kathleen Plasse, Martha Viviano, and Jeanne Esposito deserve recognition for their help testing the children, and Margaret Beeman, Ann Champion, and Diana Nomanbhoy for their work as research assistants.

REFERENCES

Anderson, R. C., & Freebody, P. (1985). Vocabulary knowledge. In H. Singer & R. B. Ruddell (Eds.). *Theoretical models and processes of reading* (3rd. ed.) (pp. 343-371). Newark, DE: International Reading Association.

Anglin, J. M. (1993). Vocabulary development: A morphological analysis. *Monographs of the Society for Research in Child Development,* (Serial No. 238). Chicago: University of Chicago Press.

Ben-Dror, I., Bentin, S., & Frost, R. (1992). *Semantic, phonological, and morphological awareness in children with reading disability and normally achieving readers: Evidence from speech perception and production.* Unpublished manuscript, Hebrew University, Jerusalem.

Berko, J. (1958). The child's learning of English morphology. *Word, 14,* 150-177.

Bowey, J. A., & Patel R. K. (1988). Metalinguistic ability and early reading achievement. *Applied Psycholinguistics, 9,* 367-383.

Bradley, L., & Bryant, P. E. (1983). Categorising sounds and learning to read—A causal connection. *Nature, 301,* 419-421.

Brittain, M. M. (1970). Inflectional performance and early reading achievement. *Reading Research Quarterly, 6(1),* 34-48.

Brown, R.; (1973). *A first language: The early stages.* Cambridge: Harvard University Press.

Carlisle, J. F. (1988). Knowledge of derivational morphology and spelling ability in fourth, sixth, and eighth graders. *Applied Psycholinguistics, 9,* 247-266.

Carlisle, J. F., & Nomanbhoy, D. (1993). Phonological and morphological development. *Applied Psycholinguistics, 14,* 177-195.

Cazden, C. (1976). Play with language and meta-linguistic awareness. In J. Bruner, A. Jolly, & K. Sylva (Eds.), *Play: Its role in development and evolution.* New York: Basic Books.

Clark, E. V. (1978). Awareness of language: Some evidence from what children say and do. In A. Sinclair, R. J. Jarvella, W. J. M. Levelt (Eds.), *The child's conception of language* (pp. 17-43). Berlin: Springer-Verlag.

Clark, E. V. (1982). The young word-maker: A case study of innovation in the child's lexicon. In E. Wanner & L. Gleitman (Eds.), *Language acquisition: The state of the art.* Cambridge: Cambridge University Press.

Clark, E., & Cohen, S. (1984). Productivity and memory for newly formed words. *Journal of Child Language, 11,* 611-625.

Clay, M. M. (1982). The development of morphological rules in children of differing language backgrounds. In *Observing young readers: Selected papers* (pp. 103-112). Portsmouth, NH: Heineman.

Derwing, B. L. (1976). Morpheme recognition and the learning of rules for derivational morphology. *Canadian Journal of Linguistics, 21(1),* 38-66.

de Villiers, J. G., & de Villiers, P. A. (1973). A cross-sectional study of the acquisition of grammatical morphemes in child speech. *Journal of Psycholinguistic Research, 2(3),* 267-278.

Feldman, L B., & Andjelković, D. (1992). Morphological analysis in word recognition. In R. Frost & L. Katz (Eds.), *Orthography, phonology, morphology, and meaning* (pp. 343-360). Amsterdam: Elsevier.

Fischer, F. W., Shankweiler, D., & Liberman, I. Y. (1985). Spelling proficiency and sensitivity to word structure. *Journal of Memory and Language, 24,* 423-441.

Fowler, A. E. (1988). Grammaticality judgments and reading skill in grade 2. *Annals of Dyslexia, 38,* 73-94.

Gleitman, L. R., & Rozin, P. (1977). The structure and acquisition of reading I: Relations between orthographies and the structure of the language. In A. S. Reber & D. L. Scarborough (Eds.), *Toward a psychology of reading* (pp. 1-53). Hillsdale, NJ: Lawrence Erlbaum Associates.

Gombert, J. E. (1992). *Metalinguistic development.* Chicago: University of Chicago Press.

Goodman, Y. M. (1986). Children coming to know literacy. In W. H. Teale & E. Sulzby (Eds.), *Emergent literacy: Writing and reading* (pp. 1-14). Norwood, NJ: Ablex.

Hammill, D., & Newcomer, P. (1982). *Test of Language Development, Primary.* Austin, TX: ProEd.

Jones, N. K. (1991). Development of morphophonemic segments in children's mental representations of words. *Applied Psycholinguistics, 12,* 217-239.

Karlsen, B., Madden, R., & Gardner, E. F. (1984). *Stanford Diagnostic Reading Test* (3rd ed.). New York: Harcourt Brace.

Leong, C. K. (1989). Productive knowledge of derivational rules in poor readers. *Annals of Dyslexia, 39,* 94-115.

Liberman, I. Y., Shankweiler, D., & Liberman, A. M. (1989). The alphabetic principle and learning to read. In D. Shankweiler & I. Y. Liberman (Eds.), *Phonology and reading disability* (pp. 1-33). Ann Arbor: University of Michigan Press.

MacWhinney, B. (1978). The acquisition of morphophonology. *Monographs of the Society for Research in Child Development, 43* (1-2, Serial No. 174).

Mattingly, I. G. (1984). Reading, linguistic awareness, and language acquisition. In J. Downing & R. Valtin (Eds.), *Language awareness and learning to read* (pp. 9-26). New York: Springer-Verlag.

Nagy, W. E., & Anderson, R. C. (1984). How many words are there in printed school English? *Reading Research Quarterly, 19(3),* 304-330.

Rosner, J. (1975). *Helping children overcome learning difficulties.* New York: Walker & Co.

Rubin, H. (1988). Morphological knowledge and early writing ability. *Language and Speech, 31(4),* 337-355.

Rubin, H., Patterson, P. A., & Kantor, M. (1991). Morphological development and writing ability in children and adults. *Language, Speech, and Hearing Services in Schools, 22,* 228-235.

Templeton, S., & Scarborough-Franks, L. (1985). The spelling's the thing: Knowledge of derivational morphology in orthography and phonology among older students. *Applied Psycholinguistics, 6,* 371-390.

Tunmer, W. E., & Herriman, M. L. (1984). The development of metalinguistic awareness: A conceptual overview. In W. E. Tunmer, L. Pratt, & M. L. Herriman (Eds.), *Metalinguistic awareness in children: Theory, research, and implications* (pp. 12-35). New York: Springer-Verlag.

Tunmer, W. E., Herriman, M. L., & Nesdale, A. R. (1988). Metalinguistic abilities and beginning reading. *Reading Research Quarterly, 23(2),* 134-158.

Tyler, A., & Nagy, W. (1989). The acquisition of English derivational morphology. *Journal of Memory and Language, 28,* 649-667.

Valtin, R. (1984). The development of metalinguistic abilities in children learning to read and write. In J. Downing & R. Valtin (Eds.), *Language awareness and learning to read* (pp. 207-226). New York: Springer-Verlag.

Van Kleeck, A. (1982). The emergence of linguistic awareness: A cognitive framework. *Merrill Palmer Quarterly, 28(2),* 237-265.

Wysocki, K., & Jenkins, J. (1987). Deriving word meanings through morphological generalization. *Reading Research Quarterly, 22,* 66-81.

9 Linguistic Influences on the Spelling of ASL/English Bilinguals

Vicki L. Hanson
IBM Research Division, Thomas J. Watson Research Center

An experiment is described here that focuses on deaf college students' skill with derivational morphology. Results indicated an awareness of morphological relationships, although a number of the syntactic errors suggested an incomplete mastery of the syntactic functions of derivations. The ability to use derivational morphology was highly correlated with spelling and reading proficiency. Additional findings converge on previous evidence that deaf students make use of a variety of linguistic information (orthographic, phonological, and morphological) when reading printed English.

INTRODUCTION

When deaf spellers make errors, the misspellings they produce are quite different than those of hearing spellers. For example, a common misspelling of the word *mortgage* by deaf spellers is *mortage* (Hanson, Shankweiler, & Fischer, 1983). Compare that misspelling with the common misspelling of *mortgage* by hearing spellers, which is *morgage*. Both misspellings leave out one letter from the correct spelling. They differ notably, however, in which letter is left out. The common error by hearing spellers is consistent with how *mortgage* is pronounced. The common error by deaf spellers is not.

Researchers have long noted that the spelling strategy for hearing persons is largely one of writing words the way they sound (Fischer, Liberman, & Shankweiler, 1985; Hanson et al., 1983; Masters, 1927; Simon & Simon, 1960, Treiman, 1993). These spellers, particularly the better spellers, then check possible letter sequences against other information, such as orthographic constraints and morphological history, to arrive at the correct spelling. Predominant misspellings for both children and adults overwhelmingly reflect the tendency of hearing spellers to write what they hear, and errors are typically due to incomplete or inaccurate knowledge of orthographic rules or morphological history.

How does a person profoundly deaf from birth spell English words? Is their spelling guided, like hearing subjects, by the phonological structure of words? Let us consider the language environment of a profoundly deaf signer. For many deaf individuals, American Sign Language (ASL) is the first language they learn. Research by linguists and psychologists over the past 25 years has shown that ASL is a language distinct from English, both lexically and grammatically (see, for example, Emmorey, this volume). Thus, in research on spelling it is important to note that deaf spellers not only are writing a language they cannot hear but are also writing a language that is commonly not their first language. The complexities added by modality and second language suggest reasons why deaf spellers might have an incomplete understanding of the linguistic structures of English.

The spelling of deaf students has been much less investigated than their reading. In part, this may stem from observations that spelling is less problematic for deaf students than is reading. On the whole, deaf children and adults are quite good spellers (Cromer, 1980; Gates, & Chase, 1926; Hanson et al., 1983; Templin, 1948). When they do make misspellings, however, the misspellings differ characteristically from those of hearing spellers. As evidenced by the misspelling *mortage*, the misspellings of deaf spellers are often not consistent with the intended word's pronunciation (Dodd, 1980; Hanson, 1982; Hanson et al., 1983; Hoemann, Andrews, Florian, Hoemann, & Jensema, 1976; Padden, in press). For example, Hanson et al. (1983) selected groups of deaf and hearing college students who were matched for spelling proficiency. They found that the type of errors distinguished the two matched groups of subjects. For the deaf subjects, 53.7% of the misspellings were not consistent with the pronunciation of the target word. In contrast, only 18.4% of the misspellings by the hearing subjects were not consistent with the word's pronunciation.

Interestingly, deaf spellers sometimes produce misspellings that contain an error in the ordering of one or more letters, resulting in misspellings that do not preserve the pronunciation of the intended word (Hanson et al., 1983; Smith, 1987). This type of misspelling is rare for hearing spellers. Comparing their matched groups of spellers, Hanson et al. (1983) found that 13% of the misspellings of deaf subjects contained such transpositions. In contrast, only .9% of the misspellings of the hearing subjects did. Most dramatically, the letter transpositions of deaf spellers often violate the syllabic integrity of the intended word (Hanson, 1980; Hanson et al., 1983; Padden, in press). For example, several subjects in the Hanson et al. (1983) study made misspellings such as *vingear* for *vinegar*. The transposition of the letter *e* across the syllable boundary resulted in a misspelling that had only two syllables, whereas the intended word contained three syllables. Other examples of misspellings by deaf spellers, many that involve transpositions across syllable boundaries, are given in Table 1. As these examples indicate, misspellings of deaf signers do not always preserve the pronunciation of the intended word.

The misspellings of deaf subjects, although not consistent with the pronunciation of the intended word, are not random. A more detailed look at the misspellings of deaf subjects suggests that deaf spellers are sensitive to orthographic, phonological, and morphological information. As can be seen from even the examples in Table 1, the misspellings produced by deaf subjects tend to contain only allowable letter sequences. That is, the resulting letter strings are pronounceable and orthographically legal. Only 4% of the misspellings obtained by Hanson et al. (1983) violated phonological and orthographic constraints. Moreover, when presented with letter strings in which these constraints are violated, deaf subjects tend to "err" in recall by inserting vowels and other letters necessary to make the strings pronounceable and orthographically legal (Hanson, 1982).

Rules about orthographic and phonological constraints on word spellings are apparently learned quite early by deaf children. Padden and Hanson (unpublished) found that deaf children as young as 5 years of age could reliably indicate that illegal letter strings (e.g., *BRFD)* were not "good words." Similarly, misspellings of young deaf children show that they are sensitive to orthographic constraints governing allowable letter doubling and word-initial clusters (Padden, in press).

TABLE 1. *Examples of spelling errors by deaf subjects (drawn, in part, from Hanson, 1980; Hanson et al., 1983).*

Correct Spelling	Misspelling
vehicle	vechile
psychological	psylogical
cashier	chasier
interrupt	interput
cantaloupe	cantapole
reptile	replite
thirsty	thristy

Patterns of letter substitutions in misspellings indicate that deaf spellers are also sensitive to phonological information. For example, in the previously mentioned study by Hanson et al. (1983), a common misspelling of *repetition* by both hearing and deaf spellers was *repitition*. This misspelling involves the substitution of the letter *i* for the letter *e*. This type of vowel substitution is a common spelling error for hearing subjects and is typically considered to result from the greater complexity for vowels than consonants in mapping phonological segments to print (Fischer et al., 1985; Fowler, Liberman, & Shankweiler, 1977; Masters, 1927; Seymour & Porpodas, 1980). This same pattern of more letter substitutions on vowel segments than on consonant segments is also characteristic of deaf spellers (Hanson et al., 1983).

Not only do both orthographic and phonological information influence the spelling of hearing as well as deaf spellers, there is now also evidence that morphological information impacts on their spelling ability. We know that both hearing and deaf spellers appreciate morphological relatedness between words (Camp, 1982; Carlisle, 1988; Fischer, 1980; Fischer et al., 1985; Hanson et al., 1983; Waters, Bruck, & Malus-Ambramowitz, 1988). Studies have found, for example, that children and adults are better able to spell morphologically derivable words, such as *grammar* (in which the spelling of the unstressed vowel can be disambiguated by reference to the derivationally related word *grammatical*), than to spell irregular words, such as *champagne*. Moreover, Fischer et al. (1985) and Camp (1985) have reported that morphological ability is an excellent predictor of overall spelling ability. In their studies with hearing sixth graders (Camp, 1982) and hearing college students (Fischer, 1980; Fischer et al., 1985), they asked subjects to spell four types of words: words whose spelling was predictable based on the words' pronunciation (e.g., *plastic*), words whose spelling was predictable based on orthographic rules (e.g., *beginner*, which required final consonant doubling), words whose spelling was predictable based on derivational history (e.g., *grammar*), and words whose spellings were irregular in English (e.g., *champagne*). Camp and Fisher tested groups of good and poor hearing spellers in their studies. Both researchers found that ability to spell the morphologically derivable type of words (e.g., *grammar*) distinguished the good from the poor spellers more than did the other three word types.

Carlisle (1988) has reported that hearing children's ability to take advantage of derivational morphology is influenced by both orthographic and phonological factors. As part of a comprehensive study of developmental changes in spellers' ability to use derivational morphology, Carlisle examined the degree to which hearing fourth, sixth, and eighth graders were influenced by orthographic and phonological transformations in forming morphologically complex derivations. Carlisle developed a derivational test that had two parts: a morphology test and a spelling test. For each item in the morphology test, the subjects listened to a base item followed by a carrier sentence (see also, Carlisle, this volume). For example, *"Swim. She was a strong _____."* That is, the base form was first said, followed by the carrier sentence. The subjects' task was to verbally supply the correct morphological form of the base word.

Across all three grades tested in the morphology production task, Carlisle (1988) found that changes involving both orthographic and phonological transformations (e.g., *decide - decision*) produced more errors than changes involving either of these transformations alone. Apparently, neither an orthographic nor a phonological transformation alone was so difficult that it resulted in impaired ability to supply the correct suffix to base words. The combined complexity, however, of the two transformations did cause problems for the students. Thus, both orthographic and phonological information influenced their ability to generate morphologically complex words, but only when the two were used in combination (see also Fowler and Liberman, this volume).

EXPERIMENT 1

An experiment was designed to address two main questions about how the spelling of deaf college students might be influenced by their knowledge of derivational morphology. First, for deaf students, is there a correlation between spelling proficiency and ability to produce derivationally complex forms? Recall that research with hearing spellers has shown that good spellers are more aware of principles of derivational morphology than are poor spellers (Camp, 1982; Fischer et al., 1985). Second, do orthographic and/or phonological transformations affect deaf college students' ability to derive and spell morphologically complex words?

Using a procedure that was a written adaptation of the morphology production tests of Carlisle (1984, 1988), subjects in this experiment were asked to write the derived forms of specific target words. The derived forms differed from the target words by prescribed orthographic and phonological transformations.

The subjects were 16 prelingually, profoundly deaf students at Gallaudet University. All had a hearing loss of 85 dB or greater, better ear average, and all were signers of ASL. Twelve of these subjects had deaf parents. All subjects were given the Stanford Test of Academic Skills spelling subtest (1978, Form E, Level 2). This standardized test uses a multiple choice format. The mean number of correct responses for the subjects corresponded to a grade equivalent of 11.7 (range: grade 6.9 to past high school). Additionally, they were given the Gates-MacGinitie Reading Tests comprehension subtest (1978, Level F, Form 2). The median reading grade equivalent on this test was 9.5 (range: 4.4 - 12.9+). There was a significant correlation between raw scores on the reading and spelling proficiency tests ($r = .67$), indicating that the best readers were also the best spellers.

Morphological test items were the stimuli from the Derived Forms Morphology Test of Carlisle (1984, 1988). There were 40 items in the test, 10 in each of four conditions. The four conditions were defined in terms of the spelling change required to transform the base word into the derived form. In the No Change (NC) condition, neither the orthography nor the phonology changed from the base to the derived form (e.g., *enjoy - enjoyment, precise - precisely, care - careful*). In the Orthographic Change (OC) condition, only the orthography changed from the base (e.g., *begin - beginner, active - activity, happy - happiness*). In the Phonological Change (PC) condition, only the phonology changed from the base (e.g., *heal - health, magic - magician, express - expression*). In the Both Change (BC) condition, both the orthography and the phonology changed from the base (e.g., *deep - depth, decide - decision, type - typical*).

The words in the four conditions were matched, as closely as possible, for length and for frequency. The OC and BC words were also comparable in terms of degree of orthographic overlap between the base and derived form of the word. For example, in the OC condition, the derived form *happiness* changed one letter of the base form, *happy*. Similarly, in the BC condition the derived form *typical* changed one letter of the base form, *type*. In only one case, the BC type *deep - depth*, did the orthographic change involve a change of more than one letter. By definition, the base and derived words had complete orthographic overlap in the NC and PC trial types. Additional details about the stimuli are supplied in Carlisle (1984, 1988).

The morphology test used a written presentation format. The 40 target items were tested using the carrier sentences given in Carlisle (1984). The instructions to the subjects stated that they would see an underlined word, followed by a sentence with a blank at the end. They were to write the form of the underlined word that finished the sentences correctly. The following three examples were then presented:

> *farm. My uncle is a _____.*
> *friend. Her dog is very _____.*
> *agree. The businessmen signed an _____.*

It should be noticed that both derivational knowledge and spelling proficiency were tested with this written procedure. When scoring the responses, therefore, the errors were categorized as being either an error of choosing the correct suffix (e.g., *endurement* for *endurance* or *adventurely* for *adventurous*) or an error primarily related to spelling of either the base or suffix (e.g., *deepth* for *depth*, *expandation* for *expansion*, or *humorus* for *humorous*). Non-responsive answers, such as blanks or writing the wrong word (e.g., *at last* written in response to the base word *final*), were excluded from analysis. Only 3% of responses were excluded.

An analysis of variance was conducted on the number or errors for the factors of word type (NC, OC, PC, BC) and error type (suffix, spelling). There were significant main effects of both word type [$F(3,45) = 6.49, p < .001$, for subjects; $F(3,34) = 2.65, p < .06$, for items] and error type [$F(1,15)= 23.47, p < .001$, for subjects; $F(1,34) = 16.84$, $p < .001$, for items]. There was no significant interaction of these variables.

As shown in Table 2, the main effect of word type was reflective of more errors on BC trials than on other trial types (Newman-Keuls, $p < .05$). The finding suggests an influence of both orthographic and phonological information on the ability of the deaf subjects to perform morphological transformations. The result is particularly striking with the present written procedure. It might be expected that phonology would influence morphological production in an auditory test, such as that used by Carlisle (1988), but that the influence of orthography would dominate over phonology in a written test. Contrary to that expectation, OC trials, in which the stem of the base and derived form differed by only an orthographic change, did not produce more errors than the NC trials (cf. Derwing, Smith, & Wiebe, this volume). Rather, the BC trials, which had a phonological complexity as well as an orthographic complexity, were the most difficult type of morphological transformations to spell. In summary, as with the hearing children tested by Carlisle (1988) and by Fowler and Liberman (this volume), neither phonological nor orthographic transformations alone resulted in an elevated error rate. The complexity of both an orthographic and a phonological change, however, did lead to significantly more errors.

While it does not seem implausible that hearing subjects might be influenced by phonological information when attempting to generate and spell morphologically complex words, it is more difficult to come to understand why deaf subjects would be using similar phonological information. Perhaps the deaf subjects' difficulty with the BC trials can be explained solely by orthographic factors, without resorting to a phonological dimension. Such an explanation would be credible if the orthographic changes in the OC trials were smaller in magnitude than the orthographic changes in the BC trials. Recall, however, that the stems of the base and derived forms of the OC and BC words had comparable orthographic overlap, yet the mean errors rates indicate that the subjects made significantly more errors on the BC trials than the OC trials. Therefore, a strictly orthographic explanation of the effect is invalidated.

TABLE 2. *Mean percentage of suffixation and spelling errors for the four different trial types.*

	NC	OC	PC	BC
Suffixation Errors	23.1	19.0	22.8	40.2
Spelling Errors	4.6	3.9	3.7	9.2

English syntax typically is problematic for deaf students (e.g., Quigley, Power, & Steinkamp, 1977), and the present study was no exception. The main effect of error type indicated considerably more errors of suffixation than of spelling. There was a mean of 26.3% errors related to suffixation, but a mean of only 5.3% errors related to spelling.

In order to gain some understanding into the type of suffixation errors made by the subjects, each error was categorized as being of one of the following three types:

> *Context error:* These were errors in which the answer's suffix was incorrect for the sentence context. All these responses were allowable English words (e.g., *healing* instead of *health, happily* instead of *happiness,* and *appears* instead of *appearance*) but violated word class constraints imposed by the sentence.

> *Lexical error:* These were errors in which an allowable English suffix was affixed to the base word, but the resulting string was not an English word (e.g., *magicer* instead of *magician, humorable* instead of *humorous,* and *permitly* instead of *permission*).

> *Unclassifiable:* These were errors that could not be classified along any describable morphological dimension. Some examples of responses falling into this category were *glorissem* instead of *glorious* and *precisus* instead of *precisely.*

The results of this classification indicated that the majority of suffixation errors fell into the category of context errors: 65.3% were context errors, 30.7% were lexical errors, and 4% were unclassifiable. There was a high degree of correlation between each subject's context and lexical errors ($r = .77$), indicating that an individual subject did not tend to make only one type of error. That is, if the subject had trouble with suffixation, they made both context and lexical errors.

The suffixation errors indicated that these subjects have not fully mastered how different suffixes relate to specific meanings. This was clear from the large number of suffixation errors in which the attached suffix did not result in the correct part of speech. Taking a look at the suffixation errors that were categorized as context or lexical errors, we find that 61.3% of these errors had a suffix that was not syntactically correct for the carrier sentence. While subjects used a wide variety of suffixes in their responding, it is worth noting that more than a third (34.2%) of the cases involving a syntactically incorrect suffix used the suffix -*ly*. It appears that these subjects had some tendency to use -*ly* when uncertain about the correct suffix.

Correlations between deaf subjects' suffixation errors on the morphology test and their general reading and spelling proficiency suggest that skill with derivational morphology is associated with proficiency in both reading and spelling. Table 3 shows the interrelatedness of these measures.

TABLE 3. *Correlations of the mean suffixation errors on the morphology test with the scores on the reading and spelling proficiency tests. Also shown are the correlations of the categorized suffixation errors with these measures.*

	Morphology	Spelling	Reading	Context errors	Lexical errors	Syntax errors
Spelling	-.86*					
Reading	-.83*	.73*				
Context Errors	.94*	-.74*	-.72*			
Lexical Errors	.91*	-.89*	-.75*	.77*		
Syntax Errors	.95*	-.77*	-.76*	.94*	.80*	
Unclassifiable	-.16	-.04	.26	-.20	-.09	-.03

*Note: * $p < .01$, two-tailed*

There were significant correlations between the total number of errors on the morphology test and the measures of both spelling proficiency ($r = -.81$) and reading proficiency ($r = -.83$). The direction of these correlations indicated that those who made the fewest errors on the morphology test had the highest scores on the reading and spelling tests. Thus, the better readers and spellers were also those who demonstrated the greater facility with derivational morphology. This is an interesting finding, consistent with evidence that ability to appreciate morphological relationships distinguishes good from poor hearing spellers (Camp, 1982; Fischer, 1980; Fischer et al., 1985).

Suffixation errors categorized as content, lexical, and syntactic were each significantly correlated with both reading and spelling, as shown in Table 3. The directions of these correlations suggest that the better readers and spellers are less likely to make each of these types of suffixation errors than poorer readers and spellers. The (few) unclassifiable errors did not correlate significantly with the measures of reading and spelling proficiency, nor with the frequency of other suffixation errors.

The spelling errors on the morphology test did not correlate significantly with either reading or spelling proficiency. Given the extremely small number of errors of this kind in the data, it is difficult to draw any conclusions about the absence of a significant correlation.

SUMMARY

The subjects in the present study demonstrated an awareness of principles of derivational morphology (see also Hanson, 1993; Hanson & Wilkenfeld, 1985; Volterra & Bates, 1989). The fact that the majority of the responses in the present experiment were correct attests to the ability of deaf college students' ability to apply these principles. In addition, the fact that all of their errors, except the small percentage of unclassifiable errors, had legal suffixes attached to the base word, attests to their understanding of ways in which English words are analyzable into parts. The problems the subjects did have involved providing the correct suffix. As the lexical errors showed, they sometimes attached a suffix to a base that resulted in a string that was not an English word. This pattern may be indicative of a lack of exposure to specific derived forms in English and is consistent with the often-cited finding of English vocabulary deficiencies in deaf populations (see, for example, Karchmer, Milone, & Wolk, 1979; LaSasso & Davey, 1987; Silverman-Dresner & Guilfoyle, 1972).

It also appears that the mastery of the syntactic function of derivational suffixes is not complete for the subjects of this study, all of whom were college students. This can be seen in the number of errors in which the suffix was syntactically incorrect. This difficulty with syntactic function may be related to difficulties encountered in learning a second language. Volterra and Bates (1989) present evidence that problems with derivational morphology are characteristic of second language learners and are not the result of hearing loss.

In addition to providing evidence as to the derivational morphology ability of deaf college students, the present study suggests that ability to master derivational morphology is related to spelling skill. Not only are deaf students more able to spell morphologically derivable words than irregular words (Hanson et al., 1983), but, as the present work shows, overall spelling proficiency is highly correlated with ability to master derivational morphology. While there can be little doubt that appreciation of derivational morphology is acquired through formal education (Derwing et al., this volume), the obtained correlations between performance in the morphology test and reading and spelling are likely also reflective of a causal relationship between morphological knowledge and reading/spelling proficiency. For example, understanding of derivational relationships could enhance vocabulary (Tyler & Nagy, 1989; White, Power, & White, 1989) and be useful in disambiguating the spelling of words that are phonologically ambiguous (Fischer, 1980; Fischer et al., 1985).

The present results add to the growing body of evidence which indicates that deaf spellers are guided by several forms of linguistic information. Orthographic, phonological, and morphological information each have their influence. Although misspellings of deaf subjects suggest that deaf spellers may not be guided by a word's pronunciation when spelling, phonological information does, apparently, influence deaf spellers in other ways. First, there is the evidence that misspellings are legal letter strings, indicating a sensitivity to phonological constraints (Hanson, 1982; Hanson et al., 1983). Second, the results of the present study showed that the subjects had difficulty providing correct responses when the base and morphologically complex form of a word differed both orthographically and phonologically. A strictly orthographic interpretation was ruled out.

We must, therefore, consider how deaf signers would have knowledge of phonological information and what role it might play in their processing of English print. The ability to use phonological information may come through experience with speaking and/or lipreading, or through experience with print. In this connection, we might think of a phonological code for a deaf person as primarily visual or kinesthetic in nature. This is not incompatible with the form of phonological codes that hearing persons employ. For example, the "McGurk Effect" shows that when visual and auditory information are in conflict, hearing subjects may report that they "hear" phonemes that they, in fact, actually only see (McGurk & MacDonald, 1976). This type of evidence indicates a visual component to the phonological code of hearing persons and, therefore, suggests one form that a phonological code could take for deaf persons.

We know that some deaf signers use phonological information when reading (Hanson 1991; Lichtenstein, 1985). Hanson, Goodell, and Perfetti (1991), for example, demonstrated that deaf native signers of ASL (all college students) had more difficulty making semantic acceptability judgments about tongue-twister sentences than about sentences that were phonologically dissimilar. That is, sentences such as *The spacious zoo sits beside a sandy seashore* were more difficult for subjects than were sentences such as *The amusement park was beside a rocky beach*. Moreover, when these subjects had to retain in memory a string of numbers while reading the sentences, the phonological structure of the numbers in memory influenced subjects' performance. Specifically, if the numbers were composed of the same subset of phonological elements as the tongue-twister sentence, (such as the numbers 6, 7, 63, 74, 17, for the sample tongue-twister sentence given above), then the semantic acceptability task was more difficult than if the phonological content of the numbers and the sentence were unrelated. We see from that study that deaf signers were using phonological information during sentence comprehension. Most likely, this phonological information is used in reading for maintaining words in working memory to enable the processing of individual words and the assembly of individual words into phrases and sentences.

In connection with spelling, one intriguing possibility is that deaf spellers who use sign language might use a type of "manual phonology." It has been noticed that deaf spellers often make reference to fingerspelling (Hanson, 1980, 1982; Hanson et al., 1983). Fingerspelling is a manual communication system in which a word is spelled out, letter by letter, on the hand. Signers will sometimes try out spellings of words on their hand before writing. This trying out sometimes involves visual feedback, with the speller watching his or her own hand while working on the spelling. Often, however, this visual feedback is absent as the spellers try out different letter combinations for words with their hands held underneath the table, suggesting the involvement of a proprioceptive component. Such a manual phonology could serve to monitor for legal letter sequences. Just as speakers are aware of what is or is not pronounceable in English, so, too, might fingerspellers be aware of what is "pronounceable" manually. In this regard, if asked to fingerspell nonwords that are orthographically and phonologically illegal (e.g., *fternaps*), deaf signers have noticeable difficulty fingerspelling the illegal segments (Hanson, 1982).

Phonology and fingerspelling might also interact in another interesting way. Very often deaf signers will "mouth" words as they fingerspell (or sign) them. This mouthing looks much like the signer is speaking the word, although there is no accompanying voicing. In a situation such as the morphology test described above, phonological transformations may influence the speller in terms of the mouthing that accompanies the fingerspelling. This is less direct than saying that deaf spellers spell from a word's pronunciation. Here they are deriving and spelling a word not directly from the phonetic structure of the word but rather from the fingerspelling that has been influenced by the accompanying mouthing. For BC changes, where both orthographic and phonological changes are required, the accompanying mouth movement may reflect the pronunciation of the stem, thus making it more difficult to derive the correct transformations.

In closing, it is worth returning to the point that several types of linguistic information influence deaf spellers. Orthographic, phonological, and morphological information each play a role. Early researchers tended to ascribe deaf spellers' skill to rote memorization of individual words (Gates & Chase, 1926; Templin, 1948). We have argued here, however, that this is definitely not the case. Deaf spellers spell analytically, taking advantage of linguistic information for English sometimes using information similar to that used by hearing spellers and sometimes using linguistic (e.g., fingerspelling) specific to their bilingual language experience. Research is only beginning to uncover the ways in which the linguistic structures of English impact on deaf language processing.

ACKNOWLEDGMENT

This research was supported, in part, by Grant NS-18010 from the National Institute of Health to the author. I would like to thank Deborah Kuglitsch for her help with testing subjects.

REFERENCES

Camp, L. W. (1982). *Acquisition of reading and spelling in relation to linguistic ability.* Paper presented at the 20th annual meeting of the Academy of Aphasia, Lake Mohonk, NY.

Carlisle, J. F. (1984). *The relationship between knowledge of derivational morphology and spelling ability in fourth, sixth, and eighth graders.* Unpublished doctoral dissertation, University of Connecticut.

Carlisle, J. F. (1988). Knowledge of derivational morphology and spelling ability in fourth, sixth, and eighth-graders. *Applied Psycholinguistics, 9,* 247-266.

Cromer, R. F. (1980). Spontaneous spelling by language-disordered children. In U. Frith (Ed.), *Cognitive processes in spelling* (pp. 405-421). London: Academic Press.

Dodd, B. (1980). The spelling abilities of profoundly pre-lingually deaf children. In U. Frith (Ed.), *Cognitive processes in spelling* (pp. 423-440). London: Academic Press.

Fischer, F. W. (1980). *Spelling proficiency and sensitivity to linguistic structure.* Unpublished doctoral dissertation, University of Connecticut.

Fischer, F. W., Shankweiler, D., & Liberman, I. Y. (1985). Spelling proficiency and sensitivity to word structure. *Journal of Memory and Language, 24,* 423-441.

Fowler, C. A., Liberman, I. Y., & Shankweiler, D. (1977). On interpreting the error pattern in beginning reading. *Language and Speech, 20,* 162-173.

Gates-MacGinitie Reading Tests (2nd ed.) (1978). Boston: Houghton Mifflin.

Gates, A. I., & Chase, E. H. (1926). Methods and theories of learning to spell tested by studies of deaf children. *Journal of Educational Psychology, 17,* 289-300.

Hanson, V. L. (1980). Implications of research on sign languages for theories of reading. In B. Frokjaer-Jenson (Eds.), *The sciences of deaf signing.* Copenhagen, Denmark: Audiologopedic Research Group.

Hanson, V. L. (1982). Use of orthographic structure by deaf adults: Recognition of fingerspelled words. *Applied Psycholinguistics, 3,* 343-356.

Hanson, V. L. (1991). Phonological processing without sound. In S. Brady & D. Shankweiler (Eds.)., *Phonological processes in literacy: A tribute to Isabelle Y. Liberman.* Hillsdale, NJ: Lawrence Erlbaum Associates.

Hanson, V. L. (1993). Productive use of derivational morphology by deaf college students. *Bulletin of the Psychonomic Society, 31,* 63-65.

Hanson, V. L., Goodell, E. W., & Perfetti, C. A. (1991). Tongue-twister effects in the silent reading of hearing and deaf college students. *Journal of Memory and Language, 30,* 319-330.

Hanson, V. L., Shankweiler, D., & Fischer, F. W. (1983). Determinants of spelling ability in deaf and hearing adults: Access to linguistic structure. *Cognition, 14,* 323-344.

Hanson, V. L., & Wilkenfeld, D. (1985). Morphophonology and lexical organization in deaf readers. *Language and Speech, 28,* 269-280.

Hoemann, H. W., Andrews, C. E., Florian, V. A., Hoemann, S. A., & Jensema, C. J. (1976). The spelling proficiency of deaf children. *American Annals of the Deaf, 121,* 489-493.

Karchmer, M. A., Milone, M. N., Jr., & Wolk, S. (1979). Educational significance of hearing loss at three level of severity. *American Annals of the Deaf, 124,* 97-109.

LaSasso, C., & Davey, B. (1987). The relationship between lexical knowledge and reading comprehension for prelingually, profoundly hearing-impaired students. *Volta Review, 89,* 211-220.

Lichtenstein, E. H. (1985). Deaf working memory processes and English language skills. In D. S. Martin (Ed.), *Proceedings of the conference on cognition, education, and deafness: Directions for research and instruction.* (pp. 111-114). Washington, DC: Gallaudet College Press.

Masters, H. V. (1927). *A study of spelling errors.* Iowa City: University of Iowa Studies in Education, IV(4), 1st Series #138, September 1, 1927.

McGurk, H., & MacDonald, J. W. (1976). Hearing lips and seeing voices. *Nature, 264,* 746-748.

Padden, C. (in press). Lessons to be learned from the young deaf orthographer. *Linguistics and Education.*

Quigley, S. P., Power, D. J., & Steinkamp, M. W. (1977). The language structure of deaf children. *Volta Review, 79,* 73-84.

Seymour, P. H. K., & Porpodas, C. D. (1980). Lexical and non-lexical spelling in dyslexia. In U. Frith (Ed.), *Cognitive processes in spelling* (pp. 443-473). London: Academic Press.

Silverman-Dresner, T., & Guilfoyle, G. R. (1972). *Vocabulary norms for deaf children.* Washington, DC: Alexander Graham Bell Association for the Deaf.

Simon, D. P., & Simon, H. A. (1973). Alternative uses of phonemic information in spelling. *Review of Educational Research, 43,* 115-137.

Smith, J. L. (1987). Characteristic errors of pupils. *American Annals of the Deaf, 42,* 201-210.

Stanford Test of Academic Skills. (1982). New York: Harcourt Brace.

Templin, M. (1948). A comparison of the spelling achievement of normal and defective hearing subjects. *Journal of Educational Psychology, 39,* 337-346.

Treiman, R. (1993). *Beginning to spell.* New York: Oxford University Press.

Tyler, A., & Nagy, W. (1989). The acquisition of English derivational morphology. *Journal of Memory & Language, 28,* 649-667.

Volterra, V., & Bates, E. (1989). Selective impairment of Italian grammatical morphology in congenitally deaf: A case study. *Cognitive Neuropsychology, 6,* 273-308.

Waters, G. S., Bruck, M., & Malus-Ambramowitz, M. (1988). The role of linguistic and visual information in spelling: A developmental study. *Journal of Experimental Child Psychology, 45,* 400-425.

White, T. G., Power, M. A., & White, S. (1989). Morphological analysis: Implications for teaching and understanding vocabulary growth. *Reading Research Quarterly, 24,* 283-304.

10 Diachronic and Typological Properties of Morphology and Their Implications for Representation

Joan Bybee
University of New Mexico

This paper presents certain diachronic and typological facts that bear on the issue of the representation of morphologically complex words. It is argued in particular that a gradient model is necessary, and this model has the following properties: Words have varying degrees of lexical strength, depending upon their text frequency; complex words have multiple connections to related words, and parallel phonological and semantic connections constitute morphological relations; lexical connections may vary in strength; both irregular morphologically complex words and high frequency regular complex words are stored in the lexicon, but regular low frequency words may be produced componentially.

INTRODUCTION

As a background to the study of morphological processing it is important to be aware of the range of morphological types found in human languages around the world and the way morphology is created in these languages. A viable theory of morphological storage and processing should be able to predict the direction of change in morphology and be consistent with the range of variation found in the world's languages.

DIACHRONIC PROCESSES AND LANGUAGE TYPOLOGY

The Formation of Affixes

The vast majority of affixes in the languages of the world evolve from independent words by a gradual process of change called 'grammaticization' or 'grammaticalization' (Bybee, Perkins, & Pagliuca, 1994; Heine, Claudi & Hünnemeyer, 1991; Heine & Reh, 1984; Heine & Traugott, 1991). In the gradual progression from a lexical morpheme to a grammatical one, changes occur in the phonological shape of the morpheme, its meaning, and its grammatical behavior. A well-documented instance of this type of change is the development of the future tense in Romance languages such as Spanish and French. A periphrastic construction in Latin consisting of an inflected auxiliary *habere* 'to have' and an infinitive yielded a meaning of obligation or predestination:

> *amare habeo*   'I have to love, I am to love'
> love+inf aux+1s

The auxiliary reduces phonologically and comes to appear consistently after the infinitive (where previously it could occur in various places in the clause). In Old Spanish we find the construction indicating future:

> *amar he*   'I will/shall love'
>   love+inf aux+1s

The auxiliary is written separately from the infinitive because at this stage other morphemes could come between the two; for instance, the object pronoun:

> *amar lo he*   'I will love him'
> love+inf him aux+1s

Later this possibility disappears and the auxiliary becomes an actual suffix to the verb:

> *lo amaré*   'I will love him'

In this process the grammaticizing morpheme undergoes phonological reduction (e.g., from *habeo* to *he* to *é*), its position becomes fixed, it fuses with the verb, and the whole construction takes on a more abstract, grammatical meaning.

A similar process leads to the development of derivational affixes. However, in this case the process begins with compounding. If the same element occurs in a number of compounds, it can reduce phonologically and change semantically in such a way that it becomes a derivational affix. For instance, the Modern English suffix *-ly* derives from a noun, which in Old English was *lice* meaning 'body.' The compound *mann-lice* originally meant 'having the body or appearance of a man' whence it generalized to 'having the characteristics of a man,' the modern sense of *manly*. Since *-lic* was used in so many combinations, it lost its stress and reduced to *-ly* by losing its final consonant. Its meaning had already generalized in Old English to sometimes just mean 'pertaining to' as in the form *heofon-lice* 'heavenly.' In Modern English *-ly* is used to derive adjectives, as in *friendly*, and to derive manner adverbs, as in *cleverly*, but it occurs in many other uses as well: Consider *daily, weekly, cowardly, possibly,* and so on. Most derivational affixes in English and other languages can similarly be traced back to independent words where evidence is available.

One interesting aspect of the grammaticization process is that it is unidirectional: Affixes are regularly formed from erstwhile words, while only in the rarest and most special of cases is an affix transformed into a word. (Some possible examples are words such as *pros* and *cons,* but these can also be considered clippings or shortenings, such as *lab* from *laboratory.*) Moreover, the process is not discrete but continuous; grammaticization in the form of semantic change and further phonological reduction and fusion continues even after grammatical status is achieved, and even after affixation occurs. This means that we can categorize morphemes for their 'degree of grammaticization.' Non-affixed forms such as auxiliaries are less grammaticized than affixes; affixes are more grammaticized if they are more reduced (e.g., shorter), cause changes in the stem, or undergo changes caused by the stem. As one instance of this continuing development, consider the Spanish future forms discussed previously. Some time after affixation had occurred, the new suffixes began to condition changes in certain verbs. Thus the combination *veniré* 'I will come' changed to *vendré*; *quereré* 'I will want' changed to *querré*; *teneré* 'I will have' changed to *tendré*. Such changes can be taken to indicate increased fusion between the stem and the suffix.

Another point worth mentioning here is that affixation is not just a matter of form. While it is true that two elements that occur together very frequently will have a tendency to fuse to one another, the formation of a true affix requires that there be a degree of conceptual coherence between the two elements. Thus tense and aspect markers tend to fuse with verbs, while case, gender, and definiteness markers tense to fuse with nouns (Bybee, 1985). In contrast, English contractions such as *I'll, I've, he's, we're*, etc., tend not to produce true affixes because of the lack of conceptual coherence between the subject and auxiliary.

Morphological Typology

It has long been observed that languages tend towards different types in their morphological expression (Sapir, 1921). This typology is largely a matter of the degree of fusion among morphemes, but there is also a measurable difference in the degree of grammaticization of morphemes. Some languages allow no affixation; all words consist of single morphemes. An example of such a language, referred to as analytic or isolating, is Mandarin Chinese. In Mandarin, most words are monomorphemic, although compounds do exist, and a few suffix-like morphemes are developing from compounds in the way described above. Nouns and pronouns do not change in form in subject and object functions, verbs do not agree with nouns, and there are no obligatory categories (inflections) marked on verbs or nouns or any word forms at all.

Synthetic languages, or languages which do have polymorphemic words and inflections, are divided into types according to how much fusion exists among the morphemes of a word. In agglutinative languages, morphemes are more loosely strung together; it is relatively easy to divide a word into morphemes, as there is little phonological fusion at boundaries between morphemes, and morphemes do not vary in their shape greatly. Consider the following example from Turkish.

> *demizlerimizde*   'in our oceans'
> *deniz - ler - im - iz - de*
> ocean plural 1st plural in

Fusional languages do not exhibit such neat separability of morphemes, but rather show some of the following characteristics: (i) Several grammatical morphemes may be expressed in a single consonant or vowel; e.g., in Spanish *canté* 'I sang,' the vowel *é* expresses the conjugation class (First Conjugation),' the Preterite aspect and First Person Singular; (ii) a number of different variants may occur for a single meaning, as in Latin, where the Nominative Singular could be marked by *-a, -us, -um, -is, ū, ēs* or zero; (iii) the same meaning may be distributed over various parts of the word, rather than residing in a single morpheme, as in the following analysis from Matthews (1991, pp. 170-179) of the Greek verb *elelýkete,* 'you had unfastened':

		(root)	*Perfective*	*Indicative*	*Active*
Past	*Perfective*	*Perfective*	*Active*	*Past Active*	*2nd Plural*
e	le	ly	k	e	te

In this example it is notable that Past is expressed twice while Perfective and Active are indicated three times each. One could easily conclude that there is more to this word than the simple concatenation of meaningful elements.

Sapir (1921) originally argued that languages differ not only in morphological form but also in the types of grammatical meanings that are expressed. It follows that if a language does not have inflection it does not express inflectional meaning. Thus if Mandarin Chinese does not have obligatory categories, it cannot express the same sense of tense as does English, which obligatorily expresses tense. Instead, Mandarin expresses more specific aspectual notions using auxiliaries and compounds. Bybee, Pagliuca, and Perkins (1991) have shown that languages which have less fusion and less grammaticization of form also express meanings that are less grammatical (i.e., more lexical). It appears that part of what is behind morphological typology is a tendency for some languages not to carry grammaticization as far as other languages do. This finding raises the very important issue of what drives grammaticization and what language-specific properties could encourage or inhibit the process.

Languages With Various Types of Morphological Structures

Because grammaticization is an ongoing process at all times, languages often have structures of different morphological types coexisting, often even expressing very similar meanings. Hopper (1991) has pointed out that the renewal of morphology leads to a situation in which newer and older structures create 'layers' in a language. One of his examples concerns the various ways that past tense is expressed in English. The oldest layer still surviving is that represented by the strong verbs, such as *break, broke, sing, sang, know, knew,* etc., which conserve the Proto-Germanic method of forming past tense through vowel changes.[1] Of course, this oldest method is preserved only in the most frequent lexical items. The next method of past tense formation which developed, also before the Old English period, arose from a periphrastic construction in which the past form of the verb *do,* the predecessor of modern *did,* followed the main verb to signal past tense. This auxiliary suffixed to the verb to give modern -*ed*, which, as the productive past tense suffix, has gradually been replacing the older vowel-change method. The newest development echoes the previous one: *did* is used preceding the unmarked verb to signal past tense in questions, negative clauses, and emphatic clauses. Note that the age of the construction correlates with the degree of fusion between grammatical marker and stem. The oldest method shows the greatest fusion, since it is a vowel change in the stem, the next method is more agglutinative as it uses suffixation, and the newest method is the most analytic.

In this particular case the three structures all express the same meaning, but it is more common to find that different structural types correspond to different meanings. In particular, a less grammaticized construction will express a meaning that is more specific and lexical in its content, while a more grammaticized construction will express a meaning that is more abstract. Compare the less grammaticized English *keep on dancing* and *used to dance* with *is dancing* and *danced.*

MORPHOLOGY VERSUS SYNTAX

A tendency exists in structuralist linguistics to view morphology as analogous to syntax—morphemes are strung together to form words just as words are strung

---

[1]I claimed earlier that most grammatical morphology develops from whole words reducing to affixes. What then of these strong verbs in English? It is very likely that they also have their source in the regular grammaticization process. Affixes could have conditioned these stem changes and later been lost from the verbs, leaving only the stem change to signal past tense meaning.

together to form clauses. The numerous ways in which morphology differs from syntax, however, strongly suggest a different type of processing, in particular, that full words, even multimorphemic ones, can be stored in the lexicon. The reason that morphology resembles syntax, I would argue, is that it is *old* syntax, since affixes were previously separate words (Givón, 1979). The point I want to highlight is that affixes would not develop the properties that distinguish them from independent words unless they were somehow processed differently.

The traditional criteria for determining whether a grammatical morpheme is an affix or an independent word or particle are the following:

(i) affixes occur in a fixed position with regard to the lexical stem; they are not free to change their position or their scope;

(ii) no open class items (other nouns, verbs, adjectives, or adverbs) intervene between the affix and the stem; compare English auxiliaries, which allow adverbs to come between them and the verb: *I have really tried.*

(iii) there is a high degree of interdependence between affix and stem, such that certain stems choose certain affixes: *cats, mice, oxen.*

(iv) there may be phonological fusion between affix and stem in the form of assimilation (as in [kæts] but [dɔgz]) or the coalescence of segments (as in *decide + ion* giving [dɪsɪʒən]); and

(v) the stem plus affix combination behaves phonologically like a word, for instance by acting as the domain for phonological processes such as vowel harmony or by being stressed as a single word rather than as two words.

All of these criteria reflect a very high degree of fusion or bonding between stem and affix. The initial bonding and the continued increase in the degree of fusion that is characteristic of affixal development over time indicate that speakers take the stem-affix combination to be a single unit, traditionally called a word, and that this unit has the status of a stored cognitive entity, which we would regard as a stored lexical representation. If morphologically complex words are stored in the lexicon, then some mechanisms for representing their internal complexity, the regularity of certain patterns, and the ability to form new words must be postulated. We now turn to these matters.

MORPHOLOGY IN THE LEXICON

Human beings appear to have (at least) two important capacities that make language possible: (i) the ability to store tens, perhaps hundreds, of thousands of individual lexical items with detailed information about their behavior and meaning; and (ii) the ability to concatenate series of linguistic units to form meaningful utterances. The fact that morphology differs from syntax by exhibiting a greater bonding between units suggests that the first ability is being made use of for storing and processing morphology perhaps to a greater extent than the second ability.

Linguists have objected to the idea that morphologically complex words are stored in the lexicon for two reasons: First, they fear the loss of important generalizations concerning word structure and phonological alternations, and second they argue that in morphologically complex languages the number of words is too great for lexical storage of all words. But these objections are based on an oversimplified view of the lexicon as resembling a dictionary, where words are set down permanently, in an arbitrary order, and each one is isolated from all others. If we view the lexicon as part of the human memory bank, the analogy with the dictionary fails. Rather, three important properties apply to lexical storage: Some stored items are stronger than others, there are multiple relationships among stored items, and generalizations may be formed over properties of stored items, or properties of relationships among items. These general properties of memory can account for much of what has traditionally been viewed as morphological phenomena, and in addition, they can account for aspects of morphological structure that have been traditionally ignored by structural linguists. But before explaining how these properties can capture the generalizations that linguists consider important, let us consider the question of the number of words that are plausibly stored in the lexicon.

Hankamer (1992) argues against the position that *all* possible words of a language are stored in the lexicon on the basis of agglutinative languages such as Turkish, where by his calculations a single verb root has the theoretical possibility of having over a million forms. Sadock (1980) makes similar arguments for languages in which incorporation of a noun into a verb form is a common practice. Of course, not all of the possible words in these languages would actually be semantically or pragmatically plausible, and only some of them would be in common usage. Thus, the model of Bybee (1985) proposes that morphologically complex words may be stored in the lexicon, even if they are regular, but that words of high frequency are more likely to be stored whole, while regular formations of lower frequency are more likely to be formed by combination and not stored. The complex words that the speaker uses frequently and which are entered in the lexicon serve as the basis for the formation of the unstored, less frequent words, in a way that I explain in the next section.

Lexical Connections

Let us now consider the model that follows from the three properties of memory mentioned above: that some stored items are stronger than others, that there are relations among stored items, and that generalizations may be formed over stored items. In Bybee (1985) I proposed a model of morphology based on the notions of *lexical strength* and *lexical connection*. This model has some features of models of lexical storage developed about the same time in cognitive studies (Langacker, 1987) and some properties of processing proposed for connectionist frameworks (Dell, 1991; Rumelhart & McClelland, 1986). I adopt some terminology from these studies in the description of this model.

First, I assume that memory for linguistic units is superpositional; as I argued in Bybee (1985), every time a word or a larger linguistic unit (a phrase or idiom) is processed, it is mapped onto, or superimposed on, some existing representation (unless, of course, it is being heard for the first time). If meaning and phonological form of the word in processing matches a stored representation, then it is mapped onto that representation, which is consequently strengthened. As a result, high frequency words will have greater *lexical strength* than low frequency words; this will account for their relatively greater ease of activation, and other properties as well, as we shall see in the next section.

If, on the other hand, meaning and phonological shape only partially match a stored representation, then the mapping can only be partial, and instead of a direct mapping of the item in processing with a stored representation, the new item goes into storage with the partial mapping to other stored forms represented by *lexical connections*.[2] Lexical connections are of both a semantic and a phonological nature. Thus, synonyms such as *fast* and *quick* will have semantic connections but no phonological ones. Homophones such as *plane* and *plain* will have phonological but no semantic relations. Related words such as *cat* and *kitten* have partial semantic connections and some (unsystematic) partial phonological ones. Parallel phonological and semantic connections, if they represent a pattern found in multiple sets of items, constitute morphological relations.[3] Thus, the word *started* maps only partially onto *start*, with the suffix not matching any material in *start*. However, the suffix itself can map onto other occurrences of the same suffix, creating a complex of morphological relations as in Figure 1:[4]

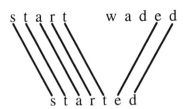

FIGURE 1. Lexical connections among regularly inflected words.

[2]A form that is directly mapped onto a stored form may also form partial connections, particularly if it is morphologically complex.

[3]This statement is a correction of the statement made in Bybee (1985, 1988), where I said that parallel semantic and phonological connections constitute morphological relations. If there were only one pair of items with such connections this would not be regarded as constituting a morphological relation. What is considered morphological apparently needs to apply to multiple sets of relations.

[4]These schematic representations using orthography are not intended to make any statement about the nature of phonological segmentation.

The existence of lexical connections for partial mappings yields an internal morphological analysis of complex words without any other mechanisms being necessary. The analysis of *started* into two 'morphemes' is represented by the connections that word has with the stem *start* and other instances of the suffix *-ed*. Such a representation captures the fact that we only learn that words are morphologically complex by comparing them to other related words. This model, then, allows the storage of whole words as well as information about their internal complexity. It does not insist, as a morpheme-based model would, however, that all words be exhaustively divisible into morphemes and thus allows for the unproblematic representation of complexity even in words where some constituent parts do not actually have morpheme status, words such as *cranberry* (consisting unmistakably of *berry*, but with the non-morpheme *cran* as its other part) or the days of the week such as *Tuesday, Wednesday,* and so on (Bybee, 1988).

In this model, then, morphemes do not have independent status and representation. They are rather seen as epiphenomenal or 'emergent' in the sense of Hopper (1987). Other models with this property are the 'word and paradigm' models of Matthews (1972, 1991) and Anderson (1992). Such models account naturally for the type of inflected word analyzed in the section on Morphological Typology. The Greek word *elelykete,* 'unfastened,' does not display a one-to-one relation between the meanings expressed in it and the form; rather, the notion of perfective is distributed over three elements in this word, as is the notion of active. The greater semantic and phonological fusion exhibited in a single word, the less attractive a strict morpheme-by-morpheme description appears to be.

The current model is quite appropriate for Semitic languages, where lexical roots consist only of consonants and much derivational and some inflectional morphology is expressed by changing the vowel pattern of the word and to a much lesser extent, the consonants of the root themselves. Lexical connections can be made between the consonants of two forms of the same root, as shown in Figure 2, while independently the vowel patterns of words of the same morphological category can be related, as shown in Figure 3.

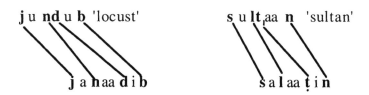

FIGURE 2. Lexical connections between two Arabic nouns and their plurals.

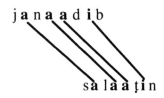

FIGURE 3. Lexical connections between two Arabic plural nouns.

Bentin and Frost (this volume) present evidence that suggests for Hebrew that derivatives of a root are each listed in the lexicon, but that their representations are also interrelated.

Moreover, they find evidence that the vowel pattern and the root are separated in the process of word identification even though neither are listed separately. Such conclusions are totally compatible with the type of representation depicted in Figures 2 and 3. In the section on the Treatment of Patterns in the Lexicon, we discuss the way that recurrent patterns, such as multiple instances of Semitic nouns that are pluralized by the same vowel pattern, are treated in this model.

Lexical connections also easily accommodate agglutinative morphology, such as that illustrated by Turkish earlier, since the constituent parts of words, in this case the suffixes, map onto instances of these same suffixes in other words. The Turkish lexicon will of course look rather different from the Greek or Semitic lexicon, but the difference in structure will be entirely due to the nature of the linguistic material that is entered in the lexicon. The basic principles of lexical strength and lexical connection remain the same.

Considerable evidence exists for differential strengths of lexical connections. On the phonological side, lexical connections can be computed simply from shared phonological features, although the possibility that some shared features create stronger lexical connections than others cannot be ruled out. (Thus, a general feature such as syllabic will be less important to morphological relatedness than a more specific one, such as velar or round.) With semantic features, the number of identical matches will of course be an important determinant of morphological relatedness, but here the evidence is good that sharing some features produces stronger morphological relations than sharing others. In particular, shared features that are more 'relevant' to the stem, in the sense of Bybee (1985), comprise stronger relations than those that are less relevant. Thus, for verbs, aspect and tense distinctions are more relevant to the verb and produce larger meaning changes than person/number agreement. We expect, then, that verb forms in the same tense or aspect category are closely related despite differences in person and number. While this hypothesis awaits experimental testing (but see Stanners, Neiser, Hernon, & Hall, 1979, and Bybee & Pardo, 1981, for applicable experimental results), there is considerable linguistic evidence for it: A strong cross-linguistic pattern shows morphophonemic differences aligned with tense and aspect categories, rather than person/number categories. This can be illustrated with Spanish examples, where morphophonemic differences in the verb tend to coincide with the important aspectual distinction of perfective/imperfective:

Imperfective (Past)		Perfective	
	tener 'to have'		
ten-ía	ten-íamos	tuv-e	tuv-imos
ten-ías	ten-íais	tuv-iste	tuv-isteis
ten-ía	ten-ían	tuv-o	tuv-ieron

In a substantial set of high frequency verbs, stem changes produce the result that there is one common stem for the imperfective and one for the perfective. The person/number forms within each aspect are very similar to one another, being very closely related. On the other hand, since person/number agreement is a minor semantic dimension for verbs, forms sharing the same person/number, such as first person *tenía* and *tuve*, are not as closely related.

Lexical Strength

The proposal that lexical items differ in their relative lexical strength is based very simply on the idea that much-used items are more ingrained or entrenched in memory that lesser used items. This notion accounts for a number of psycholinguistic, diachronic, and typological facts about morphology. I have already mentioned that lexical strength can account for the relatively greater ease of access of frequent words over infrequent ones. In the following I mention other phenomena that can be accounted for with a notion of lexical strength.

First, there is a universal tendency for morphological irregularity to be restricted to the highest frequency forms of a language. Thus, irregular verbs tend to have such frequently used meanings as 'come,' 'go,' 'have,' and 'be.' Or, if there is a large number of irregular verbs, their meanings will not so much be predictable as their relatively high frequency. Thus, among the 30 most frequent verbs of English, 22 are irregular according to Francis and Kučera (1982). Nouns with irregular plurals are commonly the words for man, woman, child, or common livestock animals. Also, irregular plurals tend to reside in nouns in which the plural is much used—nouns designating objects that come in pairs or groups (*mice, feet, teeth, oxen, geese*) (see Tiersma, 1982, and discussion following).

Much morphological irregularity develops naturally as the byproduct of phonological change. For example, a general voicing of fricatives (such as *s, f,* and *th*) between vowels in Middle English gives us an alternation in singular/plural pairs such as *wife, wives, leaf, leaves,* and *house, hou*[z]*es.* Again in Middle English, the shortening of vowels before certain consonant clusters yielded irregularity in *sleep, slept, keep, kept, weep, wept*, and *leap, leapt*, among others. An irony long noted by historical linguists is that regular sound changes create irregular morphology. A further irony is that re-establishment of the morphological regularity undoes the phonological regularity. That is, it is common for the morphological regularity to reassert itself and for new regular forms to appear (formed on the basic form of the paradigm, see following discussion). For instance, new regular past tense forms *weeped* and *leaped* are considered acceptable in current English.

One of our interests in this diachronic process of regularization lies in the fact that infrequent words tend to regularize before frequent ones. Thus, while *weeped* and *leaped* are acceptable as past tense forms, the highly frequent **keeped* and **sleeped* clearly are not (Hooper, 1976). In fact, the entire pattern of regularization of strong verbs in the last millennium in English shows that infrequent verbs regularize and the frequent ones maintain the vowel change as the indicator of past tense and past participle status (Bybee, 1985, pp. 119-120). This diachronic pattern of regularization then leads to the synchronic pattern (which is cross-linguistically valid) in which only the relatively high-frequency forms tend to be irregular.

The notion of lexical strength determined by frequency accounts for this pattern in the following way: If frequent words have stronger representations than infrequent ones, they are more easily accessed and there is no need to create new regular forms. If, on the other hand, infrequent irregulars are only weakly represented, they are not so easily accessed and are thus more likely to be replaced by newly formed regulars. (More discussion of the treatment of regulars and irregulars in this model follows.)

The other relevant fact about the regularization process, which can also be accounted for by lexical strength, is the fact that the direction of change in morphological regularization is usually predictable. When there is an alternation or allomorphy in a morpheme—that is, when a morpheme has two variants— such as *house, hou*[z]*es* or *weep, wept*, regularization entails the loss of one of the allomorphs or variants, accomplished by the replacement of one variant for the other. (This is also known as 'analogical leveling' in historical linguistics.) Interestingly, we are often able to predict which variant survives and replaces the other—it is usually the variant in the category member that is the most basic, the least marked, and the most frequent (Kuryłowicz, 1968; Mańczak, 1980).

Thus, in nouns we expect the variant used in the singular to replace the one used in the plural; so many people say *hou*[s]*es* for the plural, but no one tries *hou*[z] for the singular noun. In languages with case marking the nominative is usually the basic member, and in European gender systems, the masculine is basic. For verbs, the present indicative is more basic than the past or future or other moods (see Greenberg, 1966). Thus, for English we find the regularization of the past tense form in *weeped* and *leaped* and not a change in the base or present form giving **wep* and **lep*.

While some (Jakobson, 1957; Kuryłowicz, 1968) would argue that markedness or basicness is a purely structural dimension, Greenberg (1966) has shown that a major correlate of markedness is frequency. That is, the basic or unmarked member of a category is the most frequently occurring member of the category. Moreover, Tiersma (1982) has shown that the frequency criterion can predict apparent exceptions to the rule that the least marked member survives in leveling, while the structural account cannot. In West Frisian (a dialect of a West Germanic language, spoken primarily on islands off the coasts of The Netherlands) singular and plural forms of many nouns have vowel alternations: *hoer, hworren,* 'whore,' *koal, kwallen,* 'coal,' and these tend to regularize with the stem of the singular replacing that of the plural: *hoer, hoeren* and *koal, koalen.* However, some nouns regularize in the opposite direction, with the stem of the plural replacing that of the singular: thus *earm, jermen,* 'arm,' becomes *jerm, jermen* and *goes, gwozzen* becomes *gwos, gwozzen.* Tiersma argues that nouns which more frequently occur in texts in the plural because their referents more commonly occur in the real world in pairs or groups have the plural as their "least marked" or "basic" form. The nouns that regularize on the basis of the plural are 'arm' and 'goose' as shown above and 'animal horn,' 'stocking,' 'tooth,' 'wood shaving or splinter,' 'thorn,' and 'tear.' Thus, it is actually frequency which determines the member that survives in regularization and not a structural relation.

Since members of paradigms differ in their token frequency, they also differ in their lexical strength; the more frequent member(s) will be easier to access than the less frequent ones, as shown in Sereno and Jongman (1991). If the less frequent members of a paradigm are not accessible, a speaker would have to create a new form on the basis of the one that is available, regularizing on the basis of the most frequent form of the paradigm. This would be particularly likely to happen if the whole paradigm is low in frequency.

The differential lexical strength of members of paradigms leads to a hierarchical structure for paradigms in which more frequent members dominate the less frequent members. We return in the next section to a discussion of paradigm-internal relations.

Further evidence for lexical strength is found in the creation and maintenance of suppletive paradigms. I am using the term "suppletion" in its narrowest sense, in which it refers to synchronic inflectionally related forms that come from different roots historically. In English the examples from verbs are *go, went* and *is, be, were*; in French we find *va, allons,* etc., 'go,' as well as *être, suis,* etc., 'be.' In adjectives suppletion occurs in *good, better, best; much, more, most; bad, worse, worst*; cf. Spanish *bueno* 'good' and *mejor,* 'better, best,' *mal,* 'bad,' and *peor,* 'worse, worst.' The first fact to observe about suppletion is that it occurs only in the most frequent paradigms (Rudes, 1980). For our purposes, the way suppletion arises is of considerable interest: In order for a suppletive paradigm to develop, it is necessary for a form that once belonged to one paradigm to split away from that paradigm and join another. For instance, *went* was formerly the past tense form for *wend*, meaning to go turning or winding along. Now *went* has no semantic or morphological relation with *wend* but rather is associated with *go*. In order for that to have happened, *went* had to have lexical autonomy from *wend*, which would be possible if it became very frequent (eventually more frequent than *wend*) and had a high degree of lexical strength. The possibility of a split of a non-basic form of a paradigm from the basic form indicates that it must have had its own lexical representation despite the strong phonological relation between the two. The fact that only frequent paradigms have suppletion suggests that frequency is important in determining lexical representation. Suppletion also helps us understand the relation between lexical strength and lexical connections, which we turn to in the next section.

Interaction of Lexical Strength with Lexical Connections

The notion of lexical connection is based on the idea that linguistic units (like other units of perception and memory) are often understood and remembered in terms of other linguistic units. However, high frequency units are available enough in the input to be remembered as autonomous items. Members of high frequency paradigms, then, will all have a high degree of lexical strength and be less dependent upon connections with other members of the paradigm, while low frequency paradigms will be characterized by stronger lexical connections among the members.

The evidence for this inverse relation between lexical strength and lexical connections come from diachronic splits among related items, both in inflection, where it results in suppletion, and in derivation, where it results in divergent meaning among historically related forms, such as *awe, awful,* and *awfully.* As mentioned above, it is clear that inflectional suppletion is heavily determined by frequency. Splits among derivationally related items are much more common, but frequency appears to play an important role in this process as well. Infrequent derived forms will tend to maintain a close relation with the base from which they derived, but frequent derived forms will diverge in both meaning and form and tend to become autonomous (Bybee, 1985, pp. 88-89). Words beginning with the prefix *pre-* in English show this trend clearly. Pagliuca (1976) studied the 323 words with this prefix listed in the Shorter Oxford English Dictionary and, using the definitions provided there, rated them as having transparent or opaque meaning according to whether or not their sense was a simple combination of the meaning 'before' with the stem's meaning. A strong association between frequency and opacity emerged, as did an association with the extent of vowel reduction, as shown in Table 1.

These facts suggest that phonological fusion of prefix to stem and reduction of the prefix (phonological opacity) are related to the development of unpredictable meaning (semantic opacity), and both of these factors are related to token frequency.

TABLE 1.

Vowel Quality	Percent of Words with Average Frequency	Percent of Words with Predictable Meaning	Example
[iy]	5.74	74.76	predecease
[i]	2.54	59.52	predestine
[ɪ]	49.80	3.30	prediction
[ɛ]	81.32	2.89	preface

Since related forms may maintain a close relation or diverge gradually over time, the lexicon contains a range of types of relations among forms; on one end of the scale are the forms with the strongest lexical connections, i.e., the semantically and phonologically transparent words in pairs such as *happy, happiness* or *pure, purity*. Going down the scale, lexical connections weaken because of lessened phonological or semantic similarity, or the high frequency of derived forms. *Opaque, opacity* have a lesser phonological similarity, *recite, recital* have a lesser semantic similarity (one does not necessarily recite at a recital), and *face, facet* differ phonologically and also semantically, or at least their range of usage is so different that people rarely view them as related; *awe* and *awful* are phonologically transparent and not radically semantically divergent, but their frequency disparity weakens their connectedness (*awful* is three times as frequent as *awe* according to Francis & Kučera, 1982). A similar scale can be applied to inflection (see Bybee, 1985, pp. 91-96).

In this model, then, regular and irregular morphological relations, productive and nonproductive relations among words are represented using the same mechanisms. The differences among them, from which we derive our notions of regularity and productivity are due to the type frequency of the various morphological relations and the ease with which language users can construct generalizations over these relations.

The Treatment of Patterns in the Lexicon

Given the superpositional mapping of items in processing onto stored items, inflectional affixes will accumulate considerable lexical strength. The higher type frequency of English plural *-(e)s* over irregular plural *-en* accounts for the former's greater availability for new formations. The allomorph *-en* occurs in the very frequent word *children*, but given the irregularity of this word (vis à vis its singular counterpart) and its very high frequency, any lexical connections it might have to the suffix in *oxen* would be very weak and would not contribute to the strength of this allomorph. It is the type frequency of affixes that determines their relative productivity, not their token frequency (see MacWhinney, 1978, and Bybee, 1985, pp. 132-134).

Lexical connections also provide a means for representing minor lexical patterns that arise because small groups of words share some salient characteristics. Among English strong verbs there is one class that exhibits some productivity, given a verb of the appropriate phonological shape: Many past tense verbs end in the vowel [ʌ] plus a velar and/or a nasal, e.g., *stung, strung, hung, stuck, struck, dug,* etc. This partial similarity in the rhymes of these verbs paired with the meaning 'past tense' produces a series of connections describable as a schema, which then is applicable to other items, such as *sneak* yielding *snuck,* or *drag* yielding *drug* in some American dialects.

In Bybee and Moder (1983) we pointed out that the formation of such a schema depended upon there being a critical mass of words exhibiting the pattern (the minimum being around six or eight, see Bybee & Pardo, 1981) and that the participating words not be of such high frequency that they form no connections, or only form weak ones, for without lexical connections no schema could emerge.

Thus, regular and irregular patterns are treated the same way in this model. The difference between them is an automatic consequence of the number of items that participate, the relative frequency of the items and, in the case of minor patterns, the degree to which participating items resemble one another. Approaches that treat regular and irregular patterns as governed by different *types* of processing, i.e., rules vs. schemas (Marcus, Pinker, Ullman, Hollander, Rosen, & Xu, 1992) or as processing at different levels (Kiparsky, 1982) fail to account for the fact that regular patterns have wider applicability, while in the current model this is accounted for by the strength of the regular pattern, which is totally derivative of its applicability or type frequency.[5] The traditionally cited evidence that regular patterns are best accounted for with disembodied symbolic rules, while irregular patterns may be lexical, is the overgeneralization of regular patterns found in children's speech and the rarity of generalization of irregular patterns. However, Marcus et al. (1992) have found in a massive study of the generalization of regular past tense in English that overgeneralization of regular past tense to irregular verbs occurs in only 2.5% of irregular productions during the period in which children are overgeneralizing. This low level of generalization of the regular pattern does not suggest rule-governed behavior but rather is more consistent with the treatment of even regular patterns as lexical generalizations.

---

[5]A case is made in Clahsen and Rothweiler (1992) that the productive German participle ending *-t* does not have a higher type frequency than the suffix *-en,* but this case depends upon counting the German verbs with separable prefixes as different types. This is comparable to counting English *break up, break down, break in two,* etc., as different verbs rather than considering them all to be instances of the verb *break.* If such instances are counted as examples of one type, then the suffix *-t* does have a substantially higher type frequency than *-en.*

The Treatment of Regular Inflected Forms

While many researchers agree that there are good reasons to list irregular morphological forms in the lexicon, as I have just mentioned, regular formations are usually treated as derived by combinatory rules. In the model being described here it is proposed that high frequency forms are treated the same, whether they are regular or irregular. Even regular forms may develop a greater lexical strength due to a high level of usage. On the other hand, the lexical patterns that emerge from the lexical connections yield a means by which lower frequency regular forms may be produced by combination. Thus, both lexical access and combinatory generation are available in this model, with frequency determining the method to be used, which is the reason that Losiewicz (1992) refers to the current model as a 'dual-access frequency-dependent' model.

Stemberger and MacWhinney (1986, 1988) demonstrate that in naturally occurring and experimentally induced speech errors involving English verbs, high-frequency regular items have a lower error rate than low-frequency items. They interpret this to mean that at least high-frequency inflected regulars are stored in the lexicon. However, their evidence does not bear on the question of whether or not low-frequency regularly inflected forms are stored in the lexicon.

Losiewicz (1992) presents experimental results indicating that high-frequency inflected forms are stored lexically while low-frequency forms are not. Her experiments were based on a previous finding by Walsh and Parker (1983), who reported that morphemic /s/ in English words such as *laps* is significantly longer than non-morphemic /s/ in words such as *lapse*. Losiewicz hypothesized that if high-frequency inflected forms were lexically stored but low-frequency forms were not, then the suffix (in this case past tense /d/) would be longer in the latter words than in the former. This is exactly the result that she obtained; when comparing verbs such as *needed / kneaded* and *covered / hovered*, she found a difference in length in the predicted direction for every subject and every verb pair.

Losiewicz interprets this result in the current framework in which both whole words and their connections to other words are stored in the lexicon. She says:

> For high frequency multi-morphemic words, the most highly primed, and activated, item would be the whole word representation. For low frequency words, the multi-morphemic word would not have a strong lexical representation (i.e., would not be highly primed), so a construction process of stem + affix would be the most readily available, and fastest, processing route. (p. 50)

As for the reason for the length difference in the suffix, my own interpretation of this is that an affix is more highly fused to the stem in a frequent combination than in an infrequent one.[6] Thus, the attached affix in the stored representation of a word would be shorter than the stronger, more autonomous representation of the affix.

The Representation of Paradigms

A paradigm is a set of inflectionally related words sharing the same stem. In English, paradigms are relatively simple: Each count noun has two forms, a singular and a plural, and since most of these are regular, the plural form need not be strongly represented. For verbs there are several forms: *play, plays, playing,* and *played,* and for irregulars sometimes there is a difference between the past tense and the past participle form. Still, this amounts to only five forms for each verb, with four being much more common. But other languages have much more complex paradigms for verbs, and sometimes for nouns as well. How are these paradigms accommodated within the current model?

Paradigms are represented as clusters of highly connected words. The strongest words may be thought of as bases around which other words cluster. Especially in languages with complex morphology, there may be more than one strong form per paradigm. Evidence from acquisition and morphophonemic patterning and change in Spanish and Portuguese suggests that in these languages the Present tense of a verb has a base or strong form (usually the third singular form), and the Preterite may have two strong forms (the first and third singular forms). In Bybee and Brewer (1980) we showed what emerged as the base forms in Preterite paradigms in diachronic restructuring were also the most frequent forms in these paradigms.

The following paradigm is the standard Spanish Preterite for First Conjugation and the result of largely regular phonological changes applied to the Latin Perfect:

	Singular	Plural
1st	canté	cantámos
2nd	cantáste	cantásteis
3rd	cantó	cantáron

In various dialects of the Iberian Peninsula, changes have occurred in paradigms of this sort. The most common change is the change of first plural to *cantémos.* This change can be analyzed as the formation of a new first plural on the basis of the stronger first singular form *canté,* with the suffix *-mos,* which is perfectly regular in every first plural form, added to it. Another common change is the construction of a new second singular on the basis of the third singular, again a low frequency form being rebuilt on the basis of a high frequency form.

---

[6]This claim perhaps reminds the reader of Zipf's (1935) demonstration that frequent words strongly tend to be shorter than infrequent ones. Zipf was apparently unaware that the mechanism that creates this correlation is gradual phonetic reduction and fusion.

These changes show that both the first and third singular are strongly represented in these Preterite paradigms, and the lower frequency forms are either weakly represented as connected to the stronger forms or they are created on-line by applying schemas to the stronger forms. The diachronic evidence suggests, then, that a single paradigm, even of a regular stem, can have multiple strongly represented forms. In the case just discussed, in addition to the representation of the Preterite, the Present, Imperfect, and other tenses will also have to be represented. Moreover, the evidence presented in the section on Lexical Strength concerning the role of frequency in determining lexical strength shows that different paradigms, even if they are structurally the same, can have a different organization in the lexicon. For instance, in most noun paradigms the singular will be the strongest member, but in others, such as the nouns denoting 'arms,' 'geese,' or 'horns' the plural could be the strongest form.

Losiewicz (1992) points out that in this model, since parts of words may be connected or strengthened by repetition, stems will be highly primed as well as the frequent words that contain them. This accounts for the fact that the frequency of both the stem and the inflected forms of a word contribute to its latency in lexical decision tasks (Burani, Salmaso, & Caramazza, 1984; Nagy, Anderson, Schommer, Scott, & Stallman, 1989). Moreover, while some restructuring can be analyzed as the addition of affixes to existing words, as in the case of *cantémos* produced from the word *canté*, there are cases in languages in which stems seem to play a role in the creation of new forms.

SUBSTANCE DETERMINES STRUCTURE

In the model being described here the substance of words—their actual phonological and semantic substance—determines not only their structure but the larger structure of the lexicon and morphology into which they fit. There are no predetermined modules or levels of description; all the structure that is built up in the lexicon emerges precisely from the words or phrases that are stored there.

The lack of modules or strict components separating rules from representations means that the model is capable of handling various sorts of gradient phenomena as well as languages of different morphological types. I have already pointed out that regular and irregular patterns are handled in the same way, with the only difference between them being the number of items involved, which determines how strong or entrenched the pattern is.

Similarly, inflectional and derivational morphology are treated the same way; the differences between them emerge from the fact that inflectional forms tend to be more closely related semantically, and they tend to fit into highly entrenched patterns (see Bybee, 1985). The fact that derivational processes at times do have the properties of inflection, that is, they can also be highly productive and make small meaning changes, and the fact that some high frequency inflected forms are very irregular and can even split apart from related forms means that we cannot draw a strict line between inflection and derivation and proposals such as Anderson's (1982, 1992), which assign inflection and derivation to different components of the grammar, cannot be maintained.

Another gradient phenomenon that this model can accommodate well is the gradual nature of grammaticization. As grammaticizing elements reduce and begin to develop into affixes, we must allow for a gradual passage from independent to dependent status. The current model, which does not insist that units be strictly categorized as 'in' the lexicon or 'out of' the lexicon, would allow a newly developing affix to be stored with its stem if it is a high frequency combination; a sufficient number of such combinations would lead to the generalization that the unit has become an affix. Further fusion between stem and affix serves as evidence that the new word is taken to be a coherent semantic, phonological, prosodic, and indeed, lexical unit.

Finally, the typological differences among languages in this view derive from the differences in substance that give rise to differences in structure. The amount of morphological complexity in a language will be measured by the number of related words and the complexity of their connections to one another. An agglutinative language will be characterized by highly entrenched regular affixes with few variants and by less overlap in connections at boundaries. A fusional language will have more complex relations and more variations on relations, including a wider range of patterns and more irregular forms that do not participate in dominant patterns.

ACKNOWLEDGMENT

I would like to thank Carol Fowler and Beth Losiewicz for valuable comments on an earlier version of this chapter.

REFERENCES

Anderson, S. (1982). Where's morphology? *Linguistic Inquiry, 13,* 571-612.

Anderson, S. (1992). *A-morphous morphology.* Cambridge: Cambridge University Press.

Burani, C., Salmaso, D., & Caramazza, A. (1984). Morphological structure and lexical access. *Visible Language, 18,* 342-352.

Bybee, J. (1985). *Morphology: A study of the relation between meaning and form.* Amsterdam: John Benjamins.

Bybee, J. (1988). Morphology as lexical organization. In M. Hammond & M. Noonan (Eds.), *Theoretical Morphology.* New York: Academic Press.

Bybee, J., & Brewer, M. (1980). Explanation in morphophonemics: Changes in Provençal and Spanish preterite forms. *Lingua, 52,* 271-312.

Bybee, J., & Pardo, E. (1981). On lexical and morphological conditioning of alternations: A nonce-probe experiment with Spanish verbs. *Linguistics, 19,* 937-968.

Bybee, J., & Moder, C. (1983). Morphological classes as natural categories. *Language, 59,* 251-270.

Bybee, J., Pagliuca, W., & Perkins, R. (1991). Back to the future. In E. Traugott & B. Heine (Eds.), *Approaches to grammaticalization.* Amsterdam: John Benjamins.

Bybee, J., Perkins, R., & Pagliuca, W. (1994). *The evolution of grammar: Tense, aspect, and modality in the languages of the world.* Chicago: University of Chicago Press.

Dell, G., & Juliano, C. (1991). Connectionist approaches to the production of words. *Cognitive Science Technical Reports CS-91-05.* Urbana, Illinois: The Beckman Institute.

Francis, W. N., & Kučera, H. (1982). *Frequency analysis of English usage.* Boston: Houghton Mifflin.

Givón, T. (1979). *On understanding grammar.* New York: Academic Press.

Greenberg, J. (1966). *Language universals.* The Hague: Mouton.

Hankamer, J. (1992). Morphological parsing and the lexicon. In W. Marslen-Wilson (Ed.), *Lexical representation and process.* Cambridge, MA: MIT Press.

Heine, B., Claudi, U., & Hünnemeyer, F. (1991). *Grammaticalization: A conceptual framework.* Chicago: University of Chicago Press.

Heine, B., & Reh, M. (1984). *Grammaticalization and reanalysis in African languages.* Hamburg: Helmut Buske Verlag.

Heine, B., & Traugott, E. (Eds.). (1991). *Approaches to grammaticalization.* Amsterdam: John Benjamins.

Hooper, J. (1976). Word frequency in lexical diffusion and the source of morpho-phonemic change. In W. Christie (Ed.), *Current trends in historical linguistics.* Amsterdam: North-Holland.

Hopper, P. (1987). Emergent grammar. *Proceedings of the Thirteenth Berkeley Linguistic Society Meeting,* 139-157.

Hopper, P. (1991). On some properties of grammaticization. In E. Traugott and B. Heine (Eds.), *Approaches to grammaticalization.* Amsterdam: John Benjamins.

Jakobson, R. (1957). Shifters, verbal categories and the Russian verb. Reprinted in *Roman Jacobson, Selected Writings, III.* The Hague: Mouton.

Kiparsky, P. (1982). Lexical phonology and morphology. In I.-S. Yang (Ed.), *Linguistics in the morning calm.* Seoul: Hanshin.

Kuryłowicz, J. (1968). The notion of morpho(pho)neme. In W. Lehmann & Y. Malkiel (Eds.), *Directions in historical linguistics.* Austin: University of Texas Press.

Langacker, R. (1987). *Foundations of Cognitive Grammar* (Vol. I). Stanford: Stanford University Press.

Losiewicz, B. (1992). *The effect of frequency on linguistic morphology.* Doctoral dissertation, University of Texas, Austin.

MacWhinney, B. (1978). *The acquisition of morphophonology.* Monographs of the Society for Research in Child Development, *43* (Serial No. 174).

Mańczak, W. (1980). Laws of analogy. In J. Fisiak (Ed.), *Recent developments in historical phonology.* The Hague: Mouton.

Marcus, G., Pinker, S., Ullman, M., Hollander, M., Rosen, T., & Xu, F. (1992). *Overregularization in language acquisition.* Monographs of the Society for Research in Child Development, *57* (4, Serial No. 228).

Matthews, P. (1972). *Inflectional morphology: A theoretical study based on aspects of Latin verb conjugation.* Cambridge: Cambridge University Press.

Matthews, P. H. (1991). *Morphology: An introduction to the theory of word structure* (2nd ed.). Cambridge: Cambridge University Press.

Nagy, W., Anderson, R., Schommer, M., Scott, J., & Stallman, A. (1989). Morphological families in the internal lexicon. *Reading Research Quarterly, 24,* 262-282.

Pagliuca, W. (1976). *PRE-fixing.* Unpublished master's thesis, SUNY, Buffalo, NY.

Rudes, B. (1980). On the nature of verbal suppletion. *Linguistics, 18,* 655-676.

Rumelhart, D., & McClelland, J. (1986). Learning the past tenses of English verbs: Implicit rules or parallel distributed processing? In B. MacWhinney (Ed.), *Mechanisms of language acquisition.* Hillsdale, NJ: Lawrence Erlbaum Associates.

Sadock, J. (1980). Noun incorporation in Greenlandic. *Language, 56,* 300-319.

Sapir, E. (1921). *Language.* New York: Harcourt Brace.

Sereno, J. A., & Jongman, A. (1991, January). *Inflectional morphology in the mental lexicon.* Paper presented at the Annual Meeting of the Linguistic Society of America.

Stanners, R., Neiser, J., Hernon, W., & Hall, R. (1979). Memory representation for morphologically related words. *Journal of Verbal Learning and Verbal Behavior, 18,* 399-412.

Stemberger, J., & MacWhinney, B. (1986). Frequency and the lexical storage of regularly inflected forms. *Memory & Cognition, 14,* 17-26.

Stemberger, J., & MacWhinney, B. (1988). Are inflected forms stored in the lexicon? In M. Hammond & M. Noonan (Eds.), *Theoretical morphology.* New York: Academic Press.

Tiersma, P. (1982). Local and general markedness. *Language, 58,* 832-849.

Walsh, T., & Parker, F. (1983). The duration of morphemic and non-morphemic /s/ in English. *Journal of Phonetics, 11,* 201-206.

Zipf, G. K. (1935). *The psycho-biology of language.* Boston, MA: Houghton Mifflin.

11 Phonological and Lexical Constraints on Morphological Processing

Joseph Paul Stemberger
University of Minnesota

Phonological processing and lexical access, and their interactions, have their own characteristics and impose their own constraints and biases on the expression of morphology. Phonological and lexical processing with attention to the ways in which they mold morphological processing are explored in this chapter. Many phenomena in language production that have been attributed to morphology may actually reflect phonological and lexical processing. There is currently no unequivocal evidence that morphological rules are present in language production.

INTRODUCTION

Language is a complex cognitive domain with many different components. Morphology is a microcosm of this complexity, interacting with semantics, pragmatics, syntax, phonology, and the lexicon. Within linguistic theory, the phonological aspects of morphology are heavily emphasized, with major research areas such as Lexical Phonology (Kiparsky, 1982) and Prosodic Morphology (McCarthy & Prince, 1993) dedicated to exploring the interactions of phonology and morphology. Linguists posit that morphology and phonology are part of the same component of grammar and interact heavily; studying morphology without reference to phonology would be unthinkable. In contrast, in studies of psycholinguistic processing and language acquisition, morphology is often studied by itself, with less consideration of the contributions of phonology. In language acquisition, for example, the development of morphology is most often studied without reference to phonological development (e.g., Kuczaj, 1977; Marcus et al., 1992).

Little can be learned about morphology per se (in acquisition or in processing) until we have sorted out the contributions from other areas of language. Whenever several components work together (as they do in morphology), there is ambiguity about the source of any effect. If we wish to interpret an outcome as evidence about morphology, possibly as part of an argument that there are morphological rules, we must be sure that the outcome is not a by-product of general morphology-independent processing in some other language component. It is not enough to show that the outcome could possibly be due to morphology, or that it is reasonable for it to be due to morphology. Such arguments are very weak. To be certain of our conclusions, we need to explore and eliminate alternative explanations.

In this chapter, I focus on phonological processing and lexical access, especially in language production, exploring characteristics that are independent of morphology and considering what impact they might have on morphological processing. Phonological processing is relevant because morphologically complex words must ultimately be pronounced, and the phonological components of morphological affixes are subject to phonological effects. Lexical access is relevant because the accurate production of morphologically complex words is possible only when lexical access proceeds successfully. Phonological processing and lexical access can also interact in interesting ways that impact on morphological processing.

The most prominent issues in morphology today are whether there are two routes for processing morphologically complex forms (rules vs. lexical storage) and which routes are possible for regular vs. irregular forms. Many researchers hold that there is only one route: either rules (e.g., Kiparsky, 1982) or lexical storage (e.g., McClelland & Rumelhart, 1986). Two-route models are also common and generally distinguish between regular and irregular forms: Irregular forms use only lexical storage, but regular forms use either both rules and storage (Butterworth, 1983; Stemberger & MacWhinney, 1988) or just rules (Pinker, 1991). Most of the relevant research has centered on differences between regular and irregular inflected forms; Pinker (1991) provides a useful catalog of the phenomena that have been used, many of which I address later. Importantly, the contribution of phonological processing to the regularity issue has not been sufficiently explored (partly because phonological processing itself is still being explored). Accordingly, it is not clear that regular and irregular forms are morphologically different because phonological and lexical differences between regular and irregular forms may underlie the apparent morphological differences. In this chapter, I focus primarily on phonological and lexical constraints on morphological aspects of language production in adults and in children learning their first language but also discuss some implications for language comprehension.

PHONOLOGY CONSTRAINS MORPHOLOGY

Phonology has clear effects upon morphology, whether we are discussing psycholinguistic or processing grammar. I first review some of the well-known grammatical effects of phonology on morphology, including addition to or loss from affixes of segments for phonological reasons and suppletion of affixes for phonological reasons. I then turn to child language acquisition, where regular forms are strongly affected by the child's phonological system. I then discuss some biases in phonological processing (vowel dominance, a bias for vowel substitution over consonant addition, and global similarity effects) in both adult and child speech and show how they impact on regular and irregular forms. Finally, I argue that regular and irregular forms show predictably different patterns when phonological characteristics are considered.

Within phonological theory, there is much evidence showing how phonology can constrain morphology (e.g., Kiparsky, 1982). Phonological rules can apply after an affix is added to a base form in such a way as to alter the phonological form of the affix. In English, for example, the plural forms of the words *cat* and *match* are usually analyzed as underlyingly /kæ:t-z/ and /mæ:č-z/, but phonological rules devoice the /z/ (in [kʰæ:t-s]) or epenthesize a schwa (in [mæ:č-əz]). In some cases, all the phonological material of the affix can be deleted. For example, in Swedish present tense forms such as *kör* [çö:r] 'drive' (from underlying /çö:r-r/), the sequence of two /r/'s is simplified by deleting the /r/ of the suffix. The only reason to suspect that an affix is present at all is that /r/ is present in all other phonological contexts, as in [se:r] 'see' (from /se:-r/) (e.g., Stemberger, 1981). In most cases, it is possible to apply the affix first, then to apply phonological rules. This is compatible with a modular system in which the output of the morphological component is fed into the phonological component. Although it is not certain that the details of any particular linguistic analysis of these facts correspond in any direct way to what goes on in performance, the analyses do identify the essential factors of the phenomena.

In some cases it is clear that the phonology determines the application of morphological rules because some affixes are restricted to base forms with a particular phonological shape. In English, for example, comparative *-er* and superlative *-est* cannot be added to adjectives with three syllables (*horrible-est*), only to adjectives with one syllable (*blue-er*) or with two syllables in which the second syllable ends in a vowel or syllabic consonant (*happy-er*, *rotten-est*, but *secret-er*); this restriction is to avoid sequences of unstressed syllables (especially complex ones). Seri (a Hokan language spoken in Baja California) contains many such affixes, with highly idiosyncratic phonological restrictions (Marlett & Stemberger, 1983). In addition, in some cases, phonological changes to the base morpheme must occur before an inflectional morpheme is added. To handle such cases, phonological and morphological information must be available at the same time, and phonology and morphology must belong to the same module (Kiparsky, 1982).

In English, the phonology does not radically alter the phonological form of the affix. In most words, an affix is pronounced (not deleted), with strong phonetic similarities between the different allomorphs of the affix. As in most languages, an affix tends to be of a phonological shape that is compatible with the general phonology of the language, so that it is not generally deleted or altered beyond recognition. Preservation of the affix's phonological information is useful for listeners processing the information that the affix encodes. However, having a phonological form that is both compatible with the adult phonology and consistent enough for listeners to use will not necessarily be true for young children who have not yet mastered the phonology of the language. Due to constraints on production, the phonological system of a given child is greatly reduced compared to the adult system, so that morphological affixes often cannot be encoded. There are many phonological phenomena that are common across children's productions (e.g., Ingram, 1986), including:

a) word-final consonant deletion: e.g., *hide* [hay], *please* [pʰi:]
b) consonant cluster simplification: e.g., *last* [yæ:s], *box* [bak]
c) unstressed syllable deletion: e.g., *pocket* [ba:], *sister* [si:]

These phenomena are often present when an English-learning child first attempts to produce morphologically complex forms (Smith, 1973; Stemberger, 1991a). Consider the output of a child whose phonology includes (a-c) above: All words are reduced to a single stressed syllable, and all word-final consonants are deleted. Listening to such a child, one would be unable to differentiate *any* of the regular inflected forms of English:

[wa:] 'walk,' or 'walks,' or 'walked,' or 'walking'
[wa:] 'rock,' or 'rocks'

Here, all of the phonological material in the affixes is deleted, for reasons that have little to do with morphology. In contrast, the child would be capable of producing most irregularly inflected forms, at least so that they could be differentiated from other forms of the same word:

| *throw/throws* | [sow] | *foot* | [fa:] |
| *threw* | [su:] | *feet* | [fi:] |

The phonological difference between most irregular forms and their corresponding base forms lies in the stressed vowel rather than a final consonant (or syllable). All children can produce stressed vowels. The vowel system also tends to develop faster than the consonant system (Stoel-Gammon & Herrington, 1990) and is therefore more adult-like. Because it is the stressed vowel that differentiates base forms from irregularly inflected forms, most children can produce recognizable irregular inflected forms, even when the phonological abilities needed to produce regular inflected forms are absent.

Studies of morphological development generally provide little information about the child's phonological abilities (see, for example, Marcus et al., 1992, the largest study on past tense forms to date). This omission can influence the ways that we interpret the patterns observed in data. For instance, suppose a child varies between correct *ran* [wæ:n] and an apparent base form used as past tense *run* [wʌn] (an early pattern for most children; see Marcus et al., 1992, for discussion). At a later point, the child stops using the base form *run* [wʌn] and starts using the regularization *runned* [wʌnd] (also a usual pattern). The change from [wʌn] to [wʌnd] is usually interpreted as a morphological event, the point where the child starts to use a general rule of *-ed* in the past tense. However, suppose that previously the child had had no final /nd/ clusters in words such as *round* [wawn]. In that case, the form [wʌn] is ambiguous because it also could represent the regularization *runned* with deletion of the final /d/. When [wʌnd] finally appears, it might be a phonological event, with [nd] now present for all words that end in /nd/ in adult speech, including *round* [wawnd]. In order to determine that the change was a morphological event and not a phonological event, one must show that similar changes in the phonology did not occur at the same time. Because no studies have included this contrast, we have no way to tell whether developmental changes such as this have any bearing on morphology.

For a second example, it has long been observed that children tend to mark past tense *-ed* in English long before marking present tense *-s* (e.g., Brown, 1973). Explanations have tended to focus on semantic differences between the tenses or on the fact that past tense is marked in English much more frequently than present tense. Ingram (1991), however, observed that children tend to develop word-final stops (found in *-ed*) earlier than word-final fricatives (found in *-s*); children often pass through a developmental period where fricatives are deleted but stops are produced. He pointed out that this might underlie the observed order of development. Because phonological factors have not been investigated, it is difficult to tell. A third example appeared in Pinker and Prince (1988), where they interpreted pronunciations such as [bak] for *box* as back-formations: the child apparently interpreted the final /s/ as the plural suffix *-s*, removed it, and used the inferred (incorrect) singular form *bock*. However, the deletion of the final /s/ (and /z/, in clusters and after vowels) is a common phenomenon for purely phonological reasons. To show that it was a back formation, Pinker and Prince would have had to show that the child produced *bocks* [baks] as the plural form. Because Pinker and Prince do not report on *bocks*, this may not be an example of back-formation but may simply be consonant deletion for phonological reasons.

It is often observed that the allomorphs of an affix are not all mastered simultaneously and that allomorphs are acquired in a particular order. A common observation (e.g., Berko, 1958; Bybee & Slobin, 1982) is that the syllabic allomorphs of -*ed* and -*s* are acquired later than the other allomorphs:

cried	[kʰrayd]	*flies*	[flayz]
walked	[wa:kt]	*cats*	[kʰæ:ts]
needed	[ni:d]	*horses*	[hɔrs]

Various explanations have been proposed for why the syllabic allomorphs are acquired later in some children. The most common explanation is that because base forms like *horse* and *need* already end in /s/ or /d/, the child assumes that they are already marked for plural or past tense and does not add -*s* or -*ed* because this would lead to marking the words twice (Bybee & Slobin, 1982; MacWhinney, 1978; Stemberger, 1981. Pinker and Prince (1988) suggest that dissimilation is involved, with the /z/ or /d/ being deleted when it follows a segment that is almost identical. Stemberger (1991a) has suggested that the lateness of the syllabic allomorphs could involve the following three developments in the child's phonological system:

a) acquisition of word-final single consonants
b) acquisition of word-final clusters ending in /s/, /z/, /t/, /d/
c) acquisition of word-final closed unstressed syllables

If (a) and (b) occur first, we derive the lateness of the syllabic allomorphs for general phonological reasons independent of morphology or dissimilation. Stemberger notes that, if the capabilities develop in a different order (such as (a) and (c) before (b)), other patterns of development are possible:

cried	[kʰrayd]	*flies*	[flayz]
walked	[wa:k]	*cats*	[kʰæ:t]
needed	[ni:dəd]	*horses*	[hɔrsəz]

In this case, the ability to produce final unstressed syllables develops before the ability to produce final consonant clusters, and the syllabic allomorphs are produced better than some other allomorphs. This second pattern of development has been observed (Smith, 1973; Stemberger, 1991a). It remains to be seen whether the late occurrence of forms like [ni:dəd] and [hɔrsəz] in the speech of some children is truly a morphological phenomenon rather than a phonological one.

Children sometimes produce an affix twice, as in *walkeded* [wa:ktəd], and this is universally treated as a morphological phenomenon. Rumelhart and McClelland (1986) suggest that this double marking of an affix may be more likely when the base has certain phonological characteristics. In an unpublished study, I have data in which this is clearly the case. At the time, the child could produce any consonant after a vowel or approximant, but consonant clusters were limited to those ending in /s/ or /z/ or those with a nasal (pronounced fairly long, as in Italian but not as in adult English) followed by a voiceless stop, including /nt/ (left column):

seed	[si:d]	*round*	[wawn]
hide	[hayd]	*act*	[æ:k]
beard	[bird]	*last*	[læ:s]
held	[hɛwd]	*lift*	[lɪf]
jump	[zʌmp]		
ant	[ʔæ:nt]		

All other clusters (right column) were simplified by retaining the first consonant and deleting all that followed. The distribution of doubled -*ed* follows these two categories exactly: There was no doubling if the -*ed* followed a vowel or approximant or could create a cluster made up of a nasal plus voiceless stop (left column); there was doubling if any other cluster resulted (right column).

peed	[pʰi:d]	*turned*	[tʰr̩ ndəd]
cried	[sayd]	*keeped*	[tʰi:ptəd]
scared	[sɛrd]	*walked*	[wa:ktəd]
smelled	[fɛwd]	*kissed*	[tʰɪstəd]
jumped	[zʌmt]	*hugged*	[hʌddəd]
		buzzed	[bʌzdəd]
		jumped	[zʌmptəd]

There is one form in the left column that had an unpronounceable cluster: the /mpt/ in *jumped*; the child sometimes doubled the affix here, but sometimes resolved the cluster by deleting the /p/, creating the new cluster [mt] that fit the nasal/voiceless-stop pattern of the existing clusters [mp], [nt], [ŋk]. The same patterns were observed for regularizations:

see-ed	[si:d]	*sleeped*	[si:ptəd]
flied	[fayd]	*breaked*	[veyktəd]
heared	[hird]	*losed*	[lu:zdəd]
falled	[fawd]	*winned*	[wɪndəd]
drinked	[ziŋt]	*drinked*	[ziŋktəd]

The child had the phonological capabilities to pronounce the past tense forms in the left column and so pronounced them correctly. The child did not have the phonological capabilities to pronounce the past tense forms in the right column and so could not pronounce them correctly. The most common solution across children for these unpronounceable clusters seems to be to delete the phonological material in the affix, but an alternative solution is to create a new syllable for those final consonants. In the right column, the new syllable was created by doubling the affix. These data suggest that double-marking is not a purely morphological phenomenon (though it must clearly be influenced by morphology, because this child doubled only -ed and never in a simple /nd/ such as in *round* *[wawndəd]).

Phonological processing is relevant to the processing of inflected forms in at least two other ways, as will be demonstrated. First, elements which are easier to access for phonological reasons should be processed more accurately, with fewer errors. Second, it has been shown that phonological processing in language production is sensitive to global phonological similarity with other words in the lexicon (e.g., Dell, 1986); processing of a given word or segment is affected by other words that are phonologically similar in that they have the same vowels, consonants, number of syllables, stress patterns, etc. Because these factors affect processing in general, they should also affect morphological processing.

Stemberger (1992a) reports that there are biases in the mispronunciation of vowels in speech errors that involve the misordering of sounds between words. The following biases are present:

a) front vowels are replaced by back vowels
b) mid vowels are replaced by high or low vowels
c) unrounded vowels are replaced by rounded vowels
d) infrequent vowels are replaced by frequent vowels

The first three biases affect vowels that differ only along the dimension noted. However, vowels can differ along several dimensions, and this can lead to conflicts between the biases; for example, by bias (a) /æ:/ (front) might be expected to be replaced by /o:/ (back), but by bias (b) /o:/ (mid) would be expected to be replaced by /æ:/ (low). When biases (a)-(c) conflict, bias (d) holds: the less frequent vowel is replaced by the more frequent vowel. (In this example, /æ:/ is replaced by /o:/.) These biases should be present in any situation in which there is competition between two vowels, whether in two adjacent words or in two words competing for lexical access.

Stemberger (1993) points out the relevance of these observations to irregular past tense forms, in particular to regularizations such as */fa:ld/ in place of correct *fell*, and */getəd/ in place of correct *got*. Consider the regularization errors in relation to the changes in the vowel that take place. In */fa:ld/, the /ɛ/ of *fell* is replaced by /a:/; this is covered by (a) because /ɛ/ is front and /a:/ is back and by (b) because /ɛ/ is mid and /a:/ is low. As a result, phonologically, */fa:ld/ is an expected type of error. (Technically, /fa:l/ is the expected error; see Stemberger, 1993, 1994, for discussion of the addition of -ed.) In */getəd/, however, the opposite occurs: The /a:/ of *got* is replaced by /ɛ/, which goes against the biases in both (a) and (b). As a result, phonologically, */getəd/ is an unlikely type of error. Regularizations should be common if they are in accord with the biases in (a-d), rare if they conflict with them. Stemberger (1993) shows that this is the case with regularizations in child language. In the most extreme case (Abe from 2;5-3;0), verbs that were in accord with (a-d) showed a regularization rate of about 80% (defined as the number of attempts that were regularized divided by the total number of productions), while verbs that conflicted with (a-d) showed a regularization rate of about 15%. The effect of bias was separate from and slightly more powerful than the effect of lexical frequency (with a lower regularization rate on high frequency verbs). Evidently, phonological biases contribute to morphological processing.

In the speech of adults and children, other differences between regular and irregular forms might be attributable to phonological differences as well, such as overtensing errors including *didn't ate* and *didn't wanted* (Stemberger, 1992b). Most overtensing errors involve irregular forms, and this has been used as evidence that irregular forms are stored in the lexicon, whereas regular forms are not (e.g., Maratsos & Kuczaj, 1978). Stemberger asked whether irregular forms such as *ate* might be commonly involved because the vowel is different from that of the correct form (*didn't eat*), while regular forms such as *helped* might be uncommon because the vowel doesn't change (*didn't help*). In other words, maybe speakers tend to make vowel substitution errors (replacing the /i:/ of target *eat* with /ey/ to get *ate*) more than they tend to add word-final consonants (adding /t/ to target *help* to get *helped*). Stemberger (1992b) showed experimentally with adults that vowel-change irregular forms such as *ate* are more often involved in overtensing than regular past tense forms. Moreover, vowel-change irregular forms are also involved more than suffixing irregular forms such as *fallen*, where the irregular suffix *-en* is added to the base form of the verb. Suffixing irregular forms were only slightly more likely to be involved in overtensing errors than regular forms (and this small difference might be due to a phonological effect, with the nasal of *-en* in words such as *blown* forming a tighter phonological sequence with the vowel than the stop of *-ed* in *glowed,* as Treiman, 1988, has shown for uninflected forms in English). Stemberger concluded that phonological effects underlie the apparent effect of rule regularity, and that there may be no effect of regularity per se.

In work in progress, I have found that the vowel biases noted above hold for adult speech, for both regularization and overtensing. Regularization errors are more common on those verbs whose past tense vowels are biased to be replaced by their base vowels (such as *fall-fell*); this is because the vowel of the base form shows up in the error. In overtensing, however, the vowel of the past tense form shows up in the error, and consequently such errors are more common on the group of verbs in which the vowel of the base form is biased to be replaced by the vowel of the past tense form (such as *get-got*). Phonological factors affect morphological processing in both adults and children.

The phonological differences between regular and irregular forms would produce the observed pattern if the phonological system were more prone to errors that change the vowel than to errors that add a consonant. A phonological bias would make overtensing errors more likely if the vowel changes (in irregular forms) than if a consonant is added (in regular forms). In unpublished data in my corpus of speech errors (both adult and child errors; see Stemberger, 1989, for details of the corpus), if one word ends in a VC sequence, and another nearby word ends in a VC sequence where the consonant is one found in a regular inflectional suffix (/s, z, t, d/), I find vowel errors (*this stiff - stuff*; n=14) but no consonant addition errors (such as *this stuffS*). This suggests a bias in which the system is more prone to getting a vowel wrong than to adding a final consonant—a vowel bias that also makes the system more prone to errors with irregular forms than with regular forms.

A second phonological factor is the global similarity between words. In phonological speech errors, this is referred to as the Repeated Phoneme Effect (Dell, 1986). When a phoneme is misordered between two words, the error is more likely if the two words have a phoneme in common. For example, the word *made* is more likely to be mispronounced [beyd] before the word *bake*, which has the same vowel [ey] as *made,* than before the word *back,* which has no phonemes in common with *made.* Stemberger (1991b) has shown that the strength of this effect (i.e., how much the error rate is increased relative to contexts in which there is no repeated phoneme) can vary with phonological factors. The Repeated Phoneme Effect is small in errors on word-initial consonants (the most common type of error). The error rate doubles if the vowels are the same but there is only a small increase if word-final consonants are the same. In contrast, the Repeated Phoneme Effect is large in errors on word-final consonants (a less common type of error): The error rate quadruples if the vowels are the same and doubles if word-initial consonants are the same. In summary, common errors show weak global similarity effects, while uncommon errors show strong effects. An intuitive account is that things that the system is prone to do will happen without any facilitation from the similarity effects, but things that the system is not prone to do generally will not happen unless they are facilitated by other factors.

Global phonological similarity effects have also been observed with irregular verbs. Irregular verbs fall into phonologically similar groups; verbs with the same past tense vowel also tend to have similar consonants, as with the word-final velars, word-final nasals, and word-initial /s/ in *sang, stank, sank, swam,* etc. (Bybee & Moder, 1983; Bybee & Slobin, 1982). Stemberger and MacWhinney (1988) report that regular forms that rhyme with these irregular forms (e.g., *thank* rhymes with *sank,* and *joke* rhymes with *broke*) tend to be produced without the *-ed*; they are assimilated to the irregular verb classes. Pinker and Prince (1988) suggest that something similar happens diachronically: Verbs that were originally regular have become irregular but only if they shared consonants with the older verbs of the class that they joined. Such effects have been called hypersimilarity (or family resemblance) effects. In contrast to irregular forms, regular forms do not seem to show hypersimilarity effects. Regular forms can be of any shape. Phonological similarity between irregular verbs and regular verbs does not seem to make irregular verbs prone to become regular. The differences between the irregular verbs and regular verbs in terms of whether they show these global similarity effects has been used to argue that irregular forms and regular forms are processed in different ways (e.g., Pinker & Prince, 1988; Stemberger & MacWhinney, 1988); in particular, irregular forms are stored in the lexicon (so similarities between verbs can easily be computed) but regular forms are created by rule each time one is needed, so that global similarity between regular verbs cannot be computed.

Stemberger (1991b) points out that the Repeated Phoneme Effect and the Hypersimilarity Effect are very similar. Ideally, it would be appealing to reduce them to a single effect, but even if they are distinct, one might expect them to have similar characteristics. The Repeated Phoneme Effect varies in strength as a function of how likely a phenomenon is. Hypersimilarity effects would be expected to vary in strength in a similar fashion. The language system is much less likely to output irregular inflectional patterns than regular patterns. Irregular forms have a much greater error rate than regular forms, even with errors in which the base form is used in place of the inflected form (Stemberger & MacWhinney, 1988). Irregular verbs are often regularized, but regular verbs are rarely irregularized. The regular *-ed* pattern constitutes something that the system is prone to do, and global similarity effects should consequently be weak; though some effect of hypersimilarity is expected, it may be too small to detect easily. The system is not prone to produce irregular patterns, so global similarity effects should be larger than with regular patterns, and hypersimilarity effects should be easier to detect than for regular patterns. As noted above, this is the case. The observed differences between regular forms and irregular forms are not necessarily correlated with regularity per se but might rather be due to inherent characteristics of the phonological factor of global similarity and the way in which that effect varies in magnitude as a function of how likely an output is.

In summary, phonological factors have been neglected in the study of morphology in language production. They predict many phenomena, including many of the differences between regular and irregular forms that have been observed.

LEXICAL ACCESS CONSTRAINS MORPHOLOGY

Another aspect of language that must be addressed in relation to morphology is lexical access. There are two basic classes of models for lexical access: search models and spreading activation models. In search models (Forster, 1979), the speaker has a template for a particular word. The template is compared to each lexical entry, and when a match is found, the speaker accesses that word for further processing. Search is generally serial, one word at a time. In spreading activation models, the template broadcasts activation to words in the lexicon simultaneously, with each feature of the template contributing a small amount of activation to each word that has that same feature. Many words will receive some amount of activation, but the word that has more activation than any other is eventually accessed, either by an external mechanism that selects the most activated item (McClelland & Elman, 1986) and/or intrinsically via a mechanism such as inhibition (McClelland & Rumelhart, 1981). Here, I assume a spreading-activation scheme with inhibition to select among competitors, but these comments should be compatible with a wide range of models.

Perhaps the most important characteristic of lexical access is that high-frequency lexical items are processed more rapidly and accurately than low-frequency words. This is encoded in activation-based models by setting things up so that high-frequency items need less activation to be accessed. All other things being equal, we expect that high-frequency inflected forms would be accessed faster and more accurately than low-frequency inflected forms. This has been shown to be the case with irregular past tense forms in English, both with adult (Prasada, Pinker, & Snyder, 1990; Seidenberg & Daugherty, 1992; Stemberger & MacWhinney, 1988) and child (Bybee & Slobin, 1982; Marcus et al., 1992) language production where measures include error rates in spontaneous speech and reaction time and error rates in experimental tasks (such as morphonaming, in which the subject is presented with one form of a word, such as *was choosing,* and is asked to change it into a different form of the same word, such as past tense *chose,* as rapidly as possible). However, it appears that regular past tense forms show far weaker frequency effects (Stemberger & MacWhinney, 1988), and some studies have failed to detect them at all (Prasada et al., 1990). One interpretation of the difference between regular forms and irregular forms is lexical: Irregular forms are stored in the lexicon and so each irregular form has a stored frequency, whereas regular forms are produced only via rules, so that there is no locus in the system for storing the frequency of a particular inflected form.

Frequency effects may not be of the same magnitude for all classes of words because of the way class size and other factors interact. In connectionist models, similar words form groups that mutually reinforce each other in such a way as to increase the accessibility of their parts. Groups are not defined a priori but arise spontaneously as a function of both semantic and phonological similarity. The phonemes of a given lexical item are not accessed just via its meaning, which is dependent on the token frequency of the individual lexical item, but also via other verbs in the group. Consequently, the type frequency of the group (the number of lexical items in the group) is also important (and possibly also the summed token frequencies of the members of the group). As group size increases, group activation offsets the effects of lexical frequency for an item. Seidenberg and Daugherty (1992) demonstrate with a simulation that group effects reduce frequency effects on morphologically regular inflected forms (see also Stemberger, 1994). A verb in an inflectional group with few members (such as any particular group of irregular verbs) is accessed primarily through the verb itself, and there are large frequency effects. In contrast, inflectional groups with many members (such as regular verbs) receive a large boost from the group, and frequency effects are much smaller (small enough usually to be undetectable, just as global phonological similarity effects are too small to detect). Thus, differences in the magnitude of frequency effects do not implicate lexical differences between regular and irregular forms, other than differences in group size.

Another basic issue in lexical access in language production is what Levelt (1989) has called the hypernym problem. A hypernym is a word with a general meaning that has basically the same meaning as a more specific word. For example, *dog* is a hypernym, while *collie* and *chihuahua* are more specific subordinate terms. The hypernym tends to be a basic-level category that is used by speakers with high frequency; speakers usually refer to collies and chihuahuas as dogs, rather than using the subordinate terms, which are consequently of relatively low frequency. This difference in frequency is the crux of the hypernym problem: Speakers have difficulty accessing subordinate terms because of interference from hypernyms. When the speaker wishes to talk about chihuahuas, the word *dog* always matches the main part of the semantic template for *chihuahua*, lacking only the more specific characteristics that chihuahuas do not share with other types of dogs. As a result, the word *dog* always becomes highly activated. Because the word *dog* is so much more frequent than the word *chihuahua*, the system has a tendency (at all times) to access the word *dog* rather than the target word *chihuahua*. The word *chihuahua* receives more activation than the word *dog,* however, because it matches all the features of the semantic template. For correct performance, the system must be carefully balanced, so that the extra activation to *chihuahua* from the additional semantic features offsets the additional inhibition from *dog* that derives from the difference in frequency.

The hypernym problem is relevant to morphology because, at least in a language such as English, base forms are general in meaning while particular inflected forms are more specific. In English, the base form of a verb, such as *walk,* is used as an imperative, in non-third-person present tense uses, in infinitives, and embedded under modals (*can't walk*); it is even used in past tense contexts when embedded under an auxiliary (*didn't walk*) or another lexical verb (*continued to walk*). In contrast, *walked* is used only in past tense contexts. As a relatively high-frequency hypernym, the base should be more accessible than the past tense form, and speakers should have a tendency to access the base form rather than the past tense form. In spontaneous speech, this would be apparent in errors such as *yesterday I eat one* (instead of *ate one*). This is indeed the case, both in child language (Bybee & Slobin, 1982; Kuczaj, 1977) and in adult language (Stemberger & MacWhinney, 1988). One could argue that the hypernym problem should be worse with inflected forms than with other subordinate category members because the meaning differences are small compared with the meaning differences between *dog* and *chihuahua,* for example.

The hypernym problem may be relevant to compound nouns in English, with some interaction with phonological constraints. There is some possibility that irregular plurals, like *mice,* can appear as the first member of a compound. However, few such forms are actually used by speakers (such as *teeth-marks* and *lice-ridden*); speakers prefer to use base forms (as in *mouse-eater*) rather than plurals (as in *mice-eater*). Pinker (1991) reports that forms such as *mice-eater* evoke grammaticality ratings from speakers of English that are relatively low but nonetheless higher than those obtained for regular plurals such as *rats-eater.* Gordon (1985) reports that children frequently produce compounds such as *mice-eater* when the form *mice* has just been used by the child but rarely produce compounds such as *rats-eater* when the form *rats* has just been used. Following Kiparsky (1982), Pinker and Gordon argue that irregular forms like *mice* are stored in the lexicon, that any lexical entry can appear as the first member of a compound, and that regular forms like *rats* are not stored in the lexicon and so cannot appear as the first member of a compound. But such an account fails to explain why speakers prefer base forms in compounds. It is probable that the basic compounding process uses the base form (the more accessible hypernym), and that plural forms are acceptable only insofar as they can compete well with the base form. The hypernym problem should affect regular forms and irregular forms equally, but irregular forms may be marginally more acceptable in compounds for phonological reasons. Specifically, as noted above, the phonological system may be more prone to substitute one vowel for another (as in irregular forms) than to add a consonant to the end of the word (as in regular forms). Singular forms may be preferred in compounds, but plurals that differ from singulars in ways that agree with the biases of the phonological system would sound better than other plurals. This account would explain the difference in acceptability between compounds containing irregular plurals and regular plurals, without reference to morphology.

The hypernym problem is not present, of course, when there is no hypernym. As a result, defective inflected forms like *suds,* which appear to be regular plurals except that they can never be used in the singular (**sud*), will not be subject to the hypernym problem. Because there is no singular form **sud* to access in its place, *suds* is accessed easily. Consequently, forms like *suds* appear freely as the first member of a compound: *suds-eater, pants-pocket, glasses-case,* etc. Pinker (1991) explained this fact by assuming that *suds* is stored in the lexicon (like an irregular plural) and hence is available for compounding. However, treating *suds* like an irregular form does not explain why *mice-eater* is less acceptable (in speakers' grammaticality judgments) than *suds-eater.* What is relevant here is that *suds* has no competing singular form, while *mice* does; *mice,* but not *suds,* is subject to the hypernym problem. Full consideration of the hypernym problem allows us to account for the differences without positing differences in lexical storage.

Children suffering from a developmental disorder known as Specific Language Impairment (SLI) also show differences between regular and irregular inflected forms: The base form is used erroneously in place of the inflected form more often for regular forms than for irregular forms. Pinker (1991) has used this as evidence that regular forms are produced via rules but irregular forms are not and that rules are impaired in SLI children. This account is incomplete because it incorrectly predicts that irregular forms should be produced correctly on all attempts; as noted, however (e.g., Gopnik & Crago, 1991, Leonard McGregor, & Allen, 1992), irregulars are subject to base form errors and regularizations in a large proportion of attempts. We might alternatively assume that SLI children have an exacerbated hypernym problem, so that base forms are more often accessed than inflected forms. If the hypernym problem interacts with the phonological characteristics of the inflected forms, then the problem could be greater for regular forms than for irregular forms. This also accounts for why irregular forms are affected at all.

While my focus has been on language production, lexical access would also have an impact on morphological processing in perception, given a model in which lexical access begins as soon as phonological information becomes available (as opposed to waiting until the end of the word to begin accessing the word), such as the cohort model (Marslen-Wilson & Welsh, 1978) or TRACE (Elman & McClelland, 1985). The first phoneme activates all words in the lexicon that begin with that phoneme. When the second phoneme is accessed, all words that contain that phoneme remain activated, while those that do not are deactivated (the exact mechanism for and extent of this deactivation is unimportant here). This process continues until a single lexical candidate remains; the point at which this occurs is called the recognition point in the cohort model. After the recognition point the listener does not need to pay close attention to the acoustic information but only need monitor it roughly to make sure that it is consistent with the word that has been accessed. If a mispronunciation error occurs early in the word, before the recognition point, it affects lexical access and tends to be noticed by the listener. However, if the mispronunciation error occurs late, after the recognition point, it tends not to be noticed because the speaker is not listening as attentively to phonemes after the recognition point.

If the hypernym problem is also relevant for perceptual processing, the listener, aware of contextual appropriateness, might tend to hear (more frequent) hypernyms than (less frequent) subordinate terms. In general, this would not be a problem. Because there is little phonological similarity between most hypernyms such as *dog* and subordinate terms such as *chihuahua*, only the subordinate word could be heard. The hypernym is quickly eliminated as a candidate for lexical access for phonological reasons. When listening to an inflected form of a word, however, there will be a problem. When the /k/ in *walk* is heard, all morphological variants are possible, including the hypernym *walk* and the subordinate terms *walks, walked,* and *walking*. If there is a bias to access hypernyms, the listener may decide that *walk* has been heard, and then may only monitor poorly after that point. If monitoring is poor enough, the listener may not be aware that a different inflected form has appeared (especially for affixes with less salient phonetic material, such as stops).

I have suggested that SLI children might have a more pronounced hypernym problem, and it is thus possible that they do not always perceive regular affixes. Leonard et al. (1992) have shown that SLI children have some difficulty perceiving phonetic material in nonwords that is similar to the phonetic material of the English affixes (e.g., final stops, unstressed final syllables). This perceptual difficulty is not insurmountable and probably merely makes the difficult phonetic material less salient to the child. This perceptual problem may be exacerbated by the hypernym problem. Note that the child might be able to consistently perceive the phonemes in morphologically simple words where there is no hypernym problem; the word *box* should be heard as [ba:ks] because there is no word *bock* to compete with it and be selected in lexical access. Only in morphologically complex words, where the hypernym can be accessed, would there be a problem; the word *rocks* [ra:ks] could be heard as *rock* [ra:k], without the /s/ being noticed. As a result, the child might leave such affixes out of their language production simply because they do not always hear them. In contrast, with irregular forms such as *mice* and *ran,* the hypernym is removed (*mouse* and *run*) as a possible candidate when the vowel is processed, so that the child always hears that the form is plural or past tense. The greater accuracy of irregular forms in production might reflect greater accuracy in perception. Again, there is thus no reason to assume that the differences between regular forms and irregular forms reflect morphological differences because the confounded phonological differences lead to differences in auditory lexical access. Interestingly, this explanation entails that one cannot rule out phonological effects by comparing phonologically similar words that are morphologically simple: *Box* is not a good control for *rocks* because the phonological differences interact with lexical access. The words *box* and *rocks* are phonologically comparable but not lexically comparable.

A similar interaction between phonological processing and lexical access may occur in everyday language production. Stemberger (1992c) argues that phonological processing in natural child speech may show special phenomena when the word that is being processed combines several difficult elements (reflected in error rates in adult speech and in the order of acquisition in child language acquisition). It was noted above that three elements that cause difficulty in child speech are word-final consonants, word-final consonant clusters, and word-final unstressed syllables. Words that have more than one of these characteristics often show special properties. For example, if a child can produce word-final consonants and word-final unstressed syllables, the child may still be unable to produce word-final unstressed syllables that end in a consonant. Stemberger (1992c) reported such a pattern in two English-learning children:

	Adult	Child 1	Child 2
a) stressed with consonants:	hʊt	hʊt	hʊt
b) unstressed, no consonants:	kʰʊri	tʰʊdi	tʰʊdi
c) unstressed, consonants:	pʰa:kət	pʰakə	pʰa:

Child 1 produced the unstressed syllable but deleted the final consonant, while Child 2 deleted the whole unstressed syllable that contained the final consonant.

The hypernym problem entails that accessing a past tense form or plural form is more difficult than accessing a base form. The difficulty inherent in inflected forms should interact with other factors. In particular, the hypernym problem should exacerbate problems with phonological encoding, especially for those phonological elements that are less accessible to begin with, such as final consonants (/s, z, t, d/), final consonant clusters, and unstressed syllables with final consonants (/əz, əd, ɪŋ/). The interaction between the hypernym problem and phonological accessibility should, in principle, lead to especially poor processing of regular inflected forms. Thus, we might find base form errors, such as loss of the consonant of the affix (in *rocks*) or of the unstressed closed syllable (in *needed*) in inflected forms, whereas there might be no deletion in morphologically simple forms (such as *box* or *naked*), which are less difficult in terms of lexical access. Irregular forms would be relatively spared; they are subject to the hypernym problem in lexical access but are phonologically simpler than regular forms. In summary, because regular forms combine lexical and phonological difficulties, while irregular forms have only lexical difficulties, we would anticipate that irregular and regular forms might behave differently. SLI children's deficit with regular inflected forms may also derive from this interaction in language production.

Lexical access can have a large impact on morphological processing in both production and comprehension. In particular, the phonological differences between regular and irregular morphological forms can interact with lexical access to yield qualitatively different outcomes, whether regular and irregular forms are all stored in the lexicon or all produced via rules.

CONCLUSIONS

Studies of morphology have generally given insufficient attention to other aspects of language, such as phonological processing and lexical access. An apparent characteristic of morphology may in fact be due to lexical access or to phonological processing, or to their interaction. Before we can attribute an outcome to morphological processing, we must eliminate alternative accounts.

I have reviewed some aspects of phonological processing and lexical access and explored their impact on morphological processing. Typically, regular and irregular inflected forms produce different effects and these differences have been attributed to morphology. However, such a conclusion cannot be accepted without more detailed justification, as the differences are derivable from natural confounds between phonological factors and morphological regularity. Aspects of phonological processing may directly lead to the observed differences between regular and irregular forms. Alternatively, characteristics of lexical access, specifically with the hypernym problem, yield differences between regular and irregular forms, both in production and in perception.

Because the contributions of phonological processing and lexical access have not been adequately considered in studies of morphology, there is little unequivocal evidence for morphological rules, and future research must identify effects that cannot be attributed to other factors. We may ultimately determine that morphology exists as a separate domain of human language. Alternatively, we may discover that it does not. Perhaps all inflected forms of all words are simply listed in the lexicon as independent words, and different words show different types of behavior depending on their lexical and phonological characteristics. Either possible outcome is interesting in its own right.

The true test of a theory is how well it makes correct predictions that lead us to new data. If the observed characteristics of morphology derive from phonological processing and lexical access, the following predictions arise: (1) Global phonological similarity effects (the Repeated Phoneme Effect in phonology and the Hypersimilarity Effect in morphology) should be linked: If a given speaker shows no Repeated Phoneme Effect, there should also be no Hypersimilarity Effect for irregular forms. To test this, we need to examine extensive data from both phonological and morphological processing. This may be especially worthwhile for child language. Stemberger (1989) suggests that children tend to show weaker Repeated Phoneme Effects than adults, which suggests that they may also show weaker Hypersimilarity Effects than adults. If the two similarity effects are not correlated, then the case for morphological rules is strengthened; (2) Irregular forms in which a suffix is added to the base (e.g., *burn-t, fall-en*) should be more similar to regular forms than to irregular forms in which the vowel changes. We need to contrast these more systematically with regular forms, controlling for more subtle phonological differences and for differences in group size. If suffixing irregular forms still differ from regular forms, the case for morphological rules is strengthened; (3) In some other language in which regular and irregular forms both involve affixation or both involve vowel changes, differences due to irregularity that cannot be attributed to subtle phonological differences or to differences in group size would strengthen the case for morphological rules.

In conclusion, the characteristics of phonological processing and lexical access, as well as their interaction, have a profound impact on the processing of inflected forms. Phonological and lexical factors provide a serious challenge to accounts involving morphological rules. Compelling arguments for morphological rules await unambiguous evidence that reasonable alternative accounts such as those presented here can be eliminated.

ACKNOWLEDGMENT

This research was supported in part by NSF Research Grant #DBS-9209642.

REFERENCES

Berko, J. (1958). The child's learning of English morphology. *Word, 14,* 150-177.

Brown, R. (1973). *A first language.* Cambridge, MA: Harvard University Press.

Butterworth, B. (1983). Lexical representation. In B. Butterworth (Ed.), *Language Production: Vol. 2. Development, writing, and other language processes* (pp. 257-294). London: Academic Press.

Bybee, J., & Moder, C. (1983). Morphological classes as natural categories. *Language, 59,* 251-270.

Bybee, J. L., & Slobin, D. I. (1982). Rules and schemas in the development and use of the English past tense. *Language, 58,* 265-289.

Dell, G. S. (1986). A spreading activation theory of retrieval in sentence production. *Psychological Review, 93,* 283-321.

Forster, K. I. (1979). Accessing the mental lexicon. In E. Walker (Ed.), *Explorations in the biology of language* (pp. 139-174). Montgomery, VT: Bradford Books.

Gopnik, M., & Crago, M. B. (1991). Familial aggregation of a developmental language disorder. *Cognition, 39,* 1-50.

Gordon, P. (1985). Level-ordering in lexical development. *Cognition, 21,* 73-93.

Ingram, D. (1986). Phonological development: Production. In P. Fletcher & M. Garman (Eds.), *Language acquisition* (pp. 223-239). Cambridge, MA: Cambridge University Press.

Ingram, D. (1991). *The acquisition of the English past and plural morphemes.* Unpublished manuscript, University of British Columbia.

Kiparsky, P. (1982). From cyclic phonology to lexical phonology. In H. van der Hulst & N. Smith (Eds.), *The structure of phonological representations* (Part 1) (pp. 130-175). Dordrecht, Holland: Foris.

Kuczaj, S. A. (1977). The acquisition of regular and irregular past tense forms. *Journal of Verbal Learning and Verbal Behavior, 16,* 589-600.

Leonard, L. B., McGregor, K. K., & Allen, G. D. (1992). Grammatical morphology and speech perception in children with specific language impairment. *Journal of Speech & Hearing Research, 35,* 1076-1085.

Levelt, W. J. M. (1989). *Speaking: From intention to articulation.* Cambridge, MA: MIT Press.

MacWhinney, B. (1978). The acquisition of morphophonology. *Monographs of the Society for Research in Child Development, 43* (1, Serial No. 174).

Maratsos, M., & Kuczaj, S. A. (1978). Against the transformational account: A simpler analysis of auxiliary overmarkings. *Journal of Child Language, 5,* 337-345.

Marcus, G. F., Pinker, S., Ullman, M., Hollander, M., Rosen, T. J., & Xu, F. (1992). Overregularization in language acquisition. *Monographs of the Society for Research in Child Development, 57* (4, Serial No. 228)

Marlett, S., & Stemberger, J. P. (1983). Empty consonants in Seri. *Linguistic Inquiry, 14,* 617-639.

Marslen-Wilson, W., & Welsh, A. (1978). Processing interactions and lexical access during word recognition in continuous speech. *Cognitive Psychology, 10,* 29-63.

McCarthy, J. J., & Prince, A. (1993). *Prosodic morphology I.* Unpublished manuscript, MIT.

McClelland, J. L., & Elman, J. L. (1986). The TRACE model of speech perception. *Cognitive Psychology, 18,* 1-86.

McClelland, J. L., & Rumelhart, D. E. (1981). An interactive activation model of context effects in letter recognition: Part 1. An account of basic findings. *Psychological Review, 88,* 375-407.

Pinker, S. (1991). Rules of language. *Science, 253,* 530-535.

Pinker, S., & Prince, A. (1988). On language and connectionism: Analysis of a Parallel Distributed Processing model of language acquisition. *Cognition, 28,* 73-194.

Prasada, S., Pinker, S., & Snyder, W. (1990). *Some evidence that irregular forms are retrieved from memory but regular forms are rule-generated.* Paper presented at the Annual Meeting of the Psychonomics Society, New Orleans.

Rumelhart, D. E., & McClelland, J. L. (1986). On learning the past tenses of English verbs. In J. L. McClelland, D. E. Rumelhart, & the PDP Research Group (Eds.), *Parallel Distributed Processing: Explorations in the microstructure of cognition. Vol. 2: Psychological and biological models* (pp. 216-271). Cambridge, MA: Bradford Books.

Seidenberg, M. S., & Daugherty, K. (1992). *Rules or connections? The past tense revisited.* Paper presented at the 33rd annual meeting of the Psychonomic Society, St. Louis.

Smith, N. (1973). *The acquisition of phonology.* Cambridge: Cambridge University Press.

Stemberger, J. P. (1981). Morphological haplology. *Language, 57,* 791-817.

Stemberger, J. P. (1989). Speech errors in early child language production. *Journal of Memory and Language, 28,* 164-188.

Stemberger, J. P. (1991a). *Morphological aspects of child phonological processing.* Unpublished manuscript, University of Minnesota.

Stemberger, J. P. (1991b). *Global similarity effects in phonological and morphological processing.* Unpublished manuscript, University of Minnesota.

Stemberger, J. P. (1992a). Vocalic underspecification in English language production. *Language, 68,* 492-524.

Stemberger, J. P. (1992b). *Overtensing, regularity, and the unreality of rules.* Paper presented at the 33rd Annual Meeting of the Psychonomic Society, St. Louis.

Stemberger, J. P. (1992c). *Resource limitations in child phonology and morphology.* Paper presented at the Child Phonology Conference, Champaign-Urbana.

Stemberger, J. P. (1993). Vowel dominance in Overregularization. *Journal of Child Language, 20,* 503-521.

Stemberger, J. P. (1994). Rule-less morphology at the phonology-lexicon interface. In R. Corrigan, G. Iverson, & S. Lima (Eds.), *The reality of linguistic rules* (pp. 147-169). Amsterdam: John Benjamins.

Stemberger, J. P., & MacWhinney, B. (1988). Are inflected forms stored in the lexicon? In M. Hammond & M. Noonan (Eds.), *Theoretical morphology* (pp. 101-116). San Diego, CA: Academic Press.

Stoel-Gammon, C., & Herrington, P. B. (1990). Vowel systems of normally developing and phonologically disordered children. *Clinical Linguistics and Phonetics, 4,* 145-160.

Treiman, R. (1988). The internal structure of the syllable. In G. Carlson & M. Tanenhaus (Eds.), *Linguistic structure in language processing* (pp. 27-52). Dordrecht, Holland: Kluwer.

PART 4

Structural and Statistical Issues in Morphological Processing

12 Morphological Factors in Visual Word Identification in Hebrew

Shlomo Bentin and Ram Frost
Hebrew University, Jerusalem
Haskins Laboratories

This chapter offers an overview of Hebrew morphology emphasizing its distinctive aspects. The potential advantage of using these special properties for understanding universal principles of morphological organization of the lexicon and the involvement of morphological factors in visual word processing and reading are illustrated in a review of recent studies. These studies suggest that young children are sensitive to morphological units and that adult readers are aware of the morphological structure of words even when the morphemic constituents are not phonological units themselves. It is suggested that the morphological analysis is necessary for activating the meaning of a morphologically complex word and that this occurs after a phonological representation in the lexicon has been accessed.

INTRODUCTION

The identification of written words involves analysis of orthographic structures aimed at extracting phonologic, semantic, morphologic, and syntactic linguistic information. This information is used to integrate words into meaningful phrases and sentences that, in normal verbal communication, convey informative messages. Although there are models of visual word recognition which stipulate that letter strings may gain access to their meaning directly (e.g., Jared & Seidenberg, 1991), our premise is that access to meaning is mediated by the phonological lexicon. According to this premise, letters activate orthographic and phonological units which are associated with nodes in a semantic network.

In our model, we consider the lexicon to be the part of semantic memory in which phonological units are the kernels of word entries. Lexical entries may be enriched through learning, but the nature of the information added to the lexicon is still under debate. For example, it is accepted that literacy adds knowledge about the orthographic structure of words to their phonological lexical entries.[1] More controversial, however, is the way morphology is represented and processed in the lexicon. Some models assume that lexical entries contain only word-stems along with a set of affixation (or word-formation) rules (e.g., Taft, 1985; Taft & Forster, 1975, 1976). Such models suggest that the orthographic input has to be parsed into constituent morphemes before it can gain access to the lexicon. Other models suggest that morphologically complex words are represented by separate and complete lexical entries which can be directly addressed and are nuclearly organized around a nominative (e.g., Lukatela, Gligorijević, Kostić, & Turvey, 1980). Still other models distinguish between the lexical representation of inflectional and derivational morphology, suggesting that "base words" and their inflections share a common lexical entry while derivatives have separate but related entries (e.g., Stanners, Neiser, Hernon, & Hall, 1979; see also Feldman, in press).

Models of word processing, however, may not be independent of the language to which they apply. Psycholinguistic studies in languages other than English have revealed that the nature of lexical representation and lexical processes may differ across different languages. Most of these studies focused on phonological and orthographic codes for lexical access, as illustrated in the concept of orthographic depth (e.g., Frost, in press; Frost, Katz, & Bentin, 1987; Katz & Feldman, 1983). The influence of morphologic language-specificities on word identification has been relatively less investigated although there are data consistent with such a claim. For example, Lukatela et al.'s (1980) "satellite" model, in which the nominative singular case of the noun serves as a frequency counter for all the other cases of that noun (cf. Kostić, this volume), is more plausible in the richly inflected Serbo-Croatian noun system than in English. As another example, the lexical representation and parsing of morphologically complex words which are possible in languages with an agglutinative word structure such as Turkish[2] must be different than those in a language with a nonconcatenative morphology such as Hebrew, in which different inflections and derivatives are formed by infixing word-patterns within the consonantal

---

[1]This position is not different in essence from that assuming two separate lexica, one phonological and one orthographic (e.g., Morton, 1984), as long as such a model allows for within-level bi-directional connections between comparable entries in the two lexica.

[2]In agglutinative languages the process of affixation is extremely productive, so that each word is composed of a base to which a series of affixes can be linearly concatenated and the phonologicalal form of the affix can vary according to properties of the base.

string that forms the root morpheme. In the present chapter we discuss some special properties of Hebrew morphology and review several studies in which the consequences of these morphological factors on word identification and reading processes in Hebrew have been investigated.

ROOTS AND WORD-PATTERNS: AN INTRODUCTION TO HEBREW MORPHOLOGY[3]

Hebrew is a Semitic language. In the following description we refer only to Hebrew, but the reader should remember that what is described for Hebrew may be applicable in principle and in specific for other Semitic languages as well (e.g., Arabic).

Derivational Morphology

As a rule, word formation in Hebrew is based on mounting a "word-pattern" of vowels and consonants onto a "root" which is (usually) a skeleton of consonants.

In contrast to the base-morpheme or stem in English, the Hebrew root is never a word by itself. In fact, the root is not even a phonological unit. Rather, it is an abstract linguistic entity represented by a sequence of usually three (but sometimes four) phonemes (viz., consonants). Roots convey general semantic information which is, in many cases, transparent to the reader. A specific meaning, however, cannot be accessed unless a word is formed by mounting a particular word-pattern on a root. Nevertheless, a speaker of Hebrew can form new words by mounting other word-patterns on the same root and can usually deduce the meaning of new words by extracting the root. For example, the root קשׁר (the letters **Kuf Shin Reish**)[4] refers to the concept of 'connection.' Mounting the word-pattern [- e - e -][5] on this root, the homographic noun קשׁר (**kesher**) that means either 'knot' or 'connection' or 'conspiracy' is formed. Mounting a different word-pattern such as [- a - a -] may form the noun קשָׁר (**kashar** - 'radio operator'). Other words can be derived form the same root, such as תִקְשׁוֹרֶת (**tikshoret** - 'communication'), קוֹשֵׁר (**kosher** - 'conspirator' or present masculine singular of the verb 'to tie'), and many more.

There are two major types of word-patterns, verbal and nominal. The organization of verbal patterns is relatively more systematic so we begin by describing them.

---

[3]For a detailed description of Hebrew morphology, see Lewis (1989).

[4]We refer to letters of the Hebrew alphabet by their Hebrew names. For the convenience of the English reader, the approximate sound of each letter will be emphasized using bold characters.

[5]Note that in Hebrew the vowels are represented in print by diacritical marks that are placed below, above, or within the letters. Thus, although the English transcription of the word-patterns contain letters (vowels), in Hebrew these vowels do not break the orthographic integrity of the root.

In Hebrew, there are seven main verbal word-patterns. Each verbal pattern determines the form in which a verb can be conjugated (called *binyan*, plural *binyanim*). The different *binyanim* are labeled by the pattern used to form the verb in the past tense, third person masculine singular.[6] The verbal pattern modulates the basic meaning conveyed by the root. For example, there are three active verbal patterns { [- *a* - *a* -], [- *i* - *e* -], and [*hi* - - *i* -] }, three passive verbal patterns { [- *u* - *a* -], [*ni* - - *a* -], and [*ho* - - *a* -] } which vary in relative strength of passiveness and activeness, and one reflexive pattern [*hit* - *a* - *e* -]. In addition to the grammatical roles described above, different verbal patterns mounted on the same root may considerably change the meaning of the verbs that they form. For example, the root שׁמר (**Shin Mem Reish**) refers to the concept of 'keeping,' 'watching,' or 'guarding.' Mounting the word pattern [- *a* - *a* -] on this root forms the verb שָׁמַר (*shamar*), which means 'watched' or 'guarded.' On the other hand, mounting the word-pattern [- *i* - *e* -] on the same root forms the verb שׁמר (*shimer*), which means 'preserved.' In this example, the semantic relationship between the two verbs is transparent. However, this is not always the case. Consider, for example, the root גדר (**Gimel Dalet Reish**) which refers to the concept of 'frame.' Mounting the word-pattern [- *i* - *e* -] on this root forms the verb גדר (*gider*), which means 'built a fence around,' while mounting the word-pattern [*hi* - - *i* -] on the same root forms the verb הגדיר (*higdir*), which means 'he defined. The common origin of the last two verbs may be quite easily deduced, but their semantic relationship is not completely transparent. In effect, mounting different verbal patterns on the same root may change the meaning so that the psychological reality of the semantic relationship between the resulting verbs is in question.

Most roots are not lexically represented in all seven patterns; that is, the system has many gaps. In addition, there are irregularities in derivations of verbs that involve defective roots in which, as a result of phonological changes, not all three consonants are pronounced. For example, there are several consonants that, according to morpho-phonetic rules, are not pronounced in all phonological environments. Such consonants may be silent in particular roots. The same consonants may be completely missing from the printed form of verbal roots. An example of the first kind of irregularity is the root מצא (**Mem Tzadi Aleph**), which refers to the concept of 'finding.' Note that the last letter of this root is silent: Cast in the verbal pattern [- *a* - *a* -] it forms the verb מָצָא ('found') which is pronounced /matza/, whereas cast in the verbal pattern [*ni* - - *a* -] it forms the verb נמצא ('was found'), which is pronounced /nimtza/. An example of the second form of irregularity is the root נזק (**Nun Zain Kuf**), which refers to the concept of 'damage.' Cast in the verbal pattern [*hi* - - *i* -] it forms the verb הזיק (*hizik*, 'he damaged') in which the first consonant of the root is dropped.

---

[6]Thus, unless otherwise specified, all the examples are of verbs in the past tense, third person masculine singular.

Nominal word-patterns (called *mishkalim*) are more numerous (about three dozen) and less systematic than verbal patterns. Some nominal patterns contain only vowels represented by diacritical points that are appended to the root consonants. In this case the phonological process of infixation does not break the orthographic integrity of the root. Other nominal patterns also contain vowel-letters that are infixed between the root-consonants, as is typical of a nonconcatenative morphology. Finally, there are nominal patterns that include consonants in addition to vowels. These consonants are usually prefixed or suffixed.

A large category of nominal patterns are related to the verbal system. For example, the same phonological unit used to denote the present tense of a verb can also be used as a noun and/or an adjective (accordingly, the present tense is labeled *Beinoni* which means 'intermediate'). When used as a noun it usually denotes an agent (i.e., the person performing the action),[7] but the same phonological unit is used in the verbal system to denote the action (in the present tense). For example, the root זכר (*Zayn Kaf Reish*) refers to 'memory.' Mounting the word-pattern [*hi - - i -*] on it we get the verb הִזְכִּיר (*hizkir*), which means 'he reminded.' The present form of the verb 'to remind' (masculine singular) is obtained by mounting the word-pattern [*ma - - i -*] on the same root: מַזְכִּיר (*mazcir*). Used as a noun, however, this word means 'male secretary.' The action-nominal is an example of a noun directly derived from a verb form.[8] Note, however, that a different word-pattern is used to denote the action-nominal for each one of the seven verbal patterns.

Although they are not very transparent, it is possible to distinguish some semantic consistency across different nominal patterns, which the Hebrew reader (and speaker) may or may not be aware of (e.g., Clark & Berman, 1984). For example, the pattern [- *a- a* -] is frequently used to form agents with roots that are not used to form verbs. Thus, נַגָר (*nagar*) means 'carpenter,' כַּנָר (*kanar*) means 'violinist,' גַנָן (*ganan*) means 'gardener,' etc. However, the same word-pattern may also be used to form adjectives such as חַלָשׁ (*halash*) meaning 'weak,' or חָזָק (*hazak*) meaning 'strong.' Other semantic categories of word patterns may be found. To give one additional example, the ending [*ia*] in various word patterns is frequently used to name the place in which the action

---

[7]Note that the present tense is only one of the possible mechanisms for forming agents from a verbal root. Other patterns that are frequently used to form agents are [*a - - an*], such as in *rakdan* ('dancer'; whose root is *Reish Kuf Dalet* which refers to 'dancing') and [- *a -a* -], such as in *ganav* ('thief'; whose root is *Gimel Nun Beit* which refers to 'stealing').

[8]To get the flavor of how the derivational system works, here are several additional examples of words derived form the same root: זִכָּרוֹן (*zicaron*), which means 'memory'; מַזְכֶּרֶת (*mazkeret*), which means 'souvenir'; the verb זָכַר (*zachar*), which means 'remembered'; and the adjectives מוּזְכָּר (*muzcar*), which means 'mentioned/cited,' and זָכוּר (*zachur*), which means 'remembered.'

takes place. For example נַגָּרְיָה (*nagaria*) is a 'carpenter shop,' סִפְרִיָּה (*sifria*) is a 'library,' and צָרְכָנִיָּה (*tzarkania*) is a 'grocery store' (the root of the latter is צרכ (*Tzadi Reish Kaf*), which refers to the concept of 'needs'). A final example is the pattern [- *a* - *e* - *et*] which is frequently used to denote diseases.

There are numerous exceptions to these rules, and the semantic categories of nominal word-patterns are very loose. There are, moreover, word-patterns that are not semantically informative. Nevertheless, despite the high variability and uncertainty regarding the semantic role of word-patterns, Hebrew speakers tend to agree on what word-pattern should be used to form words of a particular semantic category, and colloquial new words are frequently formed using predictable patterns.

What is common to the processes of derivation described above is that the word-pattern (or at least most of it) is infixed into the root to form a word. Once a word is formed, however, its inflection usually requires the addition of suffixes and/or prefixes (and vowel change inside), much as in English. We now briefly describe, in brief, the inflectional system in Hebrew.

Inflectional Morphology

The inflectional system of the Hebrew language is richer and more complex than that of English. Verbs are inflected for person, number, gender, and tense, and adjectives are inflected for number and gender. In addition to number and gender, nouns are also inflected for relations such as locative and possessive, as well as a specific construct state which forms compound words. In contrast to the derivational process, in which the basic constituents (the root and the word-pattern) are not words, in Hebrew, as in other languages, inflectional variants are usually formed by attaching prefixes and suffixes to real words. However, due to morphophonemic and phonotactic rules, the process for inflection may also require some changes to the word pattern. Let us first consider the inflectional system for verbs.

As mentioned above, in the process of conjugation, verbs are inflected to denote person, number, gender, and tense. Because the verb includes all this information, pronouns are usually not necessary and therefore frequently are omitted. The inflection of verbs is very systematic. In the past tense, the person is denoted by suffixes added to the basic verbal form (third person masculine singular). In the future tense, the person is denoted mainly by prefixes (in all cases) and suffixes (in some cases) added to a basic future form. Table 1 presents the conjugation of the verb based on the root שמר (*Shin Mem Reish*), which refers to the concept of 'watching,' 'guarding,' or 'keeping.'

In Hebrew, there is no unequivocal verb form for the present tense. As we have mentioned previously, the phonological unit that is used to denote the present tense may also be used as a noun or an adjective. In the present tense the verb does not change with person, but it is inflected for gender and number. For example, in the present tense masculine singular the verb 'to watch' (conjugated in Table 1) is שׁוֹמֵר (*shomer*), which is also the noun 'guard.' The inflection of this verb for the feminine gender and the plural number requires the use of suffixes also used for nouns and adjectives, to which we now turn.

Common inflections for nouns and adjectives specify gender and number. Some nouns (mostly living things) have both a masculine and a feminine form. Objects, on the other hand, are either feminine or masculine. Both types of inflections are achieved by adding specific suffixes to the masculine singular form. However, because of morpho-phonemic and phonotactic rules, gender inflection may result in some phonemic changes in addition to affixation. The feminine singular usually requires either the suffix [*et*] or the suffix [*a*]. So, for example, a 'female guard' is denoted by שׁוֹמֶרֶת (*shomeret*). However, the masculine noun יֶלֶד (*yeled*), which means 'boy,' is inflected and phonemically altered to form יַלְדָּה (*yaldah*), the feminine, 'girl.' The plural usually requires the suffix [*im*] for masculine and [*ot*] for feminine. Thus 'male guards' are שׁוֹמְרִים (*shomrim*) and 'female guards' are שׁוֹמְרוֹת (*shomrot*). There are, however, some exceptions to these rules.[9]

TABLE 1. *The past and future tense conjugations of the verb 'to guard.'*

Past			Future		
(I) watched	שָׁמַרְתִּי	(shamarti)	(I) will watch	אֶשְׁמֹר	(eshmor)
(you, ms)	שָׁמַרְתָּ	(shamarta)	(you, ms)	תִּשְׁמֹר	(tishmor)
(you, fs)	שָׁמַרְתְּ	(shamart)	(you, fs)	תִּשְׁמְרִי	tishmeri)
(he)	שָׁמַר	(shamar)	(he)	יִשְׁמֹר	(yishmor)
(she)	שָׁמְרָה	(shamra)	(she)	תִּשְׁמֹר	(tishmor)
(we)	שָׁמַרְנוּ	(shamarnu)	(we)	נִשְׁמֹר	(nishmor)
(you, mp)	שְׁמַרְתֶּם	(shmartem)	(you, mp)	תִּשְׁמְרוּ	(tishmeru)
(you, fp)	שְׁמַרְתֶּן	(shmarten)	(you, fp)	תִּשְׁמְרוּ*	(tishmeru)
(they)	שָׁמְרוּ	(shamru)	(they)	יִשְׁמְרוּ	(yishmeru)

*There is an older form for the future feminine plural תִּשְׁמֹרְנָה (*tishmorna*), which is not used in colloquial Hebrew.

---

[9]For example, an 'egg' (which is feminine) is בֵּיצָה (*beitza*), but the plural form follows the masculine form בֵּיצִים (*beitzim*).

The possessive case is formed by adding suffixes (possessive pronouns) that vary with person. For example 'my guard' is שׁוֹמְרִי (*shomri*), 'your guard' is שׁוֹמְרְךָ (*shomrcha*), 'his guard' is שׁוֹמְרוֹ (*shomro*), etc.[10] Several suffixes may be concatenated—for example, 'my (female) guard' is שׁוֹמְרָתִי (*shomarti*)—but in colloquial speech these forms are rarely used. Instead, alternative unaffixed forms are used, such as שׁוֹמֶרֶת שֶׁלִי (*shomeret sheli*, where *sheli* means "my'). To specify definiteness, the prefix [*ha*] is used. Thus, 'the guard' is הַשׁוֹמֵר (*hashomer*) in the masculine and הַשׁוֹמֶרֶת (*hashomeret*) in the feminine.

Nouns are also inflected to form a compound-like structure—the *construct nominal* (Levi, 1976). This form is very frequent in the Hebrew nominal system and is a morpho-syntactic construction formed of two nouns, of which the first is the head (which is usually inflected) and the second is the modifier. The construct nominal in Hebrew is used for many purposes. Most frequently it replaces the possessive particle 'of' (שֶׁל, *shel*), as in בֵּית חוֹלִים (*beit holim*) rather than בֵּית שֶׁל חוֹלִים (*bayt shel holim*) which means 'hospital' but literally translated is 'house of sick persons.' Other uses of the construct nominal are, for example, to substitute for the relations 'have' (e.g., *lev arieh*, 'lion-heart'[11]) 'use' (e.g., *maghezt eydim*, 'steam iron'), 'be' (e.g., *kadur sheleg*, 'snow ball'), 'in' (*aruhat boker*, 'morning-meal' or 'breakfast'), and 'for' (e.g., *naaley bayt*, 'house-shoes' or 'slippers').

This description of Hebrew morphology is by no means complete. Nevertheless, it was our intent to provide the reader with the flavor of its distinctive properties and with sufficient background for understanding its implications for written word identification and reading. To summarize, the main aspect in which Hebrew diverges from non-Semitic languages is its process of derivation. If we consider both the root and word-pattern to be morphemes, almost all Hebrew words are at least bi-morphemic. A second distinctive characteristic is its process of infixation, which compromises the continuity of the root. Hebrew is thus an example of a nonconcatenative language in which there are no base morphemes that function as uninterrupted phonological units.

The inflectional system of Hebrew is more similar to that of non-Semitic languages than its derivational system, in that it includes all three kinds of affixes (prefixes, infixes, and suffixes). It is, however, richer and more complex than that of English. In the following sections we examine the implications of the Hebrew morphological system for word identification and provide some evidence for its psychological reality.

---

[10]In colloquial speech these forms are rarely used except with certain kinship terms (my brother, my father, etc.). Mostly, possessive cases are conveyed by adding the possessive pronoun.

[11]Although the Hebrew construct nominal has the head noun first, for the ease of reading the literal translation will reflect the normal order for English nominal of modifier first and head noun second.

The Psychological Reality of Roots and Word Patterns

Because the root-structure of Hebrew words is explicitly taught in school, finding sensitivity to roots and word patterns in children younger than school age may provide strong evidence for the natural emergence and for the psychological reality of this morphological system. Relevant data have been published in a number of studies.

The development of morphological structures and the productive use of such structures in children's language was examined with children as young as two years old (Levy, 1988). Results of a longitudinal study in which the spontaneous speech of two children was recorded and analyzed revealed that the children commanded a wealth of inflectional forms. They used all tenses, a variety of persons, both genders, and both number forms. All seven verbal structures (*binyanim*) were present, and the frequency of use was fairly similar to that observed in adult speech. Additional insight into the children's morphological ability was obtained by analyzing their errors. For example, in forming the feminine singular gender of present tense verbs children occasionally substituted an inappropriate feminine suffix (usually the [*a*]) for the other [*et*]. Similarly, for defective roots children tended to apply inflectional patterns to the regular root when an irregular was appropriate (Berman, 1980, 1982). The pattern of errors, even more than their correct speech, suggests that children as young as 2 years apply inflectional rules to roots and do not simply mimic adult speech.

As has been described above, morphosyntactic agreement rules in Hebrew require the sentential components to agree in gender and number. Both verbs and nouns are inflected accordingly. A study of the development of plurals for Hebrew nouns (Levy, 1983) showed that children started by assigning the masculine plural suffix to all nouns, regardless of their gender or number. Only later did they gradually become sensitive to the distinction between masculine and feminine plural suffixes. It is interesting to note that they first used stringent rules, assigning the feminine plural suffix /ot/ to all singular nouns that end in /a/ and the masculine plural suffix /im/ to all other nouns (masculine or feminine). By the middle of the second year, the children started to use the feminine plural suffix for feminine singular nouns ending with /et/ as well, and by age 3, they mastered the gender of all plural nouns that were not exceptions.

An additional insight relevant for the present discussion is provided by errors related to the internal phonological vowel changes that are required to change singular nouns into the plural. Apparently, children did not master these internal vowel changes as early as they mastered the proper suffixes. However, once they began to introduce vowel changes it was not done randomly. Rather, they drew upon their knowledge of derived forms and tried them out as a possible basis for these changes. The early development of noun gender-appropriate plural inflection is remarkable because this process could not be motivated solely by the need to communicate better. Note that the initial use of the /im/ (masculine) plural suffix is sufficient for the child to convey his/her intentions. In the case of gender agreement as well, children systematize the data on some formal non-semantic basis before they understand the semantic notion carried by this linguistic distinction. The pattern of gender and number development thus supports the view that the morphological system is psychologically real and is not only parasitic on the child's need to communicate (for an alternative view see Ninio & Snow, 1988).

The psychological reality of the derivational system in Hebrew is demonstrated by a study of Clark and Berman (1984). In that study children from 3 to 7 years old were asked to produce innovative (i.e., nonexistent) agents and instruments from real verbs presented in the infinitive form. Verbs were presented to the children by the experimenter in the context of a question in which the activity of the agent or the use of the instrument was described. In order to increase the probability that children would produce novel forms, the selected verbs represented activities that had no conventional agent or instrument noun. Following the production test, a perception (comprehension) test was administered in which the same children were asked to describe the characteristic activity of the innovative agent or the use of an innovative instrument. The materials were formed by mounting the conventional word-patterns (which in these particular cases were not appropriate) on existing roots.[12] Adults used as a control group in this study were able to perform the perception tests with 100% accuracy.

The results showed that the children were able to comprehend the agents and the instruments well above chance. Among preschoolers, the comprehension of agents ranged from 59% in the 3-year-olds to 87% in the 5-year-olds. The comprehension of instrument-nouns was slightly worse, 42% in the 3-year-olds and 68% in the 5-year-olds. Note that successful comprehension of the innovative nouns could not be based on prior word knowledge. In order to interpret these nouns, the children had to be able to extract the consonantal skeleton root that was combined with an affixal word-pattern. Because more than one type of word-pattern may be used to form agents or instruments, there was more than one "correct" response for each verb. If we add together all the responses in which the noun was produced by mounting a correct word-pattern on the correct root, the performance ranged between 46% for the youngest group and 79% for the five-year-olds (compared with 88% in adults). Hence, although developmental trends were found in both tests, even the youngest children

---

[12]To illustrate the manipulation, a nominal pattern frequently used to form agents is [- a - - an], while [ma - - e - a] is often used to form instrument nouns. From the infinitive לדפוק(lidfok), which means 'to knock,' and the two word-patterns above, one could form the agent דפקן(dafkan) and the instrument מדפקה(madfeka). Although morphologically correct and semantically understandable, they do not exist in the Hebrew lexicon.

showed significant awareness of both roots and word-patterns and above-chance ability to manipulate these morphological units.

Summing up, the following picture emerges: Hebrew-speaking children establish inflectional and derivational paradigms which are independent of their semantic role. These paradigms may be observed as early as the children can be tested (at 2 years of age) and reflect their ability to separately manipulate roots and word-patterns. In speech, this ability develops naturally, without the intervention of explicit teaching. In the following sections we examine the influence of morphological relations on fluent reading.

STUDIES OF VISUAL WORD PROCESSING IN HEBREW

Parsing Words into Morphemes

Ample evidence suggests that subjects are aware of the constituent structure of morphologically complex words during visual word recognition. Data derive from studies in English (Kelliher & Henderson, 1990; for a review of earlier literature, see Stolz & Feldman, this volume; Taft, 1985) as well as Italian (Caramazza, Laudanna, & Romani, 1988; Laudanna, Badecker, & Caramazza, 1992), Dutch (Bergman, Hudson, & Eling, 1988; Schreifers, Zwitserlood, & Roelofs, 1991), and Serbo-Croatian (Feldman, Kostić, Lukatela, & Turvey, 1982). Typically, morphologically complex words in these languages are constructed by appending affixes to a stem which is often a word by itself. In contrast, the root and word-pattern of which Hebrew words are composed have no independent existence as words. It is possible, therefore, that roots and (derivational) word-patterns, because they are always combined to form words, are never decomposed during visual word processing, while the root and inflectional affixes added to form words are decomposed. On the other hand, because both the roots and word-patterns are productive and carry semantic information, identifying inflectional words may require decomposing them into their morphemic constituents.

The psycholinguistic aspects of Hebrew morphology are still at an early stage of investigation. Nevertheless there are some data, which are summarized in the present chapter. We begin our review by describing the case in which Hebrew is fairly similar to other languages, that is, studies in which the relevant morphemic units were inflectional prefixes.

Studies in English have revealed that very common function words (such as *the, an,* and *of*) tend to conceal their constituent letters. This effect is typically demonstrated by a significantly higher percentage of omissions for function words than for content words in letter cancellation tasks (e.g., Corcoran, 1966; Drewnowsky & Healy, 1977; Proctor & Healy, 1985) and was therefore labeled "the missing letter effect" (Healy, 1976). Several interpretations of this effect have been suggested. One is based on the assumption that, because the function words in which target letters appear are very frequent in the language, their whole-word orthographic pattern activates a unitized representation, thus bypassing analysis of their lower level, constituent letters (Drewnowsky & Healy, 1980; Healy & Drewnowsky, 1983). Other accounts of the missing letter effect suggest that subjects may not carefully attend to function words because they are highly predictable and redundant in text. Hebrew morphology provides an opportunity to examine this phenomenon because in Hebrew many syntactic and morpho-syntactic functions are achieved by the addition of an inflectional prefix (such as the definite article "הַ" (ha)) to the root. The representation of functors by prefixes is as frequent as by separate function words. Moreover, a sequence of several functors (such as *from the* or *and that from the*) may be represented in Hebrew by a sequence of several prefix-letters sequentially appended to the word. In a series of studies (Greenberg & Koriat, 1991; Koriat & Greenberg, 1991, 1993; Koriat, Greenberg, & Goldshmid, 1991) the missing letter effect was found for Hebrew prefixes as well as for Hebrew function words: The same letter was omitted significantly more often when it served as a prefix (as for example the "מ" in מכאן (*mekan*), 'from here') than when it was part of the root (as for example in מלון (*melon*), 'melon'). Similar effects were found for prefixes appended to nonsensical roots (nonwords). From the morphological perspective, these findings are evidence that the inflectional prefix is analyzed separately from the root and word-pattern, viz., separately from the word to which it is affixed. Note, however, that this analysis does not occur to lexical access, as was suggested by Taft (1981), because when several functor-prefixes are sequentially appended to one word (e.g., וּמֵהַכֶּרֶם (*umeihakerem*), 'and from the vineyard'), the missing-letter effect was found primarily for the initial functors (Koriat & Greenberg, 1993). This result contradicts the claim that stems are stripped of all their affixes prior to lexical access.

Evidence that Hebrew readers are sensitive to both roots and word-patterns during visual word processing comes from a recent study in which a "segment shifting task" was used (Feldman, Frost, & Pnini, in press). The segment shifting task was developed by Feldman and her associates to compare subjects' ability to segment words along morphemic boundaries with their ability to break unitary morphemes (Feldman, 1991; Feldman & Fowler, 1987). In this task, the subject is provided with a source word followed by a target word. The task is to take part of the source word and attach it to the target, forming a morphologically complex word, and to name the resulting word as rapidly as possible. The main manipulation is on the morphemic structure of the source word from which the segment gets shifted. In one condition the segment is an affixed morpheme (such as the /en/ in *harden*), whereas in the other condition the segment is part of the stem morpheme (such as the /en/ in *garden*). The dependent variable is the time necessary to shift the designated segment from the source to the target, measured from the onset of the target display to the onset of naming. Previous studies in Serbo-Croatian (a highly inflected language) revealed that shifting latencies were faster when the segment was a suffix than when it was part of the stem (Feldman, 1994). Similar results were found in English (Feldman et al., submitted; Stolz & Feldman, this volume). These results suggest that in English as well as in Serbo-Croatian it is easier for subjects to segment and shift letter sequences from the source to the target when the sequence constitutes a morphological unit in the source than when it does not.

As noted previously, both English and Serbo-Croatian are example of concatenative morphologies in which affixes are usually appended to stems. Moreover, in all previous studies in these languages, all the segments that had to be shifted took the form of final syllables. In Hebrew morphology, on the other hand, infixation of the word pattern results (at least at the phonological level) in "breaking up" the consonantal root; thus, Hebrew is an example of a nonconcatenative morphology. If morphological effects generalize across different types of morphologies and over segments that are not final syllables then similar results are expected in the segment shifting task with Hebrew material. If shifting infixed segments in Hebrew shows the same pattern of results as shifting suffixes in English and Serbo-Croatian, this would indicate an effect of morphological organization on parsing words that cannot be attributed to a simple visual analysis of the letter string.

In contrast to the segment shifting studies in English and Serbo-Croatian, in the Hebrew version of this task the shifted segment was always the word pattern; hence, it was always a morpheme (at least by some linguistic accounts). However, it was not a phonological unit concatenated to the base. These word patterns were combined either with roots that could take other patterns as well (productive roots) or with roots that were unique in the sense that there is only one Hebrew word in which they can appear (nonproductive roots). Thus, the distinction between word pattern and root in the second type of words, although linguistically valid, may not have been psychologically real.

The subjects were native Hebrew speakers. Each trial was composed of two stages. First a source word with vowels (pointed) was presented. This word contained either a productive or a nonproductive root combined with a regular nominal word pattern. In the second stage the word disappeared and a meaningless string of unpointed consonants was presented. The subject's task was to name the string of consonants using the word pattern of the source word. By a morphological account it should be easier to detach word patterns from productive roots than from nonproductive roots because the morphological parser typically parses the former type of words. In addition to demonstrating that roots and word-patterns are psychologically distinct, such a result would also support the view that these two morphemes actually are separated during the process of word identification. A second departure of the Hebrew paradigm from the original segment shifting task was that the target stimulus was not a word. In fact, it was not even a meaningful root. Therefore, mounting the shifted word pattern on the target root always formed a pseudoword. This procedure ensured that the effects that were found could not be accounted for by pure lexical factors or by syntactic factors such as similarity (or dissimilarity) in word class between the source and the target.

As predicted by the morphological account, the targets were named faster if the root of the source word segment was productive than if it was not productive. This pattern was observed both when the word-pattern was comprised of vowels only (e.g., [- a - a -] in גַּנָּב - 'thief'), in which case the orthographic integrity of the root remained intact (because the vowels were represented by diacritics appended below the consonants), and when the word-pattern was comprised of vowels represented by letters in addition to diacritics (/o/ = "ו", /i/ = "י"), in which case the orthographic integrity of the root was compromised (e.g., מוֹקֵד (moked), 'focus'). The effect was in fact strongest when the word pattern included consonants in addition to vowels (e.g., [ma - - e - et] in מַזְכֶּרֶת - 'souvenir'). This comparison must be interpreted with caution, as different word patterns were included in the two sets.

The segment shifting effect in Hebrew provides empirical evidence that Hebrew word identification includes a stage in which roots and word-patterns are decomposed. In addition, it contributes to our understanding of the segment shifting effect in English and Serbo-Croatian, suggesting that morphological parsing is indeed one of its stages. In particular, since similar effects were observed for both Hebrew pseudoword and English and Serbo-Croatian real-word targets, it is unlikely that syntactic or morpho-syntactic compatibility between the source and the target in the morphemic condition and incompatibility in the non-morphemic condition plays a role. In addition, since both meaningful and meaningless stimuli showed an effect of morphology in this task, it is unlikely that the effect reflects lexical or semantic processing. Finally, it is significant that the effect occurred in Hebrew, where the shifted segment was distributed across syllables, as well as in English, where it was a phonologically and orthographically coherent unit. This finding makes it unlikely that phonological and/or orthographic coherence of the to-be-shifted sequence is a major factor accounting for the segment shifting effect.

Repeating a Morpheme

Many studies have demonstrated that the processing of repeated stimuli is faster and more accurate than processing the same stimuli for the first time (e.g., Forbach, Stanners, & Hochhous, 1974; Scarborough, Cortese, & Scarborough, 1977). In addition to an effect with identical repetitions (full repetition), facilitation has also been observed when some but not all structural or formal aspects of the stimulus are repeated (partial repetition; e.g., Bentin, 1989; Fowler et al., 1985). The word that is presented first in such a pair is labeled the "prime" and the word presented second the "target." Partial repetition has been used to examine the processing and lexical organization of morphologically complex words. Significant facilitation has been observed when prime and target preserved the morphological stem and had different inflections or derivatives. This effect is known as the "morphological repetition effect" (Feldman, 1992; Feldman & Fowler, 1987; Feldman & Moskovljević, 1987; Fowler, Napps, & Feldman, 1985; Kemply & Morton, 1982; Monsell, 1985; Murrell & Morton, 1974; Stanners, Neiser, Hernon, & Hall, 1979; Stanners, Neiser, & Painton, 1979).

The morphological repetition effect in Hebrew was recently examined in two studies (Bentin & Feldman, 1990; Feldman & Bentin, 1994). In both, the root was repeated, each time with a different word-pattern. The first study (Bentin & Feldman, 1990) compared semantic priming with morphologic repetition priming. Taking advantage of the large number of words in which a Hebrew root may appear and the semantic variability among those words, the authors formed three types of prime-target pairs. The same target word was paired with a semantically but not morphologically related prime in the "semantic relation" condition (S), with a morphologically but not semantically related prime in the "morphologic relation" condition (M), and with a prime that was related both morphologically and semantically in the "semantic plus morphologic relation" condition (SM). Morphologically related words were words formed combining the same root with different word-patterns. For example, the target מִגְדָל (*migdal,* 'tower' derived from the root *Gimel Dalet Lamed*) was paired with the prime צְרִיחַ (tzeriah, 'turret') in the S condition, with the prime גָדוּל (*gydul,* 'tumor') in the M condition and with the prime גָדוֹל (*gadol,* 'big') in the SM condition. The lexical decision latency from the onset of the target in each of these conditions was compared with an "unrelated" condition in which the same target was paired with an unrelated prime. Facilitation in lexical decision was examined when the target followed the prime immediately (short-lag condition) and when separated by 15 intervening items (long-lag condition). The same prime-target pairs appeared for different subjects at long and at short lags.

Repetition at short-lag facilitated lexical decision in all three relatedness conditions. The effect of semantic priming in the S condition (48 ms) was similar to that in the SM condition (51 ms), and both were significantly greater than the effect in the M condition (21 ms). With long-lag repetition, on the other hand, targets were facilitated only in the M and SM conditions (24 ms and 28 ms, respectively). That is, in contrast to the effect at short-lag, pure semantic priming did not facilitate lexical decision when the target was separated from the prime by 15 intervening stimuli.

Because the morphological relationship in this study was based on the repetition of the root, the results of this study provide further support for the claims that subjects were sensitive to the root during the process of word identification. Moreover, since neither the root nor the word pattern could have independent lexical entries, it is unlikely that the extraction of the root occurs prior to lexical access. The long-lasting morphological repetition effect cannot be accounted for by a semantic relationship, because semantic priming does not exist at long lags and because the magnitude of the long-lag facilitation in the SM condition was similar to that measured in the M condition. Finally, it is unlikely that orthographic similarity between prime and target, which is characteristic of repetition of the root, could account for the observed pattern of facilitation. Support for the latter claim was provided by Bentin (1989), who demonstrated that pure orthographic repetition (repetition of the consonants in different words that are not morphologically related, e.g., מֶלַח (melah, 'salt') and מַלָּח (malah, 'sailor')) did not facilitate lexical decision for the target (for similar findings in English, see Henderson, Wallis, & Knight, 1984; Murrell & Morton, 1974). The conclusion is, therefore, that the derivatives of a root are interrelated in the lexicon and that this organization is not necessarily dependent on the semantic network. A detailed description of the morphological organization of the lexicon must await additional research (but see Bybee, this volume).

Additional insight into the morphological organization of the lexicon and further evidence against an orthographic account of partial (morphological) repetition effects comes from a recent study of repetition effects in Hebrew (Feldman & Bentin, 1994). In that study the authors asked whether the effect of morphological repetition in Hebrew is different when the root is orthographically continuous (i.e., combined with word-patterns containing only diacritic vowels which do not disrupt the consonantal sequence of the root) and when it is orthographically disrupted (i.e., combined with word-patterns that include at least one letter-vowel which is inserted between the consonants of the root) and whether it is different for inflections and derivations based on the same root. In English the evidence for inflections vs. derivations is inconclusive. As briefly mentioned in the introduction to the present chapter, Stanners et al. (1979) found that word-stems used as targets were primed by inflections as strongly as by full (identity) repetitions. In contrast, although derivatives of those stems also produced significant facilitation, the priming effect was significantly smaller than the effect of full repetition. Consequently, those authors concluded that inflections share the same lexical entry as the stem, whereas derivatives are lexically represented by different but interrelated entries. This suggestion was challenged, however, by Fowler et al. (1985), who found that when episodic memory for the prime was controlled, the facilitative repetition effect for identity, derivational, and inflectional repetition was similar. Repetition of the root across inflectional and derivational, word patterns in Hebrew provides an ideal opportunity to examine this issue further because it allows good control over the orthographic and morpho-syntactic similarity between the prime and the target in the derivational and inflectional relation conditions.

Feldman and Bentin (1994) compared the magnitude of the repetition effect (at variable lags ranging between 7 and 13 intervening items) caused by identity, inflection, and derivation repetition. The results revealed that all three types of primes facilitated lexical decision for the target similarly. This outcome was obtained with primes that had orthographically continuous roots as well as with disrupted roots. These results were replicated in additional experiments in which the morphological structure of nonwords was manipulated (nonwords contained meaningful roots and legal word patterns which were improperly combined). Thus, even when the lexical decision could not have been based solely on the analysis of the root, inflection, derivation, and identity primes produced equivalent facilitation. Results were similar for words with continuous roots and for words with disrupted roots.

CONCLUSION

In the present chapter a brief but comprehensive description of Hebrew morphology aimed at psycholinguists and experimental psychologists who are interested in word perception processes is offered. For pure linguistic purposes the description is probably insufficient, because we emphasized primarily the special properties of Hebrew word formation, omitting those morphological and morpho-syntactic processes that are more or less universal.

Clearly, the root and word-pattern system particular to Semitic languages, in combination with the specific manner in which vowels are represented in print, is the most interesting aspect of Hebrew word formation. The possibility of using concatenated prefixes to substitute for most function words is useful for testing theories of orthographic processing and may provide an interesting tool for the investigation of phrase and sentence processing and their relation to the lexicon. Finally, the richness of most roots and some word patterns, their differential semantic transparency, and the fact that neither of these two types of morphemes is independently represented permit elegant investigations of the independent contributions of morphologic, semantic, and lexical phonological/orthographic processes to word identification.

At the present time, only a few studies have taken advantage of the promising potential of Hebrew morphology. Much more needs to be done. Nevertheless, a few conclusions can already be drawn. First, our data do not support models of prelexical morphologic decomposition. Rather, it appears that all the possible derivations of one root (i.e., all the possible words that are formed by mounting different word-patterns on one root) are represented by separate but interrelated lexical entries. Hence, there is evidence that the organization of the lexicon includes morphological principles. Other authors have shown that phonological factors such as rhyming may also influence the processing of words, suggesting phonologically based lexical organization (Lukatela & Turvey, 1991). The multitude and the complexity of the inter-lexical relationship among words may suggest that each lexical entry can participate in separate networks that may co-exist in parallel in the lexicon. Second, there are strong indications that the root and the word-pattern are probably considered separately during the process of word identification. It is possible that this separation is required in order to find the meaning of the word, suggesting the possibility that the semantic network interacts with the lexicon via an interface in which roots and word patterns are independent nodes.

Obviously, additional investigation needs to be done. We hope that the present chapter will stimulate additional word processing research in Hebrew and promote international cooperation in which linguistic rules and mechanisms for word perception will be compared across languages.

ACKNOWLEDGMENT

This study was supported by a grant from Israeli Foundation Trustees. The description of the Hebrew morphology gained from comments made by Benny Shanon, Yael Ziv, Yonata Levi, and Neomi Goldbloom, to whom our thanks are extended. The comments made by Joan Bybee, Avital Deutsch, and Laurie Feldman on a previous version of this chapter are appreciated.

REFERENCES

Bentin, S. (1989). Orthography and phonology in lexical decision: Evidence from repetition effects at different lags. *Journal of Experimental Psychology: Learning, Memory, and Cognition, 15,* 61-72.

Bentin, S., & Feldman, L. B. (1990). The contribution of morphological and semantic relatedness to repetition priming at short and long lags: Evidence from Hebrew. *The Quarterly Journal of Experimental Psychology, 42A,* 693-711.

Bergman, M. W., Hudson, P. T. W., & Eling, P. A. T. M. (1988). How simple complex words can be: Morphological processing and word representation. *The Quarterly Journal of Experimental Psychology, 40A,* 41-72.

Berman, R. A. (1980). Child language as evidence for grammatical description: Preschoolers' construal of transitivity in the verb system of Hebrew. *Linguistics, 18,* 677-701.

Berman, R. A. (1982). Verb pattern alternation: The interface of morphology, syntax, and semantics in Hebrew child language. *Journal of Child Language, 9,* 169-191

Caramazza, A., Laudanna, A., & Romani, C. (1988). Lexical access and inflectional morphology. *Cognition, 28,* 297-332.

Clark, E. V., & Berman, R. A. (1984). Language structure and language use in the acquisition of word-formation. *Language, 6,* 542-590.

Corcoran, D. W. J. (1966). An acoustic factor in letter cancellation. *Nature, 210,* 658.

Drewnowsky, A., & Healy, A. F. (1977). Detection errors on *the* and *and*: Evidence for reading units larger than the word. *Memory & Cognition, 5,* 636-647.

Drewnowsky, A., & Healy, A. F. (1980). Missing *-ing* in reading: Letter detection errors on word endings. *Journal of Verbal Learning and Verbal Behavior, 19,* 247-262.

Feldman, L. B. (1991). The contribution of morphology to word repetition. *Psychological Research, 53,* 33-41.

Feldman, L. B. (1992). Morphological relationships revealed through the repetition priming task. In M. Noonan, P. Downing, & S. Lima (Eds.), *The linguistics of literacy* (pp. 239-254). Amsterdam: John Benjamins.

Feldman, L. B. (1993). Bi-alphabetism and the design of a reading mechanism. In D. M. Willows, R. S. Kurt, & E. Corco (Eds.), *Visual process in reading and reading disabilities* (pp. 237-261). Hillsdale, NJ: Lawrence Erlbaum Associates.

Feldman, L. B. (1994). Beyond orthography and phonology: Differences between inflections and derivatives. *Journal of Memory & Language, 33,* 442-470.

Feldman, L. B., & Bentin, S. (1994). Morphological analysis of disrupted morphemes: Evidence from Hebrew. *Quarterly Journal of Experimental Psychology.*

Feldman, L. B., & Fowler, C. A. (1987). The inflected noun system in Serbo-Croatian: Lexical representation of morphological structure. *Memory & Cognition, 15,* 1-12.

Feldman, L. B., Frost, R., & Pnini, T. (in press). Morphemes need not be syllabic units.

Feldman, L. B., Kostić, A., Lukatela, G., & Turvey, M. T. (1982). An evaluation of the "basic orthographic syllabic structure" in a phonologically shallow orthography. *Psychological Research, 45,* 55-72.

Feldman, L. B., & Moskovljević, J. (1987). Repetition priming is not purely episodic in origin. *Journal of Experimental Psychology: Learning, Memory, and Cognition, 13,* 573-581.

Fowler, C. A., Napps, S. E., & Feldman, L. B. (1985). Lexical entries are shared by regular, irregular, and morphologically-related words. *Memory & Cognition, 13,* 241-255.

Forbach, G. B., Stanners, R. F., & Hochhous, L. (1974). Repetition and practice effects in a lexical decision task. *Memory & Cognition, 2,* 337-339.

Frost, R. (1994). Prelexical and postlexical strategies in reading: Evidence from a deep and a shallow orthography. *Journal of Experimental Psychology: Learning, Memory, and Cognition, 20,* 116-129.

Frost, R., Katz, L., & Bentin, S. (1987). Strategies for visual word recognition and orthographical depth. *Journal of Experimental Psychology: Human Perception and Performance, 13,* 104-115.

Greenberg, S. N., & Koriat, A. (1991). The missing-letter effect for common function words depends on their linguistic function in the phrase. *Journal of Experimental Psychology: Learning, Memory, and Cognition, 17,* 1049-1059.

Healy, A. F. (1976). Detection errors on the word THE: Evidence for reading units larger than letters. *Journal of Experimental Psychology: Human Perception and Performance, 2,* 235-242.

Healy, A. F., & Drewnowsky, A. (1983). Investigation of the boundaries of reading units: Letter detection in misspelled words. *Journal of Experimental Psychology: Human Perception and Performance, 9,* 413-426.

Henderson, L., Wallis, J., & & Knight, D. (1984). Morphemic structure and lexical access. In H. H. Bouma & D. Bouwhuis (Eds.), *Attention and Performance X* (pp. 211-224). Hillsdale, NJ: Lawrence Erlbaum Associates.

Jared, D., & Seidenberg, M. S. (1991). Does word identification proceed from spelling to sound to meaning? *Journal of Experimental Psychology: General, 120,* 358-394.

Katz, L., & Feldman, L. B. (1983). Relation between pronunciation and recognition of printed words in deep and shallow orthographies. *Journal of Experimental Psychology: Learning, Memory, and Cognition, 9,* 157-166.

Kelliher, S., & Henderson, L. (1990). Morphologically based frequency effects in the recognition of irregularly inflected verbs. *British Journal of Psychology, 81,* 527-539.

Kemply, S., & Morton, J. (1982). The effects of priming with regularly and irregularly related words in auditory word recognition. *British Journal of Psychology, 73,* 441-454.

Koriat, A., & Greenberg, S. N. (1991). Syntactic control of letter detection: Evidence from English and Hebrew nonwords. *Journal of Experimental Psychology: Learning, Memory, and Cognition, 17,* 1033-1048.

Koriat, A., & Greenberg, S. N. (1993). Prominence of leading functors in function morpheme sequences as evidenced by letter detection. *Journal of Experimental Psychology: Learning, Memory, and Cognition, 19,* 34-50.

Koriat, A., Greenberg, S. N., & Goldshmid, Y. (1991). The missing letter effect in Hebrew: Word frequency or word function? *Journal of Experimental Psychology: Learning, Memory, and Cognition, 17,* 66-80.

Laudanna, A., Badecker, W., & Caramazza, A. (1992). Processing inflectional and derivational morphology. *Journal of Memory and Language, 31,* 333-348.

Levi, J. N. (1976). A semantic analysis of Hebrew compound nominals. In. P. Cole (Ed.), *Studies in modern Hebrew syntax and semantics* (pp. 9-55). Amsterdam: North Holland.

Levy, Y. (1983). The acquisition of Hebrew plurals: The case of the missing gender category. *Journal of Child Language, 10,* 107-121.

Levy, Y. (1988). The nature of early language: Evidence from the development of Hebrew morphology. In Y. Levy, I. M. Schlesinger, & M. D. S. Braine

(Eds.), *Categories and processes in language acquisition*. Hillsdale, NJ: Lawrence Erlbaum Associates.

Lewis, G. (1989). *The grammar of modern Hebrew*.

Lukatela, G., Gligorijević, B., Kostić, A., & Turvey, M. T. (1980). Representation of inflected nouns in the internal lexicon. *Memory & Cognition, 8*, 415-423.

Lukatela, G., & Turvey, M. T. (1991). Phonological access of the lexicon: Evidence from associative priming with pseudohomophones. *Journal of Experimental Psychology: Human Perception and Performance, 17*, 951-966.

Monsell, S. (1985). Repetition and the lexicon. In A. W. Ellis (Ed.), *Progress in the psychology of language* (Vol. 2, pp. 147-196). Hillsdale, NJ: Lawrence Erlbaum Associates.

Morton, J. (1982). Disintegrating the lexicon: An information processing approach. In J. Mehler, E. C. T. Walker, & M. Garrett (Eds.), *Perspectives on mental representation* (pp. 89-110). Hillsdale, NJ: Lawrence Erlbaum Associates.

Murrell, G., & Morton, J. (1974). Word recognition and morphemic structure. *Journal of Experimental Psychology, 102*, 963-968.

Ninio, A., & Snow, C. E. (1988). Language acquisition through language use: The functional sources of children's early utterances. In Y. Levy, I. M. Schlesinger, & M. D. S. Braine (Eds.), *Categories and processes in language acquisition*. Hillsdale, NJ: Lawrence Erlbaum Associates.

Proctor, H. D., & Healy, A. F. (1985). A secondary task analysis of a word family effect. *Journal of Experimental Psychology: Human Perception and Performance, 3*, 286-303.

Scarborough, D. L., Cortese, C., & Scarborough, L. H. (1977). Frequency and repetition effects in lexical memory. *Journal of Experimental Psychology: Human Perception and Performance, 3*, 1-17.

Schreifers, H., Zwitserlood, P., & Roelofs, A. (1991). The identification of morphologically complex words: Continuous processing or decomposition? *Journal of Memory and Language, 30*, 26-47.

Stanners, R. F., Neiser, J. J., Hernon, W. P., & Hall, R. (1979). Memory representation for morphologically related words. *Journal of Verbal Learning and Verbal Behavior, 18*, 399-412.

Stanners, R. F., Neiser, J. J., & Painton, S. (1979). Memory representation for prefixed words. *Journal of Verbal Learning and Verbal Behavior, 18*, 733-743.

Taft, M. (1981). Prefix stripping revisited. *Journal of Verbal Learning and Verbal Behavior, 20*, 289-297.

Taft, M. (1985). The decoding of words in lexical access: A review of the morphological approach. In D. Besner, T. G. Waller, & G. E. MacKinnon (Eds.), *Reading research: Advances in theory and practice* (Vol. 5, pp. 83-124). Academic Press.

Taft, M., & Forster, K. I. (1975). Lexical storage and retrieval of prefixed words. *Journal of Verbal Learning and Verbal Behavior, 14,* 638-647.

Taft, M., & Forster, K. I. (1976). Lexical storage and retrieval of polymorphemic and polysyllabic words. *Journal of Verbal Learning and Verbal Behavior, 15,* 607-620.

13 The Representation of Bound Morphemes in the Lexicon: A Chinese Study

Marcus Taft and Xiaoping Zhu
University of New South Wales

In three experiments the representation of bound morphemes in lexical memory is examined. Using an interactive-activation framework, four options were considered for the storage of morpheme and whole word representations. To test these options, an experimental paradigm was adopted whereby subjects responded to individually presented bound morphemes which could either only occur in the initial position of a word or only in the final position. The Chinese language is ideal for such a paradigm because it is possible to find compound words whose two morphemes (i.e., two characters) each only ever occur in that one word (called a "binding word"). Characters that only occur in second position took longer to name than ones which only occur in first position (whereas there was no effect in a character decision task). It was concluded that such bound morphemes were not associated with their pronunciations in the lexicon independent of the whole word. However, a further experiment revealed that this was only true for binding words and, therefore, that an independent morphemic representation does exist when the morpheme can be used in a variety of word contexts. It was proposed that the contrast of different contexts allows the morpheme to develop a semantic function which leads to the development of a representation in the lexicon.

INTRODUCTION

It does not seem to be a particularly challenging suggestion to claim that an affixed word like *unhooked* is in some way analyzed in lexical processing as *un + hook + ed*, nor that a compound word like *daydream* is analyzed as *day +*

293

dream, and there is much evidence to support such a position (e.g., Andrews, 1986; Stanners, Neiser, Hernon, & Hall, 1979; Stanners, Neiser, & Painton, 1979; Taft, 1979a; Taft & Forster, 1976). What is less appealing, though, is the idea that such morphological analysis occurs even when it generates units which are not words in their own right (i.e., "bound morphemes," as opposed to "free morphemes"), for example, analyzing *replenish* as *re + plenish* or *henchman* as *hench + man.* Nonetheless, there is evidence to suggest that morphological analysis does take place when the stem morphemes are bound (e.g., Stanners, Neiser, & Painton, 1979; Taft, 1979a, 1981; Taft & Forster, 1975; Taft, Hambly, & Kinoshita, 1986). Indeed, evidence for morphological processing in languages like Hebrew (e.g., Bentin & Feldman, 1990), Italian (e.g., Burani & Laudanna, 1992), and Serbo-Croatian (e.g., Feldman & Moskovljević, 1987; Lukatela, Gligorijević, Kostić, & Turvey, 1980) would seem to necessitate such a view since morphemes in those languages are almost always bound, in the sense that the root morpheme must always combine with an affix to form a word. What then is the best framework in which to think about morphological processing?

The account which I, the senior author, originally advocated was couched within the framework of a serial search model (cf. Forster, 1976). In this account (Taft & Forster, 1975), lexical access takes place via a representation of the stem of the word stored in an orthographic access file, regardless of whether that stem is free or bound. Access to the stem makes available the full information about all words containing that stem, from which the correct word can be selected. The stem itself needs to be isolated from the rest of the word prior to any attempt at access. This can be achieved by stripping off any prefixes and searching on a left-to-right basis for the stem (which means that any suffixes need not be stripped off). When it comes to compound words, which essentially have two stems, it was proposed (Taft & Forster, 1976) that access takes place via a representation of the first stem. Subsequently, however, it became apparent that the second stem might play some role as well (Andrews, 1986; Sandra, 1990; Taft, 1985, 1991).

More recently (Taft, 1991), I have adopted a rather different framework for thinking about lexical processing, utilizing the notions of an interactive-activation model (e.g., Glushko, 1979; McClelland, 1987; McClelland & Rumelhart, 1981). In this account, there are sets of units which can become activated when a word is visually presented. These units exist at different levels of representation, potentially ranging from single letters up to whole words, with activation passing up (and back down) the different levels. The links by which the activation passes have different connection strengths depending on the frequency with which the particular link is used. There are both orthographic and phonological units linked together at each level. When a word is visually presented, activation passes up through the orthographic units, as well as passing across to the phonological units via the orthographic/phonological links.

There are various ways of conceptualizing the lexical processing system within this interactive-activation framework depending upon which levels one includes. The simplest version would be one whereby low-level units map directly onto meaning. This is depicted in Figure 1. The focus of this chapter is on the contrast between bound and free morphemes, so the example of *henchman* is used in illustrating the models, as it contains both a bound and a free constituent.

For explanatory purposes, the lowest level depicted here is a "sub-morpheme level" in which onset/body structure is represented. The "body" (or orthographic "rime") of a monosyllable is the vowel plus all following consonants (e.g., the *and* of *stand*), while the "onset" comprises all consonants preceding the vowel (e.g., the *st* of *stand*). Onset/body structure has been shown to play a role in the lexical processing of monosyllabic words (e.g., Bowey, 1990; Glushko, 1979; Kay & Bishop, 1987; Treiman & Chafetz, 1987; Treiman & Zukowski, 1988), and the notion has recently been extended to polysyllabic words (Taft, 1992) whereby each orthographic syllable is seen as having an onset/body structure (e.g., the word *standard* includes the bodies *and* and *ard*). The "concept level" summarizes what might actually be a constellation of units representing the meaning of the word.

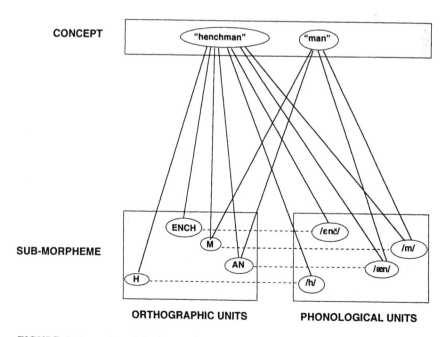

FIGURE 1. A version of the interactive-activation model where there are only concept and sub-morpheme levels.

The model presented in Figure 1 indicates that activation in the onset units *h* and *m*, and body units *ench* and *an* leads to activation of the meaning "henchman." The pronunciation, if required, is constructed from low level phonological units. However, there would have to be additional adjustment rules when the phonemic form is converted into an articulatory form, since the pronunciation of the whole word might deviate from the pronunciation derived from a mere concatenation of phonemes. For example, *henchman* is usually pronounced /hɛnčmən/ rather than /hɛnčmæn/, and therefore the /æ/ must be reduced to an /ə/.

Although there is no explicit representation of morphemes in this version of the model, it may be possible to account for evidence favoring morphological processing. This is because morphemic structure can be indirectly represented in the onset/body structure. In particular, the body could refer to the body of the morpheme (or at least the body of a syllable of the morpheme), with *ench* being the body of the first morpheme and *an* being the body of the second (see Taft, 1992). So, for example, if it were demonstrated that a bound morpheme like *hench* seems to have lexical representation by virtue of the fact that it is difficult to say that it is not a word (cf. Taft & Forster, 1975, 1976), this could be explained in terms of the joint activation of the sub-morphemic units *h* and *ench* leading to activation in the concept unit.

Where such a view faces difficulty, however, is when it is shown that morpheme frequency influences processing, independently of word frequency. For example, Taft (1979a), Bradley (1979), and Burani, Salmaso, and Caramazza (1984) have observed that the frequency of the stem of an affixed word can influence lexical decision times when word frequency is controlled. For example, Taft found that prefixed words like *dissuade* took longer to respond to than those like *reproach*. While these two words have the same frequency of occurrence, the bound stem *suade* is less frequent than *proach* because *persuade* is less frequent than *approach*. Now, according to the model presented in Figure 1, there are only two types of frequency that would seem to be relevant to processing. First, the amount of activation at the concept level could depend on the frequency with which all of the relevant sub-morphemic units are activated together (e.g., *r*, *e*, *pr*, and *oach*, or *ap*, *pr*, and *oach*). The frequency with which only *pr* and *oach* alone are activated together, however, should have no impact at the conceptual level, and therefore, the frequency of the morpheme should be irrelevant.

Second, since common bodies might be activated more rapidly than rarer bodies, one may seek to explain the morpheme frequency effect in terms of an inadvertent confounding of body frequency with morpheme frequency (e.g., the *uade* of *suade* being of lower frequency than the *oach* of *proach*). Inspection of the items used in the 1979a experiment, however, do not show any obvious systematic bias in this way. The mean log frequency of the bodies of the high frequency stems was .7659 (from Carroll, Davies, & Richman, 1971),[1] while that of the low frequency stems was .6181, a difference which was not significant, $t(13) = 0.68$, $p > .1$.

Therefore, it seems that a model where activation passes straight from sub-morpheme units to conceptual units would appear to be unlikely. In order to account for results like the morpheme frequency effect, it would seem necessary to include a morpheme level of representation. This is illustrated in Figure 2.

By the morpheme account, both bound and free morphemes have a representation. Activation in both the *hench* and *man* morpheme units will in turn activate the concept "henchman," though the bound morpheme will presumably provide a greater contribution than the free morpheme, since the latter will set up competing activation in other concept units (i.e., "man," "postman," "manpower," etc.). The pronunciation of the word is again constructed from sub-lexical units, though there still needs to be adjustments at articulation to reduce the /ə/ to an /æ/.

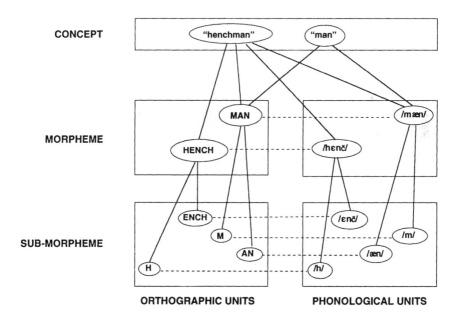

FIGURE 2. A version of the interactive-activation model where there are concept, morpheme, and sub-morpheme levels.

---

[1]The frequency of the body of a stem was calculated by adding up the log frequency of all the monosyllabic words and stems that included that body. Four of the item pairs used by Taft (1979a) were not analyzed since they included polysyllabic stems for which it was unclear what unit to take as the body.

Words like *breakfast* (i.e., brɛkfəst/), whose pronunciation cannot be determined from the combined pronunciations of the two stem morphemes (*break* and *fast*), might have to be considered to be monomorphemic in this model, so that the whole pronunciation can be represented at the morpheme level. Alternatively, there might be two phonological representations linked to the *break* morpheme (i.e., /breɪk/ and /brɛk/), with activation passing down from the concept unit for "breakfast" to the /brɛk/ phonological unit.

An alternative approach would be to replace morpheme units in the model with whole word units. In this way, morphemes are included, but only when they are free morphemes, since free morphemes are also words. Figure 3 depicts a version of the interactive-activation model that includes free morphemes.

Notice that within a single level, namely, the word level, there is cross-activation between words which share a free morpheme (e.g., *henchman* and *man*). This is essentially equivalent to having a separate monomorphemic word level (including *man, break, and fast,* for example) and polymorphemic word level (including *henchman* and *breakfast,* for example), with activation passing from the former to the latter.

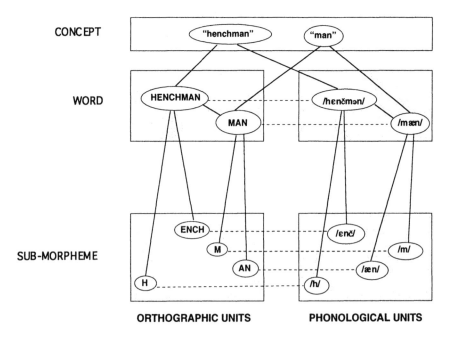

FIGURE 3. A version of the interactive-activation model where there are concept, word, and sub-morpheme levels.

In the version of the model presented in Figure 3, the pronunciation of the whole word is available, and therefore, irregularities like the pronunciation of *breakfast* as /brɛkfəst/ would cause no problems. The fact that irregular words (e.g., *pint*) actually do take longer to name than regular words (e.g., *pink*), at least when they are of low frequency (e.g., Andrews, 1982; Baron & Strawson, 1976; Seidenberg, Waters, Barnes, & Tanenhaus, 1984; Stanovich & Bauer, 1978) must be explained in terms of conflicting pronunciation being generated at the sub-morpheme level. Activation of these sub-morphemic phonological units would allow one to pronounce a letter-string that turned out to be a non-word (e.g., *rint*).

There is one result, however, which seems to be problematical for the version of the interactive-activation model depicted in Figure 3. This is the finding of Taft (1979a), discussed previously, where the frequency of the bound morpheme stem (e.g., *suade* or *proach*) has an effect on word recognition responses. According to the model, the frequency with which the sub-morpheme units *pr* and *oach* activate the word unit *reproach* will be independent of the frequency with which they activate the word unit *approach,* and therefore, the frequency of *approach* should have no impact on the activation level of *reproach;* that is, there should be no effect of bound morpheme frequency.

Perhaps, then, what we need to consider is one final variation on the model, namely, the most comprehensive case where there is both a word and a bound morpheme level. This is presented in Figure 4.

Such a model is able to handle all of the available evidence, though it does so by sacrificing economy. Word frequency effects are explained because there are word units, and morpheme frequency effects are explained because there are morpheme units.

We see, then, that at least four variations of the interactive-activation model are possible, differing on the levels of representation posited. For ease of reference, the four versions of the model will be given labels: Figure 2 depicts the "Morpheme" variation, Figure 3 the "Word" variation, Figure 4 the "Word+Morpheme" variation, and Figure 1 the "Neither" variation. The experiments presented in this chapter address themselves to the question of whether a bound morpheme level, a word level, or both levels should be a part of one's model of lexical processing.

The paradigm adopted in these studies examines a situation where it is possible to ascertain whether a bound morpheme is being named on the basis of the phonology of the whole word in which it typically occurs or on the basis of the phonology of the bound morpheme alone. If the former were shown, it would clearly demonstrate that the whole word level exists (i.e., the Word or Word+Morpheme models would be supported).

Consider the word *zigzag*. For the sake of explanation, let us assume here that *zig* and *zag* are both bound morphemes, neither of which can combine with any other morpheme. *Zig* is always followed by *zag,* and *zag* is always preceded by *zig.* Now, if the Morpheme model is correct (i.e., a model which represents bound morphemes but not whole words), then *zig* will be associated with the phonological unit /zɪg/ to exactly the same degree as *zag* is associated with /zæg/. This means that the time taken to initiate the pronunciation of *zig* should be the same as the time taken to initiate the pronunciation of *zag*. Note that the same result would obtain if the Neither model were correct since both *zig* and *zag* would be pronounced on the basis of sub-morpheme units.

On the other hand, if the Word or Word+Morpheme model is correct (i.e., where the whole word is also explicitly represented), a different result is possible. It may be the case that word level phonological information is used in naming the letter-string if it is advantageous to do so. It is an easy matter to generate the pronunciation of *zig* from the representation for *zigzag,* as one simply pronounces the first half of /zɪgzæg/. It is not so easy, however, to generate the pronunciation for *zag,* as one needs to ignore the first half of /zɪgzæg/ and commence one's pronunciation halfway through. Accordingly, there may be an advantage in pronouncing *zig* at the word level rather than at the sub-lexical level, but not so for *zag* Such a situation would be reflected in longer naming responses to *zag* than to *zig.*

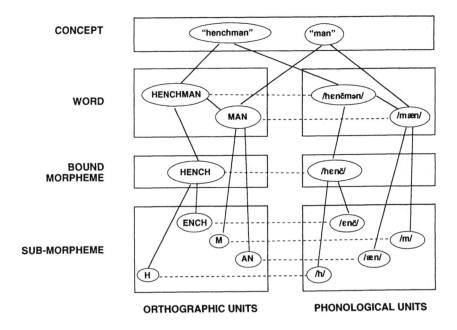

FIGURE 4. A version of the interactive-activation model where there are concept, word, morpheme, and sub-morpheme levels.

There does exist at least some evidence to support the claim that naming responses are preferentially based on word level phonology than on sub-lexical phonology. This comes from the work of McCann and Besner (1987) and Taft and Russell (1992), who demonstrated that nonwords which are homophonic with real words (e.g., *gaim*) can take less time to pronounce than those not homophonic with any word (e.g., *raim*). What this result means is that it is advantageous to pronounce a letter-string on the basis of whole word phonology (i.e., /geɪm/, the pronunciation stored for *game*) as opposed to constructing this pronunciation from sub-lexical phonological units (i.e., from /g/ plus /eɪm/). If sub-lexical units were used exclusively, the homophony of *gaim* with *game* would not have affected naming responses.

It seems very possible, then, that evidence can be garnered for the existence of a whole word level of representation for polymorphemic words using a paradigm whereby bound morphemes are to be named. The problem in carrying out such an experiment in English, however, is that words like *zigzag* have a highly dubious status as polymorphemic words. Examples like *hurdy-gurdy* and *holus-bolus* are perhaps more convincing because of the hyphen, but even so, it is hard to state exactly why such items should be considered to be polymorphemic. Perhaps one can say that the meaning is conveyed to some extent by the sound. For example, the sounds of *zig* and *zag* suggest the backward and forward shape of a zigzag, and the rhyming of *hurdy* and *gurdy* conjures up the sounds created by a hurdy-gurdy. However, just because the *-ash* of *crash, splash, gash, slash, smash,* etc., appears to convey the meaning of 'a rapid action,' it does not mean that it should be thought of as a morpheme. Hence, it is hard to justify morphemic structure on the basis of onomatopoeia alone.

Thus, English is a less than ideal language in which to examine the status of bound morphemes in lexical memory using the proposed naming paradigm. The Chinese (Mandarin) language appears to offer a better opportunity for an understanding of the issue. In Chinese there is no doubt about the internal orthographic and phonological structure of a word. Every word is made up of one or more (usually two) characters, where each character is pronounced as a monosyllable. A character typically provides semantic information about the word, and for this reason, Chinese characters are said to be equivalent to single morphemes (e.g., Chao, 1968; Chen, 1992; Hoosain, 1992; Li & Thompson, 1981; Zhang & Peng, 1992). As an example, the word 沐浴 is pronounced *mù yù*[2] and means 'a bath.' The constituent character 沐 is pronounced *mù* and means 'cleanse,' while 浴 is pronounced *yù* and means 'bathe.'

Most characters are composed of two components: a "semantic radical" which is typically on the left side and provides a guide to the meaning of the word, and

---

[2]The pinyin alphabetic transcription of Mandarin is used throughout to represent pronunciation.

a "phonetic radical" which typically occurs on the right side and provides a guide to pronunciation. In the case of 沐, the left-hand radical 氵 means that the character has something to do with 'water,' while the right-hand radical 木 is pronounced *mù* when used in isolation. Not all radicals, though, are as regular as these.

While a character may represent a morpheme, not all characters are free morphemes, despite the fact that they are spatially distinct. For example, 浩 (*hào*) means 'vast' but is never used on its own and is, therefore, a bound morpheme. If one wants to convey the meaning 'vast' in a sentence, one uses 浩大 (*hào dà*) (where 大 means 'big'). What is of most interest here, though, are words like 蚯蚓 (*qiū yǐn*), which we call "binding words." The important feature of *qiū yǐn* is that 蚯 only occurs in first position and is always followed by 蚓, while 蚓 only occurs in second position and is always following 蚯. That is, both 蚯 and 蚓 could be said to be bound morphemes, and this is what will be assumed at this stage of the argument. 蚯蚓 means 'earthworm,' and each of the two characters conveys something of this meaning in the sense that each includes the semantic radical 虫 which refers to 'creepy-crawly animals.'[3]

We see then that the Chinese language provides more fertile ground for studying bound morphemes than does the English language, at least when using the paradigm where bound morphemes are to be named. In addition to the greater number of binding words in Chinese, there is the fact that in English the stimuli to be named are nonwords (e.g., *zig*), whereas in Chinese, they are real characters.

EXPERIMENT 1

In Chinese text, all characters are evenly spaced, so there is every reason to believe that all characters are treated in the same way regardless of whether they belong to binding words or not. That is, it seems reasonable to suppose that there is a character level of representation in lexical memory, and if so, this is equivalent to saying that morphemes are represented. Such an account would favor the Morpheme model (Figure 2) or Word+Morpheme model (Figure 4) for Chinese. The Chinese version of the Morpheme model is shown in Figure 5.

The "character level" is equivalent to the "morpheme level" of Figure 2, while the "radical level" is equivalent to the "sub-morpheme level." The Chinese situation is somewhat more complex than English, though, in that it is possible for the sub-morphemic units to be associated with a meaning. Furthermore, it is possible for both the character and its phonetic radical to activate the same phonological unit (as in the case of 蚯 and 丘, shown in Figure 5). However, in many cases the character and the phonetic radical will activate different phono-

---

[3]This radical is usually said to refer to insects but in fact embraces worms, crustaceans, spiders, snails, amphibians and reptiles, etc.

logical units (e.g., 尴 is pronounced *gān*, while the phonetic radical 监 is pronounced *jiān*). Support for the conceptualization of orthographic/phonological relationships in Chinese shown in Figure 5 comes from research which shows that naming times to a character are delayed when the pronunciation of that character conflicts with the pronunciation of its phonetic radical (e.g., Fang, Horng, & Tzeng, 1986; Seidenberg, 1985; Zhu, 1988).

An alternative possibility to the model depicted in Figure 5 is one in which characters do not have their own representations, and this is illustrated in Figure 6. This is the Chinese equivalent of the Word version of the interactive-activation model illustrated in Figure 3.

In order to compare the models depicted in Figures 5 and 6, a naming experiment was conducted in Chinese whereby subjects were required to pronounce single characters each of which was either the first character of a binding word (e.g., 蚯, 尴, 徘, 珊) or the second (e.g., 蚓, 尬, 徊, 瑚).

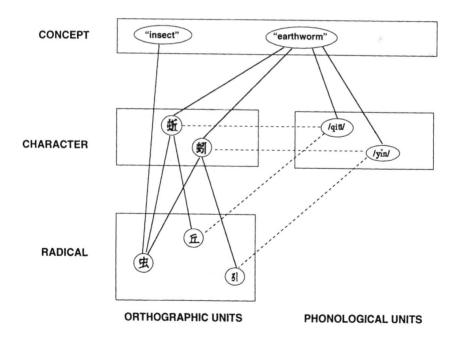

FIGURE 5. The Morpheme version of the interactive-activation model for Chinese, where there are concept, character, and radical levels.

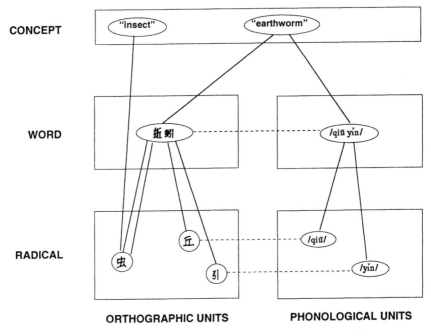

FIGURE 6. The Word version of the interactive-activation model for Chinese, where there are concept, word, and radical levels.

The two conditions (First Position and Second Position) were necessarily matched on character frequency, since they occurred in the same words. In addition, they were designed to be approximately matched on the number of strokes used to compose the character and on the consistency of the pronunciation of the phonetic radical with the pronunciation of the whole character.

There were two groups of 14 subjects. One saw, for example, 蚯 (First Position) and 蚓 (Second Position), and the other saw 尴 (First Position) and 尬 (Second Position), where 蚯蚓 and 尴尬 are binding words. Altogether 36 binding words were used, and therefore, each subject named 18 First Position characters and 18 Second Position characters. No subject saw both characters from the same binding word.

The subjects were all native speakers of Mandarin from northern China and were graduate students at the University of New South Wales. They were instructed to read aloud each of the characters that they saw as quickly but as accurately as possible. Characters were presented in random order in the standard simplified form as used in Mainland China. Each character was presented on a visual display unit for 1.5 s, with an inter-trial interval of 3.5 s. Vocalization onset times were measured using a voice-key.

The results from the naming task are summarized in Table 1.

TABLE 1. *Naming latencies in ms (and percentage errors) for Experiment 1. Standard deviations of item means in parentheses.*

CONDITION	EXAMPLE	LATENCIES	ERRORS
First Position	蚯	984 (124.8)	28.0%
Second Position	蚓	1038 (119.4)	26.2%

The time taken to name the Second Position items was significantly slower than the time taken to name the First Position items, $F_1(1,26) = 12.32$, MSe = 3111, $p < .001$; $F_2(1,34) = 5.20$, MSe = 975, $p <. 05$. Although the two conditions did not differ on error rates, $Fs <1$, it was noticeable that the pattern of errors was different for the two conditions. Many of the errors made on Second Position items involved the subject giving the pronunciation of the character that preceded it (i.e., naming 蚓 as *qiū* when it should be *yǐn*), while the reverse situation was very rare (where a First Position character was given the pronunciation of the character that followed it). The most common error in both conditions, however, was the misassignment of lexical tone.

The fact that it takes longer to name a character that only occurs in second position within a word than one which only occurs in first position strongly supports the view that each character (at least each character of a binding word) does not have its own lexical representation with associated pronunciation. Instead, one needs to activate the whole word in order to determine the pronunciation of the individual characters (i.e., see Figure 6). The pronunciation cannot be reliably based on the phonological units that are associated with the phonetic radicals alone, since it is frequently the case (81.5% of the time; Zhu, 1988) that a character and its phonetic radical are not pronounced identically (though they happen to be pronounced identically in 蚯 and 蚓, the example given in Figure 6).

Despite the compatibility of the data with the model portrayed in Figure 6, however, there is an alternative possibility. It is also possible to explain the data in terms of a First Position character actually having an independent lexical representation, while the Second Position character does not. Such an idea is in line with the original model proposed by Taft and Forster (1976). In that model, there is a discrete representation of those bound morphemes which can act as access codes. The access code is the stem of the word, or first stem if there are two. Thus, 蚯 would be an access code, but 蚓 would not. Depending upon where phonology is linked into the model, it is possible to explain why First Position characters are pronounced more quickly than Second Position characters: The pronunciation of First Position characters could be read out from the access representation, while the pronunciation of Second Position characters would have to be extracted from the whole word information in the lexicon.

Where the Taft and Forster model makes a different prediction than that of the Word model is in a character decision task, where subjects must decide whether or not a presented stimulus is a real Chinese character. According to the former model, an equivalent pattern of results that was observed in the naming task should emerge in the character decision task. That is, it should take longer to say that 蚓 is a character than to say the same of 蚯 because the former is accessible as an independent unit while the latter is not.

The Word model would make a quite different prediction. In order to decide whether a character which has no independent lexical representation is a real character, the activation from the sub-character information to a word-level representation must reach a threshold level. If it does, the stimulus must be a real character.[4] Assuming this approach to the character decision task with bound morphemes, it should be the case that 蚓 will not differ from 蚯, since the combination of activation in the radical units 虫 and 引 will activate a higher level unit (i.e., 蚯蚓) to the same extent as will the combined activation of 虫 and 丘. Thus, the Word model predicts no difference between First Position and Second Position items in the character decision task, despite there being a difference in the naming task.

EXPERIMENT 2

Performance in the character decision task was examined in Experiment 2, using the same characters as were used in Experiment 1 but mixing them with 36 non-existent characters. These non-existent characters were constructed by combining radicals inappropriately (e.g., 㤅) or by introducing non-existent radicals (e.g., 伫, 拜). Each of the two groups comprised 15 subjects who had not participated in Experiment 1. They were asked to press a "yes" button as soon as they recognized that a character really existed in Chinese or a "no" button as soon they realized that it did not.

Table 2 summarizes the results.

---

[4]It might be thought that an error would be made in this task if the left-hand radical of the first character of a binding word were combined with the right-hand radical of the second character to form a non-character, since this would activate the word-level representation just as much as would the correct combination of radicals. However, it is a feature of binding words that the left-hand radical of each of the two characters is always the same, and therefore, no inappropriate recombining of left and right radicals is possible. On the other hand, to avoid an error when a non-character is created from a combination of the two right-hand radicals (e.g., 引卩), one must assume that the connections between the radical level and character level are sensitive to radical position.

TABLE 2. *Character decision latencies in ms (and percentage errors) for Experiment 2. Standard deviations of item means in parentheses.*

CONDITION	EXAMPLE	LATENCIES	ERRORS
First Position	蚯	633 (64.4)	10.0%
Second Position	蚓	640 (49.1)	12.2%

No significant difference was found between the First Position and Second Position conditions, either on character decision times or on errors, all *F*s < 1.30. Thus, morpheme position sensitivity is only observed when a pronunciation must be produced, at least for the bound morphemes of binding words. Such a result appears to support a Word version of the interactive-activation model (Figures 3 and 6), which says that morphemes are only lexically represented when they are free morphemes, that is, when they are words in their own right.

Such a conclusion, however, needs further consideration, since it certainly cannot hold for all languages. In Hebrew, Italian, and Serbo-Croatian, morphemes are exclusively (Hebrew, Italian) or predominantly (Serbo-Croatian) bound rather than free. To handle this, we need to address the question of how the bound morphemes of these languages differ from the bound morphemes used in the present experiments in Chinese. One obvious difference is that the bound morphemes used in the Chinese experiments could only combine with one other morpheme, whereas the bound morphemes of Hebrew, Italian, and Serbo-Croatian tend to be highly productive and able to be combined with various other morphemes. That is, most roots can take on a variety of affixes, and most affixes can be used with a variety of roots (see Bentin & Frost, this volume, for a description of Hebrew morphology). This then leads to the possibility that the results obtained so far in Chinese are specific to binding words, that is, words whose constituent units can only occur in the one context.

To take an English example, while *zig* and *zag* may not be stored as units, it may be the case that *yester* is lexically represented owing to its occurrence in more than one word (*yesterday, yesteryear*). The existence of several semantically related words which share an orthographic unit suggests that such an orthographic unit contributes to the common meaning and should therefore be considered to be a morpheme.[5] This is tantamount to saying that *zigzag* and 蚯蚓 are not actually considered by readers to be polymorphemic. It may be that one needs to encounter an orthographic unit in several different contexts

---

[5]If *-ash* is not considered to be a morpheme in *crash, splash, gash, slash*, etc., it is presumably because the remaining letters are not morphemic in nature (e.g., *cr, spl*).

before a lexical representation develops for that unit. Since *zig* only occurs in the one context (i.e., followed by *zag*), no such representation will develop.

It would be very difficult to test this possibility in English, since it is rare for bound morphemes to occur in several contexts in initial position (as with *yester*). It mainly happens in final position, with prefixed words (e.g., *reproach, approach; dissuade, persuade*). The fact that stem frequency plays a role in recognizing prefixed words (Taft, 1979a) is consistent with the idea that bound morphemes are lexically represented when they occur in more than one word but is not a direct test of this hypothesis. Again, Chinese provides a better test.

EXPERIMENT 3

In Chinese it is possible to find characters which only ever occur in either first or second position but which can combine with several different characters in the other position. For example, 殉 (*xùn*) only occurs in first position but exists in several different words (e.g., 殉难, 殉职, 殉葬, meaning respectively 'die for one's country,' 'die at one's post,' and 'be buried alive with the dead'). From this range of words it is possible to extract a meaning for 殉 (i.e., something like "to sacrifice one's life"). Similarly, 侣 (*lǚ*) only ever occurs in second position but exists in several words (e.g., 僧侣, 伴侣, 情侣, meaning respectively 'monk,' 'partners,' and 'lovers').

Now, if it is the case that the range of contexts in which a character can occur influences whether a representation develops for that character, we should see this by comparing naming responses to characters which only have one possible partner (as was the case in Experiment 1) with those to characters with several possible partners. In particular, a Second Position character should be slower to name than a First Position character only when it has a unique partner. When the character has several possible partners, a representation will exist for that character (with its associated pronunciation) and, therefore, the character can be named on the basis of its morpheme-level pronunciation regardless of the position in which that character occurs in a word.

The claim that productivity of a morpheme determines whether or not it is represented in the lexicon was examined by comparing four conditions, each including 20 individual characters matched in quadruples on character frequency (according to the Modern Chinese Frequency Dictionary, 1985). Each character could appear only in the first position of a word or only in the second position, and occurred in only one possible word or in several. Thus, there were four conditions:

1) Unique First Position (e.g., 琥, *hǔ*, which only occurs in the word 琥珀, *hǔ pò*).

2) Unique Second Position (e.g., 尬, *gà*, which only occurs in 尴尬, *gān gà*).

3) Non-Unique First Position (e.g., 殉 *xùn*, which occurs in several words but only as the first character, as in 殉难, *xùn nàn*, and 殉职, *xun zhí*).

4) Non-Unique Second Position (e.g., 侣, *lǚ*, which occurs in several words but only as the second character, as in 伴侣, *bàn lǚ*, and 情侣, *qíng lǚ*).

Over the whole item set, the four conditions were approximately matched on the number of component strokes, and for the Non-Unique conditions, on the number of words containing that character (mean of 5.5 words). The consistency of the pronunciation of the character with that of its phonetic radical was also matched. Other examples of items were 珊, 玫, 鲫, 萌 (Unique First Position), 骼, 蚪, 谤, 虏 (Unique Second Position), 妖, 嗜, 迁, 翘 (Non-Unique First Position), 狡, 怂, 晞, 址 (Non-Unique Second Position). The experiment followed the same procedure as in Experiment 3.

Table 3 summarizes the results of the naming task. Looking first at response times, the most important result was that there was a significant interaction between position and uniqueness, $F_1(1,14) = 22.251, p < .001; F_2(1,18) = 5.785, p < .05$.[6] In agreement with Experiment 1, the Unique Second Position characters were named significantly more slowly than the Unique First Position characters, $F_1(1,14) = 15.567, p < .01; F_2(1,18) = 5.471, p < .05$. On the other hand, the Non-Unique Second Position characters were not named more slowly than the Non-Unique First Position characters, with a trend in the opposite direction (the item analysis was not significant), $F_1(1,14) = 5.335, p < .05; F_2(1,19) = 0.622, p > .05$.

TABLE 3. *Naming latencies in ms (and percentage errors) for Experiment 3. Standard deviations of item means in parentheses.*

CONDITION	EXAMPLE	LATENCIES	ERRORS
Unique First Position	琥	817 (85.3)	17.7%
Unique Second Position	尬	874 (87.6)	21.0%
Non-Unique First Position	殉	803 (83.8)	7.0%
Non-Unique Second Position	侣	780 (87.9)	12.7%

[6]One of the quadruplets was eliminated from the analysis of response times because the mean for the Unique First Position character was based on only four reaction times. Evidently most subjects did not know how to pronounce it.

This pattern of results strongly suggests that characters do not develop independent representations (with associated pronunciations) unless their status as a morpheme is clearly established. One could suggest that this occurs when the semantic function of the character is extracted from the comparison of the meaning of different words that include that character. Presumably the same is true in English (and, in fact, any alphabetic language), where *zig* may not have a representation but *yester* and *proach* may. It may even be the case that *hench* has a representation, not because it can form a word by combining with constituents other than *man* to form a word but because a henchman is a man, which suggests that *hench* is a morpheme. In other words, what we are suggesting is that morphemes are indeed represented in the lexicon, whether they be free or bound (i.e., Figure 2 or 4) and the reason why *zig zag,* 蚯, and 蚓 are not represented is because they are not actually taken to be morphemes. For a unit to be considered to be a morpheme, it seems that there needs to be some sense of its semantic function.[7]

In coming to this conclusion, it is assumed that the presence of the same orthographic unit in different semantically related words leads to that unit being treated as a morpheme because some sense of its meaning can be extracted. However, there are clear cases where several words might be thought to share a morpheme, yet the meaning of that morpheme is very difficult to specify. For example, the words *conceive, perceive, receive,* and *deceive* appear to contain the stem *ceive* (see Aronoff, 1976), yet it would be difficult to put into words what the relationship between their meanings is and hence what is meant by *ceive.* Indeed, Emmorey (1989) demonstrated that words which share such apparently meaningless stems prime each other in an auditory lexical decision task (while words which merely share a final syllable do not).

What could be argued here, though, is that the semantic function of the stem need not be definable in words in order to say that there is one. It was mentioned earlier that the term "concept" was being used here to summarize what might be a constellation of units representing meaning. It seems most unlikely that it would be possible to define what each of these abstract units actually represents and therefore, in turn, it may be very difficult to define what a combination of these units represents, particularly if that combination is smaller than the whole word. So, by saying that a morpheme has a semantic function, what is really being said is simply that an orthographic (or phonological) sub-lexical unit is associated with a set of units at the concept level. We propose that *ceive, yester,* 殉, and 倡 are, while *zig, zag,* 蚯, and 蚓 are not.

---

[7]The involvement of semantics in determining morphemic status is being assumed here in order to differentiate the morpheme from any other recurring unit, like the syllable (e.g., the *ve* of *vehicle, veneer, verandah, veto,* etc.).

So we see that the experiments looking at binding words are important, not so much in what they say about how such words are mentally represented per se (since such words are very unusual), but in what they tell us about non-binding words. This is based on the different pattern of results obtained for the two types of words. In contrast to binding words, it is apparent that the individual morphemes of non-binding words are represented in the lexicon. Thus, we ultimately support the Morpheme or Word+Morpheme variation of the interactive-activation model where all meaningful units (i.e., morphemes) are represented. Binding words are treated as single morphemes.

Whether the word level need be included along with the morpheme level (i.e., the Word+Morpheme variation rather than the Morpheme variation) is a moot point. The advantage of so doing is that it will readily capture any whole word pronunciation that deviates from the simple concatenation of component morphemes (as in the case of *breakfast*), though it was pointed out earlier that solutions to this problem do exist within the Morpheme framework. It is interesting to note that, in Chinese, the whole word pronunciation is predictable from the pronunciation of the component characters and, therefore, there is no justification on these grounds for the inclusion of a word level along with the morpheme level in Chinese.

On the other hand, the word level might serve another function. In particular, the existence of a hierarchy of levels might help to explain how position information is captured. For example, in the Morpheme model depicted in Figure 2, there would be as much activation in the concept unit "henchman" when *manhench* is presented as when *henchman* is presented. This would not be true in the Word+Morpheme model depicted in Figure 4, as there is no word unit *manhench*. This way of preserving position information would only run into problems when more than one valid combination of the same morphemes exists. This certainly happens, though it is very rare (e.g., *gunshot* and *shotgun*, 蜂蜜 and 蜜蜂). In order to handle such cases, there are presumably other cues. For example, if processing takes place from left to right (e.g., Taft, 1979b), the unit *gun* will be activated earlier in *gunshot* than *shotgun,* and this temporal information might somehow be utilized within the system. Alternatively, it may be that both whole word units are indeed activated but that the correct one is selected through some mechanism that verifies the activated candidates against the original stimulus (see Taft, 1991).

The variations on the interactive-activation model that have been considered here all incorporated the assumption that for every orthographic unit there is a phonological unit (at least for units above the sub-morpheme level). However, we should consider whether it is possible to explain the results without this assumption. For example, it may be the case that there actually are separate character units for 蚯 and 蚓 with no orthographic word unit for 蚯蚓, while there are no phonological morpheme units (i.e., syllable units) for *qiū* and *yǐn*,[8] but there is a phonological word unit *qiū yǐn.* Such a set-up would explain the results of Experiments 1 and 2 because the character decision responses can be made at the character level equally for First Position and Second Position characters, while the naming response would have to be generated from the whole word pronunciation, thus giving an advantage to First Position characters.

The problem with uncoupling phonological and orthographic units is that it does not handle the Non-Unique characters in a satisfactory way. In order to explain why there is no advantage of First Position over Second Position for Non-Unique characters, one would have to assume that Non-Unique characters *are* associated with a phonological representation at the syllable level where Unique characters are not. However, there is no obvious reason why only characters that can occur in a number of different words are linked with a syllable unit. A character is pronounced the same way no matter how many words it appears in. Therefore, the original conclusion appears to be more logical, namely, that the uniqueness factor influences whether the character has its own independent lexical representation or not.

Finally, something must be said about the error rates observed in Experiment 3. Given that there was no effect of position on error rates in Experiment 1, it is not surprising that there was no interaction of position and uniqueness on error rates, nor any difference between the First Position and Second Position Unique characters (all $Fs < 1$). There was, however, a significant main effect of uniqueness on error rates, with more errors when pronouncing Unique characters than Non-Unique characters, $F_1(1,14) = 18.224, p < .001$; $F_2(1,19) = 8.763$, $p < .02$. The explanation for this might be that when there is a discrete representation for a character, as is proposed for the Non-Unique characters, a pronunciation is directly associated with it. On the other hand, errors occur when the pronunciation of the character must be extracted from the pronunciation of the whole word, as is proposed for the Unique characters. In addition, when a character is contained in only one word, it is more likely that a reader will not know it or will have forgotten it than if there are several possible words in which that character occurs.

In conclusion, the results of the experiments reported in this chapter suggest that bound morphemes are represented in lexical memory but that there must be some sense of what a unit means before it is taken to be such a morpheme. Even in Chinese, which is often thought to represent morphemes in its orthography as distinct orthographic units, it seems that these distinct orthographic units (i.e.,

---

[8]Actually, these phonological units would have to exist in lexical memory because they can be used elsewhere as word units, for example in 秋 (*qiū*) meaning 'autumn' and 饮 (*yǐn*) meaning 'drink.' However, what is suggested here is that there is no link between the character unit 蚯 and the phonological unit *qiū* nor between 蚓 and *yǐn.*

characters) only function as morphemes when they have been encountered in different contexts.

ACKNOWLEDGMENT

The research reported in this chapter was supported by a grant awarded to the senior author by the Australian Research Committee. The authors thank Jishan Huang for her assistance in conducting the experiments.

REFERENCES

Andrews, S. (1982). Phonological recoding: Is the regularity effect consistent? *Memory & Cognition, 10,* 565-575.

Andrews, S. (1986). Morphological influences on lexical access: Lexical or nonlexical effects? *Journal of Memory and Language, 25,* 726-740.

Aronoff, M. (1976). *Word formation in generative grammar.* Cambridge, MA: MIT Press.

Baron, J., & Strawson, C. (1976). Use of orthographic and word-specific knowledge in reading words aloud. *Journal of Experimental Psychology: Human Perception and Performance, 2,* 386-393.

Bentin, S., & Feldman, L. B. (1990). The contribution of morphological and semantic relatedness to repetition priming at short and long lags: Evidence from Hebrew. *Quarterly Journal of Experimental Psychology, 42A,* 693-711.

Bowey, J. A. (1990). Orthographic onsets and rimes as functional reading units. *Memory & Cognition, 18,* 419-427

Bradley, D. C. (1979). Lexical representation of derivational relation. In M. Aronoff & M. L. Kean (Eds.), *Juncture.* Cambridge, MA: MIT Press.

Burani, C., & Laudanna, A. (1992). Units of representation for derived words in the lexicon. In R. Frost & L. Katz (Eds.), *Orthography, phonology, morphology, and meaning.* Amsterdam: Elsevier.

Burani, C., Salmaso, D., & Caramazza, A. (1984). Morphological structure and lexical access. *Visible Language, 18,* 342-352.

Carroll, J. B., Davies, P., & Richman, B. (1971). *The American Heritage word frequency book.* Boston: Houghton Mifflin.

Chao, Y. R. (1968). *A grammar of spoken Chinese.* Berkeley, CA: University of California Press.

Chen, H.-C. (1992). Reading comprehension in Chinese: Implication for character reading times. In H.-C. Chen & O. J. L. Tzeng (Eds.), *Language processing in Chinese.* Amsterdam: North-Holland.

Emmorey, K. D. (1989). Auditory morphological priming in the lexicon. *Language and Cognitive Processes, 4,* 73-92.

Fang, S.-P., Horng, R.-Y., & Tzeng, O. J.-L. (1986). Consistency effects in the Chinese character and pseudo-character naming tasks. In H. S. R. Kao &

R. Hoosain (Eds.), *Linguistics, psychology, and the Chinese language.* University of Hong Kong: Centre of Asian Studies.

Feldman, L. B., & Moskovljević, J. (1987). Repetition priming is not purely episodic in origin. *Journal of Experimental Psychology: Learning, Memory, and Cognition, 13,* 573-581.

Forster, K. I. (1976). Accessing the mental lexicon. In E. C. J. Walker & R. J. Wales (Eds.), *New approaches to language mechanisms.* Amsterdam: North-Holland.

Glushko, R. J. (1979). The organization and activation of orthographic knowledge in reading aloud. *Journal of Experimental Psychology: Human Perception and Performance, 5,* 674-691.

Hoosain, R. (1992). Psychological reality of the word in Chinese. In H.-C. Chen & O. J. L. Tzeng (Eds.), *Language processing in Chinese.* Amsterdam: North-Holland.

Kay, J. & Bishop, D. (1987). Anatomical differences between nose, palm, and foot, or, the body in question: Further dissection of the processes of sub-lexical spelling-sound translation. In M. Coltheart (Ed.), *Attention & Performance XII.* Hillsdale, NJ: Lawrence Erlbaum Associates.

Li, C., & Thompson, S. (1981). *Mandarin Chinese: A functional reference grammar.* Berkeley, CA: University of California Press.

Lukatela, G., Gligorijević, B., Kostić, A., Turvey, M. T. (1980). Representation of inflected nouns in the internal lexicon. *Memory & Cognition, 8,* 415-423.

McCann, R. S., & Besner, D. (1987). Reading pseudohomophones: Implications for models of pronunciation assembly and the locus of word frequency effects in naming. *Journal of Experimental Psychology: Human Perception and Performance, 13,* 13-24.

McClelland, J. L. (1987). The case for interactionism in language processing. In M. Coltheart (Ed.), *Attention & Performance XII.* Hillsdale, NJ: Lawrence Erlbaum Associates.

McClelland, J. L., & Rumelhart, D. E. (1981). An interactive activation model of context effects in letter perception: Part 1. An account of basic findings. *Psychological Review, 88,* 375-407.

Modern Chinese frequency dictionary (Xianda huayu pinlu zidian). (1985). Beijing: Beijing Language Institute Press.

Sandra, D. (1990). On the representation and processing of compound words: Automatic access to constituent morphemes does not occur. *The Quarterly Journal of Experimental Psychology, 42A,* 529-567.

Seidenberg, M. S. (1985). The time course of phonological code activation in two writing systems. *Cognition, 19,* 1-30.

Seidenberg, M. S., Waters, G. S., Barnes, M. A., & Tanenhaus, M. K. (1984). When does irregular spelling or pronunciation influence word recognition? *Journal of Verbal Learning and Verbal Behavior, 23,* 383-404.

Stanners, R. F., Neiser, J. J., Hernon, W. P., & Hall, R. (1979). Memory representation for morphologically related words. *Journal of Verbal Learning and Verbal Behavior, 18,* 399-412.

Stanners, R. F., Neiser, J. J., & Painton, S. (1979). Memory representations for prefixed words. *Journal of Verbal Learning and Verbal Behavior, 18,* 733-743.

Stanovich, K. E., & Bauer, D. W. (1978). Experiments on the spelling-to-sound regularity effect in word recognition. *Memory & Cognition, 6,* 410-415.

Taft, M. (1979a). Recognition of affixed words and the word frequency effect. *Memory & Cognition, 7,* 263-272.

Taft, M. (1979b). Lexical access via an orthographic code: The Basic Orthographic Syllabic Structure (BOSS). *Journal of Verbal Learning and Verbal Behavior, 18,* 21-39.

Taft, M. (1981). Prefix stripping revisited. *Journal of Verbal Learning and Verbal Behavior, 20,* 289-297.

Taft, M. (1985). The decoding of words in lexical access; A review of the morphographic approach. In D. Besner, T. G. Waller, & G. E. MacKinnon (Eds.), *Reading research: Advances in theory and practice* (Vol. V). New York: Academic Press.

Taft, M. (1991). *Reading and the mental lexicon.* Hillsdale, NJ: Lawrence Erlbaum Associates.

Taft, M. (1992). The body of the BOSS: Subsyllabic units in the lexical processing of polysyllabic words. *Journal of Experimental Psychology: Human Perception and Performance, 18,* 1004-1014.

Taft, M., & Forster, K. I. (1975). Lexical storage and retrieval of prefixed words. *Journal of Verbal Learning and Verbal Behavior, 14,* 638-647.

Taft, M., & Forster, K. I. (1976). Lexical storage and retrieval of polymorphemic and polysyllabic words. *Journal of Verbal Learning and Verbal Behavior, 15,* 607-620.

Taft, M., Hambly, G., & Kinoshita, S. (1986). Visual and auditory recognition of prefixed words. *Quarterly Journal of Experimental Psychology: Human Experimental Psychology, 38A,* 351-366.

Taft, M., & Russell, B. (1992). Pseudohomophone naming and the word frequency effect. *Quarterly Journal of Experimental Psychology, 45A,* 51-71.

Treiman, R., & Chafetz, J. (1987). Are there onset- and rime-like units in printed words? In M. Coltheart (Ed.), *Attention & Performance XII.* Hillsdale, NJ: Lawrence Erlbaum Associates.

Treiman, R., & Zukowski, A. (1988). Units in reading and spelling. *Journal of Memory and Language, 27,* 466-477.

Zhang, B. Y., & D. Peng (1992). Decomposed storage in the Chinese lexicon. In H.-C. Chen & O. J. L. Tzeng (Eds.), *Language processing in Chinese.* Amsterdam: North-Holland.

Zhu, X. (1988). Analysis of the cueing function of the phonetic in modern Chinese. *Proceedings of the symposium on Chinese language and character.* Beijing: Guang Ming Daily Press. (In Chinese).

14 Information Load Constraints on Processing Inflected Morphology

Aleksandar Kostić
Laboratory for Experimental Psychology
University of Belgrade

Two approaches to the processing of inflected morphology are evaluated with respect to Serbian inflected noun forms.[1] Standard approaches (as instantiated in the Decomposition Hypothesis, the Single Unit Hypothesis, and the Satellite Entry Hypothesis) cannot account for the results obtained with inflected Serbian nouns. The alternative approach presented here assumes that processing of inflected noun forms is determined by the amount of information which is derived from the average frequency per thematic role carried by a particular inflected noun form. Evaluation of the Informational Approach as performed in a series of experiments with inflected Serbian noun forms indicates that it can account for nearly all the processing variability due to noun inflection. Possible extensions of the Informational Approach to languages other than Serbian are discussed, as well as implications for a better understanding of the emergence and logic of morphological structures.

INTRODUCTION

The present study contrasts two approaches to the mental processing of inflected morphology; the standard one which is based on conventional concepts of the

---

[1]Serbian is the language spoken by Serbs in the former Yugoslavia. In the original research we referred to this language as Serbo-Croatian.

lexicon and the stages involved in processing grammatical information, and a second one which assumes that processing of inflected noun forms depends on the amount of information in the inflection, where information is specified in terms from information theory. The latter will be referred to as the *Informational Approach*. Data relevant to the contrast between the two approaches were collected using the Serbian language. Since some of the concepts of the Informational Approach derive from particular aspects of inflected morphology that have been thus far neglected, a description of the Serbian morphology and case system follows will be elaborated.

MORPHOLOGICAL PROPERTIES OF SERBIAN NOUNS

Serbian is a highly inflected, free word order language in which morphology plays a pivotal role in conveying relational aspects among sentence constituents. All open class words, as well as some types of closed class words, consist of a base morpheme to which an inflectional affix is appended. Different word types are characterized by codified sets of morphological transformations (i.e., declensions and conjugations) which indicate a word's possible thematic roles in a sentence. Nouns in the Serbian language are characterized by three grammatical attributes—case (e.g., nominative, genitive, dative, etc.), grammatical number (singular, plural), and gender (masculine, feminine and neuter). These attributes are marked by a suffix added to the base form of a noun which specifies a particular combination of the grammatical attributes. Thus, for example, if the suffix *i* is attached to the masculine noun *konj* ('horse') it will indicate the nominative plural case (*konji*). If however, the suffix *em* is attached to the same noun it will indicate the instrumental singular case. Each noun can appear in all cases, both singular and plural. In contrast, grammatical gender is an intrinsic property of a word; a particular noun can be of one gender only. Nouns of the same gender take a fixed set of transformations (i.e., declension) to specify case and grammatical number. It should be emphasized that the same sequence of letters can specify different combinations of case and grammatical number within a particular declension and can also be used with different declensions. Take, for example, the suffix *i*. If attached to a feminine noun it will indicate the dative/locative singular case, while if attached to a masculine noun it will indicate the nominative plural case (see Table 1 and Appendix 1). Moreover, because the same form of the noun can encompass several cases, an isolated noun form that corresponds to more than one case cannot be differentiated with respect to case and/or grammatical number. In such instances case specification can be provided either by context or by intonation. Noun forms for the three genders and cases they encompass are presented in Appendix 2.

In addition to inflection, in Serbian, as in all inflected languages, there is agreement among certain different word types which requires suffix coordination. Thus, for example, each Serbian adjective or possessive adjective has to agree with a noun in case, grammatical number, and gender.

TABLE 1. *Declension of Serbian nouns in three genders.*

CASE	MASCULINE Singular	Plural	FEMININE Singular	Plural	NEUTER Singular	Plural
nominative	konj	konj-i	žab-a	žab-e	sel-o	sel-a
genitive	konj-a	konj-a	žab-e	žab-a	sel-a	sel-a
dative	konj-u	konj-ima	žab-i	žab-ama	sel-u	sel-ima
accusative	konj-a	konj-e	žab-u	žab-e	sel-o	sel-a
locative	konj-u	konj-ima	žab-i	žab-ama	sel-u	sel-ima
instrument	konj-em	konj-ima	žab-om	žab-ama	sel-om	sel-ima

konj (M) - 'horse'
žaba (F) - 'frog'
selo (N) - 'village'

Likewise, verbs and personal pronouns have to agree in person, grammatical number, and sometimes gender. The agreement is often marked, and any violation, specified in terms of morphological rules, will produce an ungrammatical combination. Take, for example, the feminine noun *kuća* ('house') in the dative/locative singular case (*kući*). Any preceding adjective has also to be in the dative/locative singular (e.g., *Lepoj kući*, 'To the beautiful house'), where adjectival suffix *oj* uniquely specifies feminine dative/locative singular. If, for example, the suffix *u* which specifies the accusative case is attached to the preceding adjective (e.g., *lepu kući*) the adjective/noun combination will be ungrammatical because a basic agreement rule has been violated. By contrast, preposition-noun agreement is realized through prepositional meaning alone because prepositions are not marked for case. The agreement between a preposition and a noun is lexically defined; each preposition modifies one particular case or a particular set of cases. Any violation of this rule will generate an ungrammatical sentence.

Case Functions and Meanings

Whereas grammatical number and gender can be treated as noun attributes of minor relevance for syntax, case appears to represent the nucleus as it contains a noun's repertoire of possible syntactic functions and meanings in a sentence context. In inflected languages, by virtue of being marked, case overtly indicates a noun's syntactic potential. Take, for example, the noun form *viljušku* ('fork'). The suffix *u* indicates that it is a feminine noun in the accusative singular and it has primarily an object role in a sentence (e.g., *Uzeo je viljušku*—'He took the fork'). If, instead of *u*, the suffix *om* is attached to the same word (e.g., *viljuškom*), the case is instrumental singular. This, in turn, has consequences for its thematic role as now it becomes an instrument (*Jede viljuškom*—'He eats with a fork').

The difference between the notions of case function and case meaning should be made clear. While the term 'function' refers to the global thematic roles a case can have in a sentence (e.g., subject, object, etc.), the term 'meaning' refers to specific contextual aspects modified by case (e.g., purpose, time, manner, cause, etc.). Take, for example, the following sentences: *U svakoj školi ima profesora* ('In each school there are professors') and *To su knjige profesora* ('Those are the books of professors'). In both sentences the word *profesora* is genitive plural of the masculine noun *profesor* ('professor'). However, in the first sentence we have a partitive genitive, while in the second the genitive denotes possession. Take another example. The two following sentences contain the noun *tim* ('team') in the instrumental singular case: *Upravljao je timom* ('He was leading the team') and *Sa tim timom postao je slavan* ('With that team he became famous'). In the first sentence, the instrumental denotes an object, while in the second it has the meaning of an instrument (i.e., means). These examples indicate that the syntactic functions and meanings that a noun can have in a sentence can be specified either through case alternation or by means of contextual factors which modify the thematic role inventory of a particular case. While there are a vast number of case meanings, there are only a few case functions. The term 'thematic role' seems to capture the notions of both case meaning and case function. Therefore, in what follows, case functions and meanings are generally referred to as 'thematic roles.'

An additional modification of case meanings comes from prepositional agreement. Prepositional modification to a noun case can be treated as a 'fine tuning' of the potential meanings (or roles) a particular case can play in a sentence, in that a preposition modifies a restricted set of thematic roles carried by a particular case. For example, the instrumental case has different syntactic meanings depending on whether or not it is preceded by a preposition. Take these two sentences: *Plaši bratom*—'He/she threatens by means of (his/her) brother' and *Plaši sa bratom*—'He/she, with (his/her) brother, threatens.' While in the first sentence the noun's instrumental suffix (*om*) indicates the instrument of threatening, in the second sentence the instrumental form, with the preposition *sa* ('with'), indicates accompaniment. The accusative case, to take another example, is also modified by a large number of prepositions, each of which indicates one of the potential meanings of the accusative case (e.g., *Na kuću*—'On the house,' *Za kuću*—'For the house,' etc.). Prepositional modification of a noun case allows us to get some insight into the differentiation of case meanings. Each preposition indicates a particular syntactic relation (or set of relations) which is coded in the noun as part of the syntactic repertoire of a particular inflected case. Since each preposition modifies only a particular case (or set of cases), the relation denoted by a preposition is strictly tied to the corresponding case meaning and can be treated as part of the inventory of case meanings. The fact that a violation of preposition/case congruency will produce an ungrammatical sentence indicates that an incongruent preposition denotes a relation that is incompatible with the inventory of that case.

These properties of Serbian cases make it misleading to assume that an inflected case refers merely to a suffix which denotes the global thematic roles a noun can take in a sentence context. It would be more accurate to say that an inflected case represents a set of the potential relations that a noun can enter into, these relations being realized either in terms of global syntactic functions or in terms of fine-tuned local specifications (i.e., meanings). The number of functions and meanings (denoted as R) for each Serbian case is presented in Appendix 1. Some noun forms correspond to more than one case. The cumulative number of functions and meanings modified by a particular noun form is presented in Appendix 2 (Kostić, Dj., 1965a). It should be noted, however, that notions of case function and meaning are a matter of controversy among linguists. While they agree that functions and meanings are the principal properties of a case, it is generally acknowledged that there are no strict criteria for their unequivocal taxonomy and classification (cf. Benveniste, 1962; Diver, 1964; de Groot, 1956; Hjelmslev, 1937; Kuryłowicz, 1960). Therefore, the absolute number of case functions and meanings in Serbian reported in Appendices 1 and 2 should be taken as tentative.

STANDARD MODELS OF PROCESSING AFFIXED WORDS

In consideration of the properties of the Serbian noun system, it is appropriate to ask how the Serbian speaker processes inflected noun forms. The fact that an affixed word can be formally partitioned into its base form and an affix is the basis of controversy among linguists with respect to the way affixed words may be represented in the lexicon. While some linguists have assumed that both affixed and unaffixed words may be lexically represented as whole items, others posit a special status for affixed words (cf. Chomsky, 1965, 1970; Jackendoff, 1975). Along the lines of these arguments, some psycholinguists have assumed that the morphological processing mechanism can, at least conceptually, operate on an affixed word by partitioning it into its constituents (i.e., base form and affix). On the other hand, it is often assumed that the (bound) base form does not differ from the affixed form with respect to its *lexical* representation, in which case the factors that influence processing of the base form in isolation (unaffixed) should also affect it when it is affixed.

Most of the research on morphological processing seems to follow these intuitions. An elaboration of potential processing mechanisms proposed by Manelis and Tharp (1977) identifies three possible sequences of operations in the recognition of an affixed word. The Decomposition Approach assumes that an affixed word is decomposed into its root form and affix, followed by a search for the two constituents in the lexicon and then by an evaluation of the validity of their combination (Decomposition First). A positive outcome of this process is followed by a positive response, while a negative evaluation would require an additional search for the undecomposed item in the lexicon. The implication of this approach is that an affixed word should be recognized faster than an unaffixed one (see Hudson & Buijs, this volume). A variation on the model assumes a search for the whole word occurs first. If the word is not found in the lexicon, it is then decomposed into the root form and affix, the lexicon is searched and the congruency of the root form and the affix is evaluated (Decomposition Second). Since unaffixed words need not undergo decomposition, this approach predicts longer response latencies for affixed words.

The second approach (Single Unit Hypothesis) assumes that affixed words, like unaffixed words, are represented in the lexicon. Other factors being equal, no difference should be observed in the processing latency for affixed and unaffixed words. If, however, there is a processing difference it should be ascribed to factors other than (time-consuming) manipulations of word constituents, such as affix frequency (cf. Rubenstein, Lewis, & Rubenstein, 1971; Stanners & Forbach, 1973).

The reported research on this topic appears to be equivocal. Findings reported by Forster and Taft suggest that prefixed words are partitioned into base form and prefix, before lexical search (Taft, 1979a, 1979b, 1981; Taft & Forster, 1975, 1976). On the other hand, Manelis and Tharp (1977) reported results which favor the Single Unit Hypothesis, with little evidence for decomposition. Likewise, a number of studies suggest that affixed words may be represented as undecomposed lexical items (Feldman & Fowler, 1986; Fowler, Napps, & Feldman, 1985; Rubin, Becker, & Freeman, 1979; Stanners, Neiser, Hernon, & Hall, 1979; Stanners, Neiser, & Painton, 1979). Additional support for such an approach comes from studies with auditory word recognition (Butterworth, 1983; Cutler, 1983; Henderson, 1985; Katz, Boyce, Goldstein, & Lukatela, 1987). There are some indications, however, that in contrast to prefixed words, suffixed words may not undergo decomposition (Bergman, Hudson, & Eling, 1988).

Extended to the processing of Serbian noun forms, the Single Unit Hypothesis would predict that processing latency to an inflected noun should be determined by the frequency of its suffix, since all inflected forms have the same base (and therefore the same semantic frequency) and differ only in the relative frequencies of the various inflected forms. According to the Decomposition First (or Second) account, inflected noun processing is composed of several processing stages: Suffixed noun forms should be processed either faster (or slower) than non-suffixed ones, and processing latency differences among suffixed nouns themselves should be a function of frequency differences among suffixes. Since in Serbian the same suffix can be attached to nouns of different genders, with differing frequency in each gender (see Appendix 1), the Decomposition Hypothesis implies that the processing mechanism operates on noun forms of a particular gender and not on noun cases per se.

EXPERIMENTS IN THE SERBIAN LANGUAGE

A series of experiments with inflected Serbian nouns indicate that the forms in nominative case were processed faster than those which were not in nominative (Feldman & Fowler, 1987; Katz et al., 1987; Kostić, & Katz, 1987; Lukatela, Gligorijević, Kostić, & Turvey, 1980; Lukatela, Mandić, Gligorijević, Kostić, Savić, & Turvey, 1978; Todorović, 1988). The outcome in most of those studies indicated no conspicuous processing differences among the inflected forms that were not in nominative case, in spite of the fact that forms differed with respect to their frequency of occurrence. In order to evaluate the Decomposition Hypotheses, Lukatela and his associates directly contrasted masculine and feminine inflected noun forms (Lukatela et al., 1980). The outcome of that experiment indicated no processing differences across genders. Latency differences to the nominative and oblique (i.e., non-nominative) case forms for the masculine nouns did not differ from those for feminine nouns. Because there are significant structural differences between masculine and feminine nouns (the masculine nominative is equivalent to the base form but the feminine nominative is not), this seemed to be a crucial finding. Moreover, the oblique forms of masculine nouns are created by adding a suffix to the nominative form (the base) which has a lexical status in its own right. In contrast, both the nominative and the oblique cases of feminine nouns are created by adding a suffix to a base morpheme such that feminine base forms have no independent lexical status (cf. Appendix 1). According to an account based on decomposition of morphological structure, one would expect faster lexical recognition of masculine nouns in the nominative case than in oblique cases (as nominatives do not require decomposition), but equivalent recognition latencies for feminine nominative nouns relative to feminine oblique cases. The fact that no processing difference was observed between the two genders suggested that no decomposition of oblique noun forms occurred. Moreover, the apparent absence of any processing differences among the oblique forms themselves suggested that inflected noun processing is not frequency dependent. In other words, neither of the two pivotal factors (i.e., decomposition and/or frequency) proposed by the standard models seemed to affect processing of inflected Serbian noun forms.

Based on fastest latencies for nominative and no latency differences among oblique cases for both genders, Lukatela and his associates proposed the Satellite Entries Hypothesis: It assumes that each grammatical case of a noun has a separate entry in the lexicon. According to the model, the nominative singular functions as a nucleus around which the other inflected forms cluster. Unlike the decomposition approach, which emphasizes a discrete sequence of processing stages and a lexical search influenced by the frequencies of base form and suffix, the Satellite Entries Hypothesis implies that the observed results are due to intralexical processes and that processing differences among noun forms are determined by local intralexical structuring (cf. Lukatela et al., 1980). Additional support for the Satellite Entries Hypothesis comes from an experiment showing fastest latencies for nominative and no latency differences among oblique cases for regular nouns in both genders and for irregular feminine nouns. The experiment demonstrated that latencies for irregular feminine nouns show satel-lite-like patterning as well, in spite of the fact that their suffixes are not typical for feminine nouns. In addition, no patterning differences were observed for oblique masculine and regular feminine nouns (Lukatela, Carello, & Turvey, 1987).

The first indication that Serbian nouns may not be organized in a satellite-like fashion came from an experiment reported by Todorović (1988) who presented four forms of high, medium and low familiarity feminine nouns with a 150 ms exposure duration. The pattern of response latencies averaged across familiarity indicated faster recognition for the nominative singular, but the other forms were not uniform in latency (see Table 2). Specifically, the form containing the geni-tive singular *žabe* was processed faster than expected relative to other oblique forms. This effect was accounted for by pointing out that the genitive singular for feminine nouns is the same as the nominative plural for the same gender, and the assumption that both nominative singular and plural play pivotal roles.

The problem with this explanation is that, while it was acknowledged that the genitive form *žabe* could also be nominative plural, it was not acknowledged that it could be accusative plural as well. Moreover, the nominative *žaba* could also be genitive plural (see Table 1). In other words, neither of the two forms could be uniquely treated as nominative. Consequently, between the two forms there should be no processing difference due to the privileged status of the nominative case, unless an effect of grammatical number is assumed (i.e., singular cases are processed faster than plural ones). Additional inconsistencies between the findings of Lukatela et al. (1980) and Todorović (1988) are in the relative size of the observed difference between the nominative and genitive cases for feminine nouns (i.e., *žaba* vs. *žabe*). The reported processing differ-ence between the two forms in the Lukatela et al. (1980) experiment was approx-imately 75 ms. Todorović, on the other hand, reported only 20 ms difference between the two forms and the same difference between forms *žabe* vs. *žabi* (cf. Table 2). Thus, the results of the two experiments are inconsistent. It could be argued that different outcomes in the two experiments are due to differences in exposure duration (150 ms in Todorović, 1988, and 1,500 ms in Lukatela et al., 1980). This will prove not to be the case, however.

TABLE 2. *Reaction time for the inflected forms of feminine nouns averaged across familiarity (from Todorović, 1988).*

Form	Case	RT
žaba	nom. s. + gen. pl.	684
žabe	gen. s. + nom. pl. + acc. pl.	704
žabi	dat. s. + loc. s.	724
žabu	acc. s.	720

žaba (F) - 'frog'

The suggestion that the relatively small difference between *žaba* and *žabe* in the Todorović (1988) experiment could be due to the privileged status of the nominative plural (i.e., *žabe*) and an assumed effect of grammatical number gets some support from the experiment reported by Kostić and Katz (1987).

In that experiment subjects were presented with three cases of singular and plural nouns. Because the nouns were masculine in gender, both nominatives were morphologically unique, neither of which occurred in other cases. The results showed a main effect of grammatical number (plural forms being slower than singular) and case. There was no case by number interaction (see Table 3).

While the outcome of the experiment reported by Todorović indicated no satellite-like patterning for feminine nouns, the outcome of the Kostić and Katz (1987) experiment suggested satellite-like structuring for masculine nouns for each grammatical number. The implication of the two outcomes is that the Satellite Entries Account can be applied to masculine nouns only. This is contrary to predictions of the original model which claimed primacy of the nominative case and no difference among the oblique forms, irrespective of gender.

In order to reevaluate the Satellite Entries Hypothesis, the two pivotal experiments which supported the model (i.e., Lukatela et al., 1980, and Lukatela et al., 1987) were repeated (Kostić, A., 1991). The original pattern of experimental results failed to replicate. In the replication of the original Lukatela et al. (1980) experiment, Kostić found a case by gender interaction, suggesting processing differences between the two genders. In contrast to the masculine gender, the response latencies for feminine noun forms did not exhibit a satellite-like patterning (see Table 4).

Lukatela et al. (1987) originally reported faster recognition of the nominative singular for irregular feminine nouns (approximately 70 ms) and no significant difference between the two oblique forms. These results also failed to replicate. In the repeated version there was a much smaller difference between the nominative and the faster of the two oblique forms (25 ms) and a substantial latency difference between the two oblique forms themselves (47 ms) (see Table 5) (Kostić, A. 1991). Again, the patterning of the response latencies for feminine nouns did not exhibit satellite-like structure.

TABLE 3. *Reaction time for six forms of inflected masculine nouns (from Kostić, & Katz, 1987).*

Form	Case	RT
konj	nom. s.	679
konju	dat. s. + loc. s.	744
konjem	inst. s.	744
konji	nom. pl.	716
konje	acc. pl.	768
konjima	inst. pl. + dat. pl. + loc. pl.	758

konj (M) - 'horse'

TABLE 4. *Reaction time for masculine and feminine noun forms in replication of Lukatela et al., 1980 (from Kostić, 1991).*

Form	MASCULINE Case	RT	Form	FEMININE Case	RT
konj	nom. s.	604	žaba	nom.s .+ gen. pl.	593
konja	gen. s. + acc. s. + gen. pl.	660	žabe	gen. s. + nom. pl. + acc. pl.	604
konjem	inst. s.	674	žabom	inst. s.	622

konj (M) - 'horse'
žaba (F) - 'frog'

Replications of the two studies were conducted several times, always with the essentially same outcome. Considering the results of the two replicated versions, as well as the results of the Todorović (1988) experiment, on empirical grounds the Satellite Entries Hypothesis has to be rejected.

With the rejection of the Satellite Entries Hypothesis, it becomes necessary to reevaluate the predictions offered by the Single Unit Hypothesis and the Decomposition Hypotheses. A common prediction of the Single Unit and the Decompostion Hypotheses is that processing latencies to inflected noun forms should differ as a function of suffix frequency. It should be emphasized, however, that the only way to evaluate this prediction is to compare noun forms of a particular gender, since the same suffix can be shared by various cases and genders. The frequency values for singular and plural cases for masculine, feminine, and neuter nouns is given in Appendix 1, while the cumulative case frequency values for the noun forms of the three genders is given in Appendix 2 (Kostić, Dj., 1965b). The evaluation of the Single Unit and the Decomposition Hypotheses were performed on the findings from Todorović (1988) and on the two replications of the Lukatela et al. experiments (Kostić, A. 1991).

TABLE 5. *Reaction time for three forms of irregular feminine nouns in replication of Lukatela et al., 1987 (from Kostić, 1991).*

Form	Case	RT
strast	nom. s. + dat. /loc. acc. s.	590
strasti	gen. s. + dat. /loc. s.+ nom. pl. + gen. pl. + acc. pl.	615
strašću	inst. s.	662

strast (F) - 'passion'

Table 6 contains the critical reaction time and frequency differences from Todorović (1988). By contrasting the forms *žaba* and *žabe*, the less frequent form *žaba* is processed 20 ms faster than the form *žabe*. On the other hand, the more frequent form *žabe* is processed 20 ms faster than the form *žabi*. Basically, the magnitude of the processing difference (20 ms) is unrelated to relative frequency.

The same contrast for the replication of Lukatela et al. (1980) using three forms of masculine nouns is summarized in Table 7 (cf. Table 4). The less frequent form *konj* was processed 56 ms faster than form *konja*, while the more frequent form *konja* was only 14 ms faster than the less frequent form *konjem*.

Finally, the frequency and reaction time contrasts for the three forms of irregular feminine nouns from the replication of Lukatela et al. (1987) (Kostić, A., 1991) are given in Table 8 (cf. Table 5). Note that the less frequent form *strast* was processed 25 ms faster than the more frequent form *strasti*. On the other hand, the more frequent form *strasti* was processed 47 ms faster than *strašću*.

TABLE 6. *Reaction time and frequency differences for the oblique feminine forms (from Todorović, 1988).*

	žaba vs. žabe	žaba vs. žabi
RT differences	+20 ms	+20 ms
Frequency differences	- 2.15%	+10.41%

TABLE 7. *Reaction time and frequency differences for the oblique masculine forms in replication of Lukatela et al., 1980 (Kostić, 1991).*

	konj vs. konja	konja vs. konjem
RT differences	+56 ms	+14 ms
Frequency differences	- 5.19%	+16.12%

TABLE 8. *Reaction time and frequency differences for the oblique forms of irregular feminine nouns for the replication of Lukatela et al., 1987 (Kostić, 1991).*

	strast vs. strasti	strasti vs. strašću
RT differences	+25 ms	+47 ms
Frequency differences	- 6.91%	+19.29%

Again, there is no systematic relation between form frequency and processing latency. The same contrast also indicates no systematic relation between form frequency and processing latency for the results reported by Kostić and Katz (1987) (see Table 3 and Appendix 2).

In summary, the above outcomes suggest that differences in processing latencies to inflected Serbian nouns cannot be accounted for in terms of suffix frequency. This means that both the Decomposition Hypothesis and the Single Unit Hypothesis are also disconfirmed. Because none of the proposed models can accommodate the observed effects, the factors that determine processing variation for the inflected noun forms remain unclear.

THE INFORMATIONAL APPROACH TO THE PROCESSING OF INFLECTED MORPHOLOGY

An assumption of the standard approaches discussed previously is that variation in processing latency to suffixed words is a function of number of processing stages and/or suffix frequency. While differences in processing stages may (theoretically) account for the robust processing effects with clearly distinguishable stimulus properties (e.g., the contrast between suffixed and unsuffixed words), it is assumed that suffix frequency may be responsible for variability within a class of inflected word forms. Experiments in Serbian demonstrate that suffix frequency cannot account for the variation.

The failure of the standard models may be due to inappropriate specification of cognitively relevant stimulus properties. Rather than asking about the processing stages and mechanisms responsible for variation in processing time to the same word in its different grammatical forms, we could pose the following question: What are the relevant stimulus properties to which our cognitive system is sensitive, and in what metrics should these properties be expressed? As an operating principle, the search for the relevant stimulus properties should obey the following constraint: Properties must be expressed in a way which will allow correlation with the response latencies across different noun forms. This, in turn, may require a shift from factorial ANOVA to regression analysis. The models discussed previously assumed either discrete processing stages or structural properties which invited factorial analyses where processing variations were discussed in terms of main effects and interactions. If the stimulus properties can be quantitatively expressed, then relevant parameters can be evaluated in terms of regression analyses in which response latency is regressed on a quantitatively expressed descriptor. This will enable us to estimate the relative contribution of potential descriptors in accounting for variability in response latency.

What might be the candidates in the domain of stimulus properties that can be quantitatively expressed? An obvious one is suffix frequency which, as previously demonstrated, does not seem to provide a good prediction of processing time. At this point we could either reject frequency as an inappropriate descriptor or assume that in addition to frequency there must be another factor which influences processing of the inflected noun forms. One candidate that can be quantitatively expressed is the *number of syntactic functions and meanings* (i.e., thematic roles) that each Serbian noun case represents (see Appendices 1 and 2). It should be emphasized that for the purpose of the present study the absolute number of thematic roles is of marginal interest—it is irrelevant whether the accusative case, for example, really modifies 58 functions and meanings, as opposed to the 32 modified by the instrumental case. What is important is the *proportion of thematic roles modified by a particular case, relative to other cases* (see R% in Appendices 1 and 2).

What are the processing consequences of the two descriptors (i.e., frequency of the form and number of thematic roles)? There is reason to believe that frequency of a form and number of thematic roles may be inversely related. It is well established that the frequency of occurrence and processing latency for individual words are inversely related. In contrast, it seems plausible that the number of thematic roles and the response latency may be directly related—the greater the number of thematic roles, the longer the processing latency. Intuitively, the number of thematic roles associated with a particular noun form could be thought of as a measure of its complexity—the more roles a form modifies, the more complex it is and, consequently, the longer its processing latency. If so, then processing time should be influenced by form complexity, defined as the number of associated functions and meanings. Regression analyses, however, indicate that processing time does not vary significantly with complexity defined in terms of the number of modified form meanings (cf. Tables 2, 3, and 4 and Appendix 2). This suggests that neither of the two descriptors per se can account for a significant proportion of the variability in response latencies to inflected noun forms.

If form frequency and number of thematic roles have inverse consequences on processing, their relation can be expressed as mutually dependent influences on processing time, that is, in terms of a ratio. If we divide form frequency by the number of thematic roles a form modifies, the derived expression is the average frequency per thematic role for a particular inflected noun form (Equation 1).

$$\overline{RT}_m = f\left(\frac{F_m}{R_m}\right) \tag{1}$$

Equation 1 states that the average response latency to a particular noun form (RT_m) is some function of form frequency (F_m) divided by the number of thematic roles modified by that form (R_m). The index m stands for "morpheme," indicating that the unit of description is the noun form—the particular letters or sounds (or combination of letters and sounds) that constitutes the inflectional suffix—rather than its case.

To evaluate the predictions derived from Equation 1, response latencies to the four forms of feminine nouns reported in the Todorović (1988) experiment were regressed on values obtained from Equation 1 (see Table 2 and Appendix 2). The linear regression indicated that a significant proportion of the response latency variability was accounted for by the ratio of the frequency and the number of thematic roles: $r^2 = .953$, $F(1,2) = 40.955$, $p < 0.02$. For the reaction times obtained in the Kostić and Katz (1987) experiment with six forms of masculine nouns (see Table 3 and Appendix 2), the values derived from Equation 1 again accounted for a significant proportion of processing time variability: $r^2 = 0.872$, $F(1,4) = 27.224$, $p < 0.01$. For the replication of Lukatela et al. (1980) (Kostić, A., 1991), no significant proportion of the variance was explained either for the masculine or for the feminine noun forms (see Table 4 and Appendix 2). The same outcome was observed with the replication of Lukatela et al. (1987) (Kostić, A., 1991) with three forms of irregular feminine nouns (see Table 5 and Appendix 2).

The fact that latency for two out of the four experiments was accounted for by the values obtained from Equation 1 suggests that the subjects may be sensitive to the average frequency per thematic role carried by a particular noun form, rather than frequency of a suffix per se. The average frequency per thematic role within a particular inflected noun form appears to be a plausible descriptor of stimulus properties relevant to subject's sensitivity. However, in two experiments the values derived from the equation did not account for latency.

Frequency can also be expressed as a probability, therefore the obtained descriptor can be stated in terms of the amount of information (bits) carried by the noun form. Accordingly, the average frequency per thematic role for a particular noun form is expressed as a proportion, relative to a sum of average frequencies per thematic roles for other noun forms for a given gender. The obtained proportion must undergo a log transform which will provide us with the amount of information in bits carried by each grammatical form (Kostić, A., 1991).

$$\overline{RT}_m = f\left[-\log_2\left(\frac{\dfrac{F_m}{R_m}}{\displaystyle\sum_{m=1}^{M}\dfrac{F_m}{R_m}}\right)\right] \qquad (2)$$

Equation 2 states that the processing latency to identify an inflected noun form is some function of the amount of information derived from the average frequency per thematic role within a particular inflected form. The equation was evaluated on the same set of experiments as Equation 1. For the Todorović (1988) experiment, linear regression indicates that 99% of the variability is accounted for by Equation 2: $r^2 = 0.987$, $F(1,2) = 152.852$, $p < 0.01$ (see Table 2 and Appendix 2). Likewise, for the Kostić and Katz (1987) experiment, the values obtained from Equation 2 account for 93% of the variability: $r^2 = 0.926$, $F(1,4) = 50.328$, $p < 0.01$ (see Table 3 and Appendix 2). In contrast to Equation 1, which could not account for the replication of Lukatela et al. (1980) experiment (Kostić, A. 1991), Equation 2 could predict differences among response latencies correlated for the three forms of masculine nouns: $r^2 = 0.998$, $F(1,1) = 580.822$, $p < 0.05$ and for the three forms of feminine nouns and $r^2 = 0.996$, $F(1,1) = 260.112$, $p < 0.05$ (see Table 4 and Appendix 2). Finally, while Equation 1 did not account for a significant proportion of processing latency variability for irregular feminine nouns (Kostić, A.,1991), the values obtained from Equation 2 did: $r^2 = 0.997$, $F(1,1) = 301.201$, $p < 0.05$ (see Table 5 and Appendix 2).[2]

In summary, the values obtained from Equation 2 account for almost all of the processing variability of Serbian noun forms across four studies. The fact that so much of the processing variability of inflected noun forms can be accounted for by Equation 2 strongly suggests that the proper description of a subject's sensitivity to an inflected noun form is the amount of information (as specified in Equation 2) carried by that form.[3]

---

[2]The significant proportion of the explained variance in the four experiments suggests that the different outcomes of the experiments reported by Todorović (1988) and Lukatela et al. (1980) should not be ascribed to differences in exposure duration, since Equation 2 has no exposure variation term.

[3]It should be noted that the slope of the linear function (of RT to bits) changes across experiments (see Tables 2-5 and Appendix 2). It was demonstrated that changes in slope are systematic. Specifically, ln slope linearly decreases as a function of linear increases in the entropy of the experiment (i.e., the mean information load for forms presented). As entropy increases, processing latency per bit decreases (A. Kostić, in preparation). The regression equation provides a general formula for values of slope as a function of entropy for *any* experiment.

GENERAL DISCUSSION

The Informational Approach proposed in this study has several implications with respect to stimulus specification on one hand and processing mechanisms on the other hand. Some implications are derived from Equation 2, while others come from the metric (i.e., the amount of information) in which psychologically relevant stimulus properties should be specified. A significant proportion of explained variance implies that when processing an inflected Serbian noun subjects are sensitive to the amount of information derived from the average frequency per thematic role within a particular inflected noun form. Note that Equation 2 has no terms referring to standard linguistic attributes such as case and grammatical number. Nevertheless, it provides an almost perfect prediction for processing latency with inflected noun forms. This implies that two of the three pivotal attributes of the noun system are cognitively irrelevant and suggests that some formal aspects of language which belong to a standard linguistic taxonomy do not map directly into cognitive organization.[4]

The Informational Approach makes accurate predictions for all Serbian noun forms, including the unaffixed nominative singular masculine gender (cf. Table 3 and Appendix 2). Because Equation 2 has no decomposition term, it would not be appropriate if inflected forms were decomposed into base form and suffix. By virtue of the fact that the amount of information associated with affixed and unaffixed forms is calculated by the same equation, a mechanism of decomposition is not supported. On the other hand, extended to inflected Serbian noun forms, the Single Unit Hypothesis predicts that processing of inflected noun form should reflect its suffix frequency. This proved not to be the case. Suffix frequency does not predict latency because it does not explicitly refer to thematic role, and thematic role is an obligatory term in the equation. The term reflects substantial differences between inflectional suffixes on one hand and derivational prefixes and suffixes on the other hand because derivational affixes modify a word semantically (e.g., *teacher* from *teach*).

The frequency of an inflectional suffix is the cumulative frequency of thematic roles modified by a particular noun form.[5] Because the number of thematic roles and form frequency have inverse processing effects, an increase in the number of roles, which implies an increase in informational load, is compensated for by a frequency increase, and therefore by a decrease in informational load. However, in most cases the increase of one parameter is not necessarily paralleled by a proportional increase in the other parameter; as a

---

[4]Whereas it is certainly true for grammatical number, it is less clear how to assess the cognitive status of case since it is covertly nested in form specification.

[5]The fact that some thematic roles are more frequent than others (cf. Dj. Kostić, 1965a), is of marginal importance for estimates of the amount of information because the value of the F/R ratio is the same for both equal and unequal frequency distributions of thematic roles (see Katz et al., this volume).

consequence, the informational load for different noun forms will vary. Considering the properties of the two parameters, processing latency to identify inflected noun forms can be treated as an intersection of the two inverse processing effects. The intersection represents the relative complexity of an inflected noun form, while the amount of information serves as a quantitative expression of this complexity and, by the same token, a predictor of processing time to the inflected form. In other words, the amount of information derived from the average frequency per thematic role reflects the mutually compensatory influences of the two parameters. This should apply to any suffix which contains syntactically relevant information. If all relevant parameters are properly specified, there is good reason to believe that the amount of information could account for processing latency with inflected forms of other word types as well.

The obtained descriptor could also be applied to fixed word order languages characterized by few inflections. These languages need not have a morphologically rich inventory since most of the syntactically relevant information is embedded in word order. This, of course, does not imply that inflections in fixed word order languages should be characterized by minimal informational load. There should be no principal difference between fixed and free word order languages, since a decrease in number of thematic roles is expected to parallel a frequency decrease in inflected form. Take, for example, the suffix s in English which, if added to a noun, denotes pluralization.[6] This being the only role carried by the suffix, Equation 2 states that the difference in the amount of information between the singular and plural forms of the same noun should derive only from probability of grammatical number because the denominator is 1.[7] If the probability that an English noun appears in plural form parallels that of Serbian nouns (approximately 0.25), the amount of information carried by the suffix s would be 2 bits, as opposed to 0.415 bit carried by the null morpheme for the same noun in singular. The analogous calculation could be performed for other inflected forms in English and for other languages where the suffix carries grammatical information. Equation 2, if verified in languages other than Serbian, would capture a general principle which unifies processing of inflected words, irrespective of language. Generally it only requires the proper specification of form frequency and the number of thematic roles.

The way relevant stimulus properties have been specified, with form complexity expressed in terms of informational load (i.e., bits), may imply that searching for language specific processing mechanisms may not be fruitful. The bit, as an index of the expectation or (inversely) the surprise value of a stimulus, has been used often to describe psychological systems that are characterized by stimulus and response uncertainty (cf. Adelson, Muckler, & Williams, 1955;

---

[6]The present discussion does not include apostrophe s.

[7]This is not the case with suffixes such as -ed or -ing, for example, since they include several roles (cf. Dj. Kostić, 1965a).

Bruner, Miller, & Zimmerman, 1955; Frick, 1954; Klemmer, 1957; Miller, Heise, & Lichten, 1951; Pollack, 1959; Poulton, 1956). In the present circumstances, the fact that a subject's sensitivity to different suffixes is accounted for by information load, instead of by the ratio of frequency and number of thematic roles, suggests that morphological processing need not be considered strictly as a language specific process. Amount of information does not refer specifically to linguistic attributes, even though a language-specific term (i.e., number of thematic roles) is nested in the specification for informational load. Consequently, the processing mechanism need not be restricted to linguistic material—it has to be sensitive only to variation in informational load, specified in terms of the relevant processing parameters and their interaction. Accordingly, morphological processing may not differ from processing of other kinds of material. This may suggest that some aspect of our cognitive system operates in a uniform metric expressed in terms of the amount of information. The content (i.e., semantics) of the processed material is irrelevant—the only factor that matters is the informational load of the incoming material. If stimulation is properly specified, processing variation could be equally well predicted for tasks in which stimulation seems to be simple (e.g., CRT "choice reaction time," cf. Hick, 1952; Hyman, 1953) as well as more complex (e.g., inflected noun forms). It should be noted, however, that once stimuli are expressed in terms of the amount of information, the complexity criterion has to be altered—whether something is complex or not is relative with respect to the informational load. Any intuitions about complexity become irrelevant.

Thus far we have been interested in processing latency variation which, as demonstrated, highly correlates with informational load variability. Once this relation has been established for nouns, predictions of processing latency variation for other word types becomes a problem of proper numerical specification of parameters identified as relevant. However, in order to provide a better understanding of how inflected morphology is processed, we may ask why different inflected forms vary with respect to their informational load in the first place. One possibility is that the variability in informational load is unsystematic and therefore cognitively and linguistically uninteresting. On the other hand, it could be assumed that the observed variability is due to some global constraint (or set of constraints) that guides the distribution of informational load. If the latter were the case, what might these constraints be? The obvious candidate is processing limitations of the cognitive system. An additional and at this point hypothetical candidate could be the frequency of a particular thematic role (or set of roles) modified by a particular case, where the frequency of a thematic role would reflect its syntactic relevance.[8] It seems plausible that forms that

---

[8]The subject role is more frequent than time modification, to take an extreme example (cf. Dj. Kostić, 1965a). On the other hand, it would be hard to deny that the subject role

carry more relevant syntactic information should also be more easily accessed and therefore characterized by a smaller informational load. This, on the other hand, may imply that syntactic relevance is related to thematic role frequency: The more relevant roles should be characterized by higher frequency. Consequently, the frequency contribution for the cases that modify those roles should be greater relative to other cases and, by the same token, their informational load should be smaller. There are some indications that this may be the case with Serbian inflected noun forms. Thus, for example, forms that contain the nominative case, which modifies subject and predicate roles, have the smallest informational load in all three genders. Likewise, forms that contain the accusative case, which modifies the object role, have smaller informational load (averaged across genders) than those that contain instrumental or dative/locative cases (see Appendix 2). It could be assumed that this hierarchy may be due to the greater frequency values for subject, predicate, and object roles relative to frequencies of other thematic roles. The observed hierarchy seems to support the intuition that differences in informational load among Serbian noun forms may not be arbitrary but could reflect some optimal informational load distribution with respect to the syntactic relevance of modified roles on one hand and to limited processing capacities on the other hand.

Equation 2 indicates that this hierarchy is rooted in the ratio between frequency and number of thematic roles (i.e., an unequal contribution of the two parameters to the amount of information carried by noun case rather than noun form). Take, for example, the fact that forms in the nominative case are processed faster than other forms. While it is clear that the shorter recognition latency for those forms is due to the presence of the nominative case, the question is why is the nominative processed so easily? Inspection of frequency values and number of thematic roles carried by the nominative case indicates that the shorter processing latency is due to the value of the ratio of frequency and thematic roles which is large compared to the ratio values for other cases (see Appendix 1). This is because nominative is characterized by high frequency and few thematic roles. As a consequence, the contribution of relative frequency to informational load is disproportionately large compared to other cases, which causes its informational load to decrease and its processing latency to shorten. The important implication of Equation 2 is that the nominative case has no privileged status compared to other cases, as there is no difference in the way its information load value is calculated. If the nominative case had either a lower frequency or a greater number of thematic roles (with the other parameter held constant), its informational load would increase as would its processing speed. Therefore, it is this minimal information load that makes processing of the

---

also has greater syntactical relevance. As such, syntactic relevance of a particular thematic role could be specified post hoc with respect to its frequency of usage, rather than by an independent linguistic criterion.

nominative so fast relative to other forms. Other explanations of nominative superiority, such as a privileged status by virtue of being a citation form (cf. Burani, in press) or being non-decomposable are not supported.

Once the reason for the shorter processing latency to the nominative form relative to other forms is well understood, we may ask why this minimal number of thematic roles is paralleled by such a high frequency. Again, the numerical reason for the minimal informational load carried by the nominative form could either be a mere coincidence or it could be related to the syntactic relevance of the functions it modifies. Since the subject and predicate roles (in addition to the object role) are probably the principal thematic roles, it may be assumed that the exceptionally small amount of information carried by the nominative case is related to the syntactic relevance of thematic roles it modifies, this relevance being manifested through their disproportionally high frequency relative to other thematic roles. The same rationale could be applied to other cases as well, suggesting that the amount of information carried by a noun case is inversely proportional to the syntactic relevance of its modified thematic roles. This assumption, however, requires additional evaluation to demonstrate that the amount of information carried by a particular case is also systematically related to the frequencies of the modified thematic roles.

If the differences in the amount of information carried by various noun forms are guided by the syntactic relevance of thematic roles modified by case on one hand, and by limited processing capacities on the other hand, we could extend our intuitions and ask a somewhat broader question: What are the constraints which give rise to the observed morphological structures, assuming that those structures are the optimal means of minimizing processing load per time unit? The fact that there is a strong linear relation between RT and the amount of information (Equation 2) suggests that all inflected forms are within a range of informational load which is compatible with limitation on processing capacity. The amount of information carried by an inflected form seems to respect some upper limit since there is no evidence of an absence of processing variability for forms with extremely high informational load (Kostić, A., in preparation). This suggests that the variability in informational load across different forms may be an optimal local solution for the overall informational load distribution in a sentence, i.e., some default which is additionally modulated by preceding modifiers (prepositions, for example).[9] If some upper processing limit is the pivotal constraint which guides the informational load distribution, we may ask what happens when this limit is reached. This question points to different although related problems of the logic of morphological structures and their

---

[9]The informational load carried by a particular form could be treated as a local state of informational fluctuation within more global syntactic structures. To better understand local informational load distributions, a proper description of the informational load fluctuation in a sentence context may be required. This, however, is far beyond the scope of our present understanding.

emergence: Why is morphology structured the way it is,? Why do we have different word types and different forms of the same word? Why is there morphological agreement among some word types? And finally, how did these structures emerge? Below I will outline a possible scenario for the emergence of morphological structures and some hypotheses about the logic of morphological agreement among some word types.

Nouns in inflected languages exhibit morphological transformations (i.e., declension). Why should there be different forms of a noun in the first place? Along the lines of this study, if there existed only a single noun form within a free word order language it would have to modify a vast number of thematic roles, which might cause its informational load to exceed processing capacity. As a consequence, the noun form would become ambiguous. The solution to the problem might be to organize informational load into several inflected forms of the same noun, where each form would contain a fixed and distinguishable set of thematic roles. Obviously, there has to be an upper limit to the number of noun forms, since with too great a number, the system would face the same problem as with a single noun form. Once the upper limit (i.e., critical processing level) to the number of noun forms is reached, it has to be redistributed across different word types, which now mark syntactic potentials embedded in an inflected noun form.

Prepositional modification is an example of such a solution. Experiments with prepositional priming in Serbian indicate processing facilitation of an inflected noun form if it is preceded by a congruent modifier (Katz, Rexer, & Peter, this volume; Lukatela, Kostić, Feldman & Turvey, 1982). Since the processing of an isolated noun is determined by the amount of information it conveys, a facilitation effect indicates a reduction in the amount of information carried by a particular noun form. If so, the cognitive relevance of a modifier should reside in its reduction of informational load, i.e., its reduction of ambiguity. This, in turn, has both morphological and syntactic consequences. Decrease of a noun's informational load when preceded by a congruent preposition offers an explanation as to why in most languages prepositions precede the noun and not vice versa. Likewise, the same line of argument may offer a tentative explanation for the fact that nominative is the only case which is not modified by a preposition. Its minimal informational load makes additional load reduction unnecessary. The morphological and syntactic consequence of this fact is manifested by an absence of prepositional modification. By the same token, Equation 2 predicts that processing facilitation of the nominative case due to preceding congruent modifiers (e.g., adjectival priming or possessive adjective priming) should be negligible. The amount of information to be reduced is minimal. This prediction has been empirically supported in experiments reported by Gurjanov and his associates (Gurjanov, Lukatela, Lukatela, K., Savić, & Turvey, 1985; Gurjanov, Lukatela, Moskovljević, Savić & Turvey, 1985). It may be assumed that the grammatical priming effects observed in a number of experiments done in Serbian are due to modulation of the informational load of the target by a preceding grammatical context, rather than to some hypothetical operations ascribed to a "syntactic processor" (cf. Forster, 1979). This may be true for other aspects of morphology as well. In order to make accurate predictions it would be necessary to identify (and express in quantitative terms) the relevant properties of a grammatical context that affect form frequency and/or number of thematic roles.

The previous examples indicate that some properties of Serbian morphology (i.e., preposition/noun ordering and the absence of prepositional modification for the nominative case) may be due to modulation of informational load rather than to some idiosyncratic linguistic factor. If this conclusion is extended to morphological structuring in general, it could be argued that the logic of morphological structures in language is rooted in cognitive constraints from which they emerge as natural solutions guided by a minimum principle such as *minimization of informational load per time unit.* There are reasons to believe that the same may be true for syntactic structures. Moreover, the logic of morphological and syntactic structuring may not differ substantially from any other structuring in nature, where forms emerge as a consequence of an interplay among parameters such as volume, surface, material, gravity, etc. (cf. Schwenk, 1978; Stevens, 1974; Thompson, 1961). The consequence is that the emergence of morphological and syntactic structures need not be tied to language-specific mechanisms. If the guideline is a minimum principle which modifies local and global informational load, morphological and syntactic structures may be the product of a single global constraint on cognition which reflects processing limitations, irrespective of the material being processed and whether or not it is linguistic in nature. The observed morphological and syntactic structures can then be treated as an optimal (rather than an ideal) solution that provides compatibility between the mind's processing constraints on one hand and, on the other hand, the complexity of processing that is required to solve some particular cognitive problem. The challenge of research along these lines is to demonstrate the systematicity of a particular structural organization with respect to well defined cognitive constraints.

ACKNOWLEDGMENT

I am deeply indebted to my father, Prof. Djordje Kostić, whose extended research in the early sixties provided me with frequency values of grammatical forms in Serbian and a taxonomy of Serbian case functions and meanings. Without his efforts the Informational Approach would not be possible. I hope this study assures him that his work continues.

This research was supported in part by the National Institute of Child Health and Human Development Grant HD-01994 to Haskins Laboratories.

REFERENCES

Adelson, M., Muckler F. A., & Williams, A. C., Jr. (1955). Verbal learning and message variables related to amount of information. In H. Quastler (Ed.), *Information theory in psychology.* Glencoe, IL: The Free Press.

Benveniste, E. (1962). Pour l'analyse des functions causelles: Le genitif latin. *Lingua, 11,* 1-10.

Bergman, M., Hudson, P., & Eling, P. (1988). How simple complex words can be: Morphological processing and word representation. *The Quarterly Journal of Experimental Psychology, 40A(1)* 41-72.

Bruner, J. S., Miller, G. A., & Zimmerman, C. (1955). Discriminative skill and discriminative matching in perceptual recognition. *Journal of Experimental Psychology, 49,* 187-192.

Burani, C. (in press). The lexical representation of prefixed words: Data from production task. In K. Keifer (Ed.), *The interface between morphology and syntax.* Amsterdam: John Benjamins.

Butterworth, B. (1983). Lexical representation. In B. Butterworth (Ed.), *Language production, Vol. II: Development, writing and other language processes.* London: Academic Press.

Chomsky, N. (1965). *Aspects of the theory of syntax.* Cambridge, MA: MIT Press.

Chomsky, N. (1970). Remarks on nominalisation. In R. A. Jacobs & P. S. Rosenbaum (Eds.), *Readings in English transformational grammar.* Lexington, MA: Ginn.

Cutler, A. (1983). Lexical complexity and sentence processing. In G. B. Flores d'Arcais & R. J. Jarvella (Eds.), *The process of language understanding.* London: Wiley.

de Groot, A. W. (1956). Classification of uses of a case illustrated on the genitive in Latin. *Lingua, 6,* 8-66.

Diver, W. (1964). The system of agency of the Latin noun. *Word, 2,* 178-196.

Feldman, L. B., & Fowler, C. A. (1987). The inflected noun system in Serbo-Croatian: Lexical representation of morphological structure. *Memory & Cognition, 15(1),* 197-209.

Forster, K. I. (1979). Levels of processing and the structure of the language processor. In W. E. Cooper & E. C. Walker (Eds.), *Sentence processing.* Hillsdale, NJ: Lawrence Erlbaum Associates.

Fowler, C. A., Napps, S. E., & Feldman, L. B. (1985). Relations among regular and irregular morphologically related words in the lexicon as revealed by repetition priming. *Memory & Cognition, 13,* 241-255.

Frick, F. C. (1954). Some perceptual problems from the point of view of information theory. *Current Trends in Information Theory.* Pittsburgh: University of Pittsburgh Press.

Gurjanov, M., Lukatela, G., Lukatela, K., Savić, M., & Turvey, M. T. (1985). Grammatical priming of inflected nouns by the gender of possessive adjectives. *Journal of Experimental Psychology: Learning, Memory, and Cognition, 2(4)*, 692-701.

Gurjanov, M., Lukatela, G., Moskovljević, J., Savić, M., & Turvey, M. T. (1985). Grammatical priming of inflected nouns by inflected adjectives. *Cognition, 19*, 55-71.

Henderson, L. (1985). Towards a psychology of morphemes. In A. W. Ellis (Ed.), *Progress in the psychology of language* (Vol. I.) Hillsdale, NJ: Lawrence Erlbaum Associates.

Hick, W. E. (1952). On the rate of gain of information. *Quarterly Journal of Experimental Psychology, 4*, 11-26.

Hjelmslev, L. (1935, 1937). La categorie des cas. *Acta Jutlandica, VII*, 1, IX, 2.

Hyman, R. (1953). Stimulus information as a determinant of reaction time. *Journal of Experimental Psychology, 45*, 188-196.

Jackendoff, R. (1975). Morphological and semantic regularities in the lexicon. *Language, 51*, 639-671.

Katz, L., Boyce, S., Goldstein, L., & Lukatela, G. (1987). Grammatical information effects in auditory word recognition. *Cognition, 25*, 235-263.

Klemmer, E. T. (1957). Simple reaction times a function of time uncertainty. *Journal of Experimental Psychology, 54*, 195-200.

Kostić, A., & Katz, L. (1987). Processing speed differences between nouns, adjectives and verbs. *Psychological Research, 49(1)*, 229-236.

Kostić, A. (1991). nformational approach to the processing of inflected morphology: Standard data reconsidered. *Psychological Research, 53(1)*, 62-70.

Kostić, A. (in preparation). *Processing speed varies as a function of experimental entropy.*

Kostić, Dj. (1965a). *Syntactic roles of cases in Serbo-Croatian.* Institute for Experimental Phonetics and Speech Pathology, Belgrade.

Kostić, Dj. (1965b). *The structure of usage value of grammatical forms in Serbo-Croatian.* Institute for Experimental Phonetics and Speech Pathology, Belgrade.

Kuryłowicz, J. (1960). Le probleme du classement des cas. *Esquisses linguistiques* (pp. 131-150). Wroclaw-Krakov.

Lukatela, G., Mandić, Z., Gligorijević, B., Kostić, A., Savić, M., & Turvey, M. T. (1978). Lexical decision for inflected nouns. *Language and Speech, 21*, 166-173.

Lukatela, G., Gligorijević, B., Kostić, A., & Turvey, M. T. (1980). Representation of inflected nouns in the internal lexicon. *Memory & Cognition, 8*, 415-423.

Lukatela, G., Kostić, A., Feldman, L. B., & Turvey, M. T. (1982). Grammatical priming of inflected nouns. *Memory & Cognition, 11*, 59-63.

Lukatela, G., Carello, C., & Turvey, M. T. (1987). Lexical representation of regular and irregular inflected nouns. *Language and Cognitive Processes, 2(1),* 1-17.

Manelis, L., & Tharp, D. (1977). The processing of affixed words. *Memory & Cognition, 5(6),* 690-695.

Miller, G. A., Heise, G. A., & Lichten, W. (1951). The intelligibility of speech as a function of the context of the test materials. *Journal of Experimental Psychology, 41,* 329-335.

Pollack, I. (1959). Message uncertainty and message reception. *Journal of Acoustic Society of America, 31,* 1500-1508.

Poulton, E. C. (1956). The precision of choice reactions. *Journal of Experimental Psychology, 51,* 98-102.

Rubin, G. S., Becker, C. A., & Freeman, R. H. (1979). Morphological structure and its effect on visual word recognition. *Journal of Verbal Learning and Verbal Behavior, 18,* 757-767.

Rubenstein, H., Lewis, S. S., & Rubenstein, M. A. (1971). Evidence for phonetic coding in visual word recognition. *Journal of Verbal Learning and Verbal Behavior, 10,* 645-657.

Schwenk, T. (1978). *Sensitive chaos: The creation of flowing forms in water and air.* New York: Schoken Books.

Stanners, R. F., Neiser, J. J., Hernon, W. P., & Hall, R. (1979). Memory representation for morphologically related words. *Journal of Verbal Learning and Verbal Behavior, 18,* 399-412.

Stanners, R. F., Neiser, J. J., & Painton, S. (1979). Memory representation for prefixed words. *Journal of Verbal Learning and Verbal Behavior, 18,* 733-743.

Stevens, P. (1974). *Patterns in nature.* Atlantic Monthly Press.

Taft, M., & Forster, K. I. (1975). Lexical storage and retrieval of prefixed words. *Journal of Verbal Learning and Verbal Behavior, 14,* 638-647.

Taft, M., & Forster, K. I. (1976). Lexical storage and retrieval of polymorphemic and polysyllabic words. *Journal of Verbal Learning and Verbal Behavior, 15,* 607-620.

Taft, M. (1979a). Recognition of affixed words and the word frequency effect. *Memory & Cognition, 7(4),* 263-272.

Taft, M. (1979b). Lexical access via orthographic code: The basic orthographic syllabic structure (BOSS). *Journal of Verbal Learning and Verbal Behavior, 18,* 21-39.

Taft, M. (1981). Prefix stripping revisited. *Journal of Verbal Learning and Verbal Behavior, 20,* 289-297.

Thompson, D. (1961). *On growth and form.* Cambridge: Cambridge University Press.

Todorović, D. (1988). Hemispheric differences in case processing. *Brain and Language, 33,* 365-389.

APPENDIX 1

FREQUENCY (F) AND NUMBER OF THEMATIC ROLES (R) FOR SERBIAN INFLECTED CASES AS A FUNCTION OF NUMBER AND GENDER*

	Case	Form	F%	R	R%
Masculine nouns					
Singular	nominative	konj	12.830	3	1.604
	genitive	konja	8.560	51	27.273
	dative	konju	0.867	22	11.765
	accusative	konja	5.486	58	31.016
	instrumental	konjem	1.895	32	17.112
	locative	konju	3.768	21	11.230
Plural	nominative	konji	3.326	3	1.604
	genitive	konja	3.961	51	27.273
	dative	konjima	0.280	22	11.765
	accusative	konje	2.211	58	31.016
	instrumental	konjima	0.597	32	17.112
	locative	konjima	0.611	21	11.230
Feminine nouns					
Singular	nominative	žaba	8.841	3	1.604
	genitive	žabe	7.876	51	27.237
	dative	žabi	0.377	22	11.765
	accusative	žabu	5.480	58	31.016
	instrumental	žabom	1.939	32	17.112
	locative	žabi	3.419	21	11.230
Plural	nominative	žabe	3.577	3	1.604
	genitive	žaba	3.220	51	27.273
	dative	žabama	0.157	22	11.765
	accusative	žabe	2.750	58	31.016
	instrumental	žabama	0.734	32	17.112
	locative	žabama	0.799	21	11.230
Irregular feminine nouns					
Singular	nominative	strast	8.841	3	1.604
	genitive	strasti	7.876	51	27.237
	dative	strasti	0.377	22	11.765
	accusative	strast	5.480	58	31.016
	instrumental	straću	1.939	32	17.112
	locative	strasti	3.419	21	11.230

Plural	nominative	strasti	3.577	3	1.604
	genitive	strasti	3.220	51	27.273
	dative	strastima	0.157	22	11.765
	accusative	strasti	2.750	58	31.016
	instrumental	strastima	0.734	32	17.112
	locative	strastima	0.799	21	11.230
Neuter nouns					
Singular	nominative	selo	2.881	3	1.604
	genitive	sela	3.465	51	27.273
	dative	selu	0.312	22	11.765
	accusative	selo	2.551	58	31.016
	instrumental	selom	0.862	32	17.112
	locative	selu	1.606	21	11.230
Plural	nominative	sela	0.694	3	1.604
	genitive	sela	0.614	51	27.273
	dative	selima	0.039	22	11.765
	accusative	sela	0.728	58	31.016
	instrumental	selima	0.134	32	17.112
	locative	selima	0.212	21	11.230

---

* Frequency values (F%) and number of thematic roles based on functions and meanings (R) adopted from Kostić, Dj. (1965a; 1965b)

konj (M) - 'horse'
žaba (F) - 'frog'
selo (N) - 'village'
strast (F irr.) - 'passion'

APPENDIX 2

CUMULATIVE CASE FREQUENCY (F), CUMULATIVE NUMBER OF THEMATIC ROLES (R), AND THE AMOUNT OF INFORMATION (IN BITS) CARRIED BY SERBIAN NOUN FORMS

Form	Case	F%	R	F/R	R%	bit
konj	n.s.	12.830	3	4.277	0.920	0.433
konja	g.s.+a.s.+g.p.	18.007	109	0.165	33.746	5.128
konju	d.s.+l.s.	4.635	43	0.108	13.313	5.774
konjem	i.s.	1.895	32	0.059	9.907	6.608
konji	n.p.	3.326	3	1.109	0.929	2.381
konje	a.p.	2.211	58	0.038	17.957	7.243
konjima	d.p.+l.p.+i.p.	1.488	75	0.020	23.220	8.185
žaba	n.s.+g.p.	12.061	54	0.223	14.439	1.464
žabe	g.s.+n.p.+a.p.	14.201	112	0.127	29.947	2.280
žabi	d.s.+l.s.	3.796	43	0.088	11.497	2.803
žabu	a.s.	5.480	58	0.094	15.508	2.705
žabom	i.s.	1.939	32	0.061	8.556	3.346
žabama	d.p.+l.p.+i.p.	1.690	75	0.023	20.053	4.773
selo	n.s.+a.s.	5.432	61	0.089	18.885	1.272
sela	g.s.+n.p.+g.p.+a.p.	5.501	112	0.049	34.675	2.130
selu	d.s.+l.s.	1.918	43	0.045	13.313	2.269
selom	i.s.	0.862	32	0.027	9.907	2.997
selima	d.p.+l.p.+i.p.	0.385	75	0.005	23.220	5.389
strast	n.s.+a.s.	14.321	61	0.235	18.885	0.995
strasti	g.s.+d.s.+l.s.+n.p. +g.p.+a.p.	21.219	155	0.137	47.998	1.773
straću	i.s.	1.939	32	0.061	9.907	2.909
strastima	d.p.+l.p.+i.p.	1.690	75	0.023	23.220	4.336

Note: The number of thematic roles for Serbian noun cases has been obtained from five grammar books. Only those functions and meanings that were invariant across all grammar books were taken into consideration.

15 Distributional Properties of Derivational Affixes: Implications for Processing

Alessandro Laudanna and Cristina Burani
Istituto di Psicologia CNR, Roma

This chapter deals with the processing of derivational morphology. The focus is on the constraints imposed on the processing of printed words by properties of derivational affixes (both prefixes and suffixes). The effects on processing of both distributional properties (e.g., word frequency, orthographic confusability) and properties re-defined in distributional terms (e.g., length, productivity) are considered. Some recent results from visual lexical access experiments in Italian are presented, along with a discussion of empirical correlations among distributional properties of derivational affixes in that language. The possible interactions among linguistic/distributional properties, experimental data, and processing hypotheses are outlined. Finally, some methodological consequences derived from the experimental investigation of the complex factors affecting affixes' distribution are discussed.

INTRODUCTION

Most of the research on the role of morphological structure in lexical processing has been devoted to providing an answer to the following question, usually cast in dichotomous terms: Are morphologically complex words mentally represented and accessed as whole forms, or do their representation and access reflect the constituents of which they are composed?

The focus of this chapter is on another related question which, in our view, should be asked about both representation and access. It concerns primarily derived words. When formulated in broad terms (articulated later in the chapter), the question might be posed as follows: Are the mental representations of the constituents of derived words to be defined in strictly linguistic terms, or do they embody distributional properties of linguistic signals? By "distributional properties" we mean quantitative parameters defined either on the basis of the individual characteristics and/or occurrences of morphemes (e.g., length/frequency of derivational suffixes) or on the basis of the conditioned co-occurrences with other morphemes in the language (e.g., number or types of derivational prefixes which occur in combination with bound roots).

The point we would like to make is that in the attempt to answer the latter question, the theoretical proposals should not be stated in the typical dichotomous way (decomposition vs. non-decomposition). On the contrary, a more useful hypothesis might be entertained that, especially when considering their distributional properties, different types of morphological units may have different consequences for the lexical processing system. In order to refine our hypotheses about the factors that putatively influence the properties of lexical representations and the way in which they are accessed, we should start to single out these factors and submit them to experimental investigation.

In the present chapter, we try to sketch out some of these factors and describe some initial experiments carried out on Italian that investigated the role of such factors in the access to and representation of derived words. First, it is crucial to emphasize that our considerations mainly focus on one component of the lexical system, the access mechanism, which, accordingly to the Augmented Addressed Morphology (AAM) model, (Caramazza, Laudanna, & Romani, 1988; see also Burani & Caramazza, 1987; Caramazza, Miceli, Silveri, & Laudanna, 1985; Laudanna & Burani, 1985) is characterized as an activation system where the degree of activation of an orthographically defined access representation is a function of the graphemic similarity between an input letter string and the stored representation. In this component, letter strings simultaneously activate both whole word access representations when available (that is, units for known words) and morphemic access units (that is, units for the morphemic constituents which form a word). The process of activation is sensitive to the surface characteristics of word structure: The threshold value is reached when a stimulus pattern matches a whole-word access unit (and this is what happens in most cases because whole word access representations are assumed to be faster in accessing a lexical representation) and/or one or more access units corresponding to the morphemic constituents of the word.

Variables Affecting Access and Representation of Derivatives

The representational format and the organization of lexical entries may differ for different types of morphemes. This is particularly evident in the case of derivational affixes that are less homogeneous than inflectional affixes. Despite their heterogeneity, derivatives might be organized in some way: If it is the case, the problem is to determine their organizational dimensions. To date, the experimental research on this issue has not focused on differentiating hypotheses on representation and access of derived words according to the types of morphemes they include. When concerned with such possible distinctions, psycholinguistic research has either stated the criteria on intuitive grounds or borrowed them from linguistics (examples taken from a variety of researchers are Beauvillain & Segui, 1992; Fowler, Napps, & Feldman, 1985; Marslen-Wilson, Tyler, Waksler, & Older, 1994; Stanners, Neiser, & Painton, 1979).

We think there is need to investigate not only (or not necessarily) linguistically defined types of words but also types characterized on the basis of other dimensions of psycholinguistic relevance, which should be considered for their specific roles as well as for their interactions. These dimensions include a number of quantitative and distributional parameters that characterize the multiple occurrences of words and morphemes in a given language (such as word and morpheme frequency, word and morpheme length, quantitative relationships between affixed and pseudo-affixed forms, etc.). Strictly speaking, some of these parameters (e.g., length, prefixedness) are not distributional when referred to a single word or morpheme. Nevertheless, they may be treated as distributional when their configurations of values in a large sample of words are considered.

In the following section we discuss the role of several distributional and linguistic factors as it emerged from some experiments carried out in Italian in our laboratory. Before describing these experiments, however, we would like to point out that the relative importance of the factors we discuss may vary across languages with implications for how words are represented and organized in the lexicon. One such implication is the following: If the distributional and linguistic parameters of derivational morphology are relevant in shaping the organization of the mental lexicon and, in particular, the mechanisms which allow access to lexical representations, then it follows that as the range of values of those parameters vary from one language to another, the more they may lead to varying organizations of the lexical access systems across different languages (or language types). Stated differently, the procedures devoted to accessing the lexical representations corresponding to words should be sensitive to the regularities inherent in the words and the sub-lexical units. This does not mean that an exhaustive, statistical description of the input is automatically equivalent to a model of the lexical access system with no more internal structure than that provided by the orthographic regularity encountered. On the contrary, we assume that the access system is also affected by linguistic and cognitive constraints on the form and organization of mental representations. As is the case for many cognitive abilities, the type and amount of information extracted from the input is constrained by the level of representation under consideration as well as by the general architecture of the lexical processing system.

In summary, in order to guide our investigations of the variables relevant to psycholinguistic research on derivatives, our hypotheses should take into account at least two issues:

1) (language-specific) *input characteristics*: One of the most interesting consequences of studying the distributional properties of words and affixes is that theoretical proposals are to be characterized, at least initially, as specific to a given language, even though there might be universal cognitive constraints that apply across every language (see below). In other words, if it is true that the lexical processing system models itself on the basis of exposure to a particular language, then its organization should be affected by some relevant characteristics of the language under investigation.

2) *cognitive constraints:* By this, we mean all constraints independent of language deriving from properties of processes and representations such as the computational space available to process lexical information, the storage capacity of buffers, etc. One focus of interest here is on constraints on processing, including, for instance, avoiding incorrect as well as inconsistent decompositions (as it is the case for pseudo-affixed forms), the constraints on the number and/or types of possible outputs following from the use of any processing procedure (e.g., the number of morphemes that can be computed in the same word, following from decomposition procedures), and constraints on the means that the system must provide for dealing with the problem of morphological ambiguity resolution (for instance, favoring mechanisms of competitive inhibition among homographic stems; see Laudanna, Badecker, & Caramazza, 1989). Definitely, if one assumes the above sets of constraints, it seems quite implausible that one fixed procedure for affix processing (for instance an affix stripping procedure of the type proposed by Taft & Forster, 1975) can be at work irrespective of the differences among affixes and among languages (or language types).

Derivational Affixes in Italian: Some Quantitative Data on Prefixes

Preliminary empirical measures of the set of affixes in Italian show that the variables we are interested in (affix length, affix frequency, orthographic confusability (or ambiguity) of affixes, productivity of affixes) show quite peculiar patterns and non-linear intercorrelations among each other. In this section we give a brief description of the quantitative relationships between some variables of occurrence of prefixes which are all derivational in Italian. We limit our discussion to a few variables relevant to the experiments to be described and outline some problems that their quantitative patterns pose for processing.

Let us start with orthographic ambiguity (or confusability). By orthographic ambiguity of a prefix, we mean that orthographic/phonological strings corresponding to prefixes in prefixed words (e.g., *pre-* in *predire*, 'to predict') may also correspond to non-morphemic sequences (henceforth, pseudoprefixes) in non-prefixed words (e.g., *pre* in *predare*, 'to plunder'). This alternation holds true for almost all prefixes in Italian: The exceptions are a few orthographic sequences that correspond to long prefixes and never occur as pseudo-prefixes.

The empirical index by which we measure the numerical relationship between each prefix and its homographic pseudo-prefix in the language may be calculated either over word-types or word-tokens. In the first case, it is given by the ratio between the number of word-types (or lemmata) including a given prefix and the number of non-prefixed word-types with the same initial sequence in the language. In the second case, the ratio is between the cumulative frequency of occurrence of prefixed word-forms with a given prefix and the cumulative frequency of occurrence of non-prefixed word-forms with the same initial sequence. More or less marked discrepancies between the two measures may occur, and it is an empirical matter to decide which of the two, if either, better approximates dimensions of relevance for processing. Another measure of the orthographic ambiguity is given by the number (or the number of occurrences) of prefixed words over the total number (or the number of occurrences) of words with the same initial sequence. It goes without saying that, for both measures, less ambiguous prefixes will be those that will get higher values.

Preliminary counts on the whole set of orthographic sequences that correspond to two- and three-letter prefixes show that in Italian the overall number of prefixed words-types over the total number of word-types beginning with homographic sequences is 49%. The percentage falls to 33% when the number of words is weighted for token frequency: This follows from the fact that pseudo-prefixed words are widely represented in the high/medium bands of frequency. Note that these estimates are in some sense over-estimates because: i) we considered words formed by a prefix and a bound stem as prefixed (see Taft & Zhu, this volume), and ii) we excluded monographemic prefixes (e.g., *a-*, *s-*), where floor effects may be found (that is, percentages of prefixed word-types and word-forms tending to lower limits of the distribution); their inclusion would have a strong effect on the whole counts, since the number of words beginning with those monographemic segments is much higher than the number of words beginning with longer sequences (from two to six graphemes). On the contrary, while it is obviously true that, as prefixes become longer, the percentage of their pseudoprefixed counterparts tends to be smaller and smaller, there is an equally strong tendency for the absolute number of prefixed words in Italian to decrease as an inverse (probably logarithmic) function of the number of letters contained in the prefix. Hence, the high ratio of truly prefixed words in words containing longer prefixes affects the overall count far less than the low ratio in shorter words.

The data on orthographic confusability of Italian prefixes appear potentially relevant for processing and worthy of experimental investigation. They show, for instance, that a prefix-stripping procedure (such as the one proposed in Taft and Forster's model), when applied to Italian words, would very often encounter pseudo-prefixed words. Therefore, the result of stripping off an orthographic sequence which is homographic with a prefix is an orthographic sequence that does not correspond to a root morpheme. (On the basis of extensive lexical statistics, Schreuder & Baayen, 1994, show similar patterns for prefixes in Dutch and English.)

We emphasized that some importance should be attached not only to individual variables such as orthographic confusability but also to their interrelations with other variables related to the same population of affixes. In the case of orthographic confusability of Italian prefixes, we summarize very briefly its interrelation with two other variables that will be taken up again later in the chapter: prefix length and prefix frequency. The relationship between orthographic confusability and length has already been sketched: The probability that a given orthographic string homographic with a prefix occurs as the beginning of the word decreases as the prefix gets together. We find rather fixed correlational effects at the extremes of the length distribution, with monographemic prefixes tending to have the maximum confusability (percentage of truly prefixed word-types and truly prefixed word-tokens tending to have the lowest values of the distribution), and six-letter prefixes tending towards the minimum confusability (percentage of truly prefixed word-types and truly prefixed word-tokens near to 100%). The distributions of values for orthographic confusability in prefixes from two to five letters are partially overlapping, with percentages of truly prefixed words for longer prefixes progressively shifting toward higher means and more negatively skewed distributions (see Table 1). The shift is most dramatic between three and four letters. In summary, unambiguous prefixes tend to be longer, but the relationship between confusability and length is not fixed, if one eliminates the extremes of the distribution: the only prefixes that occur as prefixes 100% of the time are some of the longest ones; the only prefixes that occur as prefixes close to 0% of the time are some of the shortest ones.

The bidimensional space given by the intersection of the two described variables becomes more complex when frequency is added to the picture. Basically, frequency differently affects the two components of the conditioned, bidimensional distribution of prefix length by confusability. On the one side, length and frequency show a highly negative correlation, with shorter prefixes tending to be exponentially more frequent than longer prefixes:

TABLE 1. *Orthographic confusability for prefixes of different lengths in Italian.*

Length	Number of prefixes	Range of confusability	Median
2	15	4 - 81	43
3	18	12 - 79	35
4	19	25 - 98	71
5	22	36 - 100	84

Length: Prefix length in number of letters.

Number of prefixes: Number of prefixes for each class of length.

Range of confusability: Extreme values of confusability for each class of length. (For each prefix the value is based on the percentage of really prefixed word-types over the total number of word-types beginning with the same orthographic sequence.)

Median: Median value of confusability for prefixes in each class of length.

Frequency ordered by length displays a leptokurtic distribution, with two-letter prefixes at the mode. On the other side, less confusable prefixes (that is, prefixes occurring in higher percentages of truly prefixed words) tend to be more frequent. In this case, however, the relation is neither as strong as in the case of the two previously described simple correlations nor linear: It occurs for a number of reasons that we do not examine in detail here. We simply emphasize that the most important reason is that the interaction between confusability and frequency is constrained by a third-order interaction with length. Specifically, the correlation between percentage of prefixed words and frequency holds true only for two- and three-letter prefixes. This correlation disappears when longer prefixes that, on the contrary, are largely both infrequent and unambiguous, are considered. This higher order interaction exemplifies the point made earlier and that we will take up again later in the final section on methodology: The intercorrelations between the distributional variables of potential interest for processing of derivational affixes are sometimes so complex that it is very hard to answer questions on the functional role of one of them without considering the simultaneous effect of the others.

EXPERIMENTS ON DISTRIBUTIONAL VARIABLES OF AFFIXES IN ITALIAN

In this section we describe some recent experiments from our laboratory, which show the role of distributional parameters of derivational affixes in determining the content and the organization of the mental lexicon. The results mainly pertain to the role of prefixes, although some preliminary data on derivational suffixes are also described.

The specific aim of the experiments described below is to provide empirical content to the concept of *affix salience*, which is at the heart of the set of theoretical hypotheses developed in this chapter. By affix salience we mean the likelihood that a derivational affix will serve as a processing unit. This likelihood is based, in turn, on a conglomerate of inherent characteristics (e.g., affix length) as well as distributional parameters referring to both the occurrences within the language of the affix itself (e.g., affix frequency) and its co-occurrences with other relevant sub-lexical units (e.g., distributional configurations of the bases with which the affix can be combined). In the present experiments, we have begun uncovering some of the parameters which determine affix salience.

The first two experiments (Laudanna, Burani, & Cermele, in press) show an effect of orthographic ambiguity (or confusability) of a prefix, that is, the empirical relationship between prefixes and homographic pseudoprefixes. The third (Laudanna & Iacobini, in preparation) replicates the first result and reveals the dominant role of prefix length in lexical processing.

In recent research on prefix processing (Laudanna et al., in press), we evaluated the role of two quantitative features of Italian prefixes. As discussed previously, the two variables were the number of word-types in which a given prefix occurs and the ratio between prefixed and pseudo-prefixed word-types in which an orthographic sequence corresponding to a prefix appears.

At the basis of that research were three ideas:

1) Prefixed words dictate that they not be treated as a homogeneous class. Modeling of lexical organization for prefixed words should consider their diversity.

2) The distribution of derivational affixes (mainly prefixes) in Italian has been neglected by most researchers in the field. The potential importance of distributional factors is tied to increasing (or decreasing) the orthographic salience of some morphemic units over others; this, in turn, might enhance the likelihood of morphemes being represented as access units in the lexical access system.

3) In establishing a prefix as a potential unit for morphological processing and representation, the lexical processing system might follow some functional principles of processing by minimizing, for instance, the number of incorrect decompositions. These still largely unexplored principles may give rise to the

processing and representational differences among prefixes noted here. Finally, distributional characteristics may make units more or less plausible candidates for morphological decomposition.

Based on these premises, one can define a program of research to determine the type of experience necessary to establish an access unit for a given prefix in the lexical processing system. In planning the first experiment in Laudanna et al. (in press), we hypothesized that the likelihood of establishing an access unit for a given prefix might be a function of two empirical factors. Accordingly, their respective roles were evaluated.

First, we considered the number of word-types in the language that share a given prefix. This factor, which reflects subjects' experience with that prefix across different word contexts, might influence the likelihood that the orthographic pattern corresponding to that prefix is abstracted over time, so that it becomes a permanently stored access unit in the lexical processing system. It can be hypothesized that the number of word types in which a prefix occurs plays a role in storing and/or strengthening the activation level of the access representation for that prefix. The more words containing a given prefix, the higher the probability of establishing a processing unit which corresponds to that prefix.

Secondly, we know that the orthographic strings which in some words do correspond to prefixes, do not in other words: Decomposing the orthographic pattern corresponding to a non-prefix in a printed pseudo-prefixed word (e.g., the initial letters *re-* in English *religion,* are identical to the prefix *re-* in words like *reload*), would constitute a false alarm in the lexicon, because the letter string resulting from the pseudo-affix stripping (*-ligion*) does not correspond to a root-morpheme entry. We also know that the quantitative relationships between prefixed and pseudo-prefixed words vary to a large extent depending on the prefix considered and on other variables (for instance, length). The proportion of times that a full lexical representation is addressed following the correct decomposition of the prefixed word appeared to us potentially important for prefix processing: When the proportion (or the proportion of occurrences) of truly prefixed word-types (or word-tokens) beginning with a given prefix is large with respect to the total number (or the number of occurrences) of word-types (or word-tokens) in which the same initial orthographic sequence is present, the process of morphological decomposition would be more often successful. Thus, prefixes enhancing the success rate of the morphological parsing procedure (no matter how it is modeled) by virtue of this empirical proportion are, in principle, more likely to be represented in the lexical processing system.

The goal of the two experiments in Laudanna et al. (in press) was to determine to what extent the two variables (number of prefixed word-types, ratio between prefixed and pseudo-prefixed words) predicted the likelihood that a prefix is stored as an access unit in the visual lexical access system and is activated during word processing for addressing the orthographic lexicon.

We chose as the dependent variable in all experiments reaction time in a lexical decision task on printed stimuli; the first experiment was based on a multiple regression design in which the two independent variables served as predictors, and reaction times and errors constituted the criteria. The prefixes selected for investigation allowed the evaluation of single as well as combined effects of the predictors on subjects' performance, in that the prefixes which were compared had divergent values on one or both of the predictors.

Italian prefixes differ from each other greatly with respect to both parameters (i.e., number and percentage of truly prefixed words). The 24 two- and three-letter prefixes from which the experimental prefixes were sampled showed that the number of word-types sharing a given prefix varies from 20 to 2,281. The data base on which these counts are based is an Italian dictionary (Zingarelli, 1984) including 127,000 entries. The percentages of truly prefixed words relative to the total number of (prefixed and pseudoprefixed) words sharing the same initial orthographic sequence ranged from 4% to 81%.

Prefix Orthographic Ambiguity

We compared lexical decision times to non-words composed of a real prefix and a real word (e.g., *riviale,* formed by the combination of the prefix *ri-* with the noun *viale* ('avenue')) to non-words in which the same word was preceded by a non-morphemic sequence of the same length and the same bigram or trigram frequency (e.g., *paviale*). The reason for using non-words as experimental stimuli is the following: According to the AAM model (Caramazza et al., 1988), input letter strings activate—when available—both whole-word and morphemic access representations; furthermore, the activation of a whole word access representation is faster than the activation of the two or more access representations corresponding to the word's constituent morphemes. Consequently, for known words lexical representations (which in the model are assumed to be morphologically decomposed) are usually addressed through the activation of the whole-word address procedure. For words never encountered before and non-words whose morphemic components are known, access takes place through the morpheme address procedure. In summary, clearer effects of morphological structure are evident in non-words, although under some experimental conditions the effect of morphological structure on word processing may also be seen (Beauvillain & Segui, 1992; Burani & Caramazza, 1987; Feldman & Andjelković, 1992; Laudanna, Badecker, & Caramazza, 1989; 1992; Marslen-Wilson et al., 1994).

The results showed that reaction time differences between prefixed and control non-words were highly correlated with the ratio between prefixed and pseudo-prefixed words sharing the same initial orthographic sequences: The higher the proportion of truly prefixed words for a prefix, the slower the reaction times for non-words containing that prefix when compared with control non-words. For instance, non-words containing the prefix *ri-,* which has a high percentage of really prefixed word-types (81%), were 26 ms slower than their control non-words, while non-words containing the prefix *co-,* which has a low percentage of really prefixed word-types (18%), were 15 ms faster than their control non-words.

These results are consistent with a lexical access procedure in which morpheme access units are activated, thereby producing a processing difference between prefixed and non-prefixed non-words (e.g., *riviale* and *paviale,* respectively). The difference between the two is that the former, but not the latter, will activate the access unit for a prefix *(ri-)* and will allow for the exhaustive morphological parsing of the input letter string as well as for the subsequent access to the orthographic lexicon, where information about the legality of a combination is stored. This processing difference explains the slower reaction times for prefixed as opposed to non-prefixed non-words. The difference crucially depends on the likelihood that an access unit for the prefix is activated. It, in turn, is tied to the salience of the prefix itself. Salience is provisionally defined in terms of the values for one relevant independent variable, that is, the ratio between prefixed and pseudo-prefixed words in the language.

In the second experiment, the internal structure of both experimental and control stimuli was the same as in the first experiment, although the effect of the two independent variables was evaluated within a factorial design. Given that the distributions of values of the two variables tend to be correlated, the reason for changing the experimental design was to disentangle experimentally their respective impacts on prefix processing. The cost associated with the choice of factorial designs, at least for the population of affixes we are examining, is that such designs are possible only with a limited set of items. To give one example, the factorial design in the second experiment was possible by using only prefixes spelled with two or three letters, therefore the result is generalizable only to that subpopulation (actually, indeed, the correlation among the two variables investigated disappears when shorter or longer prefixes are considered; see Smith, 1988, and the final section of this chapter for a discussion of the limits of factorial designs in this domain).

Acknowledging the limits of our preliminary choice, in the second experiment we selected some extreme values in the distributions of the two independent variables and crossed them, selecting three experimental categories which significantly diverged from each other for the values of at least one of the independent variables. The three categories comprised: 1) prefixes which are included in a *low* number of prefixed word-types in the language and in a *low* proportion of truly prefixed words with respect to pseudo-prefixed words beginning with the same sequence (e.g., *sin-*), 2) prefixes which occur in at least a *low* number of prefixed word-types in the language but in a *high* proportion of truly prefixed word-types (e.g., *sub-*), and 3) prefixes which occur in a high number of prefixed word-types that also constitute a *high* proportion of word-types beginning with that orthographic sequence (e.g., *dis-*). The results of the second experiment confirmed the major role played by the ratio between prefixed and pseudoprefixed words: response latencies and percentage of errors were higher in the second and third categories, where non-words included an orthographic sequence corresponding to a prefix that occurs in a high proportion of truly prefixed words, regardless of the absolute number of word-types.

Prefix Length

Some of the considerations that inspired the two experiments previously described also motivated one further experiment (Laudanna & Iacobini, in preparation) in which a wider set of quantitative factors in Italian prefixes was investigated. We turn to a brief summary of this experiment, whose results confirm and extend those already reported. As we have stated, the set of prefixes is heterogeneous with respect to a number of distributional factors. Our working hypothesis is that some of those factors, subsumable under the construct of salience, are relevant in determining the representational status of prefixes. The results in Laudanna et al. (in press) shed light on one of those factors, namely the orthographic confusability, defined in quantitative terms, of prefixes with homographic, non-prefixal sequences in the language. In subsequent research (Laudanna & Iacobini, in preparation), the role of both the orthographic confusability of prefixes and the number of word-types was evaluated, but this time the range of variables under investigation was enlarged by including and manipulating experimentally three additional characteristics of prefixes: frequency, length in letters, and productivity.

By checking the distribution of Italian prefixes with regard to these variables, it is evident that their values are distributed over a numerically large range of data. By relying on a frequency count for Italian based on 1,500,000 occurrences mainly drawn from literary texts and newspaper articles (Istituto di Linguistica Computazionale del CNR, Pisa, 1988), we found that the cumulative frequency of the individual prefixes in Italian (that is, the summed frequencies of the words in which a given prefix is included) goes from 0 (no word forms represented in the frequency count and containing a given prefix) to about 15,000 occurrences. Length of prefixes ranges from 1 to 6 graphemes (and from 1 to 3 syllables). As to the productivity of prefixes, it is quite difficult to provide a quantitative estimate of this dimension which is, by definition, the *possibility* for language users to create countless new words with a given affix. We circumvented this difficulty by using as an estimate for the productivity of the various prefixes a measure of its empirical consequence, namely, the number of neologisms containing a given prefix that were created from 1963 to date and reported in one of four recent dictionaries of neologisms for Italian. In our view, this measure is not completely satisfactory, and it should not be understood as a parametric measure. Nevertheless, it provides a rough correlation with the productivity of prefixes as formulated in linguistic terms (see Schultink, 1961), and, at the very least, it permits a gross distinction between non-productive and very productive prefixes situated at the extremes of the distribution, whose values range from 0 to about 100 new word-types (for another measure of productivity suitable when statistical differences in productivity among affixes have to be assessed, see Baayen, 1991).

The main point is that the three additional parameters investigated in Laudanna and Iacobini (in preparation) are not only important per se but also in their interrelations, which allow us to test a wider set of hypotheses about prefix processing. While the two variables examined previously (Laudanna et al., in press) were positively although nonlinearly correlated, when frequency, length, and productivity are added, it becomes clear that prefixes stand in a multidimensional space, defined by multiple quantitative relationships of different forms and subsumed by different underlying functions. Given this complex picture, if the lexical processing system has to establish a consistent metric on the basis of (some of) those variables in order to treat prefixes properly during access, this means that it has to reach some "optimal" balancing of information from the different variables. For instance, the information provided by a given variable may be disregarded when it is already predictable from other variables, or, given two variables, x and y, the functional role of x for purposes of lexical access may be given more weight than y.

The experiment we conducted for assessing the respective roles of a wider cohort of variables on prefix recognition (Laudanna & Iacobini, in preparation) was based on a multiple regression design like Experiment 1 in Laudanna et al. (in press), and employed the same types of experimental stimuli (prefixed and non-prefixed non-words) and the same task (visual lexical decision). The five independent variables used as predictors were those described previously: prefixed/pseudo-prefixed word ratio (which ranged from 4% to 95% in the prefixes selected for the experiment), number of word-types including a given prefix (ranging from 5 to about 1,300), cumulative prefix frequency, ranging from 2 to about 13,000 over a frequency count of 1,500,000 occurrences), prefix length (ranging from 2 to 5 letters), prefix productivity (ranging from 0 to 103 neologisms). The numerical values of the 10 prefixes chosen to form the morphologically complex non-words were as independent as possible from one variable to another, in order to allow better detection of both single effects and potential complex interactions. Some of the discontinuities actually reflected inherent idiosyncratic relationships between two variables; some others were intentionally selected within otherwise orthogonal variables. The results for errors showed that the percentages of errors varied as a function of prefix length, with non-words including longer prefixes giving rise to more errors than nonwords including shorter prefixes when compared with their respective controls. The results for reaction times showed that lexical decision latencies varied as a function of both length and ratio between prefixed and pseudo-prefixed words in the language. Non-words containing longer and/or less orthographically confusable prefixes displayed longer latencies than other prefixed non-words. In summary, these results confirm the role of orthographic confusability of prefixes and show that prefix length also contributes to prefix salience, which, in turn, is a multidimensional factor enhancing the likelihood that affixes become represented as units for orthographic access. However, we still do not know enough about the details of the specific functional interactions between length and confusability, and this is promising ground for deeper investigations.

As to the length of prefixes, it is noteworthy that by varying the proportion of whole word length covered by prefix and base, respectively, we probably would obtain differential effects of prefix activation in the access mechanism. This hypothesis captures not only the role of prefixes per se but also the differential balance between prefix and base (or whole word) length. Additional reasons for investigating this issue further follow from the observation of different, although correlated, distributional phenomena. For instance, that longer words tend to be more often prefixed than short words, and tend to show lower proportions of pseudo-prefixed items.

The results we have described also seem noteworthy, because they do not show effects of either affix frequency or productivity. We have to be very cautious in the interpretation of such null results. After all, they might arise from experimental errors, or from insensitivity of the task employed or, finally, from the fact that the impact of these two variables is hard to detect, especially when a large portion of the experimental variance is accounted for by "heavier" factors such as length. However, some comments are possible:

1) The apparently counterintuitive absence of a frequency effect on prefixes, if replicable, would constitute evidence that the distributional characteristics of the orthographic contexts for prefixes are in some sense more crucial than their parameters of occurrence;

2) The difficulty in finding an effect of productivity may be because productivity exerts an influential role elsewhere than at access. For instance, it may affect the output component or the component in which morphosyntactic and/or semantic requirements for the combinability of derivational affixes with new bases are represented (see Feldman, 1991, and Stolz & Feldman, this volume, for a significant role played by affix productivity in segmenting an orthographic string);

3) The role of productivity may be different according to the type of derivational affix considered. In Italian, as well as in many other languages, while derivational prefixes do not change the grammatical category of the words to which they attach, derivational suffixes usually do. In a sense, derivational suffixes create new words differently from prefixes that simply add some

semantic features to their base words. Thus, we would expect a role of productivity, if any, mainly in the processing of suffixed derived words.

Affix Productivity

There is a more specific sense in which affix productivity, or its empirical consequence on the distribution of words within a language, may exert a role in lexical processing and be relevant for a model of lexical access. Following Baayen (see Baayen, 1991; Baayen & Lieber, 1991), we may consider the case of two derivational affixes which have the same (or analogous) cumulative frequency (i.e., which occur in the same number of word tokens), where one is still productive in the language, while the other is not. This may have the statistical implication that the productive affix occurs in the language in a greater number of word-types (or lemmas), which have a lower mean frequency. By contrast, the non-productive affix would tend to occur in fewer word-types which have a higher mean frequency (this is another way of stating the tendency for words with unproductive affixes to be more likely to be lexicalized as whole words, in comparison to words including a productive affix). Thus, one may make the hypothesis that, if the frequencies of both the whole-word and the morphemes constituting the word do contribute to addressing the lexicon, words with more productive affixes (and lower mean frequency as words) are better candidates to be accessed through the morphemic access procedure than words with less productive affixes (and higher mean frequency as words); for further considerations on this issue, see Burani (1993), Burani and Laudanna (1992), Frauenfelder and Schreuder (1991).

In a pilot study (Burani & Thornton, 1992), the factor of affix productivity was investigated with reference to Italian derivational suffixes. The same empirical measure of productivity described previously was used. The experimental logic was analogous to that adopted by Laudanna et al. (in press) and by Laudanna and Iacobini (in preparation). Suffixed and non-suffixed printed non-words were used in a lexical decision task. Suffixed non-words included suffixes which were either productive or non-productive. The few suffixes investigated, although having the same (high) frequency, were selected at the two extremes of productivity (e.g., both -ismo (English -ism, as in symbolism, racism) and -ezza (English -ness or -ity, as in tenderness, clarity) were included, with -ismo being extremely productive and -ezza not productive at all). The main difference from previous studies on prefixes was that nonsense orthographic sequences were combined with real suffixes (and with non-morphemic control sequences), in order to avoid semantic interpretation. Furthermore, affix productivity is probably larger for suffixes than for prefixes in the language: When calculated on the basis of the measure described above, suffix productivity ranges from 0 (no new formation in the last 30 years) to 417.

By the first measure, suffix productivity seems to contribute to make the suffix a better candidate for morphological parsing. However, and in support of the previous findings, a clear predictor of a suffix being accessed as a unit is its orthographic confusability with respect to pseudo-suffixed words. Less confusable (or more unambiguous) suffixes are more likely to function as access units. Orthographic confusability also plays a role for suffixes, even though they are homogeneous than prefixes in that they are usually less orthographically ambiguous because there are fewer pseudo-suffixed words (for another experimental approach to the issue of suffixation vs. pseudo-suffixation, see the *segment shifting* experiments described in Feldman, 1991, and in Stolz & Feldman, this volume).

Affix Salience

The main conclusion from the experiments we have reviewed is that affix salience plays a central role in accounts of morphological processing. This can be defined as the property of an affix to encode some relevant distributional characteristics (such as affix length and orthographic confusability) that allows to emerge from the orthographic noise as a unit of processing for lexical access. These characteristics may be understood as affecting the probability that an affix is activated within the orthographic strings in which it appears. To enhance this probability, the contribution of some quantitatively defined properties of occurrence (or co-occurrence) in a given language is perhaps necessary. These properties may pertain to both the distribution of individual affixes within a language and to the relations between an affix and the word contexts in which it occurs. Furthermore, what we have called orthographic confusability can be measured both on word-types (or lemmas) and word-tokens (or occurrences of word-types). All of these measures are potentially relevant for processing. What their specific role is, and which complex relationships holds among them, is a matter for further investigation.

SOME METHODOLOGICAL AND STATISTICAL CONSEQUENCES

In the final part of this chapter we would like to consider some methodological consequences deriving from the issues already discussed. They fall into two classes of problems: 1) the difficulty of submitting to an experimental test the role of a single variable without considering its implications for other variables, and 2) the need for multivariate experimental designs as opposed to factorial designs. This follows in some degree from problem 1), but also from two other factors: The underspecification of our models which do not allow strong experimental hypotheses and the failure to identify at this stage of research, the role played by other variables that should not be excluded a priori from investigation.

Smith (1988) has argued that the experimental designs and statistical analyses of many experiments involving morphologically complex words have been inadequate. We agree with the analysis provided by Smith, but we try to develop it further as it applies to derived words and derivational affixes. The methodological and statistical problems raised by Smith may be summarized as follows: Matched-pair designs are inefficient in several situations, and "standard analysis-of-variance procedures lack power in situations where performance on the stimuli may be influenced by many 'nuisance' variables" (Smith, 1988, p. 701); these experimental models do not use all the relevant information available.

In the cases we have reviewed, a further type of consideration must be added to the above statistical claims: Manipulations of the independent variables (the distributional properties of affixes) are not completely under the control of the experimenter or, more often, they cannot all be under control at the same time. In other terms, the different values of the independent variables reflect inherent properties of the affixes, arranged in non-linear distributions, which sometimes reflect largely overlapping, but sometimes mutually exclusive pieces of information.

Control of the independent variable occurs when the researcher varies the independent variable in a known and specified manner. In our case, he/she may just select the desired values of a variable from a number of values that already exist. When the values of the independent variable are selected, a constellation of values for other potentially relevant variables become specified. Some of the latter values may be randomly assigned to experimental groups, others do not.

Let us imagine planning an experiment on Italian prefixes, in which prefix length represents the independent variable. Three classes of prefixes are selected: prefixes of one or two letters, prefixes of three or four letters, and prefixes of five or six letters. Let us further imagine selecting three subgroups of prefixes which differ in length, and attempting to randomize across a number of extraneous variables over the subgroups. However, in doing so, we have also manipulated those variables systematically, in such a way that now the subgroups of prefixes differing in length also differ, say, in orthographic confusability and frequency (see the section on some quantitative data on prefixes for a description of the relationships among the three variables). The point is that, given the quantitative relationships among the three variables, prefixes chosen on the basis of their length cannot but differ in a biased manner along the other two dimensions: Longer prefixes will also be less confusable and less frequent. Given the confounded nature of both variable control and stimulus selection, we would not know which variable, or combination of variables, is responsible for possible differences in dependent variable scores (reaction times and/or errors). In synthesis, we can conclude that non-words containing long prefixes take longer to be rejected than non-words containing short prefixes, but we cannot conclude that prefix length alone is responsible for the effect.

If the previous considerations are correct, they are not without consequences for the inferential techniques employed in situations in which several variables act as possible predictors. If we seriously consider the complexity of the phenomena under consideration, we cannot continue to make use of either experimental designs and data analysis procedures which are too simplistic. They assume a normally distributed aggregate of variables, in which every variable is normally distributed with respect to the others, so that it is possible to select one of them for investigation while keeping the values of the others constant or randomized. We have argued, instead, that in some cases other possible sources of variance are not controlled and have been neglected (see also Smith, 1988, and his re-analysis of the results of some experiments carried out by Taft). It is for this reason that we propose to give preference to multivariate designs and procedures of analyses, that allow us to partial out the effect of confounding variables, which otherwise would be ignored.

ACKNOWLEDGMENT

The research reported here was supported by a grant (Progetto Bilaterale) from the Consiglio Nazionale delle Ricerche (C. N. R.) to the first author. We would like to thank Laurie B. Feldman, Claudio Iacobini, Robert Schreuder, and Anna M. Thornton for their helpful comments on a first version of this chapter.

REFERENCES

Baayen, H. (1991). Quantitative aspects of morphological productivity. In G. E. Booij & J. van Marle (Eds.), *Yearbook of morphology.* Dordrecht: Foris.

Baayen, H., & Lieber, R. (1991). Productivity and English derivation: A corpus-based study. *Linguistics, 29,* 801-843.

Beauvillain, C., & Segui, J. (1992). Representation and processing of morphological information. In R. Frost & L. Katz (Eds.), *Orthography, phonology, morphology, and meaning* (pp. 377-388). Amsterdam: Elsevier.

Burani, C. (1993). What determines morphological relatedness in the lexicon? In G. T. M. Altmann & R. C. Schillcock (Eds.), *Cognitive models of speech processing: The Sperlonga Meeting II.* Hillsdale, NJ: Lawrence Erlbaum Associates.

Burani, C., & Caramazza, A. (1987). Representation and processing of derived words. *Language and Cognitive Processes, 2,* 217-227.

Burani, C., & Laudanna, A. (1992). Units of representation of derived words in the lexicon. In R. Frost & L. Katz (Eds.), *Orthography, phonology, morphology, and meaning* (pp. 361-376). Amsterdam: Elsevier.

Burani, C., & Thornton, A. M. (1992, July). *Productivity of derivational affixes as a factor in the processing of derived words.* Paper presented at the Workshop on psycholinguistic approaches to the lexical representation of morphological structure. 5th International Morphology Meeting. Krems, Austria.

Caramazza, A., Laudanna, A., & Romani, C. (1988). Lexical access and inflectional morphology. *Cognition, 28*, 297-332.

Caramazza, A., Miceli, G., Silveri, M. C., & Laudanna, A. (1985). Reading mechanisms and the organization of the lexicon: Evidence from acquired dyslexia. *Cognitive Neuropsychology, 2*, 81-114.

Feldman, L. B. (1991). The contribution of morphology to word recognition. *Psychological Research, 53*, 33-41.

Feldman, L. B., & Andjelković, D. (1992). Morphological analysis in word recognition. In R. Frost & L. Katz (Eds.), *Orthography, phonology, morphology, and meaning* (pp. 343-360). Amsterdam: Elsevier.

Fowler, C. A., Napps, S. E., & Feldman, L. B. (1985). Relations among regular and irregular morphologically related words in the lexicon as revealed by repetition priming. *Memory & Cognition, 13*, 241-255.

Frauenfelder, U. H., & Schreuder, R. (1991). Constraining psycholinguistic models of morphological processing and representation: The role of productivity. In G. E. Booij & J. van Marle (Eds.), *Yearbook of morphology*. Dordrecht: Foris.

Istituto di Linguistica Computazionale del CNR di Pisa. (1988). *Corpus di Italiano contemporaneo*. Unpublished manuscript.

Laudanna, A., Badecker, W., & Caramazza, A. (1989). Priming homographic stems. *Journal of Memory and Language, 28*, 531-546.

Laudanna, A., Badecker, W., & Caramazza, A. (1992). Processing inflectional and derivational morphology. *Journal of Memory and Language, 31*, 333-348.

Laudanna, A. & Burani, C. (1985). Address mechanisms to decomposed lexical entries. *Linguistics, 23*, 775-792.

Laudanna, A., Burani, C., & Cermele, A. (in press). Prefixes as processing units. *Language and Cognitive Processes*.

Laudanna, A. & Iacobini, C. (in preparation). On some distributional properties of prefixes affecting processing of prefixed words.

Marslen-Wilson, W., Tyler, L. K., Waksler, R., & Older, L. (1994). Morphology and meaning in the English mental lexicon. *Psychological Review, 101*, 3-33.

Schreuder, R., & Baayen, H. (1994). Prefix stripping re-revisited. *Journal of Memory and Language, 33*, 357-375.

Schultink, H. (1961). Produktiviteit als morfologisch fenomenon. *Forum der Letteren, 2*, 110-125.

Smith, P. T. (1988). How to conduct experiments with morphologically complex words. *Linguistics, 26*, 699-714.

Stanners, R. F., Neiser, J. J., & Painton, S. (1979). Memory representation for prefixed words. *Journal of Verbal Learning and Verbal Behavior, 18*, 733-743.

Taft, M., & Forster, K. I. (1975). Lexical storage and retrieval of prefixed words. *Journal of Verbal Learning and Verbal Behavior, 14,* 638-647.

Zingarelli, N. (1984). *Vocabolario della lingua Italiana.* Bologna: Zanichelli.

16 Are Morphemes Really Necessary?

Philip T. Smith
Department of Psychology, University of Reading, England

From an anglocentric point of view, the functional value of a morphemic level of description distinct from a word level of description seems slight: Acquiring complex morphemic systems poses formidable problems for the learner, and, in the adult language user, a separate level of morphemic description seems just as likely to interfere with lexical access as to facilitate it. These prejudices have been examined with a simple connectionist model of language learning (using back-propagation). By systematically varying the degree of morphemic involvement in the models and the regularity of the morphemic processes, it is possible to assess the value of a morphemic level to an efficient running of the systems. While, in general, regular morphemic systems do appear to offer advantages to the language user, irregularities have a wide range of effects throughout the entire system and models of adult language use may need to take this more fully into account.

INTRODUCTION

"I would rather decline two drinks than decline one German adjective."
—attributed to Mark Twain

Why do languages have a morphemic level of description distinct from a word level of description? From a psychological perspective the advantages are not obvious. Some languages (e.g., Chinese) get on perfectly well without

365

inflections, the problems of learning as a first or second language a highly inflected system seem daunting, and it is not clear that significant savings, in time or storage space, are achieved by working with morphemes rather than with words. We spell out this point of view more carefully.

There can be only two reasons for favoring a linguistic device such as a distinct morphemic level of description: The device makes the learning of a language easier, and/or once the language has been learned, it makes language use more effective. On the learning side, I sometimes think, as I stand phrasebook in hand trying to hold a conversation in an unfamiliar language, that morphemic systems were designed by some malevolent genius deliberately to confuse people. In languages that have few bound morphemes, why are the same phonemic or written forms used for several quite different functions? Why does English -s signal the plural, the possessive, and the third person singular present; why does German use -en to indicate masculine singular for adjectives, dative plural for most nouns and adjectives, infinitive and first and third person plural present for many verbs? In languages where there are many bound morphemes, what is there to be gained from such profligacy? The hours of rote learning I put in as a schoolboy to master the dozens of forms of *amare* could have been better spent if the Romans had used one form of the verb *to love* together with a few helpful auxiliaries, like *is, was, have,* and *shall.*

When it comes to efficient use of the adult language, morphemes again come out poorly. The most effective argument against Taft's (1981) prefix stripping theory, it seems to me, is its lack of functional value. In English we need full lexical entries for words like *atheoretical, dissatisfied,* and *mistaken,* first because we need to know such forms are possible in English (and *distheoretical* and *asatisfied* are not) and we need to know what they mean (the meaning of *mistaken* is not readily predicted from the meanings of *mis-* and *taken*). Speeding access to such a lexicon is hardly likely to be assisted by an intermediate stage that splits a word into its constituent morphemes when, if the splitting is carried out on low-level phonemic or orthographic criteria, the result will often be an inappropriate non-morphemic structure (the so-called 'pseudo-prefixed' words, such a *pre-carious* and *re-gal*).

Note that arguments of this sort do not undermine the usefulness of words or phonemes or letters. A new item in one's vocabulary may render a cumbersome verbal description into a more succinct form that can be more easily manipulated in working memory (e.g., replacing *people who regularly travel substantial distances between their home and place of work* by *commuters*). And building thousands of words from a few dozen letters or phonemes greatly simplifies the encoding and decoding problems of language producers and perceivers.

The sentiments of the last three paragraphs may be off-the-cuff prejudices, but, I argue in this chapter, they should be taken seriously. Even from my anglocentric viewpoint, I do not really believe that highly inflected languages are unreasonably difficult to learn and inefficient to use, but the psychologist in me is still puzzled by their apparent useless complexity.

The advent of connectionist modeling has made examination of these problems more tractable. The flow-chart models that have dominated cognitive psychology since the seventies presented cognitive processes as a series of boxes linked by arrows. Such conceptualizations have provided many successes, not least in the study of brain-damaged subjects whose difficulties can often be economically understood in terms of the malfunctioning of box processors or the severing of links between boxes in the boxes-and-arrows flow-chart (e.g., Morton & Patterson, 1980). The drawbacks of these models include a bias towards conceptualizing cognitive processes as serial in nature (whereas the brain is surely a parallel processor) and these models' considerable reticence about the details of how processing is carried out within individual boxes. Connectionism, on the other hand, is committed to parallel processing and provides a general framework for modeling cognitive processes explicitly (recognition/production = activation of units; learning = changes of strengths of connections between units).

In the area of linguistic processing, connectionist investigations started with visual word recognition and extended to speech and the problems of learning to read aloud. There has been comparatively little interest in morphemic processing, the major exception being the extensive debate that has arisen from Rumelhart and McClelland's modeling of learning the past tense in English (Pinker & Prince, 1988; Plunkett & Sinha, 1992; Rumelhart & McClelland, 1986). MacWhinney and colleagues have also been active in modeling the acquisition of German morphology (e.g., MacWhinney, Leinbach, Taraban, & McDonald, 1989).

The consensus in current connectionist modeling is that large is beautiful: Attractive emergent properties of connectionist systems will become apparent only when their size matches the size of the problem as it is successfully tackled by a human. So connectionist models of word recognition will behave like their human counterparts only when they match humans on vocabulary size (several tens of thousands of words, not the few hundred that characterize most current models). The approach in this chapter is diametrically opposed to this consensus: I build very small networks which can cope with only a handful of items. While restrictions of time and computing resources have contributed to this decision, there are some definite advantages which I hope will become apparent in the course of the chapter. The first advantage is didactic: I want to show the reader the potential of connectionist systems for handling phenomena that are well known in the morphemic processing literature, and this can be demonstrated most clearly on a simple system. The second advantage is that I do not want to model the morphemic system of any particular human language; rather, I want to address the very general issues I raised at the beginning of the chapter. It turns out (I think) that most of these general issues can be examined in a miniature system, and because the system is so small it is easier to see how it works and why it exhibits the properties it does.

The general outline of my simulations is as follows: I specify a set of *words* composed of three vectors: a pre-root vector with *i* elements, a root vector with *j* elements, and a post-root vector with *k* elements. This representation is very abstract, but it might be helpful to think of each vector as representing a syllable. Vectors are composed of zeros and ones, so for example if $i = 3$, there would be several pre-root vectors, e.g., [1,0,0], [0,1,0], [0,0,1], representing the syllables *un-, per-, vo-* (say); a vector containing all zeros (in this case, [0,0,0]) means no syllable is present. These words are each paired with a linguistic output vector with *l* elements. Again, this vector is very abstract, but it might be helpful to consider the vector representing a range of phonological, syntactic, and semantic features: For $i = 3$ one element of the vector might represent stress, one element represent part of speech, and one element represent whether the word is positive or negative. Thus, in English the word *unhappiness* might be split into three vectors representing *un-, happy,* and *-ness,* and map onto an output vector indicating it has stress on the second syllable, is a noun, and is negative.

A connectionist system can be trained to learn the pairings between word inputs and linguistic outputs as follows. The word input vectors directly excite a set of *input units,* with each element in the vectors determining the excitation of a single input unit. Via a series of weighted connections, this input leads to an output from a group of *output units,* the excitation of each output unit corresponding to a single element of the output vector. The output vector obtained in this way is compared with a *target* vector, which is the output that this particular input should have produced, had the system been perfectly trained. In general, there is a mismatch between the (obtained) output vector and the (desired) target vector, and so the weights of the connections in the system are adjusted until the mismatch between output and target is trivially small. This process is called *supervised learning.*

In this conceptualization, learning is a process of moving in an n-dimensional space described by the weights of the connections, searching for a region where the mismatch between output and target is acceptably small. (To visualize this, consider a surface, like the surface of the earth. Suppose there are just two weights: Changing one weight moves us horizontally in a north-south direction, changing the other weight moves us horizontally in an east-west direction; the height that the surface is above sea level represents the output-target mismatch; moving on this surface trying to get as near as possible to sea level represents the process of learning.) This conceptualization recasts some of the traditional issues of linguistics, such as learnability and universality: For a language to be learnable, the appropriate weight combinations must be accessible in weight space, and, for example, if the requisite combination of weights is represented by a deep valley in the output-target mismatch surface, surrounded by high mountains, such a language might not be learnable. Similarly, linguistic universals may be those features common to learnable languages. In other words, learnability and universality are emergent properties of weight space.

Weight space is determined jointly by the problem (the language as presented to the system) and the architecture of the system (what units there are in the system and how they are interconnected). Prominent in current connectionist architectures are *hidden units,* so-called because they neither receive input directly from the environment (like input units) nor send output directly to the environment (like output units). Hidden units increase the power of connectionist systems to learn complex patterns, and observation of the behavior of hidden units gives us some insight into what generalizations the system is making about the input patterns (see, e.g., McClelland & Rumelhart, 1986).

Searching weight space for satisfactory output-target mismatch minima requires an algorithm. In general there are many satisfactory minima, and different algorithms may be differentially biased to find some minima rather than others. The algorithm used in this paper is the back-propagation algorithm, which is widely used in connectionist modeling. We concede, however, that we do not fully understand what biases it shows in searching weight space (a language that was not learnable with the back-propagation algorithm might be learnable with a different algorithm). However, since one message of this chapter is that individual speakers of a particular language probably do not internalize their morphemic knowledge in the same way, and since we shall be able to show that the back-propagation algorithm also provides different solutions, it is not a serious concern that there may be other solutions we have missed which other algorithms might find.

Table 1 shows the 27-word vocabulary, its morphemic structure, and other linguistic features used in our first simulations. With regard to morphemic structure, the idea was that there should be three roots, R1, R2, R3, which could stand alone or combine with one of two prefixes, P1, P2, and/or one of two suffixes, S1, S2. We assume that distributional criteria, such as non-overlapping sets of phonemes being used to construct the prefixes, the roots, and the suffixes, would enable prefixes, roots, and suffixes to be identified as such without error. The other linguistic features are phonological (stress pattern), syntactic (noun vs. verb) and semantic (positive vs. negative). On the phonological level, it is assumed that the presence of a prefix changes the stress pattern (as it sometimes does in English, cf. the verbs *édit* and *permít*). On the syntactic level, it is assumed that by themselves R1 and R2 are nouns and R3 is a verb, but in combination with one of the suffixes (S2) they all become verbs (so S2 operates a little like English *-ify* or *-ize*). Finally, on the semantic level, the prefix P1 renders the word negative (like English *un-* or *dis-*), and all the other words are positive.

No claim is made that these structures simulate English (the examples are included simply to show this is not an implausible set of structures). The implementation is very abstract; in particular, there is no order information in the system, so the affixes could be realized as any combination of prefixes, infixes, and suffixes: It is merely expository convenience to refer to one set as prefixes and the other set as suffixes. And while it is useful to consider that linguistic features might be implicated at the phonological, syntactic, and semantic levels, the particular labels we have chosen are arbitrary.

Note that the system is entirely regular (we examine aspects of irregularity later in the chapter) but has the functional load of individual morphemes unevenly distributed. For example, while both P1 and P2 have a phonological function (altering stress) only P1 has a semantic function (changing positive to negative). This unevenness of functional load is, we assert, characteristic of natural language systems, and we investigate its effects later in the chapter.

TABLE 1. *Linguistic description of words used in the simulations.*

Word	Morphemic Structure	Linguistic Features		
w1	R1	Stress1	Noun	Positive
w2	R2	Stress1	Noun	Positive
w3	R3	Stress1	Verb	Positive
w4	P1 + R1	Stress2	Noun	Negative
w5	P1 + R2	Stress2	Noun	Negative
w6	P1 + R3	Stress2	Verb	Negative
w7	P2 + R1	Stress2	Noun	Positive
w8	P2 + R2	Stress2	Noun	Positive
w9	P2 + R3	Stress2	Verb	Positive
w10	R1 + S1	Stress1	Noun	Positive
w11	R1 + S2	Stress1	Verb	Positive
w12	R2 + S1	Stress1	Noun	Positive
w13	R2 + S2	Stress1	Verb	Positive
w14	R3 + S1	Stress1	Verb	Positive
w15	R3 + S2	Stress1	Verb	Positive
w16	P1 + R1 + S1	Stress2	Noun	Negative
w17	P1 + R1 + S2	Stress2	Verb	Negative
w18	P1 + R2 + S1	Stress2	Noun	Negative
w19	P1 + R2 + S2	Stress2	Verb	Negative
w20	P1 + R3 + S1	Stress2	Verb	Negative
w21	P1 + R3 + S2	Stress2	Verb	Negative
w22	P2 + R1 + S1	Stress2	Noun	Positive
w23	P2 + R1 + S2	Stress2	Verb	Positive
w24	P2 + R2 + S1	Stress2	Noun	Positive
w25	P2 + R2 + S2	Stress2	Verb	Positive
w26	P2 + R3 + S1	Stress2	Verb	Positive
w27	P2 + R3 + S2	Stress2	Verb	Positive

MORPHOLOGICAL SYSTEM

Learning a Totally Regular System

We wish to examine how the material in Table 1 might be learned. Specifically, we suppose that the analysis labeled "Morphemic Structure" in Table 1 is given via (say) distributional criteria, and the analysis labeled "Linguistic Features" is given by context: The machine's sole problem is to learn the pairings between the two analyses. To do this, we recode Table 1 into Table 2, which is in a form suitable for application of the back-propagation algorithm. In Table 2 a seven-feature input is mapped onto a three-feature target. The first two features of the input constitute the pre-root vector and indicate the prefixes (10 = P1, 01 = P2, and 00 = no prefix), the next three features constitute the root vector and indicate the roots (100 = R1, 010 = R2, and 001 = R3), and the last two features constitute the post-root vector and indicate the suffixes (10 = S1, 01 = S2, and 00 = no suffix). In the target vector, the first feature indicates stress (1 = Stress1 and 0 = Stress2), the second feature indicates syntactic class (1 = Noun and 0 = Verb), and the third feature indicates semantics (1 = positive and 0 = negative). 0s and 1s are used because this is the most common way of representing binary features when using the back-propagation algorithm, though there are some asymmetries introduced by using this notation (see Bankart, Smith, Bishop, & Minchinton, 1994).

All the simulations we report are carried out with the McClelland and Rumelhart (1988) package, using the default values for all the parameters that are provided in that package. As Table 2 shows, seven units are used to encode the input and three units to encode the output. The first set of simulations uses two hidden units. This was the minimum number of hidden units that permitted the system to learn successfully. Using the back-propagation algorithm, the training continues until the total sum of squares (a measure of disparity between output and target) becomes less than or equal to 0.04. At such a level there is an excellent match between output activation and target. Even at these levels, however, not all patterns are learned equally well, and this we investigate using the pattern sum of squares (pss), which equals, for a given input pattern, the squared disparities between output and target for each output unit, summed over all output units.

In our first group of simulations, we wished to find out whether some patterns were learned more readily than others. The program starts with the weights set to small values chosen at random, and different simulations rarely converge to identical solutions. Accordingly, a second aim of this group of simulations was to find out how much variation, from simulation to simulation, occurs in the solutions that are found. Finally, we wished to see how this variation is influenced by inequalities in the frequency of occurrence of the individual patterns.

TABLE 2. *Pattern file used in the back-propagation network.*

	Input	Target
w1	0 0 1 0 0 0 0	1 1 1
w2	0 0 0 1 0 0 0	1 1 1
w3	0 0 0 0 1 0 0	1 0 1
w4	1 0 1 0 0 0 0	0 1 0
w5	1 0 0 1 0 0 0	0 1 0
w6	1 0 0 0 1 0 0	0 0 0
w7	0 1 1 0 0 0 0	0 1 1
w8	0 1 0 1 0 0 0	0 1 1
w9	0 1 0 0 1 0 0	0 0 1
w10	0 0 1 0 0 1 0	1 1 1
w11	0 0 1 0 0 0 1	1 0 1
w12	0 0 0 1 0 1 0	1 1 1
w13	0 0 0 1 0 0 1	1 0 1
w14	0 0 0 0 1 1 0	1 0 1
w15	0 0 0 0 1 0 1	1 0 1
w16	1 0 1 0 0 1 0	0 1 0
w17	1 0 1 0 0 0 1	0 0 0
w18	1 0 0 1 0 1 0	0 1 0
w19	1 0 0 1 0 0 1	0 0 0
w20	1 0 0 0 1 1 0	0 0 0
w21	1 0 0 0 1 0 1	0 0 0
w22	0 1 1 0 0 1 0	0 1 1
w23	0 1 1 0 0 0 1	0 0 1
w24	0 1 0 1 0 1 0	0 1 1
w25	0 1 0 1 0 0 1	0 0 1
w26	0 1 0 0 1 1 0	0 0 1
w27	0 1 0 0 1 0 1	0 0 1

To this end we constructed 3 sets of training patterns: Set 1 consisted of the 27 patterns of Table 2 each appearing once and only once; in Set 2 the morphemically simplest words (w1, w2, w3) each occurred four times, while the other words each occurred once, and in Set 3 three other words selected at random (w6, w13, w20) each occurred four times, while the other words each occurred once. Table 3 shows the pss for a typical simulation (we specify what we mean by 'typical' later). There are only six output patterns, and for a given output pattern the pss observed for all of the inputs associated with this output are usually very similar, so in Table 3 we have averaged across the pss derived for each input.

TABLE 3. *Typical performance of the back-propagation algorithm on the patterns shown in Table 2.*

Output	Number of inputs associated with output	Pss, averaged over inputs
Stress1-Noun-Positive	4	0.0008
Stress2-Verb-Negative	5	0.0011
Stress1-Verb-Positive	5	0.0012
Stress2-Noun-Negative	4	0.0014
Stress2-Verb-Positive	5	0.0019
Stress2-Noun-Positive	4	0.0025

First note that different patterns are not all learned equally well, and in particular the Stress1-Noun-Positive pattern is learned best (a small pss means the system is less likely to produce an erroneous response for this pattern and more likely to produce a quick correct response). The Stress1-Noun-Positive pattern is not the most frequent pattern, nor are all its individual feature values the most frequent values (Stress2 occurs more frequently than Stress1). It does, however, make sense to describe Stress1-Noun-Positive as the basic *unmarked* form (it contains no affixes and Noun is the most frequent root). Markedness, introduced into linguistics by the Prague school (e.g., Trubetzkoy, 1939), and prominent in the work of Jakobson (1940) and Chomsky and Halle (1968), among many others, is a linguistic device intended to give a principled account of why some forms are easier to learn than others: When a learner evaluates the complexity of a grammar, unmarked forms are considered the least complex and will be preferred by the learner unless there is positive evidence to the contrary. So what our learning algorithm has done is to induce a structure which bears similarities to structures derived from linguistic theory; moreover, such structure is not a direct function of superficial information, such as relative frequency. The parallel with Jakobson's (1940) work goes further than this: Jakobson suggested a sequence for the emergence of phonemes, whereby the maximal oppositions occur first. (The reason, according to Jakobson, why *papa, baba,* and *mama* so frequently appear early in language development is that [a] is the archetypal back vowel, whereas [p], [b], and [m] are the maximally contrasted front consonants.) In our present simulation, note that Stress2-Verb-Negative, which contrasts maximally with Stress1-Noun-Positive is learned almost as well.

While the previous observations support the idea that traditional linguistic characteristics might appear as 'emergent properties' of our network, the considerable variation in learning solutions we have obtained is at odds with a traditional linguistic view: The linguist refers to *the* grammar of a language and does not suppose such a grammar varies significantly between individuals in a homogeneous linguistic community. To examine the variability in our data, that is, to see how the patterns of pss varied from simulation to simulation, we performed a principal components analysis with log(pss) as the dependent variable (logarithms were used to correct for skewness). The first two factors of this analysis (which account for 76% of the variance) are shown in Figure 1.

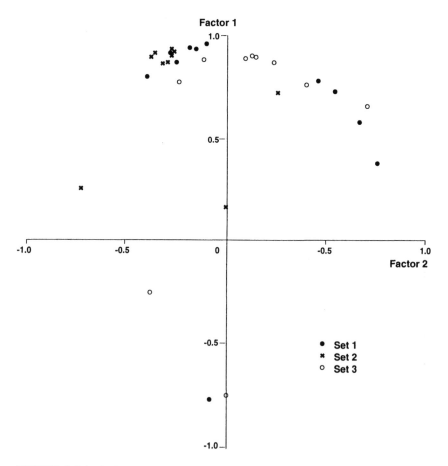

FIGURE 1. Principal components analysis of patterns pss derived from 30 simulations. Each point refers to the pattern of log(pss) derived from a single simulation.

Each point in this figure refers to a pattern of pss, derived from a single simulation, such as the pattern shown in Table 3. The first observation to make is that most of the points are clustered together and load highly on Factor 1 (we chose as the 'typical' pattern to analyze in Table 3 the pattern loading highest on Factor 1). For 50% of the simulations Stress1-Noun-Positive is learned best, and for 30% of the simulations Stress2-Verb-Negative is learned best, all corresponding to points near the top of Figure 1. This indicates there is some consistency in the simulations and it makes sense to talk of a 'typical' simulation. The second observation to make is that variations in token frequency have noticeable but relatively minor effects on the pattern of pss (Set 2, where the three simple root forms have enhanced frequency, cluster somewhat to the left of Figure 1; Set 3, where three more complex forms have enhanced frequency, cluster somewhat to the right, but the separation is not sharp). This shows that, within the range of frequency variation we have examined, changes in the frequency of individual items in the training set have only modest effects on the learning achieved. This again accords with linguistic orthodoxy, which claims that linguistic complexity, not frequency, is the principal determinant of ease of learning.

What does conflict with linguistic orthodoxy is the presence of points well separated from the main cluster which represent quite different patterns of learning. For example, in Figure 1 the point from Set 1 which loads very negatively on Factor 1 corresponds to a pattern of learning where Stress2-Noun-Positive and Stress2-Verb-Positive are learned best and the putative unmarked form Stress1-Noun-Positive is learned worst. Perhaps the best way to understand this example is to notice that all the best-learned forms involve the prefix P2, and the system is behaving as if P2+R1, P2+R2, and P2+R3 are the roots, from which all other forms, including R1, R2, and R3, are derived.

This example illustrates that the same morphological system can be learned in different ways, so different learners may differ in what they regard as easy or complex. The tendency for a few simulations to result in P2 not being treated as a prefix is in line with the low functional load associated with this prefix: Whereas P1 affects semantics and stress, P2 affects only stress. Another way to examine differences between prefixes with differing functional loads is to see how hidden units respond to them: In many of our simulations one of the hidden units seems to serve as a 'P1 detector,' responding differentially to the presence and absence of P1, but in few simulations were there clear-cut examples of hidden units differentially sensitive to P2. Incidentally, it might be useful to consider hidden units to be the repository of linguistics intuitions in the system: The system has no explicit linguistic knowledge but could make prefixedness judgments by observing how its hidden units responded to various input patterns. In such circumstances, like human subjects, the system is more likely to classify P1 as a prefix than P2.

One remark about our methodology needs to be made. All the pss in Table 3 and in the simulations represented in Figure 1 are very small, so all the patterns are learned well, and the skeptical reader might consider we are overinterpreting the small differences between patterns with different pss. Our reply to this is that these differences are present throughout most of the learning sequence, and, had we chosen to sample the system at a stage where learning was less near completion, we would have found patterns with unacceptably high pss (i.e., not learned) and these would usually be the patterns with the higher pss in Table 3, while at the same time there would be patterns with acceptably low pss (i.e., learned) and these would usually be the patterns with lower pss in Table 3. So statistics like those provided in Table 3 do provide a useful guide to the relative ease of learning of different patterns.

Learning a System with Some Irregularities

We have investigated how irregularity affects the learning of a system by randomly changing some of the features in Table 1. It turns out that even small changes have quite dramatic effects on the system. Of the seven changes of a single feature in the output that we have examined, three resulted in the system being unable to learn the patterns. We illustrate the results of changes for one of the cases where learning was possible. Table 4 illustrates the case where w8, previously coded as Stress2-Noun-Positive, is recoded as Stress2-Verb-Positive, all other words receiving the same coding as they received in Table 1. We ran 10 successful simulations, and because there was considerable variation in the solutions obtained, we then carried out a principal components analysis on log(pss), extracting three factors. Table 4 presents the highest loading simulation on each of the factors we have obtained after varimax rotation.

The main point to draw from Table 4 is that the presence of an irregularity leads to a re-alignment of the difficulties of individual patterns for the entire system: It is not just the irregular output itself, or even outputs similar to the irregular one, that have their pss changed. The most common pattern of pss obtained in the regular case (Table 3) appears with reduced frequency in Table 4 (Simulation 2) and a quite different ordering of ease of learning now predominates (Simulation 1).

The other effect of irregularity is to increase the time to learn the patterns correctly and to increase the variability of this time. For the simulations with the totally regular patterns, mean number of training epochs to reach criterion was 116, with a range of 76 to 143. For the irregular patterns, the mean was 170, and the range was 112 to 447. The difference between the means was not quite significant, but the variance of the number of epochs for the irregular set was highly significantly different from the variance for the regular set. In other words, irregularity slows the learning process down (a little) and leads to greater individual differences in learning speed (substantially).

TABLE 4. *Performance of the back-propagation algorithm on the patterns shown in Table 2, with w8 irregularly coded as a Verb. pss, averaged over all patterns with the same output, is shown. For each simulation, the frequency of occurrence of similar simulations is shown in brackets.*

Output	Number of outputs	Simulation 1 (50%)	Simulation 2 (30%)	Simulation 3 (10%)
Stress1-Noun-Positive	4	0.0012	0.0006	0.0008
Stress2-Verb-Negative	5	0.0013	0.0011	0.0022
Stress1-Verb-Positive	5	0.0010	0.0013	0.0006
Stress2-Noun-Negative	4	0.0006	0.0013	0.0012
Stress2-Verb-Positive	5	0.0016	0.0017	0.0004
Stress2-Noun-Positive	4	0.0031	0.0029	0.0018

Pseudoprefixes

In Taft's prefix-stripping model, pseudoprefixes cause particular problems. (Pseudoprefixes are words that look as though they are prefixed but are not, such as *un-der.*) Taft's prefix-stripping mechanism might strip the *un-* off *under,* and waste time searching for the non-existent root *-der* before re-processing *under* as a monomorphemic word. Taft presents evidence that pseudoprefixed words are processed more slowly than prefixed words, in line with the predictions of his prefix-stripping model.

We can examine pseudoprefixes in our micro-language in the following way. Consider the word w7, whose input structure is P2 + R1 and whose output is Stress2-Noun-Positive. If we change the output to Stress1-Noun-Positive, P2 becomes a pseudoprefix for this word because it exerts no linguistic effects, such as modifying the stress or the semantics. We may or may not wish to modify w22 and w23 in a similar way (these words also contain P2 + R1 in their inputs).

It turns out it is crucial how many words have pseudoprefixes. If we recode w7 as a pseudoprefixed word, the learning problem become quite severe (an average of 518 epochs are needed to reach criterion). On 70% of occasions w7 has a higher pss than its obvious control, w8. If we recode both w7 and w22 as pseudoprefixed, the problem still is difficult (an average of 514 epochs to criterion). On 90% of occasions w7 has a higher pss than its control, w8, and on 70% of occasions w22 has a higher pss than its control, w24. Finally, if we recode w7, w22, and w23 as pseudoprefixed, the problem becomes easier than the original totally regular patterns (an average of 102 epochs to criterion). In 97% of cases the pss for the pseudoprefixed words is *lower* than controls.

The interpretation of these results is straightforward. As long as pseudo-prefixed forms are in a minority (in comparison with the corresponding prefixed forms), they are more difficult to learn and slower to access than prefixed forms, though this effect does not appear on all simulations. However, once the number of pseudoprefixed forms becomes substantial, the system reinterprets the pseudoprefixed form as the standard form, and the prefixed forms now become more difficult. Note in this account that there is no need to appeal to a prefix-stripping mechanism.

Learning a Totally Irregular Set of Patterns

We have run simulations with the same inputs and outputs as shown in Table 2 but where the outputs were randomly permuted, so that the link between input and output was arbitrary. In this case the 'morphemic structure' has no linguistic function, and the 'morphemes' are equivalent to syllables or other groupings of phonemes within a word that have no meaning or function. Our system proved incapable of learning these pairings and never even came close to criterion on any simulation.

LEARNING TO GENERALIZE

Of all the oversimplifications present in the material learned in the previous section, the least satisfactory is that the material is self-contained and complete: There are no missing items and it is not possible to add new items to the system. A crucial characteristic of human learners is that they are able to generalize their learning to new instances: Having observed that the past tense of most of the verbs in their vocabulary is formed by adding -ed, the English speaker will expect the past tense of a new verb they encounter also to be formed by adding -ed.

To examine this phenomenon, we have extended our system as follows: The pre-root vector is extended to three elements, the root vector is extended to six elements and the post-root vector, and the output vector are left unchanged. The 27 patterns of Table 2 are retained with appropriate modification (e.g., w1, whose input vector was previously [0,0]+[1,0,0]+[0,0] becomes [0,0,**0**]+[1,0,0,**0,0,0**]+[0,0], the new features being marked in bold. This enables us to extend to nine the number of base forms (morphologically simple forms). These forms are shown in Table 5.

The investigation proceeds as follows. We train the system on all the base forms (w1-w3, w28-w33) and all the forms morphologically related to w1-w3 (w4-w27), plus *some* (possibly none) of the forms morphologically related to w28-w33. When learning has been achieved, we test how well learning generalizes to the forms morphologically related to w28-w33 which were *not* presented during training. The minimum number of hidden units needed to achieve reliable learning in these circumstances was three, and this was adopted for all our simulations.

Table 6 shows the results of this investigation. We concentrated on two of the new base forms (w28 and w31) and presented with each of them during training zero, two, or four of their related forms, chosen at random from the eight related forms associated with each of them). To obtain percent correct for forms that were not trained, we tested each output, rounding each unit's output up to one if the output was .51 or larger, and rounding down to zero if the output was .49 or less. If after rounding the output matched the target, we called this a success. Results are averaged across 10 simulations for each condition. Two aspects of Table 6 are worth comment. First, compared to chance (success rate estimated before training commenced), some generalization is achieved even if no related forms are presented with the base forms we were concerned with. Second, such generalization is very patchy (on some individual simulations performance was worse than chance) and acceptable performance is achieved only when four related forms are trained. In its limited way, this result supports other authors in this volume who claim that restricting the context in which a morpheme appears restricts its generalizability to new cases.

TABLE 5. *Base forms used in the second set of simulations. New features added to the patterns shown in Table 2 are shown in bold.*

	Input	Target
w1	0 0 **0** 1 0 0 0 **0** 0 0 0	1 1 1
w2	0 0 **0** 0 1 0 0 **0** 0 0 0	1 1 1
w3	0 0 **0** 0 0 1 0 **0** 0 0 0	1 0 1
w28	0 0 **0** 0 0 0 1 **0** 0 0 0	1 1 1
w29	0 0 **0** 0 0 0 0 **1** 0 0 0	1 1 1
w30	0 0 **0** 0 0 0 0 **0** 1 0 0	1 0 1
w31	0 0 **1** 0 0 0 1 **0** 0 0 0	1 0 1
w32	0 0 **1** 0 0 0 0 **1** 0 0 0	1 1 1
w33	0 0 **1** 0 0 0 0 **0** 1 0 0	1 1 1

TABLE 6. *Generalization performance when network trained on three base forms and all their related forms, together with six other base forms. For two of these latter base forms, zero, two, or four of their related forms are also presented at training. The table shows percent success on non-presented forms after training.*

		Number of related forms trained		
	Chance	0	2	4
Success rate	21%	63%	78%	95%

DISCUSSION

The simulations we have presented provide the following answers to the general questions we raised at the beginning of the paper:

1. *In what ways do morphemes help the learner?* A set of morphemic structures which project in a systematic way onto other linguistic features helps the learner. We have shown that, in circumstances where a totally regular pattern is learned moderately quickly, a pattern with some irregularities is learned slightly more slowly and a set of patterns without morphemic structure could not be learned. This is not to say that a set of patterns without morphemic structure cannot be learned in any circumstances: In the present case a non-morphemic structure could be learned if we gave the network more resources, in the shape of extra hidden units. What we have illustrated, however, is that for a fixed set of resources, morphemically regular systems are easier to learn. The relation between ease of learning and regularity may not be an entirely straightforward one, however: Note that in our simulations a set of patterns with several 'pseudoprefixed' words was actually learned faster than the totally regular set.

2. *Some of the evidence for prefix-stripping can be equally well handled by a network which has no prefix-stripping mechanism.* The pseudoprefix effect appears, in our work, as a direct consequence of irregularities being in general learned and processed more slowly. The simulations suggested it might be a rather fragile effect, not present on every simulation, and critically dependent on the type frequency of the pseudoprefixed forms.

3. *Morphemic processing may be an area where individual differences are substantial.* All our simulations showed major differences in the ease with which individual patterns were learned on different runs of the same program on the same set of patterns. Smith (1988) found large individual differences between subjects on a task where subjects rated English words (e.g., *unhappy, under*) for degree of prefixation. The differences related to which linguistic variables subjects took into account in their ratings: Though all subjects appeared to be using a 'semantic transparency' criterion, they differed on the extent to which they used other criteria (other forms of linguistic transparency, word length, word frequency). At the time I thought these differences might derive mainly from linguistic experience and education: You do not have to know that *breakfast* can be analyzed as *break + fast* in order to use it effectively, so some subjects may have coded it as monomorphemic and others as bimorphemic. The current simulations show, however, that even with very similar training, different 'individuals' (different runs of the same program) may show radically different structures relating morphemic patterns to other linguistic knowledge).

4. *Generalization to new instances is patchy, unless sufficient examples are given of the productivity of a given morpheme.* Informally, what our results suggested is that, given a new verb (e.g., *wug*) inflected forms such as *wugs*, *wugged*, and *wugging* may be slow to appear unless some instances of some

inflected forms are also presented (e.g., the presence of *wugs* as well as *wug* may facilitate the acquisition of *wugged* and *wugging*).

5. *When there is irregularity in a set of patterns, this affects the way the entire set of patterns is represented and processed.* This point has been accepted in the child language acquisition literature, where quite detailed simulations of past tense learning have taken into account the type and token frequencies of various irregular forms. This point does not appear to have been taken on board in the adult language processing literature, where a tripartite classification of monomorphemic, polymorphemic, and pseudopolymorphemic characterizes most studies. There is an urgent need to attempt large-scale simulations of prefixation and other morphological processes in English along the lines of the work carried out on the past tense.

REFERENCES

Bankart, J., Smith, P. T., Bishop, M., & Minchinton, P. (1994). Feature representations in connectionist systems. In G. H. Fischer & D. Laming (Eds.), *Contributions to mathematical psychology, psychometrics and methodology* (pp. 67-74). New York: Springer-Verlag.

Chomsky, N., & Halle, M. (1968). *The sound pattern of English.* New York: Harper & Row.

Jakobson, R. (1940/1968). *Kindersprache, aphasie und allgemeine lautgesetze [Child language, aphasia and phonological universals].* The Hague: Mouton.

MacWhinney, B., Leinbach, J., Taraban, R., & McDonald, J. (1989). Language learning: Cues or rules? *Journal of Memory and Language, 28,* 255-277.

McClelland, J. L., & Rumelhart, D. E. (1986). A distributed model of human learning and memory. In J. L. McClelland & D. E. Rumelhart (Eds.), *Parallel distributed processing, Volume 2.* Cambridge, MA: MIT Press.

McClelland, J. L., & Rumelhart, D. E. (1988). *Explorations in parallel distributed processing.* Cambridge, MA: MIT Press.

Morton, J., & Patterson, K. (1980). A new attempt at an interpretation, or, an attempt at a new interpretation. In M. Coltheart, K. Patterson, & J. C. Marshall (Eds.), *Deep dyslexia.* London: Routledge & Kegan Paul.

Pinker, S., & Prince, A. (1988). On language and connectionism: Analysis of a parallel distributed model of language acquisition. *Cognition, 28,* 73-193.

Plunkett, K., & Sinha, C. (1992). Connectionism and developmental theory. *British Journal of Developmental Psychology, 10,* 209-254.

Rumelhart, D. E., & McClelland, J. L. (1986). On learning the past tense of English verbs. In J. L. McClelland, D. E. Rumelhart, & PDP Research Group (Eds.), *Parallel distributed processing: Explorations in the microstructure of cognition, Vol. 2* (pp. 216-271). Cambridge MA: MIT Press.

Smith, P. T. (1988). How to conduct experiments with morphologically complex words. *Linguistics, 26,* 699-714.

Taft, M. (1981). Prefix stripping revisited. *Journal of Verbal Learning and Verbal Behavior, 20,* 281-297.

Trubetzkoy, N. S. (1939/1969). *Grundzüge der phonologie* [*Principles of phonology*]. Los Angeles, CA: University of California Press.

17   Left-to-Right Processing of Derivational Morphology

Patrick T. W. Hudson and Diana Buijs
Department of Experimental and Theoretical Psychology
Leiden University

Support for the Left-to-Right word parsing model of visual word processing is obtained in three types of experimental tasks. The first set of experiments confirmed the prediction that morphologically complex words would be recognized faster, rather than slower, than morphologically simple words using both the naming and lexical decision tasks. The second set showed that, in a syntactic category monitoring task, the category of word-internal suffixes that were inconsistent with the category of the final suffix delayed reaction times. The third set of experiments showed that in a lexical decision task the location of the illegality, manipulated by using legal stems and suffixes in illegal combinations, was significant, such that earlier illegal transitions resulted in faster response times. The Left-to-Right model is compared with connectionist models of word processing, which represent constituent order with difficulty, and with Marslen-Wilson, Tyler, Waksler, and Older (1994) model for auditory processing of morphologically complex words.

INTRODUCTION

Models for the processing of morphologically complex words range from those in which no word-internal structure is represented (Butterworth, 1986) to those which strip all words to their basic, morphological atoms in a mandatory stage prior to lexical access (Bergman, 1990; Taft, 1985). Among the analytic models, there is sufficient evidence for processing of morphological stems based on stem frequency effects (Taft, 1979; Taft & Forster, 1975) and patterns of facilitation when stems are repeated (Stolz & Feldman, this volume). Experimental evidence for processing of affixes, however, is less compelling. Moreover, the effects of prefixed and suffixed affixes are not always comparable.

Several studies have shown that pseudo-prefixed words are recognized more slowly in lexical decision than either truly prefixed or control words (e.g., Bergman, Hudson & Eling, 1988; Taft, 1981; Taft, & Forster, 1975). Rubin, Becker, and Freeman (1986) suggested that when pseudo-prefixing effects do arise they could be artifactual, due in part to subjects' strategies. Bergman et al. (1988), however, showed that there was no difference in the size of the pseudo-prefixing effect in lexical decision when either 100% or only 25% of the stimulus words were decomposable. An explanation based on strategies would predict at least some attenuation of the pseudo-prefixing effect when the proportion of decomposable items decreases by a factor of 4. This finding suggests that the analysis of prefixes is not under the control of the subject.

The results with suffixes are equivocal, however. Bergman et al. (1988) found that, in Dutch, there were no differences (551 ms and 551 ms) between agentives (e.g., *bakker,* 'baker') pseudo-agentive nouns (e.g., *poeder,* 'powder') and control nouns. Similarly, in a double lexical decision task in English (Manelis & Tharp, 1977), pairs of suffixed words (e.g., *working - helping)* were no slower than pairs of pseudo-suffixed words *(pudding - ceiling).* Failure to find an effect with pseudo-suffixes could be interpreted as evidence against affix stripping and, therefore, against the representation of morphology. However, mixed pairs consisting of one suffixed and one pseudo-suffixed form were generally slower than truly suffixed or pseudo-suffixed pairs. This finding suggests that morphological structure is relevant. Differences between prefixed and suffixed words and their pseudo-affixed controls may reflect characteristics of the processing mechanism for morphology.

Prefixes and suffixes differ along linguistic dimensions as well. Prefixes, which are always derivational, may have some effect on the meaning of words and are occasionally restricted to certain syntactic categories (e.g., *un-* only precedes adjectives and verbs). Suffixes, on the other hand, which may be either derivational or inflectional, are intimately bound with syntactic structures. Inflections are restricted to the same category and allow agreement with the immediate grammatical context, while derivational suffixes allow words to be made to fit the overall syntactic structure. In languages with derivational morphology, language users can choose between altering sentence structure to fit the syntactic characteristics of words or altering the derivational structure (and syntactic requirements) of words to fit the sentence structure. The balance between morphological and syntactic processing varies across different languages. Some languages use little morphology and rely more on word order. Other languages, such as Turkish, place more emphasis on morphology and rely less on word order. The relationship with both the syntactic and the lexical levels is what makes the study of suffixes more interesting than that of prefixes (Matthews, 1974).

When experimental work has examined suffixes, it has tended to concentrate upon inflections (e.g., Caramazza, Laudanna, & Romani, 1988; Schreuder, Grendel, Poulisse, Roelofs, & van de Voort, 1990). Because inflectional suffixes reflect syntactic processing, whereas derivational suffixes reflect both lexical choices and syntactic processing, it is surprising from a linguistic standpoint that so much of the experimental literature on visual processing of morphologically complex stimuli has concentrated upon prefixes and, apart from the present volume, has tended to neglect suffixes.

It has been suggested that the absence of a pseudo-suffix effect and the presence of a pseudo-prefix effect in visual word recognition can be explained by reference to a left-to-right parsing process and that such a model is optimal for discovering the morphological structure of a word (Bergman, 1990). In the case of potential prefixes, which come early in the word, confusion can arise when the word turns out not to be prefixed. Pseudo-suffixes, in contrast, would never produce confusion because the ambiguous letters (e.g., *ing*) would be processed as a continuation of the stem (e.g., *ceiling*). In order for a pseudo-suffix effect to arise, a right-to-left or context-free letter-parallel process would have to operate so that the pseudo-suffix would be processed without reference to the stem. In effect, pseudo-suffixed letter strings at the end of a word may look salient, but this does not necessarily imply that they are processed as independent units. In summary, differences between prefixed and suffixed words and their pseudo-affixed controls may reflect characteristics of the processing mechanism, in particular that it analyzes the letter sequence from left to right.

Experiments that reveal sequential effects in the processing of derivational morphology are the focus of the present chapter as such results are consistent with a Left-to-Right decomposition model (Hudson, 1990). This model (Hudson et al., 1984; Hudson & Bergman, 1984; Koskenniemi, 1983) can be contrasted with parallel processing models of word constituents. Here, visual word recognition, like sentence processing, is assumed to entail parsing similar to that which occurs in a recursive transition network (see Figure 1). Words are, in general, represented as strings of letter constituents at one level of representation and as morpheme constituents at another level. Stated generally, we propose that the underlying mechanisms for syntactic and lexical processing are similar, in that they are constrained by constituent order and capture commonalities between superficially separated constituents.

The Left-to-Right Processing Model

In our model, the speed of processing a single complex constituent (e.g., morpheme) is determined by the discriminability at that point. This is represented as the branching factor whose value, the number of branches, is determined by the number of alternative transitions which can follow from that point.

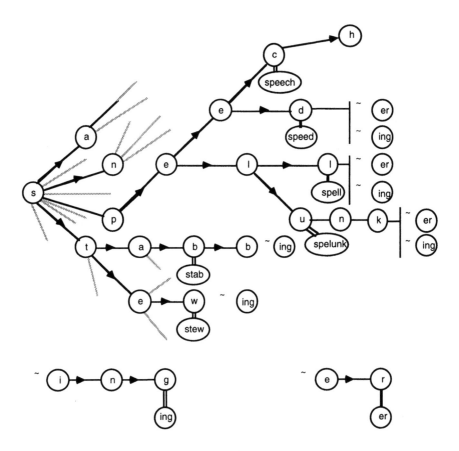

FIGURE 1. The Left-to-Right transition network model for word representation (from Hudson, 1990). The elements at lower levels are configured to determine elements at the next level (e.g., words at the phrase level, phrases at the sentence level, morphemes at the word level, and letters at the morpheme level). Morphemes are the targets for recognition.

The value will tend to be less for affixes and may even result in easier discrimination of stems because, as a result of branching, analyzing words into recognizable chunks will be beneficial relative to treating them as unanalyzed units. Consequently, morphologically complex words will be processed more rapidly than simple words of the same length. Moreover, in this model, pseudo-prefixed words will be slowed relative to simple words for two reasons: (1) At least two parses must be attempted, one treating the unit as prefix and a second treating it as part of the stem, and (2) Post-access processes that check on the legality or meaningfulness of decomposed constituents will be vulnerable to incorrect input from possible stem candidates. Finally, pseudo-suffixes, in contrast to pseudo-prefixes, will not be treated as units because they form part of the stem. Genuine suffixes are treated more rapidly that pseudo-suffixes because they require simpler discriminations. Once the stem has been recognized, the only distinctions to be made are between suffixes. Koskenniemi's (1983) concept of Continuation Classes suggests that the restrictions on possible continuing suffixes may be represented explicitly at such points.

In summary, in addition to accounting for differential processing of prefixes and suffixes, the Left-to-Right hypothesis makes an unexpected prediction. Morphologically complex words will be processed more rapidly than simple words of the same length. Intuitively, the counter hypothesis, that complex words will take longer than simple ones, is more plausible because complex words tend to be longer and lower in frequency. In the first series of experiments, simple and complex words were compared. In the latter series the sequential aspect of word-internal structure is examined.

EXPERIMENTS

Experiments Comparing Simple and Complex Words

In Experiment 1 we asked whether complex words are processed faster (or slower) than matched controls. Lexical decision and pronunciation tasks were compared in order to distinguish task-specific effects from effects that reflect lexical processing (Balota & Chumbley, 1985; Hudson & Bergman, 1985). Stimuli were presented on a PC in a semi-random order, and response times and errors were recorded. Subjects were students at Leiden University and were paid for their participation. The stimuli were Dutch words selected from the CELEX database (Burnage, 1990).

The same stimuli were used in the lexical decision and naming tasks, and different subjects (24 ss and 12 ss, respectively) took part in each task. In contrast to Bergman (1990), and consistent with Manelis and Tharp (1977), the category of the suffix was systematically varied, using both agentives and non-agentives. Simple and complex words were matched on number of letters and number of syllables, and mean word frequency was controlled by using the CELEX counts. Four groups of words defined by morphological complexity (simple/complex) and agency (agentive/nonagentive) were formed. Morphologically complex nonwords in the lexical decision condition were constructed by altering a letter in the stem of one of the suffixed words, leaving the suffix intact. Morphologically simple nonwords were constructed by changing a letter in the first syllable of the morphologically simple words. The implication of constructing materials in this way is that all the nonword decisions could be made by attending to the stem.

The results for Experiment 1 are depicted in Figure 2. In both lexical decision and naming, analyses indicated that the morphologically complex words are responded to faster than the simple words (Lexical decision $F_1(1,23) = 7.43$, $p < .05$; $F_2(1,80) = 2.87$, $p = 0.09$; Naming $F_1(1,11) = 12.5$, $p <. 01$; $F_2(1,76) = 2.59$, $p = 0.11$). For lexical decision the effect of agency was also significant although there was no interaction between agency and morphological complexity. There was no effect of agency in naming, suggesting that the agency effect may well be a post-access in nature (Balota & Chumbley, 1985). The presence of additive effects, together with the consistency of the complexity effect over tasks, suggests that the morphological complexity effects are not strategic[1] but reflect the access process itself.

In Experiments 2 and 3 we replicated the previous result with a new set of 24 morphologically complex and 24 simple words. Materials were selected from the same CELEX database, avoiding borrowed words and words with unusual spellings that may have introduced noise in Experiment 1. The stimuli in the simple and complex conditions were matched for frequency and word length in letters and syllables. In Experiment 2 the nonwords were constructed with real suffixes and alterations to the 'stems,' and lexical decisions to complex words were reliably faster than to simple words ($F_1(1,11) = 6.44$, $p < .05$; $F_2(1,46) = 4.68$, $p < .05$). In Experiment 3 the nonwords had real stems and alterations to the 'suffixes,' so as to direct attention away from the stems in the nonwords. The effect of complexity was again significant ($F_1(1,11) = 53.8$, $p < .001$; $F_2(1,46) = 7.80$, $p < .01$). The results of Experiments 1, 2, and 3 are summarized in Figure 3.

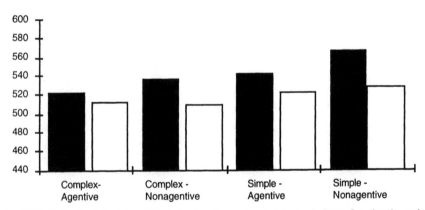

FIGURE 2. Lexical decision (black bar) and naming (white bar) times for simple and complex words, comparing agentives and non-agentives with associated controls in Experiment 1.

---

[1]It is, of course, possible that there are other strategic factors, but this is a dangerous argument to pursue as almost anything can be reduced to strategically defined post-access processing.

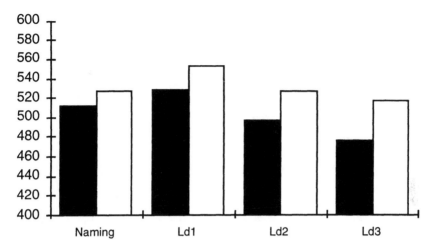

FIGURE 3. Results for Naming and Lexical decision (Ld) and experiments contrasting morphologically complex (black bars) and matched simple words (white bars).

In conclusion, it has been demonstrated in a series of three experiments that lexical decision (and naming) latencies for complex words with suffixes are faster than for simple words. This finding is consistent with a left-to-right model of processing and is not easily handled by models that treat all units in parallel. In the next series of experiments we asked whether the sequencing of morphemes can have effects on word processing.

Experiments Examining Word-Internal Structure

Syntactic Class Monitoring with Nonwords

Bergman (1990) carried out two types of experiments with Dutch materials to test the left-to-right hypothesis. In one, subjects performed a Noun-Adjective discrimination task (called Syntactic Class Monitoring; see also Monsell, 1985). The stimuli of interest were doubly suffixed words whose final and penultimate suffixes were either consistent (nominal-nominal (NN) e.g., *leiderschap;* 'motorist') or inconsistent (adjectival-nominal (AN) e.g., *waakzaamheid,* 'consistency'). In all of the words, the syntactic category is determined solely by the category of the final suffix. Inconsistency between category of suffixes could only be expected to slow down category assignment if the category of the penultimate suffix was accessed at some point during recognition. Results indicated that base morphemes with suffixes which had syntactic classes contradictory with the final and determining suffix were slowed (AN 708 ms) relative to base morphemes with consistent suffixes (NN 641 ms).

Syntactic Class Monitoring with Words

In a second syntactic class monitoring experiment, subjects were asked to decide as rapidly as possible whether a particular item was a noun or not. All stimuli were real Dutch nouns or adjectives and consisted of either morphologically simple words (A or N, e.g., *green* or *bread)* or words with one or two suffixes which determined syntactic category.

The critical comparison was between doubly suffixed nouns whose affixes were either consistent (NN e.g., *absenteeism)* or inconsistent (AN e.g., *sensibility)*. Materials consisted of 18 nouns, matched for length and word frequency, in each of the consistent and inconsistent conditions. There were also simple nouns (18) and nouns and adjectives (18 of each) with one suffix. A replication of Bergman (1990) produced significant differences between conditions $(F_1(3,33) = 12.4, p < .001; F_2(3,68) = 6.2, p < .001)$.

The experiment was also replicated with a new set of material consisting of 15 words per group (the number of usable words available in the language becomes a major constraint upon stimulus selection for replication at such a point) and 12 ss. Results indicated a significant difference between consistent and inconsistent suffixes $(F_1(3,33) = 14.50, p < .001; F_2(3,68) = 6.52, p < .001)$ such that words with AN structure were slower than words with NN structure. The results of all three experiments are shown in Figure 4. The effects in the category monitoring are important because they demonstrate morphological processing with word materials and without a lexical decision task.

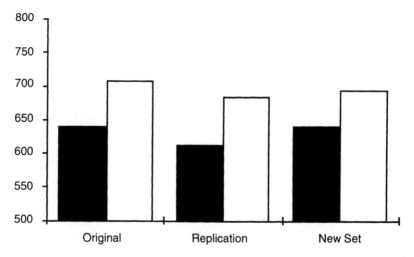

FIGURE 4. The effect of internal structure in three Syntactic Class Monitoring experiments, Bergman's original experiment and replications with the same and with new stimuli. The black bars are the stimuli with consistent suffixes (NN). The white bars are the stimuli with inconsistent suffixes (AN).

The outcome of the syntactic monitoring experiments suggests that the internal structure of stimuli composed of real morphological constituents has significant effects on processing and, moreover, that the sequencing of morphemes is important. The results place considerable constraints upon models of both morphological processing and, by extension, word processing in general. Because they were obtained in the visual domain, the results suggest that the left-to-right processing inherent in auditory processing is respected at a level of representation that is common to the two modalities (cf., Bradley & Forster, 1985). The constraint imposed by the sequencing of constituents holds even though a visual presentation preserved the entire stimulus intact.

Transition Illegality Experiments

Letter strings that are not words can be differentiated into (1) pseudowords that are very word-like (e.g., *vohicle*), (2) pseudowords that are pronounceable but not word-like (e.g., *plibikalt*), or (3) nonwords that are unpronounceable. Hudson and Bergman (1985) proposed that nonwords are rejected in lexical decision tasks by a left-to-right post-access scan of the stimulus which halts when a clear decision to accept or reject can be made. The evidence is based on the differential correlations between response times, word length (in letters and syllables), and word frequency for words presented in different nonword contexts. The assumption is that post-access strategies can be induced by the structure of the nonwords presented to subjects. Morphological transitions between stem and suffixes can be manipulated so that every morpheme is, in itself, legal but the specific combination makes a clear nonword.

In another lexical decision experiment, Bergman (1990) presented nonwords in which the illegality could be traced to a morpheme transition. Morphological constraints can produce nonwords by either a) altering one or more letters in the stem, leaving affixes unaltered, b) altering letters in the affixes, leaving the stem intact, or c) combining legal stems and affixes in an illegal combination. The present experiment used nonwords constructed from a stem and two suffixes in illegal combinations and manipulated the location of the illegality. The illegal transition was either between the stem and the first suffix (leaving the two suffixes as a legal combination -+, e.g., *workishness*), between the first and the second suffix (with the stem - first suffix transition legal +-, e.g., *greenishhood*) or between both stem-suffix and suffix-suffix transitions illegal (--, *e.g., painishness*). Results indicated that illegal transitions at the first suffix produced faster rejection times (730 ms) than illegal transitions between suffixes (779 ms). Bergman's (1990) original experiment was replicated, first with the original stimuli, albeit with a different presentation system and new subjects, and then with new materials to eliminate doubts about the generalizability.

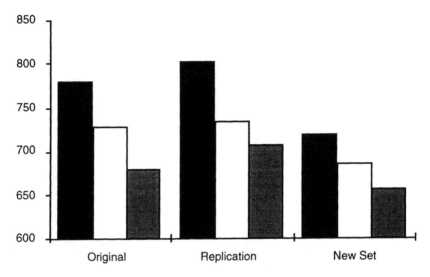

FIGURE 5. Lexical decision latencies for three types of suffix transitions. The legal-illegal transition (+-) are shown as black bars, the illegal-legal(-+) as white bars, and the illegal-illegal (--) as grey bars.

Position of the illegal transition was significant ($F_1(2,22) = 37.01$, $p < .001$; $F_2(2,87) = 12.08$, $p < .001$) as was the effect of the number of illegalities (*MinF'* $(2,71) = 16.19$, $p < .01$). The result was repeated with 20 new nonwords per condition ($F_1(2,22) = 6.02$, $p < .01$; $F_2(2,87) = 3.91$, $p < .05$).

The location of the illegality of the suffix transition was significant in three experiments. Moreover, there was an effect of the number of illegalities. This outcome may reflect an exhaustive serial search together with the possibility that the number of negative transitions biased the probability of a negative response (Bergman, 1990). Alternatively, finding a legal transition between the last and penultimate suffixes may have slowed up the rejection process. Regardless of the interpretation, what is critical here is the finding that the status of the transitions within the stimulus nonword, determined solely by the morphological rules, is reliably effective in determining response times.

SUMMARY

For many languages, the functions of suffixes are more important than prefixes because they convey syntactic class and inflectional information. Derivational suffixation allows the sentence processing mechanism to use a particular word at a particular point in a sentence without violating the syntactic constraints of the sentence. Inflectional suffixes must agree with the syntactic class which the derivational suffixes define. Prefixes have a more static role and tend to be treated as a fixed part of the word, with a semantic rather than a syntactic role (Schreuder et al., 1990). Logically it might be more appropriate to strip suffixes and leave prefixes unanalyzed (Cutler, Hawkins, & Gilligan, 1985). Our experiments originated with the paradox that while there was ample evidence for prefix stripping based on effects with pseudo-prefixes, the absence of comparable effects with pseudo-suffixes suggested that suffixes were not stripped from stems.

An interesting prediction of the left-to-right word-parsing model is that morphologically complex words should be recognized faster than matched simple words. Faster recognition of complex as compared with simple words was replicated with different stimulus sets using both the lexical decision and naming tasks. The task-independence of this 'inverse' complexity effect implied that it is not purely strategy dependent but that it arose as a result of the nature of lexical representations and the processes which operate upon them. The left-to-right model was further supported by the effects of word-internal structure in two new tasks. Syntactic class monitoring showed that the syntactic category of non-final suffixes affected judgments which could, in principle, be made solely by examining the last suffix. In a lexical decision task, the position of the illegal transition between suffixes also suggested a sensitivity to sequential aspects of morphological structure.

The effects described in this chapter have been interpreted in terms of lexical representations of morphology rather than post-access or other strategic factors. Several arguments support this account. First, there was no effect of varying the proportion of morphologically complex items (Bergman et al., 1988). Second, when simple and complex materials were contrasted, there was no effect of nonword foil structure. Third, similar patterns were found for word naming and lexical decision. Finally, the results from the Category Monitoring tasks are difficult to reconcile with a post-access account. If words are processed and accessed as wholes to start with, then the necessary information in suffixed words is directly accessible at the end of the word.

It was suggested that the lack of a suffix-stripping effect is consistent with the operation of a natural stripping process, called *word-parsing*. The term *word-parsing* was chosen to stress possible commonalties between lexical and syntactic processing. The stripping process links lexical and syntactic processing, providing syntactic information to the syntactic component (Buijs, in preparation). By analyzing representations in a left-to-right manner, word-parsing automatically avoids interference from pseudo-suffixes. In essence, they are not interpreted as potential suffixes at all.

Current connectionist models of word processing, in contrast to serial models, tend to predict either no difference between morphologically complex and simple words or slower recognition of complex words. The interactive-activation and distributed connectionist models predict that for morphologically complex words, both the affixes and the stem will become activated, generating a significant period during which the resulting competing activations have to be resolved (Phaf, v. d. Heijden, & Hudson, 1990). In the case of interactive-activation models, the resolution of competition involves a winner-takes-all inhibitory output layer. (This may also be necessary in distributed models.) The resolution of mutual inhibition is time consuming and has been be related to increased reaction times in visual attention tasks (Phaf et al., 1990).

The results of the syntactic class monitoring and transition-illegality experiments require that a connectionist account must represent morphemes explicitly, making access to syntactic information possible, and also represent the order and transition of these constituents. Both of these requirements are not found in any existing model. The problem for interactive-activation models is that they do not specify order of inputs. In speech there is a natural order defined across the time at which constituents arrive; connectionist models for speech can have order imposed upon them from outside rather than having an internal architecture which respects the order of constituents. In visual presentation this constraint does not naturally occur.

The left-to-right processing account of visually presented constituents is consistent with the account of auditorily presented materials, although there is no logical reason why visual word recognition should closely parallel auditory processing (Bradley & Forster, 1985). If visual input representations and auditory input representations are separate but share a common central lexicon (Forster, 1976; Morton, 1969), then it is reasonable to assume that the general architecture of representations in the access system could still be broadly similar for the two modalities. The Left-to-Right model of word representation (Hudson, 1990) posits that there are a number of formally similar levels of word representation, above and below the morphological level, and draws parallels between visual and auditory word recognition separate from the link between vision and audition at the superficial level of grapheme-phoneme coding.

The Left-to-Right word parsing model assumes parallels between sentence syntactic processing and morphological processing at the lexical level (Hudson, 1990). Many visual word recognition studies can be criticized either because they have conflated a number of different levels of linguistic representation onto the single word level or because, wishing to avoid these problems, they have controlled so much that linguistic effects are no longer evident. In the Left-to-Right model the prominence of word or sentence initial information and the sequential nature of analytic processing (parsing) are made explicit. Drawing parallels between the morphological and syntactic levels allows a much richer picture to emerge about how words are processed.

The data presented here are consistent with suffixing effects in the auditory processing of English words reported by Marslen-Wilson and his colleagues (Marslen-Wilson, Tyler, Waksler, & Older, 1994). Their model also exploits the ordering of constituents to explain the finding that in a cross-modal priming paradigm suffixes inhibit each other while words formed from the same base morpheme with different derivational prefixes do not. They stated that a problem for parser-type models is that for "the morphological parser to perform morphophonological inference...it will not only need to have to have access to rules of phonological alternation but also to information about the syntactic as well as phonological properties of morphemes" (p. 29). The syntactic category monitoring experiments in Dutch reported above make similar demands on the parser.

The exact nature of morphological-lexical representations and the mechanisms which process them are still unclear. We provide evidence in Dutch for a left-to-right processing constraint and suggest that this process has consequences for the nature of the representation of words as a whole. To be complete, interactive activation and distributed connectionist models must be able to represent order information.

REFERENCES

Balota, D. A., & Chumbley, J. I. (1985). The locus of word frequency effects in the pronunciation task. *Journal of Memory and Language, 24,* 89-106.

Bergman, M. W. (1990). *The visual recognition of word structure: Left-to-right processing of derivational morphology.* Unpublished doctoral dissertation, K. U. Nijmegen.

Bergman, M., Hudson, P. T. W., & Eling, P. E. (1988). How simple complex words can be. *Quarterly Journal of Experimental Psychology, 40,* 41-72.

Bradley, D. C., & Forster, K. I. (1985). A reader's view of listening. *Cognition, 25,* 103-134.

Burnage, G. (1990). *CELEX: A guide for users.* Nijmegen: CELEX.

Butterworth, B. (1983). Lexical representation. In B. Butterworth (Ed.), *Language production, Vol. II.* London: Academic Press.

Caramazza, A., Laudanna, A., & Romani, C. (1988). Lexical access and morphology. *Cognition, 28,* 297-332.

Cutler, A., Hawkins, J. A., & Gilligan, G. (1985). The suffixing preference: A processing explanation. *Linguistics, 23,* 723-758.

Forster, K. I. (1976). Accessing the mental lexicon. In E. C. T. Walker & R. Wales (Eds.), *New approaches to language mechanisms.* Amsterdam: North Holland.

Hudson, P. T. W. (1990). What's in a word? Levels of representation and word recognition. In D. A. Balota, G. B. Flores d'Arcais, & K. Rayner (Eds.), *Comprehension processes in reading.* Hillsdale, NJ: Lawrence Erlbaum Associates.

Hudson, P. T. W., & Bergman, M. W. (1984). Van spelling naar klank: Modellen voor het hardop lezen van woorden [From spelling to sound: Models for word pronunciation]. In A. J. W. M. Thomassen, L. G. M. Noordman, & P. A. T. M. Eling (Eds.), *Het leesproces.* Lisse: Swets & Zeitlinger.

Hudson, P. T. W., Bergman, M. W., Houtmans, M. J. M., & Nas, G. L. (1984). De Bestudering van Woordherkenning als basis voor het Lezen [Studying word recognition as a basis for reading]. In A. J. W. M. Thomassen, L. G. M. Noordman, & P. A. T. M. Eling (Eds.), *Het leesproces*. Lisse: Swets & Zeitlinger.

Hudson, P. T. W., & Bergman, M. W. (1985). Lexical knowledge in word recognition: Word length and word frequency in naming and lexical decision tasks. *Journal of Memory and Language, 24*, 46-58.

Koskenniemi, K. (1983). *Two-level morphology: A general computational model for word-form recognition and production*. Unpublished doctoral dissertation, University of Helsinki.

Manelis, L., & Tharp, D. A. (1977). The processing of affixed words. *Memory & Cognition, 5*, 690-695.

Marslen-Wilson, W., Tyler, L. K., Waksler, R., & Older, L. (1994). Morphology and meaning in the English mental lexicon. *Psychological Review, 101*, 3-33.

Matthews, P. H. (1974). *Morphology: An introduction to the theory of word-structure*. Cambridge: Cambridge University Press.

Monsell, S. (1985). Repetition and the lexicon. In A. W. Ellis (Ed.), *Progress in the psychology of language, Vol. II*. Hillsdale, NJ: Lawrence Erlbaum Associates.

Morton, J. (1969). Interaction of information in word recognition. *Psychological Review, 76*, 165-178.

Phaf, R. H., v. d., Heijden, A. H. C., & Hudson, P. T. W. (1990). SLAM: A connectionist model for attention in visual selection tasks. *Cognitive Psychology, 22*, 273-341.

Rubin, G. S., Becker, C. A., & Freeman, R. H. (1979). Morphological structure and its effect on visual word recognition. *Journal of Verbal Learning and Verbal Behavior, 18*, 757-767.

Schreuder, R., Grendel, M., Poulisse, N., Roelofs, A., & van de Voort, M. (1990). Lexical processing, morphological complexity and reading. In D. A. Balota, G. B. Flores d'Arcais, & K. Rayner (Eds.), *Comprehension processes in reading*. Hillsdale, NJ: Lawrence Erlbaum Associates.

Taft, M. (1979). Recognition of affixed words and the word frequency effect. *Memory & Cognition, 7*, 263-272.

Taft, M. (1981). Prefix stripping revisited. *Journal of Verbal Learning and Verbal Behavior, 20*, 289-297.

Taft, M. (1985). The decoding of words in lexical access: A review of the morphographic approach. In D. Besner, T. G. Waller, & G. E. McKinnon (Eds.), *Reading research: Advances in theory and practice. Vol. 5*. London: Academic Press.

Taft, M., & Forster, K. I. (1975). Lexical storage and retrieval of prefixed words. *Journal of Verbal Learning and Verbal Behavior, 14*, 638-647.

Author Index

Numbers in *italics* refer to reference pages.

Subject Index

Printed and bound by CPI Group (UK) Ltd, Croydon, CR0 4YY

17/10/2024

01775684-0010